DESTRUCTIVE EMOTIONS

Previous Books in the Mind and Life Series

Gentle Bridges: Conversations with the Dalai Lama on Brain Science and Buddhism
Edited by Jeremy W. Hayward and Francisco J. Varela

Consciousness at the Crossroads: Conversations with the Dalai Lama on Brain Science and Buddhism
Edited by Zara Houshmand, Robert B. Livingston, and B. Alan Wallace

Healing Emotions: Conversations with the Dalai Lama on Mindfulness, Emotions, and Health
Edited by Daniel Goleman

Sleeping, Dreaming, and Dying: An Exploration of Consciousness with the Dalai Lama
Edited by Francisco J. Varela

Visions of Compassion: Western Scientists and Tibetan Buddhists Examine Human Nature
Edited by Richard J. Davidson and Anne Harrington

The New Physics and Cosmology
Edited by Arthur Zajonc

The Mind and Life Institute is producing a video of the meeting described in this book. For further information about this video and the work of the Mind and Life Institute, and to be added to the mailing list of the Mind and Life Institute, please send an email to info@MindandLife.org and visit the following websites:

www.MindandLife.org

www.InvestigatingTheMind.org

BY THE SAME AUTHOR

The Meditative Mind
Emotional Intelligence
Working with Emotional Intelligence
Primal Leadership
(Co-author)

DESTRUCTIVE EMOTIONS

AND HOW WE CAN OVERCOME THEM

A DIALOGUE WITH

THE DALAI LAMA

NARRATED BY

DANIEL GOLEMAN

BLOOMSBURY

First published in Great Britain 2003

Published by arrangement with Bantam Books, an imprint of
The Bantam Dell Publishing Group, a division of Random House, Inc.

Art credits:
Photographs on pages 126, 127, and 129, courtesy of Paul Ekman.
Diagrams on pages 186, 193, 336, and 340, courtesy of Richard Davidson,
adapted for this book by the Hadel Studio.
Diagrams on pages 317 and 319, courtesy of Antoine Lutz.

Bloomsbury Publishing Plc, 38 Soho Square, London W1D 3HB

A CIP catalogue record for this book
is available from the British Library

ISBN 0 7475 5393 9 Hardback edition
10 9 8 7 6 5 4 3 2 1

ISBN 0 7475 6042 0 Export paperback edition
10 9 8 7 6 5 4 3 2 1

Printed in Great Britain by Clays Ltd, St Ives plc

Participants

(with titles and affiliations at the time of the meeting)

Tenzin Gyatso, His Holiness the Fourteenth Dalai Lama

Richard J. Davidson, Ph.D., William James Professor and Vilas Professor of Psychology and Psychiatry; director, Laboratory for Affective Neuroscience, University of Wisconsin–Madison

Paul Ekman, Ph.D., professor of psychology and director of the Human Interaction Laboratory, University of California at San Francisco Medical School

Owen Flanagan, Ph.D., James B. Duke Professor and Chair of Philosophy, fellow in cognitive neuroscience, and Allied Professor of Experimental Psychology, Duke University

Daniel Goleman, Ph.D., author; cochair of the Consortium for Research on Emotional Intelligence in the Graduate School of Applied and Professional Psychology at Rutgers University

Mark Greenberg, Ph.D., Bennett Chair in Prevention Research; professor of human development and family studies; director, Prevention Research Center for the Promotion of Human Development, Pennsylvania State University

Geshe Thupten Jinpa, Ph.D., president and chief editor for the Classics of Tibet Series produced by the Institute of Tibetan Classics in Montreal, Canada

The Venerable Ajahn Maha Somchai Kusalacitto, Buddhist monk and assistant abbot, Chandaram Buddhist Monastery; lecturer and deputy rector for foreign affairs, Mahachulalongkornrajavidyalaya University (MCU), Bangkok

Matthieu Ricard, Ph.D., author; Buddhist monk at Shechen Monastery in Kathmandu and French interpreter for His Holiness the Dalai Lama

Jeanne L. Tsai, Ph.D., assistant professor of psychology, University of Minnesota, Minneapolis and St. Paul

Francisco J. Varela, Ph.D., Fondation de France Professor of Cognitive Science and Epistemology at Ecole Polytechnique; director of research, CNRS, Paris; head of the Neurodynamics Unit at the Salpetrière Hospital, Paris

B. Alan Wallace, Ph.D., visiting lecturer, Department of Religious Studies, University of California, Santa Barbara

IN MEMORIAM

Francisco Varela

September 7, 1946–May 28, 2001

Good morning, my dear friend—I consider you a spiritual brother. We have a strong feeling of missing you here. So I want to express my deep feelings to you, as a brother, for your great contributions in science, especially in neurology, in the science of mind, and also in our work in this dialogue between science and Buddhist thought. We will never forget your great contributions. Till my death, I will remember you.

—THE DALAI LAMA,
May 22, 2001, via private Web TV
connection from Madison, Wisconsin,
to Francisco Varela, watching from his
bed at home in Paris,
where he died sixteen days later

Contents

DAY TWO: FEELINGS IN EVERYDAY LIFE

DAY THREE: WINDOWS INTO THE BRAIN

DAY FOUR: MASTERING EMOTIONAL SKILLS

DAY FIVE: REASONS FOR OPTIMISM

THE DALAI LAMA

Foreword

Much human suffering stems from destructive emotions, as hatred breeds violence or craving fuels addiction. One of our most basic responsibilities as caring people is to alleviate the human costs of such out-of-control emotions. In that mission, I feel that Buddhism and science both have much to contribute.

Buddhism and science are not conflicting perspectives on the world, but rather differing approaches to the same end: seeking the truth. In Buddhist training, it is essential to investigate reality, and science offers its own ways to go about this investigation. While the purposes of science may differ from those of Buddhism, both ways of searching for truth expand our knowledge and understanding.

The dialogue between science and Buddhism is a two-way conversation. We Buddhists can make use of the findings of science to clarify our understanding of the world we live in. But scientists may also be able to utilize some insights from Buddhism. There are many fields in which Buddhism can contribute to scientific understanding, and the Mind and Life dialogues have focused on several.

For instance, when it comes to the workings of the mind, Buddhism has a centuries-old inner science that has been of practical interest to researchers in the cognitive and neurosciences and in the study of emotions, offering significant contributions to their understanding. Following our discussions, several scientists have gone away with new ideas for research in their fields.

On the other hand, Buddhism can learn from science as well. I have often said that if science proves facts that conflict with Buddhist understanding, Buddhism must change accordingly. We should always adopt a view that accords with the facts. If upon investigation we find that there is reason and proof for a point, then we should accept it. However, a clear distinction should be made between what is *not found* by science and what is found to be *nonexistent* by science. What science finds to be nonexistent we should all accept as nonexistent, but what science merely does not find is a completely different matter. An example is consciousness itself. Although sentient beings, including humans, have experienced consciousness for centuries, we still do not know what consciousness actually is: its complete nature and how it functions.

In modern society, science has become a primary force in human and planetary development. In this way, scientific and technological innovations have been responsible for great material progress. However, science does not have all the answers, any more than religion did in the past. The more we pursue material improvement, ignoring the contentment that comes of inner growth, the faster ethical values will disappear from our communities. Then we will all experience unhappiness in the long run, for when there is no place for justice and honesty in people's hearts, the weak are the first to suffer. And the resentments resulting from such inequity ultimately affect everyone adversely.

With the ever-growing impact of science on our lives, religion and spirituality have a greater role to play in reminding us of our humanity. What we must do is balance scientific and material progress with the sense of responsibility that comes of inner development. That is why I believe this dialogue between religion and science is important, for from it may come developments that can be of great benefit to mankind.

When it comes to the human problems presented by our destructive emotions, Buddhism has much to say to science. A central aim of Buddhist practice is to reduce the power of destructive emotions in our lives. With that aim in mind, Buddhism offers a wide range of theoretical insights and practical methods. If any of these methods can be shown through scientific tests to be of benefit, then there is every reason to find ways to make them available to everyone, whether or not they are interested in Buddhism itself.

Such scientific assessment was one result of our dialogue. I am glad to say that the Mind and Life discussion reported in this book was more than a meeting of minds between Buddhism and science. The scientists went a step beyond and have begun programs to test several Buddhist methods that may be of benefit to all in dealing with destructive emotions.

I invite readers of this book to share in our explorations of the causes and cures for destructive emotions, and to reflect on the many questions raised that have compelling importance for us all. I hope you will find this encounter between science and Buddhism as stimulating as I did.

August 28, 2002

Prologue:
A Challenge for Humanity

There is a poignant arc between March 2000, when the events chronicled here occurred, and the completion of this book in the fall of 2001. When the dialogues at the center of this account took place, the world had, with some relief, left behind the horrors of the twentieth century, and many of us looked ahead hopefully to the human future. Then came the tragedies of September 2001, and we were faced once again with vivid reminders that calculated, large-scale inhumanity was still very much with us.

Horrific as they were, those barbarous acts represent but one more episode in history's steady stream of callous cruelty, where hatred spurs lethal action. Of all the destructive emotions, such ruthless hostility stands out as the most troubling streak in the human psyche. Most days that brand of barbarity looms offstage, lurking somewhere in the background of our collective awareness, an ominous presence waiting for its moment in the spotlight to come once again. But brutal hatred will inevitably capture center stage again and again—until, as with the rest of the destructive emotions, we understand its roots and find ways to keep cruelty at bay.

That common challenge for humanity lies at the heart of this book, which documents a collaboration between the Dalai Lama and a group of scientists to understand and counter destructive emotions. Our brief was not to confront how an individual's destructive impulses translate into mass action, nor how injustices—or their perception—spark hate-provoking ideologies. Instead we dealt at a more fundamental level, exploring how destructive emotions eat away at the human mind and heart and what we might do to counter this dangerous streak in our collective nature. And, of course, we did so with the Dalai Lama, whose life itself is an object lesson in handling historical injustice.

The Buddhist tradition has long pointed out that recognizing and transforming destructive emotions lies at the heart of spiritual practice—indeed, some hold that whatever lessens destructive emotions *is* spiritual practice. From the perspective of science, these same emotional states pose a perplexing challenge: These are brain responses that have, in part, shaped the human mind, and presumably played a crucial role in human survival. But now, in modern life, they pose grave dangers to our individual and collective fate.

Our meeting explored a range of urgent questions about that perennial human predicament, our destructive emotions. Are they a fundamental, unchangeable part of the human legacy? What makes these urges so powerful, leading otherwise rational people to commit acts they later regret? What is the place of such emotions in the evolution of our species—are they essential for human survival? What leverage points might there be for ameliorating their threat to our personal happiness and stability? How much plasticity might there be in the brain, and how might we shift in a more positive direction the very neural systems that harbor destructive impulses? Most important, how can we overcome them?

Burning Questions

The first seeds for the meeting that dealt with these burning questions were planted when my wife and I happened to be staying in a guest house in Dharamsala, India, where another guest was editing what was to become the Dalai Lama's book *Ethics for the New Millennium.* The editor asked me to comment on an early draft of the book, which sets out the Dalai Lama's proposal of a secular ethic suitable for the world community—not just for those who hold a given religion—and his wish to bring together all resources, Eastern and Western, that might benefit humanity in this effort.

As I read the draft I was struck by the relevance of new research on emotions to the Dalai Lama's thesis. A few days later I was able to review some of these findings during a short meeting with him. For instance, data on how in well-nurtured children the first signs of the capacity for empathy, so crucial for compassion, emerge early in life intrigued the Dalai Lama. I asked if he would like a fuller briefing on the most recent psychological research on emotions at some point. Yes, he answered—but specified he wanted it on negative emotions. He wanted to know, for instance, if science could tell him what the difference was at the brain level between anger and rage.

The next year we had a fleeting conversation as the Dalai Lama was waiting to speak in San Francisco; there he narrowed his request to focus specifically on *destructive* emotions. And some months later, during a brief meeting as he was about to give a religious teaching at a Buddhist monastery in New Jersey, I asked him just what he meant by "destructive." He clarified that he wanted a scientific perspective on what Buddhists call the Three Poisons: hatred, craving, and delusion. We agreed that here the Western view would differ from the Buddhist perspective, but those differences would themselves be informative.

I then took his request to Adam Engle, the chairman of the Mind and Life Institute, to see if the topic might fit in the series of ongoing meetings they had run since 1987, in which the Dalai Lama met with select groups of experts to explore Buddhist and Western scientific perspectives on a given subject, such as cosmology or compassion. I myself had co-organized and moderated the third meeting, on emotions and health, and the series seemed an ideal forum for this new topic.

After I got the go-ahead from the institute's scientific advisory board, my challenge was to find scientists whose varied expertise and perspectives could shed light on the disturbing, the distressing, and the dangerous in human nature. We needed not just the right range of expertise at the table, but people who would also raise compelling questions, engage in exploring answers, and be open to examining hidden assumptions that might be limiting their own thinking.

Both sides in this dialogue would come as learners as well as preceptors. The Dalai Lama, as always, would be eager to hear the most recent scientific findings. But the scientists themselves would be exposed to an alternative paradigm on the mind—the insights of Buddhist thought, which has explored the inner world for millennia with an extraordinary rigor. This body of expertise possesses an exacting system for probing depths of awareness that science has not yet considered, and it challenges key suppositions that guide today's psychological science. In short, this encounter would not be a mere update for the Dalai Lama, but an active, joint inquiry into deep issues of the human spirit, where he (joined by other Buddhist scholars) would also act as an interlocutor for science in ways that could stretch the thinking of the scientists themselves.

As is traditional, we would begin with a philosopher, to widen the framework for our inquiry. Alan Wallace, then at the University of California at Santa Barbara, and a scholar of Buddhism and a regular translator for the Dalai Lama at these meetings, was my cochair for philosophy, while I focused on finding the right mix of scientists.

Owen Flanagan, a philosopher of mind at Duke University, was to start our conversation by presenting Western views on a fundamental question: Which emotions—apart from the most obvious, such as anger and hatred—are to be counted among the destructive ones? Matthieu Ricard, a Tibetan Buddhist monk (who also holds a Ph.D. in biology), was to present the Buddhist perspective on destructive emotions. Our working definition going into the meeting was straightforward: Destructive emotions are those that cause harm to ourselves or to others. But as we pursued the discussion, different views emerged on just which emotions are, in fact, harmful—and when and why. The varying standards for "destructive" depended on the perspective, with moral philosophy, Buddhism, and psychology all coming up with their own set of answers.

Paul Ekman, a psychologist at the University of California at San Francisco and a world expert on the facial expression of affect, began our scientific exploration of the basic dynamics of emotions, a bedrock understanding from which to plunge into the enigma of the destructive streak in human nature. He brought a Darwinian perspective to our conversation, one suggesting that destructive emotions remain in the repertoire of the human heart as a trade-off in the evolutionary quest for survival.

For further insights from neuroscience, we turned to Richard Davidson of the University of Madison, a founder of the field of affective neuroscience. He shared findings that pinpointed the brain circuitry involved in a range of destructive emotions, from the craving of an addict to the paralyzing fears of a phobic and the out-of-control viciousness of a mass murderer. But his data also pointed to another promise: the sites in the brain that inhibit destructive urges, as well as those that replace disturbing feelings with equanimity or joy.

Though we share the gamut of feelings as part of our common human heritage, people differ in how they express or value given emotions. A cross-cultural view came from Jeanne Tsai, a psychologist then at the University of Minnesota (now at Stanford), whose research focuses on differences in how people experience emotions from culture to culture. Her findings reminded us of the need to recognize differences among people even as we pursued universal means to overcome the threat of destructive emotions.

Along with analyzing the dynamics that underlie our destructive propensities, we hoped to search for solutions. To that end, we heard from Mark Greenberg, a psychologist at the University of Pennsylvania and a pioneer in programs for social and emotional learning. He reported on school curricula for children that educate them in the basics of emotional literacy, helping them master destructive emotions rather than simply acting on those impulses. As it turned out, that report would spur us to begin to design a similar program for adults.

Our last day focused on how collaborations between advanced meditation practitioners and neuroscientists might further scientific understanding of the positive potential for emotional transformation. Francisco Varela, cofounder of the Mind and Life Institute and research director of a national neuroscience laboratory in Paris, reported on experiments dissecting the neural activity underlying a moment of perception—research he planned to collaborate on with advanced meditators, to take advantage of their expertise as observers of the mind. And Richard Davidson argued for neuroplasticity, the ability of the brain to develop throughout life, and presented data suggesting that meditation practice could produce beneficial plasticity in the brain's affective centers, inhibiting destructive emotions while fostering positive ones.

Although the topic of destructive emotions by its very nature can spawn pessimism and gloom, our endpoint was optimistic, focusing on positive steps that could be taken to counter these forces of darkness—if only within our own minds. If we are to overcome the virus of destructive emotions, we must start by inoculating ourselves against the internal chaos of feelings, such as fearful panic or blind rage, that hinder effective action. And in the scientific quest for insights into an inner balance and peace in the face of tumult, some of the early answers provide grounds for optimism—at least in the long run.

When our week ended, none of us was quite ready to leave. The questions that were raised, the possibilities that emerged, had built a momentum that carried over into a two-day follow-up meeting several months afterward at the University of Wisconsin and a later two-day conference at Harvard University, as well as several ongoing scientific projects. The intellectual exploration of destructive emotions had borne fruit in the active pursuit of further answers—and of antidotes.

A Rich Subtext

This encounter was the eighth round of the Mind and Life meetings. Like most of the other such dialogues between the Dalai Lama and a small group of scientists and philosophers, this meeting took place over five full days in the Dalai Lama's quarters in Dharamsala, India. Each morning was given over to a presentation, the afternoons to a wide-ranging pursuit of implications. Largely because of the Dalai Lama's radiant warmth and easy wit, what could have been a stiff exchange quickly mellowed into an informal atmosphere, a first-name familiarity more conducive to innovative thinking and spontaneous insights.

My appointed task in writing this book was the faithful narration of a wide-ranging collaboration between science and spirit. The organizer of each meeting has a mandate to share the proceedings with a wider public by putting together a book; this is the seventh in the Mind and Life series. (The others are listed facing the title page.) As the only full record of the dialogues, the books are meant to capture the verbatim, spontaneous flavor of the conversations.

In the service of unpacking the richness of our interaction I was also able to interview participants—including the Dalai Lama—about their own feelings and unspoken thoughts at key moments. This yielded a rich subtext to the dialogue, bringing to the printed page a stronger flavor of what it was like to be in the room, in the midst of the intellectual fireworks, probing questions, and reports from the frontiers of science.

Our conversation was an intellectual feast, offering up findings ranging from the precise insights of brain scans to observations of children on school playgrounds, from data on the emotional perspicacity of a remote tribe in New Guinea to musings on studies revealing the easygoing temperament of babies in China. We touched on a wide array of topics, from highly theoretical considerations of philosophical points to the pragmatics of teaching ways to better manage destructive impulses, from the technicalities of neuroscientific methods for exploring cognition to the fine points of cultivating compassion.

While there were no easy answers, perhaps most thrilling were the questions raised—both the cross fire of challenges from one grand tradition of thought to another and the larger enigmas for our personal lives as well as for our very future as a species. The questions were often seminal and sometimes brilliant, and they frequently suggested inviting paths for further exploration.

Of course, many readers may be more drawn to some parts of our discussions than to others, and some will no doubt pick and choose their way through. But this intellectual banquet is offered here in its entirety.

Throughout the dialogue the Dalai Lama, that beacon of peace in troubled times, had a strong effect on us all. Through his quiet influence, what began as a purely intellectual inquiry became a shared personal quest for positive antidotes to destructive emotions. That quest has already yielded some tangible results.

For one, we ended up outlining a practical application of the Dalai Lama's vision for humanity described in *Ethics for the New Millennium,* the very book I had seen in Dharamsala that was the seed for our meeting. We found ourselves pursuing the search for practical methods that could be borrowed from Buddhism or the West, the goal being to come up with a lesson plan for living with full attention and self-awareness, with self-control and responsibility, with empathy and compassion—in other words, with the skills that allow people to overcome their own destructive emotions.

Another practical fruit of the meeting has been for science itself. Buddhism has been exploring the mind and its positive potentials for millennia, with extraordinary depth and rigor; science has only engaged this same line of inquiry relatively recently. Now these two traditions have joined together in that mission. From our meeting flowed a series of experimental studies in which some of the newest, most subtle scientific instruments are taking the measure of ancient methods for cultivating positive emotional states.

Our story starts with this intriguing collaboration between a centuries-old science of mind and cutting-edge neuroscience.

Left to right: Paul Ekman, Thupten Jinpa, Jeanne Tsai, Mark Greenberg, Ven. Kusalacitto, the Dalai Lama, Daniel Goleman, the late Francisco Varela, Richard Davidson, Alan Wallace, Matthieu Ricard, Owen Flanagan

A Scientific Collaboration

Madison, Wisconsin
May 21 and 22, 2001

1

The Lama in the Lab

Lama Öser strikes most anyone who meets him as resplendent—not because of his maroon and gold Tibetan monk's robes, but because of his radiant smile. Öser, a European-born convert to Buddhism, has trained as a Tibetan monk in the Himalayas for more than three decades, including many years at the side of one of Tibet's greatest spiritual masters.

But today Öser (whose name has been changed here to protect his privacy) is about to take a revolutionary step in the history of the spiritual lineages he has become a part of: He will engage in meditation while having his brain scanned by state-of-the-art brain imaging devices. To be sure, there have been sporadic attempts to study brain activity in meditators, and decades of tests with monks and yogis in Western labs, some revealing remarkable abilities to control respiration, brain waves, or core body temperature. But this—the first experiment with someone at Öser's level of training, using such sophisticated measures—will take that research to an entirely new level, deeper than ever in charting the specific links between highly disciplined mental strategies and their impact on brain function. And this research agenda has a pragmatic focus: to assess meditation as mind training, a practical answer to the perennial human conundrum of how we can better handle our destructive emotions.

While modern science has focused on formulating ingenious chemical compounds to help us overcome toxic emotions, Buddhism offers a different, albeit far more labor-intensive, route: methods for training the mind, largely through meditation practice. Indeed, Buddhism explicitly explains the training Öser has undergone as an antidote to the mind's vulnerability to toxic emotions. If destructive emotions mark one extreme in human proclivities, this research seeks to map their antipode, the extent to which the brain can be trained to dwell in a constructive range: contentment instead of craving, calm rather than agitation, compassion in place of hatred.

Medicines are the leading modality in the West for addressing disturbing emotions, and for better or for worse, there is no doubt that mood-altering pills have brought solace to millions. But one compelling question the research with Öser raises is whether a person, through his or her own efforts, can bring about lasting positive changes in brain function that are even more far-reaching than medication in their impact on emotions. And that question, in turn, raises others: For instance, if in fact people can train their minds to overcome destructive emotions, could practical, nonreligious aspects of such training be part of every child's education? Or could such training in emotional self-management be offered to adults, whether or not they were spiritual seekers?

These very questions had been raised over the course of a remarkable five-day dialogue held the year before between the Dalai Lama and a small group of scientists and a philosopher of mind at his private quarters in Dharamsala, India. The research with Öser marked one culmination of several lines of scientific inquiry set in motion during the dialogue. There the Dalai Lama had been a prime mover in inspiring this research; in a real sense, he was an active collaborator in turning the lens of science on the practices of his own spiritual tradition.

But the experiments in Madison were merely one manifestation of that deep collective inquiry into the nature of emotions, how they become destructive, and possible effective antidotes. This book renders my account of the conversations that inspired the Madison research, of the larger questions behind the research, and of the greater implications for us all of this sweeping exploration into how humanity might counter the centrifugal drag of our destructive emotions.

Assaying the Transcendent

It was at the invitation of Richard Davidson, one of the scientists who participated in the Dharamsala dialogues, that Öser had come to the E. M. Keck Laboratory for Functional Brain Imaging and Behavior, on the Madison campus of the University of Wisconsin. The laboratory was founded by Davidson, a leading pioneer in the field of affective neuroscience, which studies the interplay of the brain and emotions. Davidson had wanted Öser—a particularly intriguing subject—to be studied intensively with state-of-the-art brain measures.

Öser has spent several months at a stretch in intensive, solitary retreat. All told, those retreats add up to about two and a half years. But beyond that, during several years as the personal attendant to a Tibetan master, the reminders to practice even in the midst of his busy daily activities were almost constant. Now, here at the laboratory, the question was what difference any of that training had made.

The collaboration began before Öser went near the MRI, with a meeting to design the research protocol. As the eight-person research team briefed Öser, everyone in the room was acutely aware that they were in a bit of a race against time. The Dalai Lama himself would visit the lab the very next day, and they hoped by then to have harvested at least some preliminary results to share with him.

With Öser's consultation, the research team agreed on a protocol where he would rotate from a resting, everyday state of mind through a sequence of several specific meditative states. To overhear that conversation would have been eye-opening for anyone who thinks of meditation as a single, vaguely defined Zen-like mental exercise. Such an assumption is akin to thinking of all cooking as the same, ignoring the vast variation in cuisine, recipes, and ingredients throughout the world of food. Likewise, there are dozens and dozens of distinct, highly detailed varieties of mental training—too loosely lumped together in English under the term "meditation"—each with its own instructions and specific effects on experience and, the research team hoped to show, on brain activity.

To be sure, there is a great deal of overlap among the kinds of meditation employed across differing spiritual traditions: A Trappist monk reciting the Prayer of the Heart, "Kyrie eleison," has much in common with a Tibetan nun chanting "Om mani padme hum." But beyond these large commonalities, there is a very wide variety of specific meditation practices, each unique in the attentional, cognitive, and affective strategies they employ, and so in their results.

Tibetan Buddhism may well offer the widest menu of meditation methods, and it was from this rich offering that the team in Madison began to choose what to study. The initial suggestions from the research team were for three meditative states: a visualization, one-pointed concentration, and generating compassion. The three methods involved distinct enough mental strategies that the team was fairly sure they would reveal different underlying configurations of brain activity. Indeed, Öser was able to give precise descriptions of each.

One of the methods chosen, one-pointedness—a fully focused concentration on a single object of attention—may be the most basic and universal of all practices, found in one form or another in every spiritual tradition that employs meditation. Focusing on one point requires letting go of the ten thousand other thoughts and desires that flit through the mind as distractions; as the Danish philosopher Kierkegaard put it, "Purity of heart is to want one thing only."

In the Tibetan system (as in many others) cultivating concentration is a beginner's method, a prerequisite for moving on to more intricate approaches. In a sense, concentration is the most generic form of mind training, with many nonspiritual applications as well. Indeed, for this test, Öser simply picked a spot (a small bolt above him on the MRI, it turned out) to focus his gaze on and held it there, bringing his focus back whenever his mind wandered off.

Öser proposed three more approaches that he thought would usefully expand the data yield: meditations on devotion and on fearlessness, and what he called the "open state."[1] The last refers to a thought-free wakefulness where the mind, as Öser described it, "is open, vast, and aware, with no intentional mental activity. The mind is not focused on anything, yet totally present—not in a focused way, just very open and undistracted. Thoughts may start to arise weakly, but they don't chain into longer thoughts—they just fade away."

Perhaps as intriguing was Öser's explanation of the meditation on fearlessness, which involves "bringing to mind a fearless certainty, a deep confidence that nothing can unsettle—decisive and firm, without hesitating, where you're not averse to anything. You enter into a state where you feel, no matter what happens, 'I have nothing to gain, nothing to lose.' " One aid to this meditation, he added, is bringing to mind these same qualities in his teachers. A similar focus on his teachers plays a key role in the meditation on devotion, he said, in which he holds in mind a deep appreciation of and gratitude toward his teachers and, most especially, the spiritual qualities they embody.

That strategy also operates in the meditation on compassion, with his teachers' kindness offering a model. Öser explained that in generating love and compassion, bringing to mind the suffering of living beings and the fact that they all aspire to achieve happiness and be free from suffering is a vital part of the training. So does the idea to "let there be only compassion and love in the mind for all beings—friends and loved ones, strangers and enemies alike. It's a compassion with no agenda, that excludes no one. You generate this quality of loving, and let it soak the mind."

Finally, the visualization entailed constructing in the mind's eye a fully detailed image of the elaborately intricate details of a Tibetan Buddhist deity. As Öser described the process, "You start with the details and build the whole picture from top to bottom. Ideally, you should be able to keep in mind a clear and complete picture." As those familiar with Tibetan *thangkas* (the wall hangings that depict such deities) will know, such images are highly complex patterns.

Öser confidently assumed that each of these six meditation practices should show distinct brain configurations. For the scientists, there are clear distinctions in cognitive activity between, say, visualization and one-pointedness. But the meditations on compassion, devotion, and fearlessness do not seem that different in the mental processes involved, though they differ clearly in content. From a scientific point of view, if Öser could demonstrate sharp, consistent brain signatures for any of these meditative states, it would be a first.

Mission Control for Inner Space

Öser's testing started with the functional MRI, the current gold standard of research on the brain's role in behavior. Before the advent of the functional MRI (or fMRI), researchers had been handicapped in observing in a fine-grained way the sequence of activity in the various parts of the brain during a given mental activity. The standard MRI, in wide use in hospitals, offers a graphically detailed snapshot of the structure of the brain. But the fMRI offers all that in video—an ongoing record of how zones of the brain dynamically change their level of activity from moment to moment. The conventional MRI lays bare the brain's structures, while fMRI reveals how those structures interact as they function.

The fMRI could give Davidson a crystal-clear set of images of Öser's brain, cross-cutting slices at one millimeter—slimmer than a fingernail. These images could then be analyzed in any dimension to track precisely what happens during a mental act, tracing paths of activity through the brain.

As Öser and the team entered the rooms where the fMRI studies would be conducted, the scene resembled a mission control room for inner space. In one room a swarm of data analysts hovered over their computers, while in the next another flock of technicians monitored their computer array as they guided Öser through the experimental protocol.

People go into an MRI fortified with earplugs to mute the incessant whine of the machine's huge, whirling magnets, a naggingly relentless *dit-dit-dit* industrial noise reminiscent of the nightmarish soundtrack in David Lynch's cult film *Eraserhead.* The sound alone can be unsettling, but even more perturbing can be the sense of confinement. Foam pads pack your head tightly in place, a cage covers your head, and as your body slides into the machine, you realize your face is bare inches away from the top of the slot.

While most people adjust as they lie in the MRI, some feel claustrophobic, and a few may feel vertigo or dizziness. While some research subjects are a bit reluctant to submit to their hour or so in the MRI, Öser's eagerness was clear; he wanted to go right in.

A Mini-Retreat

Öser, lying peacefully on a hospital gurney with his head constrained in the maws of the fMRI, looked like a human pencil inserted into a huge cubic beige sharpener. Instead of the lone monk in a mountaintop cave, it's the monk in the brain scanner.

Wearing earphones instead of earplugs so he could talk to the control room, Öser sounded unperturbed as the technicians led him through a lengthy series of checks to ensure the MRI images were tracking. Finally, as Davidson was about to begin the protocol, he asked, "Öser, how are you doing?" "Just fine," Öser assured him via a small microphone inside the machine.

"Your brain looks beautiful," Davidson said. "Let's start with five repetitions of the open state." A computerized voice then took over, to ensure precise timing for the protocol. The prompt "on" was the signal for Öser to meditate, followed by silence for sixty seconds while Öser complied. Then "neutral," another sixty seconds of silence, and the cycle started once again with "on."

The same routine guided Öser through the other five meditative states, with pauses between as the technicians worked out various glitches. Finally, when the full round was complete, Davidson asked if Öser felt the need to repeat any, and the answer came: "I'd like to repeat the open state, compassion, devotion, and one-pointedness"—the ones he felt were the most important to study.

So the whole process started again. As he was about to begin the run on the open state, Öser said he wanted to remain in each state longer. He was able to evoke the state but wanted more time to deepen it. Once the computers have been programmed for the protocol, though, the technology drives the procedure; the timing has been fixed. Still, the technicians went into a huddle, quickly figuring how to reprogram on the spot to increase the "on" period by 50 percent and shorten the neutral period accordingly. The rounds began again.

With all the time taken up by reprogramming and ironing out technical hitches, the whole run took more than three hours. Subjects rarely emerge from the MRI—particularly after having been in there for so long—with anything but an expression of weary relief. But Davidson was pleasantly astonished to see Öser come out from his grueling routine in the MRI beaming broadly and proclaiming, "It's like a mini-retreat!"

A Very, Very Good Day

Without taking more than a brief break, Öser headed down the hall for the next set of tests, this time using an electroencephalogram, the brain wave measure better known as an EEG. Most EEG studies use only thirty-two sensors on the scalp to pick up electrical activity in the brain—and many use just six.

But Öser's brain would be monitored twice, using two different EEG caps, first one with 128 sensors, the next with a staggering 256. The first cap would capture valuable data while he again went through the same paces in the meditative states. The second, with 256 sensors, would be used synergistically with the earlier MRI data.

There are only three or four other neuroscience laboratories anywhere that use 256 EEG sensors. That many readings from the brain, when analyzed by a state-of-the-art piece of analytic software called source localization, allow a triangulation that pinpoints the neural location a signal is coming from. Source localization can penetrate to sites deep inside the brain—something ordinary EEG measures, which monitor only the topmost layer of the brain, simply cannot offer.

Walking down the hall to the EEG room, Öser gamely settled in for another round of the same protocol. But this time, instead of lying in the maws of the MRI, he sat on a comfortable chair and wore a Medusa-like helmet—something like a shower cap extruding a spaghetti of thin wires. The EEG sessions took another two hours.

After the tests were done, someone asked Öser if the conditions of the MRI had disturbed his ability to meditate. "The noise was unpleasant but repetitive," said Öser. "Soon you forget about it and it does not disturb the meditation too much. I think more important is your state that day." And, as the data analyses were later to reveal, Öser's state that day—most likely any day—was very, very good.

A Feel for Science

The next morning a misty rain was falling as a sleek black car, escorted by a caravan of Madison police and cars carrying an entourage from the State

Department Office of Diplomatic Security, pulled up in front of the Waisman Center, where the Keck laboratory is located. From the black car the Dalai Lama emerged, beaming as Davidson greeted him. He would get a tour of the lab before adjourning to a nearby campus meeting center to hear the results about Öser.

Davidson escorted the Dalai Lama into a briefing room and gave him an overview of the lab's equipment and the research that went on there. He remarked that his own previous interactions with the Dalai Lama had focused his scientific attention on positive emotions—he had been particularly struck when the Dalai Lama said the mother-infant bond is an origin of compassion as well as its natural expression. Now Davidson was beginning a research program on compassion, and wondered if the Dalai Lama had some ideas about the best ways to foster compassion. The Dalai Lama, always ready to joke, laughingly suggested, "Through injection!"

As the Dalai Lama started his tour of the laboratory, the first stop was the room where graduate students manned a bank of computers, feverishly working with the sea of data accumulated the day before from Öser. Davidson showed the Dalai Lama one of the screens, displaying a brain full of Technicolor puddles, each indicating a different level of activity in various parts of Öser's brain.

There are certain scientific questions—for instance, about the nature of consciousness—that have long intrigued the Dalai Lama, and over the years he has probed whether there are methods that are able to resolve them. One of these questions—the power of the mind, or consciousness itself, to drive the brain—came up as Davidson showed him the MRI.

"We can identify with excellent spatial precision specific sources of activation in the brain as mental activity unfolds," Davidson explained. He added that the strength of the EEG is speed—just as the MRI's is spatial precision. While the fMRI can detect brain changes within a millimeter, the computerized EEG can detect changes in the brain in a thousandth of a second.

That prompted the Dalai Lama to ask, "Can you show a thought preceding the action? Can you tell if a thought comes first, before changes occur in the brain?"

In the ensuing discussion, Davidson was struck that the Dalai Lama had what seems an almost preternatural feel for data and the methods of science, a talent he has exhibited over and over in his conversations with scientists. As Davidson put it, "I've seen His Holiness penetrate into the data when everyone else but the specialists are left behind."

The Digital Whittle

From the moment Öser's fMRI data started to read out on the control room computer, the data began to be processed at multiple workstations operating in parallel. The first run at the data mathematically peeled away Öser's scalp from the image to focus on the action in the brain itself. Then another program converted the unique contours of Öser's brain to a "standard space," a mythic uniform brain that allows one person's brain to be compared to others.

This project ran on a crash deadline, compressing seven days of data analysis into a half day. Typically the schedule for such massaging of data takes weeks, competing for computer time with the twenty to thirty other research projects currently in process at Davidson's lab. But Davidson had wanted to present at least some preliminary results to the Dalai Lama the next day, at a meeting that started at 8 A.M. So the data analysis went on through the night, with the last diehard leaving the lab at 4:45 A.M. for some rest—and returning again at 7 A.M.

The fMRI data, which potentially could offer the most telling insights, was too vast and complex to tease out more than the most general patterns on such short notice. But as the afternoon session was about to begin, a bedraggled graduate student who had spent most of the last twenty-four hours at a computer massaging the data brought Davidson some first results.

Even in the broad first swipe at the MRI data that Davidson could report the next day, there were strong signs that Öser had been able to voluntarily regulate his brain activity through purely mental processes. By contrast, most untrained subjects given a mental task are unable to focus exclusively on the task—and consequently have considerable noise added to the signals that reflect their voluntary mental strategies.

But for Öser, it seemed from the preliminary analysis that his mental strategies were accompanied by strong, demonstrable shifts in the MRI signals. These signals suggested that large networks in the brain changed with each distinct mental state he generated. Ordinarily, such a clear shift in brain activity between states of mind is the exception, except for the grossest shifts in consciousness—from waking to sleep, for instance. But Öser's brain showed clear distinctions among each of the six meditations.

The Neuroanatomy of Compassion

While the fMRI findings were quite preliminary, the EEG analysis had already borne rich fruit in the comparison between Öser at rest and while meditating on compassion. Most striking was a dramatic increase in key electrical activity known as gamma in the left middle frontal gyrus, a zone of the brain Davidson's previous research had pinpointed as a locus for positive emotions. In research with close to two hundred people, Davidson's lab had found that when people have high levels of such brain activity in that specific site of the left prefrontal cortex, they simultaneously report feelings such as happiness, enthusiasm, joy, high energy, and alertness.

On the other hand, Davidson's research has also found that high levels of activity in a parallel site on the other side of the brain—in the right prefrontal area—correlate with reports of distressing emotions. People with a higher level of activity in the right prefrontal site and a lower level in the left are more prone to feelings such as sadness, anxiety, and worry. Indeed, an extreme rightward tilt in the ratio of the activity in these prefrontal areas predicts a high likelihood that a person will succumb to clinical depression or an anxiety disorder at some point in their life. People in the grip of depression who also report intense anxiety have the highest levels of activation in those right prefrontal areas.

The implications of these findings for our emotional balance are profound: We each have a characteristic ratio of right-to-left activation in the prefrontal areas that offers a barometer of the moods we are likely to feel day to day. That ratio represents what amounts to an emotional set point, the mean around which our daily moods swing.

Each of us has the capacity to shift our moods, at least a bit, and thus change this ratio. The further to the left that ratio tilts, the better our frame of mind tends to be, and experiences that lift our mood cause such a leftward tilt, at least temporarily. For instance, most people show small positive changes in this ratio when they are asked to recall pleasant memories of events from their past, or when they watch amusing or heartwarming film clips.

Though usually such changes from the baseline set point are modest, at the Madison meeting Davidson reported to the Dalai Lama some striking data from the tests the day before with Öser. While Öser was generating a state of compassion during meditation, he showed a remarkable leftward shift in this parameter of prefrontal function, one that was extraordinarily unlikely to occur by chance alone.

In short, Öser's brain shift during compassion seemed to reflect an *extremely* pleasant mood. The very act of concern for others' well-being, it seems, creates a greater state of well-being within oneself. The finding lends scientific support to an observation often made by the Dalai Lama: that the person doing a meditation on compassion for all beings is the immediate beneficiary. (Among other benefits of cultivating compassion, as described in classic Buddhist texts, are being loved by people and animals, having a serene mind, sleeping and waking peacefully, and having pleasant dreams.[2])

The data from Öser was remarkable in another way, as these were also, Davidson pointed out, most likely the first data ever gathered on brain activity during the systematic generation of compassion—an emotional state for the most part utterly ignored by modern psychological research. Research in psychology over the decades has focused far more on what goes wrong with us—depression, anxiety, and the like—than on what goes right with us. The positive side of experience and human goodness have been largely ignored in research; indeed, there is virtually no research anywhere in the annals of psychology on compassion per se.

Öser's rather amazing brain shift during the meditation on compassion raised a question bearing on scientific method: Was this a quirk of nature unique to Öser, or might it be due, as Davidson assumed, to the intensive training he had undergone? If just a quirk, then the finding is intriguing but scientifically trivial; if due to training, then it has profound implications for the potential of human development. So Davidson immediately sought the Dalai Lama's help in finding others to test who were well trained in the same method of meditation on compassion, to be sure that the findings reflected the fruit of the practice rather than being peculiar to Öser. And, as I write this, further testing is under way with a handful of highly trained meditators.

Unprecedented Findings

The Madison meeting had been arranged as a scientific briefing for the Dalai Lama on several lines of related research, all emanating from the dialogue on destructive emotions and their antidotes that had taken place a year before in his Dharamsala headquarters. Davidson's studies were one of the threads; parallel tests exploring other psychological dimensions of advanced meditation training had gone on in other laboratories.

While Davidson's data on compassion were surprising in themselves, still more remarkable results were about to be reported by Paul Ekman, one of the world's most eminent experts on the science of emotion, who heads the Human Interaction Laboratory at the University of California at San Francisco. Ekman was among the handful of scientists who had attended the Dharamsala meeting, and he had studied Öser a few months earlier in his own laboratory. In telling the Dalai Lama of his results, Ekman, too, began by emphasizing the collaborative nature of their research. "Öser was a coplanner. Many of the decisions about what we did are his."

The net result was four studies, in each of which, as Ekman said, "we found things we've never found before." Some findings were so unprecedented, Ekman admitted, he was not yet sure he completely understood them himself.

The first test used a measure that represents a culmination of Ekman's life's work as the world's leading expert on the facial expression of emotions. The test consists of a videotape in which a series of faces show a variety of expressions very briefly. The challenge is to identify whether you've just seen the facial signs, for instance, of contempt, or anger, or fear. Each expression stays on the screen for just one-fifth of a second in one version, and for one-thirtieth of a second in another—so fast that you would miss it if you blinked. Each time the person must select which of six emotions he or she has just seen.

The ability to recognize fleeting expressions signals an unusual capacity for accurate empathy. Such expressions of emotion—called microexpressions—happen outside the awareness of both the person who displays them and the person observing. Because they occur unwittingly, these ultrarapid displays of emotion are completely uncensored, and so reveal—if only for a short moment—how the person truly feels.

The six microemotions assessed are biologically fixed universals, expressed the same worldwide. While there are sometimes large cultural differences in consciously managing the expression of emotions such as disgust, these ultrarapid expressions come and go so quickly that they evade even cultural taboos. Microexpressions offer a unique window on another person's emotional reality.

From studies with thousands of people, Ekman knew that people who do better at recognizing these subtle emotions are more open to new experience, and more interested and curious about things in general. They are also conscientious—reliable and efficient. "So I had expected that many years of meditative experience"—which requires both openness and conscientiousness—"might make them do better on this ability," Ekman explained. Thus he had wondered if Öser might be better able to identify these ultrafast emotions than other people are.

Then Ekman announced his results: Both Öser and another advanced Western meditator he had been able to test were two standard deviations above the norm in recognizing these superquick facial signals of emotion (albeit the two subjects differed in the emotions they were best at perceiving). They both scored far higher than any of the five thousand other people tested. "They do better than policemen, lawyers, psychiatrists, customs officials, judges—even Secret Service agents," the group that had previously distinguished itself as most accurate.

"It appears that one benefit of some part of the life paths these two have followed is becoming more aware of these subtle signs of how other people feel," Ekman noted. Öser had superacuity for the fleeting signs of fear, contempt, and anger. The other meditator—a Westerner who, like Öser, had done a total of two to three years in solitary retreats in the Tibetan tradition—was similarly outstanding, though on a different range of emotions: happiness, sadness, disgust, and, like Öser, anger.

On hearing the results, the Dalai Lama—who had been skeptical that Ekman would find anything on this test—exclaimed with surprise, "Oh! In that case, practicing Dharma does seem to make a difference here. That's something new."

Then, trying to tease out just why meditation training might make that difference, the Dalai Lama conjectured that there seem to be two aspects of ability at play. One might be an enhanced speed of cognition, which would make it easier to perceive rapid stimuli in general. A second ability would be greater attunement to emotions in other people, which would make reading them easier. Ekman conceded the need to untangle those two abilities in order to better understand his finding, but added that he couldn't do so from these results alone.

And both Ekman and the Dalai Lama admitted to puzzlement about just why Öser is better at reading certain emotions, while the other meditator is superior on a different set. Why aren't they both better across the board? Leaving it at that, Ekman moved on to the next finding—one that was even more surprising, if not baffling.

A Spectacular Accomplishment

One of the most primitive responses in the human repertoire, the startle reflex, involves a cascade of very quick muscle spasms in response to a loud, surprising sound or sudden, jarring sight. For everyone, the same five facial muscles instantaneously contract during a startle, particularly around the eyes. The startle reflex starts about two-tenths of a second after hearing the sound and ends around a half second after the sound. From beginning to end, it takes approximately a third of a second. The time course is always the same; that's the way we're wired.

Like all reflexes, the startle reflects activity of the brain stem, the most primitive, reptilian part of the brain. Like other brain stem responses—and unlike those of the autonomic nervous system, such as the rate at which the heart beats—the startle reflex lies beyond the range of voluntary regulation. So far as brain science understands, the mechanisms that control the startle reflex cannot be modified by any intentional act.

Ekman became interested in testing the startle reflex because its intensity predicts the magnitude of the negative emotions a person feels—particularly fear, anger, sadness, and disgust. The bigger a person's startle, the more strongly that individual tends to experience negative emotions—though there's no relationship between the startle and positive feelings such as joy.[3]

For a test of the magnitude of Öser's startle reflex, Ekman took him across San Francisco Bay to the psychophysiological laboratory of his colleague Robert Levenson at the University of California at Berkeley. There they wired Öser to capture his heart rate and sweat response, and videotaped his facial expressions—all to record his physiological reactions to a startling sound. To eliminate any differences due to the noise level of the sound, they chose the top of the threshold for human tolerance—a huge sound, like a pistol being fired or a large firecracker going off near one's ear.

They gave Öser the standard instruction, telling him that they would count down from ten to one, at which point he would hear a loud noise. They asked that he try to suppress the inevitable flinch, so that someone looking at him would not know he felt it. Some people can do better than others, but no one can come remotely close to completely suppressing it. A classic study in the 1940s showed that it's impossible to prevent the startle reflex, despite the most intense, purposeful efforts to suppress the muscle spasms. No one Ekman and Robert Levenson had ever tested could do it. Earlier researchers found that even police marksmen, who fire guns routinely, are unable to keep themselves from startling.

But Öser did.

Ekman explained to the Dalai Lama, "When Öser tries to suppress the startle, it almost disappears. We've never found anyone who can do that. Nor have any other researchers. This is a spectacular accomplishment. We don't have any idea of the anatomy that would allow him to suppress the startle reflex."

Öser practiced two types of meditation while having the startle tested: one-pointed concentration and the open state, both of which were also tested during the fMRI runs at Madison. Perhaps when those data are fully analyzed they will reveal clues about which parts of the brain were involved when Öser suppressed the reflex.

As Öser experienced it, the biggest effect was from the open state: "When I went into the open state, the explosive sound seemed to me softer, as if I was distanced from the sensations, hearing the sound from afar." In fact, of all these experiments, this was the one in which Öser had the most confidence an effect would show up, so he was quite keen on doing the startle experiment in the open state. Ekman reported that although Öser's physiology showed some slight changes, not a muscle of his face moved, which

Öser related to his mind not being shaken by the bang. Indeed, as Öser later elaborated, "If you can remain properly in this state, the bang seems neutral, like a bird crossing the sky."

Although Öser showed not a ripple of movement in any facial muscles while in the open state, his physiological measures (including heart rate, sweating, and blood pressure) showed the increase typical of the startle reflex. From Ekman's perspective, the strongest overall muting came during the intense focus of the one-pointedness meditation. During the one-pointedness meditation, instead of the inevitable jump, there was a *decrease* in Öser's heart rate, blood pressure, and so on. On the other hand, his facial muscles did reflect a bit of the typical startle pattern; the movements "were very small, but they were present," Ekman observed. "And he did one unusual thing. In all others we've tested, the eyebrows go down. In Öser they go up."

In sum, Öser's one-pointed concentration seemed to close him off to external stimuli—even to the startling noise of a gunshot. Given that the larger someone's startle, the more intensely that person tends to experience upsetting emotions, Öser's performance had tantalizing implications, suggesting a remarkable level of emotional equanimity. Just such equanimity has been claimed in ancient texts as one of the fruits of these meditation practices.

To the Dalai Lama, Ekman commented, with a note of wonder in his voice, "I thought this was an enormous long shot, that it was so unlikely that anyone could choose to prevent this very primitive, very fast reflex. Yet from what we know about meditative practice, it seemed worth a try." And it certainly was.

The Power of Lovingkindness

While Öser's data on the startle test were neurologically remarkable, the implications of his performance on the next assessment were equally profound—this time not for physiology but for social relations. In this experiment, Öser would have two discussions, confrontations about issues where he and the person he talked with disagreed. As they talked, their physiology would be measured to assess the impact of their disagreement.

His partners would both be scientists dedicated to a rationalist view, and the topics were chosen to ensure a disagreement: whether one should abandon science and become a monk (as Öser had), and reincarnation. For reasons of comparison, they chose two professors—one easygoing and the other extremely abrasive—for Öser to have this encounter with. Paul described one conversational partner, a Nobel prize winner in his mid-seventies, as "one of the most gentle professors I know"—though his views on the topics were opposite Öser's. The other partner was to be a professor who, by wide consensus, was the most argumentative, difficult person on campus. However, this professor was so obstinate that when the research date arrived, he refused to participate! So Ekman chose as second-best someone with an aggressive, rather confrontational style of disputation.

During the conversations both Öser and his partner had their physiology monitored and their faces videotaped. The result: "Öser's physiology was virtually the same no matter whom he was talking to," Ekman reported. "But his expressions were enormously different." Öser smiled more often, and more simultaneously, with the gentle professor than with the difficult person.

While the easygoing professor discussed his differences of opinion with Öser, the two were smiling, keeping eye contact, and speaking fluidly. In fact, they had such a good time exploring their disagreements that they did not want to stop.

But, said Ekman, "that was not the case with the difficult person." From the start the physiological measures of the difficult man showed high emotional arousal. Yet over the course of their fifteen-minute dispute, his arousal decreased, as talking with Öser quieted him. At the end of their talk, the typically disputatious sparring partner spontaneously volunteered, "I couldn't be confrontational. I was always met with reason and smiles; it's overwhelming. I felt something—like a shadow or an aura—and I couldn't be aggressive."

That, commented Ekman, "was exactly what I hoped might occur: When interacting with someone who does not return aggression, or returns aggression with lovingkindness, then it's beneficial to you."

Finally, in the last experiment, Ekman and Robert Levenson showed Öser two medical training films that have been used for more than three decades in emotion research simply because they are so upsetting. In one a surgeon seems to amputate a limb with a scalpel and saw—actually preparing an arm stump to be fitted with a prosthesis—and there is lots of gore and blood. But the camera focuses only on the limb, so you never see the person getting the surgery. In the other, you see the pain of a severely burned patient, who stands as doctors strip skin off his body. The main emotion evoked in the scores of research subjects who have viewed both these films during experiments is highly reliable: disgust.

When Öser viewed the amputation film, the emotion he reported feeling most strongly was the usual disgust. He commented that the movie reminded him of Buddhist teachings about impermanence and the unsavory aspects of the human body that lie beneath an attractive exterior. But his reaction to the burn film was quite different. "Where he sees the whole person," Ekman reported, "Öser feels compassion." His thoughts were about human suffering and how to relieve it; his feelings were a sense of caring and concern, mixed with a not unpleasant strong, poignant sadness.

The physiology of Öser's disgust reaction during the amputation film was unremarkable—the standard changes indicating the physiological arousal seen during that emotion. But when he spontaneously felt compassion during the burn film, his physiological signs reflected relaxation even more strongly than they had when the signs had been measured during a resting state.

Ekman ended his report of the results by noting that each of the studies with Öser had "produced findings that in thirty-five years of research I have never seen before." In short, Öser's data are extraordinary.

The Extraordinary Persons Project

In fact, Ekman had been so moved personally—and intrigued scientifically—by his experiments with Öser that he announced at the meeting he was planning on pursuing a systematic program of research studies with others as unusual as Öser. The single criterion for selecting apt subjects was that they be "extraordinary."

This announcement was, for modern psychology, an extraordinary moment in itself. Psychology has almost entirely dwelt on the problematic, the abnormal, and the ordinary in its focus. Very rarely have psychologists—particularly ones as eminent as Paul Ekman—shifted their scientific lens to focus on people who were in some sense (other than intellectually) far above normal. And yet Ekman now was proposing to study people who excel in a range of admirable human qualities. His announcement makes one wonder why psychology hasn't done this before.

In fact, only in very recent years has psychology explicitly begun a program to study the positive in human nature. Sparked by Martin Seligman, a psychologist at the University of Pennsylvania long famous for his research on optimism, a budding movement has finally begun in what is being called "positive psychology"—the scientific study of well-being and positive human qualities. But even within positive psychology, Ekman's proposed research would stretch science's vision of human goodness by assaying the limits of human positivity.

Ever the scientist, Ekman became quite specific about what was meant by "extraordinary." For one, he expects that such people exist in every culture and religious tradition, perhaps most often as contemplatives. But no matter what religion they practice, they share four qualities.

The first is that they emanate a sense of goodness, a palpable quality of being that others notice and agree on. This goodness goes beyond some fuzzy, warm aura and reflects with integrity the true person. On this count Ekman proposed a test to weed out charlatans: In extraordinary people "there is a transparency between their personal and public life, unlike many charismatics, who have wonderful public lives and rather deplorable personal ones."

A second quality: selflessness. Such extraordinary people are inspiring in their lack of concern about status, fame, or ego. They are totally unconcerned with whether their position or importance is recognized. Such a lack of egoism, Ekman added, "from the psychological viewpoint, is remarkable."

Third is a compelling personal presence that others find nourishing. "People want to be around them because it feels good—though they can't explain why," said Ekman. Indeed, the Dalai Lama himself offers an obvious example (though Ekman did not say so to him); the standard Tibetan title is not "Dalai Lama" but rather "Kundun," which in Tibetan means "presence."

Finally, such extraordinary individuals have "amazing powers of attentiveness and concentration." Here again Ekman found the Dalai Lama exemplary. As Ekman later put it, "In most scientific meetings, I and others who speak frankly readily acknowledge that our mind drifts. As you listen to someone talk, you think about where you are having dinner, your attention comes back to the talk for a few minutes, and then your mind drifts off to your own work and some experiment the discussion inspires. But when I sat with the Dalai Lama for five days in meetings, I noted that His Holiness did not miss a beat. He is one of the closest listeners I have ever encountered—he's totally concentrated. And it's contagious: When I spent those five days with him, amazingly, my mind rarely drifted for a second."

Ekman acknowledged that the list was preliminary, and asked for any suggestions from the Dalai Lama. After some conversation, the Dalai Lama made an emphatic point that the cultivation of *samadhi,* a talent for single-pointed concentration, is not necessarily a spiritual activity. "When it is conjoined to spiritual practice, it may be an important preparation or adjunct, but it is not in itself one. It's a tool that can be used for a wide variety of cognitive tasks."

But, he added, "more-spiritual states of mind, such as the practice of lovingkindness and compassion, really come when you experience empathetic states. They have an expansive focus, not a narrow one, and underlying these are a sense of confidence or courage. We need to find the brain activities that are the results of that kind of spiritual practice. In the case of Öser, they were combined. But in future research, for the sake of clarity, it may be helpful if we can devise studies that could single out the effects of these different states of mind."

In short, anyone can learn to pay attention with keen one-pointedness—and apply that ability for any human end, from caring for an infant to making war. But true empathy and a universal compassion bespeak a goodness that not only is admirable spiritually but also marks one as truly extraordinary.

The Plastic Brain

From the perspective of neuroscience, the point of all this research has nothing to do with demonstrating that Öser or any other extraordinary person may be remarkable in him- or herself, but rather to stretch the field's assumptions about human possibility. Some of these key assumptions have already begun to expand, in part due to a revolution in neuroscience's supposition about the malleability of the brain itself.

A decade ago the dogma in neuroscience was that the brain contained all of its neurons at birth and it was unchanged by life's experiences. The only changes that occurred over the course of life were minor alterations in synaptic contacts—the connections among neurons—and cell death with aging. But the new watchword in brain science is "neuroplasticity," the notion that the brain continually changes as a result of our experiences—whether through fresh connections between neurons or through the generation of utterly new neurons. Musical training, where a musician practices an instrument every day for years, offers an apt model for neuroplasticity. MRI studies find that in a violinist, for example, the areas of the brain that control finger movements in the hand that does the fingering grow in size. Those who start their training earlier in life and practice longer show bigger changes in the brain.[4]

A related issue revolves around the amount of practice that it might take in order for the brain to show such a change, particularly in something as subtle as meditation. There is an undeniable impact on the brain, mind, and body from extensive practice. Studies of champion performers in a range of abilities—from chess masters and concert violinists to Olympic athletes—find pronounced changes in the pertinent muscle fibers and cognitive abilities that set those at the top of a skill apart from all others.

The more total hours of practice the champions have done, the stronger the changes. For instance, among violinists at the topmost level, all had practiced a lifetime total of about ten thousand hours by the time they entered a music academy. Those at the next rung had practiced an average of about seventy-five hundred hours.[5] Presumably, a similar effect from practice occurs in meditation, which can be seen, from the perspective of cognitive science, as the systematic effort to retrain attention and related mental and emotional skills.

Öser, as it turned out, far exceeded the ten-thousand-hour level in meditation practice. Much of that practice came during the time he spent in intensive meditation retreats, along with the four years living in a hermitage, during the early period of his training as a monk, as well as occasional long retreats over the subsequent years.

But humility stands as one of the virtues that mark spiritual advancement. Although Öser has, for instance, done a nine-month retreat that included visualization practice every day for eight hours, he notes that he still has to construct the image in his mind part by part. This can't be compared, he says, with those among the older generation of Tibetan masters still living who have devoted ten or more years in solitary retreat to training the mind. When it comes to visualization, for instance, Öser says that there are some highly experienced practitioners who are able to visualize an entire complex image in full detail all at once. And one Tibetan yogi he knows was able to do this for a full pantheon of 722 different images. "Without false modesty," said Öser, "I consider myself a very average practitioner."

He sees himself as an ordinary person who achieved the results captured in the laboratory through sustained training and a deep aspiration to transform the mind. "The process itself," as he put it, "has some extraordinary qualities, but not necessarily the subject"—that is, himself. "The important idea is that this process is within the reach of anyone who applies himself or herself with enough determination."

Humility aside, Öser appears to point toward an extreme along a continuum of brain changes that accrue from meditation. While Öser may be a virtuoso of meditation, even raw novices start to show some of the same shifts. This was clear from other data Davidson had gathered on similar brain changes in people just beginning to practice a variety of meditation called "mindfulness"—data he had shared at the earlier Dharamsala meeting (see Chapter 14 for details).

These studies had given Davidson convincing data that meditation can shift the brain as well as the body. While Öser's results suggested just how far that shift could go with years of sustained practice, even beginners displayed evidence of biological shifts in the same direction. So the next question for Davidson to tackle was this: Can specific types of meditation be used to change circuitry in the brain associated with different aspects of emotion?

Davidson may be one of the few neuroscientists anywhere who can dare to ask this, because his lab is using a new imaging technique, diffusion tensor imaging, to help answer this question. The method shows connections among different regions in the nervous system. Until now, diffusion tensor imaging has mostly been used to study patients with neurological diseases. Davidson's lab is among a select group that use the technique for basic neuroscience research, and the only one to be using it for research on how methods that transform emotion may be changing the connectivity of the brain.

Perhaps most exciting, the images created by diffusion tensor imaging can actually track the subtle reshaping of the brain at the heart of neuroplasticity. With the method, scientists can now—for the first time ever—identify the changes in the human brain as repeated experiences remodel specific connections or add new neurons.[6] This marks a brave new frontier for neuroscience: It was only in 1998 that neuroscientists discovered that new neurons are continually being generated in the adult brain.[7]

For Davidson, who readily admits that he's entering uncharted territory here, one immediate application will be searching for new connections in the circuitry crucial for regulating distressing emotions. Davidson hopes to see if there actually are new connections associated with a person's increased ability to manage anxiety, fear, or anger more effectively.

Introspective Skill: The Crucial Piece

The final presentation was made by Antoine Lutz, a research associate of Francisco Varela, a cognitive neuroscientist and director of research at the Centre National de la Recherche Scientifique in Paris. Varela, a cofounder of the Mind and Life Institute meetings of which this session was a part, had also participated in the earlier Dharamsala meeting. But, sadly, he was too ill to come to Madison; he was suffering from the final stages of liver cancer. Confined to bed, he was observing the Madison meeting from his bedroom in Paris, connected via a video Internet link. The Dalai Lama, who had known Varela for years, began each morning of the two-day Madison briefings with an affectionate greeting to his friend lying ill in Paris.

The aim of the studies by Varela and Lutz was to refine a methodology for studying subtle states of consciousness by collaborating with keen observers of the mind, such as Öser, who are highly trained in generating specific mental states.[8] They monitored what happened in Öser's brain before, during, and after a moment of recognizing an image—a sequence that comes and goes within a half second.[9]

The images being recognized are stereograms, the pop-up illusions where a vague pattern suddenly reveals itself as a three-dimensional image (the same sort of illusions were a fad in book publishing a while back). On first glance, the eye does not perceive what's being portrayed; with more focused scrutiny, the mind suddenly recognizes the hidden image. Varela's research team has done this experiment with scores of subjects, and so they know what typically occurs throughout the brain during a moment of recognition. But with Öser, they wanted to see if meditative states would make a difference in brain activity during that moment. And so Öser tried the test during the open state, during one-pointed concentration, and during a visualization.

Varela and Lutz's observations focused on the impact of each of these meditations (which they described in more scientific terms as "attentional preparation strategies") on a subsequent moment of perception. Varela and Lutz were fishing, trying to establish what difference it might make for how one perceives if, rather than being in an everyday mental state, the person is in a specific, stable meditative state. Would there be detectable variations in how the brain operates from state to state? Their answer: There are indeed clear differences, with distinctive brain signatures for both the open state and one-pointedness.[10]

But Varela's scientific goal was not so much to identify the unique landscape of the brain patterns associated with a perception following each meditative state as to show that these distinct patterns indeed exist. The real aim of the work in Paris was—as Varela had long argued—simply to demonstrate the value of working with a highly skilled and keen observer of the mind such as Lama Öser.

The appeal for science of using a skilled meditator in a study of this kind, Varela and Lutz argued, stems from the fact that the moment of perception is being analyzed in the context of the mental state that occurs in the moment just before—the topic of Antoine Lutz's dissertation research with Varela.[11] Ordinarily, subjects approach the moment of recognition from a random potpourri of mental states. But someone like Öser can do something relatively remarkable: stay in a specific, stable state just before the perception. In that way, Varela had proposed, the researchers can control with a previously unknown precision the context of the recognition moment—the mental state mere tenths of a second before the perception occurs.

His argument speaks to a perplexing dilemma for any scientist studying links between brain activity and mental states. Neuroscientific measures such as the fMRI and EEG are our microscopes on the mind, letting scientists observe the brain during the range of mental states. But these methods too often yield only rough, even fuzzy data, since the states of mind among those they measure come in rather motley assortments. While the instrumentation has extraordinary precision, scientists are left with the frustrating limitation that their experimental subjects (typically college students who volunteer as subjects to make a bit of pocket money) can provide at best a gross account of the mental states they are observing.

Even so, most neuroscientists naively assume that simply telling a subject to evoke a given mental state—such as generating an image in the mind's eye, or reliving a vivid emotional memory—means that the person being studied is actually doing as instructed during the entire time his or her brain activity is being assayed. That leap of faith is, of necessity, a standard procedure, but the data it produces typically are plagued by large inconsistencies due to the subjects' widely varying ability to execute even such simple mental tasks accurately. In short, cognitive neuroscience lacks a crucial piece for more precise measures of mental activity: skilled observer-subjects who can not only report with sharp accuracy their mental states but reliably generate a specific mental state so that it can be studied over and over.

Indeed, what was most remarkable for neuroscience about Öser's mental performance was the consistency of each state. During the experimental sessions in Madison the protocol demanded that he generate a given state for about one minute, then shift into a neutral state for the same length of time, then back to the state for another minute—and to repeat the sequence five times. For those states that Davidson has carefully examined so far, there is a remarkable dependability to the pattern that was replicated over time. For instance, for the compassion state, the likelihood of it being pure chance that the same pattern of brain activity was observed each time was less than one in ten million.

And while less-seasoned meditators cannot be counted on to replicate reliably a specific kind of meditation, with Öser's data Davidson would not have that problem. As Davidson commented on the preliminary analyses of Öser's meditation sessions, in the tone of a connoisseur relishing a superb specimen, "In every state, massive activity throughout the brain, some focal. Beautiful laterality effects."

The Bottom Line: Train Your Mind

From the scientific perspective, what does any of this matter? Davidson summed it up by referring to a book the Dalai Lama wrote with psychiatrist Howard Cutler, *The Art of Happiness*, in which the Dalai Lama said that happiness is not a fixed characteristic, a biological set point that will never change. Instead, the brain is plastic, and our quota of happiness can be enhanced through mental training.

"It can be trained because the very structure of our brain can be modified," Davidson said to the Dalai Lama. "And the results of modern neuroscience inspire us now to go on and look at other practiced subjects so that we can examine these changes with more detail. We now have the methods to show how the brain changes with these kinds of practices, and how our mental and physical health may improve as a consequence."

Take the implications for research on meditation itself. Some studies, for instance, have used relative beginners (compared to Öser's level of expertise) and had them meditate for long periods, during which their brain states were likely to have meandered through a range of experiences.[12] Such imprecision makes brain imaging data difficult to interpret with certainty. What's more, some of these researchers have made questionable speculations, going way beyond what the data actually support—for instance, expounding on the metaphysical implications of their findings.

Davidson's aims in studying meditation are more modest, and grounded in well-accepted scientific paradigms. Rather than trying to speculate about the theological implications of his findings, he seeks to use skilled meditators to better understand what he calls "altered traits" of consciousness—transformations of the brain and personality that endure, and which foster well-being.[13]

Öser, reflecting on the data reported at the Madison meeting, put it this way: "Such results of training point to the possibility that one could continue much further in such a transformation process, and, as some great contemplatives have repeatedly claimed, eventually free one's mind from afflictive emotions. The very notion of enlightenment then begins to make sense." That possibility—freeing the mind completely from the hold of destructive emotions—surpasses any assumptions of modern psychology. But Buddhism, as well as most religions (in the archetype of the saint), holds the possibility of such inner freedom as an ideal, an endpoint of human potential.

When I asked the Dalai Lama what he made of the data on Öser—such as being able to mute the startle reflex—he replied, "It's very good he managed to show some signs of yogic ability." Here he used the term "yogic" not in the garden-variety sense of a few hours a week practicing postures in a yoga studio but in its classic sense—referring to one who dedicates his or her life to the cultivation of spiritual qualities.

The Dalai Lama added, "But there is a saying, 'The true mark of being learned is humility and mental discipline; the true mark of a meditator is that he has disciplined his mind by freeing it from negative emotions.' We think along those lines—not in terms of performing some feats or miracles." In other words, the real measure of spiritual development lies in how well a person manages disturbing emotions such as anger and jealousy—not in attaining rarified states during meditation or exhibiting feats of physical self-control such as muting the startle reaction.

One payoff for this scientific agenda would be in inspiring people to better handle their destructive emotions through trying some of the same methods for training the mind. When I asked the Dalai Lama what greater benefit he hoped for from this line of research, he replied: "Through training the mind people can become more calm—especially those who suffer from too many ups and downs. That's the conclusion from these studies of Buddhist mind training. And that's my main end: I'm not thinking how to further Buddhism, but how the Buddhist tradition can make some contribution to the benefit of society. Of course, as Buddhists, we always pray for all sentient beings. But we're only human beings; the main thing you can do is train your own mind."

The Madison meeting where all this took place had been inspired by the conversations in Dharamsala the year before. There with the Dalai Lama many of these same scientists spent five intensive days exploring the great human puzzle: the nature of destructive emotions and what humanity can do to counter them. Revisiting that dialogue and the questions it raises for us all will be the main part of our story. But before we get to Dharamsala, there's another tale to share: the untold saga of the Dalai Lama's lifelong interest in science.

2

A Natural Scientist

The lineage of the Dalai Lama dates back to the fifteenth century, but Tenzin Gyatso, the fourteenth Dalai Lama, is the first in that line to be thrust so fully beyond the circumscribed universe of Tibet into the stark realities of the modern world. In a remarkable way, he seems to have been preparing himself from childhood for his encounter with the scientific worldview that so dominates the modern sensibility.

As was clear in the Madison meetings—and in those that had taken place earlier in Dharamsala—the Dalai Lama exhibits a sophistication about methods and issues in science that is unexpected, even surprising, in a spiritual leader. I've long been curious about the source of this scientific sophistication—and the Dalai Lama was kind enough to let me interview him about his lifelong interest in science. These interviews with him and with his close associates have let me sketch, for the first time, his scientific biography. A detour into this little-known side of his personal history reveals just why he places such importance on dialogues and collaborations with scientists.

That story begins with the Dalai Lama's traditional schooling, which was extremely rigorous, covering a sophisticated system of theology, metaphysics, epistemology, logic, and several schools of philosophy. It also touched on the arts, including poetry, music, and drama. From age six onward he spent many hours each day engrossed in his studies, which included a great deal of memorization, as well as meditation and concentration—all vehicles for mental discipline.

He also received intensive training in dialectics and debate, forms at the heart of a Tibetan monastic education. Indeed, the favored competitive sport of Tibetan monks is nothing like soccer or chess: It's debate. At first glance, seeing monks debate in the courtyard of their monastery looks like the intellectual equivalent of a rugby match. A tight group of monks throng around their opponent, who assails them with an energetic volley of words—a philosophical proposition he challenges them to disprove.

The monks jockey for position to reply, sometimes scrambling their way to the front with a vigor that resembles a rugby scrum. Then, swinging their prayer beads as though to underscore their point, they let go with a high-energy logical retort, emphasizing its climactic point with a grand clap of their hands. While the physicality of the debate adds a layer of theatrics, the philosophical discourse itself is as rigorous as any Socrates or the logician G. E. Moore might have engaged in.

And then there's the pure entertainment value: A witty rejoinder, which turns an opponent's point humorously to one's own advantage, scores both merit and great appreciation from onlookers. When the Dalai Lama was growing up, watching debates was a popular pastime among lay Tibetans, who would spend part of their leisure time in a monastery courtyard observing the intellectual acrobatics of the sparring monks.

For the monks, their abilities in debate were the primary way their intellectual achievements became known, and so judged. The Dalai Lama had expert tutors—and sparring partners—in this intellectual battle from the time he was twelve. Each day the main topic of his philosophical studies would also become a subject for debate. His first public debate was at thirteen, when his challengers were learned abbots of two of the largest monasteries. It was just such debates that were the focus of the Dalai Lama's final exams, a series of grand spectacles that took place when he was twenty-four.

Imagine being questioned for ten hours by the fifty top experts in your field of study, while being evaluated by a hard-nosed panel of judges—not just once, but four times. And all that in front of huge audiences, ranging in size up to twenty thousand spectators. That was exactly the predicament of the Dalai Lama when, at sixteen, he took the traditional oral exam for the degree of *geshe,* the Tibetan equivalent of a Ph.D. in Buddhist studies. Moreover, while the course of study for this degree typically takes twenty to thirty years, the Dalai Lama stood for his exam after just twelve years of schooling.

During one exam, fifteen learned scholars took turns, in groups of three, challenging the Dalai Lama on each of five main areas of religious and philosophical studies; the Dalai Lama in turn had to challenge two erudite abbots. In another exam—this during the annual new year's festival in Lhasa—thirty scholars took turns disputing him on points of logic; another fifteen were his opponents in debates on Buddhist doctrine; thirty-five more challenged him on metaphysics and other subjects. At the conclusion of these exams, he was awarded the *geshe lharampa* degree, the highest level of scholarly accomplishment.

In Tibetan-style debate, it is as important to ask the right questions as it is to have the right answer. Indeed, at the end of a round of questioning, the Dalai Lama, as is traditional, would turn the tables to ask questions of his examiners. This art of asking the right questions is a strength the Dalai Lama has put to good service in pursuing his long-standing curiosity about science.

A Trickle of Technology

Consider the Dalai Lama's dilemma as an inquisitive and bright youngster growing up in Lhasa during the 1940s and 1950s, one eager to get a scientific education. While the traditional monastic curriculum offered him a keen understanding of the nuances of Buddhist philosophy, it offered not a hint of the scientific findings of the last thousand years. For instance, a classic Buddhist text brought to Tibet from India nearly twelve centuries earlier posited a cosmology in which the world was flat and the moon shone with its own light like the sun.

To protect its political and cultural integrity, Tibet had sealed itself off from most foreign influences for centuries. By the Dalai Lama's childhood, a few members of the families of Tibetan nobility or wealthy traders had been sent to schools run by the British in Indian towns such as Darjeeling, and so were able to speak English. But by the protocol of the time, the Dalai Lama had little or no direct contact with these English-speakers. And in any case, there was not a single Tibetan in all of Lhasa with any special training in science.

Even so, a trickle of modern technology had seeped into the environs of the towering Potala Palace and to the Norbulinka, the Dalai Lama's summer residence. Some had come as gifts to his predecessor, the thirteenth Dalai Lama (who had taken a great interest in modern technology), from diplomatic missions over the years, or in the form of goods brought from British India by traders. Among these was a small electrical generating plant that powered some electric lights, a movie projector, and three antiquated automobiles.

Others were direct gifts. In 1942 an American goodwill expedition brought as one present for the young Dalai Lama a gold pocket watch. The British legation gave him several favored toys over the years, including a red pedal car, a windup clockwork train set, and a large set of miniature metal soldiers. One of his very favorite toys was a Meccano set, small metal strips with holes for screws, along with wheels and gears, with which he spent hours constructing small feats of mechanical engineering. The elaborate cranes and railway wagons that he put together existed in his mind's eye, but nowhere in Tibet.

A third cache of Western goods was the result of a 1910 Chinese incursion into Tibet, which had sent the thirteenth Dalai Lama into exile for a brief time at the hill station of Darjeeling, in India. There the Tibetan-speaking British political officer for Sikkim, Sir Charles Bell, befriended the Tibetan leader, giving him many gifts that were eventually to find their way back to a storeroom in the Potala Palace. Three of these gifts played a special role in the fourteenth Dalai Lama's earliest scientific explorations: a telescope, a globe, and a pile of English-language illustrated books about the First World War.

A Major Discovery

Though he lacked a single basic textbook on any scientific subject, the young Dalai Lama became a science polymath, voraciously learning everything he could on his own. This intellectual drive also made him eager to read books in English; he found a Tibetan official who could help him translate the English alphabet into Tibetan phonetics, and he set himself to mastering the vocabulary in a Tibetan-English dictionary. Already accustomed to memorizing long passages of scripture, he applied the same skill to building his English vocabulary. "I learned the words by heart," he recalls.

The Dalai Lama soon became an avid reader of English-language pictorial magazines, especially a British illustrated weekly and *Life* magazine, subscriptions he received through the British legation in Lhasa. These magazines became his tutor in foreign affairs; in their pages he followed the news of the world.

The Dalai Lama had also discovered in the cache of foreign goods left by his predecessor those picture books of the First World War, which he read with a boyish enthusiasm. Despite his embrace of the Buddhist doctrine of nonviolence, it was the machines of war that caught his attention: Gatling guns, tanks, biplanes, the German zeppelins and U-boats, and British warships.

Those same books featured maps of the great battlefields of the war and of the countries involved in the grand alliances. Through studying these maps, he became familiar with the cartography of France, Germany, England, Italy, Russia—and found his interest in geography ignited.

That interest, in turn, brought the young monk to a discovery that signaled, even as a boy, his scientific bent of mind. In his private quarters there was a hand-wound mechanical clock, another gift to his predecessor, the thirteenth Dalai Lama. At first the Dalai Lama was intrigued by the mechanisms of the clockwork, which rested atop a globe that gradually moved through the day.

"The globe had some patterns on it," the Dalai Lama recalls, "but I didn't know what they were."

But as he pored over those books showing maps of Europe, a realization dawned, and in the etchings on that globe he started to recognize the outlines of the countries of Europe, and then of other countries he had read about—America, China, Japan. The Dalai Lama still remembers that startling moment when "I realized it was actually a map of the world."

The turning of the globe, he saw, was designed to indicate time zones and how they changed through the day—that when it was noon on one side of the earth, it was midnight on the other. All these insights came along with a still more fundamental discovery: He deduced that the world was round!

Growing Epiphanies

That small epiphany was one of a series of independent childhood discoveries for this budding scientific mind. Another came via a different legacy from the days of the thirteenth Dalai Lama: the telescope. Because his lofty status in Tibetan society kept him sequestered in his isolated quarters in the Potala Palace, one of the fourteenth Dalai Lama's favorite pastimes during his free hours was spying on the comings and goings of people in the city below through his telescope.

But at night he turned the telescope to the skies, studying the stars and the volcanic peaks and meteor craters on the moon. One night as he peered through the telescope, he saw that the craters and peaks cast shadows. Surely, he suspected, this means the source of that light comes from somewhere outside the moon—not from inside that heavenly body, as he had been taught in his monastic studies.

To check this hunch, he scrutinized astronomical photos of the moon in a magazine. He found they showed the same thing: a shadow to the side of the craters and peaks. His own observations were now supported by independent evidence. From that the young Dalai Lama confirmed his deduction that the moon was illuminated not by some intrinsic source but by the light of the sun.

As the Dalai Lama recalled that stark moment of confronting scientific truth, "there was some kind of awareness" that dawned: "a realization that the traditional description was not true." A twelve-hundred-year-old teaching was being contradicted by his own systematic observations!

That discovery in basic astronomy was followed by other challenges to that traditional Buddhist cosmology.[1] He saw for himself, for instance, that, contrary to what he had been taught, the sun and moon are not at the same distance from Earth, nor are they roughly the same size. These childhood discoveries were to become one seed of a principle the Dalai Lama has repeated many times since: If science can prove that some tenet of Buddhism is untrue, then Buddhism will have to change accordingly.

A Mechanical Savant

When the Dalai Lama toured Richard Davidson's state-of-the-art neuroscience lab, perhaps his favorite stop was the machine shop, where parts unavailable from suppliers are custom-made to support the lab. This room fascinated him as much or more than the high-tech brain measures. He looked carefully at the lathes, drill presses, hand tools—all part of the shop he would have loved to have had when he was growing up. Later he joked about how his hands had wanted to reach out and grab for some of those tools.

When he was a boy in Lhasa, a new toy might amuse him for a short while, but the real enjoyment started once he turned to taking it apart to figure out how it worked. The young Dalai Lama was particularly fascinated by the mechanisms in clocks—how when one gear moved here, it led to a chain of movements there. To study the principles that made his wristwatch operate, he took it entirely to pieces, and—with no guidance or help—managed to put it together again so that it still worked.

He did the same (with admitted occasional disasters) to virtually every mechanical toy he had: little cars, boats, airplanes. But as he grew older, beyond these toys awaited greater challenges. There was the gift of a movie projector run by a hand crank, his first introduction to electricity. The ancient movie projector's hand-cranked generator fueled his fascination with how the rotation of a wire coil around a magnet could create an electric current. He puzzled over the pieces for hours, unable to ask anyone how it worked—until he found out how to make it work on his own.

This bit of mechanical mastery astonished Heinrich Harrer at their first meeting. Harrer, an Austrian mountain climber, had escaped over the Himalayas from a British detention camp in India and spent the last years of World War II, and a few beyond, in Lhasa. At the request of the Dalai Lama's attendants, Harrer had set up a motion picture theater at the Norbulinka for the youngster to enjoy films and newsreels that came through from India.

One day Harrer got an urgent request to come to the theater. There, for the first time, he met the Dalai Lama, then just fourteen years old. The Dalai Lama, Harrer soon realized, was a better operator of the film projector than

Harrer himself. The boy had spent a good part of the previous winter taking it completely to pieces and then putting it together again—without recourse to an instruction manual.

Then there was the oil-fed generator that ran a few electric lights in the Norbulinka. The generator often broke down, and the Dalai Lama leaped at the opportunity to try to fix it. From this machine he discovered how internal combustion machines work, as well as how the dynamo in the generator created a magnetic field as it turned.

His next venture was transferring his new knowledge of internal combustion to the three antiquated automobiles—a 1931 Dodge and two 1927 Baby Austins—that had been dismantled in India and carried over the Himalayas into Tibet for the thirteenth Dalai Lama (and were now up on blocks, rusting). With the help of a young Tibetan who had been trained as a driver in India, he was able to get the Dodge and one of the Austins to work—a particularly exciting accomplishment.

So it was that by the time he was sixteen, the young Dalai Lama had completely dismantled or reassembled to working order the generator, the projector, and two cars.

A Science Tutor Arrives

One other early scientific fascination for the young Dalai Lama was an English-language anatomy book with precise charts of the body. Transparent pages each depicted a different biological system. Even today, the Dalai Lama says, "I remember this very clearly: You see a human body and then you can take the layers off: skin on, skin off. Then the muscles off, then you can see the tendons, then the bones. Also the internal organs. It was quite detailed."

This interest in anatomy was part of a larger fascination with biology, and with nature itself. As a child he observed the natural cycles of life, making his own empirical observations of insects, birds, butterflies, plants, and flowers. Today the Dalai Lama finds himself interested in just about every scientific field except, as he says, for the dry theories of computer science.

But in the Lhasa of his youth, this thirst for scientific knowledge went largely unquenched. Although there were ten or so Europeans living at Lhasa throughout his childhood, most were with foreign legations, and formalities kept them from seeing him much, if at all.

Harrer was the exception. Having shown up in Lhasa on his own, he became a surveyor, mapmaker, and advisor to the Tibetan government, until he finally left for his native Austria in 1950. Harrer became an informal tutor for the last year and a half of his stay in Lhasa, with a weekly meeting where the Dalai Lama would grill Harrer on wide-ranging topics.

For example, Churchill, Eisenhower, and Molotov were familiar names from the magazines the Dalai Lama had read about the Second World War, but he was puzzled by exactly how they were connected to the events of recent history. There was an avalanche of questions on mathematics, geography, world events—and, always, science. How did the atom bomb work? How are jet planes constructed? What are the chemical elements, and what are the molecular differences between metals?

Harrer's tutoring focused on lessons in English, geography, and arithmetic, drawing on a handful of English schoolbooks discovered in the thirteenth Dalai Lama's cache. Even so, in his book about his seven years in Tibet, Harrer rather sheepishly hints that the Dalai Lama often asked questions to which Harrer did not have the answers.

"At that time people in Tibet believed that all the Westerners knew everything about science," the Dalai Lama told me recently. He added with a laugh, "Later I found Harrer was basically a mountain climber—I now wonder whether he really knew much at all about science!"

A New World Opens

When the invasion of Tibet by the Chinese Communists forced the Dalai Lama to flee to India in 1959, a world of scientific sources opened up for him, both in a cornucopia of books and in conversations with knowledgeable people. Once in India during the 1960s and 1970s, whenever he managed to cross paths with a scientist, or even a science teacher, he would press his questions. Such encounters, however, were sporadic and coincidental.

Other, more pressing concerns occupied his time and set his agenda of who to meet with. There was, first of all, establishing a Tibetan government in exile and tending to the needs of the Tibetan refugees scattered in settlements throughout India. Then there were his religious duties as the head of the Tibetan branch of Vajrayana Buddhism. Add to that the press of reaching out to other governments, agencies, or individuals who could work with the exiled Tibetans on regaining a degree of freedom for his countrymen inside Tibet.

Even so, he devoured books in English on biology, on physics, on cosmology—on most any scientific topic he could find. He found cosmology of particular interest, reading all he could about astronomy and theories of the universe. At the time, he recalls, "I could remember quite a lot of factual information, like the distance of celestial bodies from Earth, Earth from the sun, the sun from the galaxies, and so on."

And, at last, he was able to have at least casual contacts with people knowledgeable about science. By nature the Dalai Lama likes to talk with people he meets about their own interests. If he meets a businessperson, he talks about business; with politicians he talks politics; with theologians, religion. Now and then his path would cross that of someone current with science—or, even better, an actual scientist. And when that happened, he would inquire with keen interest about their scientific expertise.

In 1969, for example, Huston Smith, a professor of religion at MIT, came with a film crew to Dharamsala to make a documentary on Tibetan Buddhism. The Dalai Lama remembers very clearly that during a conversation about reincarnation, it was Smith who first explained the concept of DNA to him.

In 1973 the Dalai Lama met the Oxford professor Karl Popper, a leading philosopher of science. Though their encounter was at a conference about philosophy and spirituality, it was Popper's theory of falsifiability—that to be valid, every scientific hypothesis must be stated in such a way that it can be proven wrong—that particularly appealed to the Dalai Lama's background in logic.

On his first visit to Russia in 1979, the Dalai Lama requested a meeting with scientists. There a Russian psychologist gave a detailed presentation explaining Pavlov's famous experiment in which he trained his dogs to salivate in response to the sound of a feeding bell. This classic study of conditioning was the Dalai Lama's introduction to modern psychology.

By the 1980s the Dalai Lama had a working familiarity with most branches of modern science. As he puts it, "Step by step, I found I could gain some information."

The Quantum Connection

Quantum physics, with its radical challenge to our assumptions about the nature of reality, has held a particular fascination for the Dalai Lama. He explored this interest with David Bohm, a professor at the University of London and an eminent theoretical physicist who had studied with Einstein. Bohm, who for many years had had a close relationship with Krishnamurti, the Indian spiritual teacher, had a series of private conversations with the Dalai Lama over the years as travels brought the Dalai Lama to Europe. Over lunch the two men—sometimes joined by Bohm's wife—would have long discussions about quantum physics, Buddhist thought, and the nature of reality.

At one point Bohm gave the Dalai Lama a two-page summary of Niels Bohr's philosophical views about quantum theory, which articulated the scientific case for the nonsubstantial nature of reality. A similar view has been a basic premise of Buddhist thought since the teachings of Nagarjuna, the second-century Indian philosopher whose Fundamentals of the Middle Way remains a central text in the philosophy curriculum in Tibetan monasteries. The Dalai Lama was delighted to discover that modern physics, too, was positing that we cannot find an ultimate ground for our notion of the substantial nature of reality. He further explored this convergence of physics and Buddhist thought at a meeting on the philosophical assumptions underlying quantum physics, held at the Niels Bohr Institute in Copenhagen, with Professor Bohm among the participants.

By now the Dalai Lama has had deep conversations with several quantum physicists, among them Anton Zeilinger, at the University of Vienna, and Carl Friedrich von Weizsäcker (whose branch of Germany's prestigious Max Planck Institute explored links between science and philosophy), as well as astrophysicists such as Piet Hut at the Princeton Institute for Advanced Study. These conversations have continued to pursue basic compatibilities between Buddhist views of reality and those emerging from the frontiers of physics and cosmology.

From Monastery Courtyard to Scientific Lab

I once asked the Dalai Lama why, as a Buddhist monk and scholar, he had such an intense interest in science. As he explained, for him Buddhism and science are not conflicting perspectives on the world, but rather differing approaches to the same end: seeking the truth. "In Buddhist training it is very essential to investigate reality, and science is a different way to search for truth. While the purpose may be different, the scientific search expands our knowledge, so that we Buddhists can utilize it—of course, for another purpose."

For the Dalai Lama, then, Buddhism and the scientific method offer alternative strategies in the same quest. For instance, in the Abhidharma tradition—a major Buddhist framework on the mind and reality—one primary focus of analysis is in terms of distinguishing specific characteristics from general ones. He sees this as a close parallel to scientific investigations, whether of physical properties or the mechanics of mind. And as science—particularly psychology and cognitive science—focuses on studying the mind, Buddhism has its own expertise to offer.

The spirit of Tibetan monastic debate also reflects the fierce pursuit of the truth—an attribute the Dalai Lama is drawn to in scientific inquiry. Over one of their lunches David Bohm explained in more depth Karl Popper's falsifiability thesis, which holds that statements of scientific truth can be judged in terms of whether they can be disproven—all scientific hypotheses must be testable. This basic principle of the scientific method leads to a natural scaffolding of understanding, where experimental results or new discoveries build on one another, disproving or amending a hypothesis. The principle of falsifiability thus allows the scientific enterprise to be self-correcting.

This the Dalai Lama found of great interest philosophically. He was seeing that any naive belief in the "truth" of science—including his own as a child in Lhasa—was misplaced. The speculative nature of the scientific enterprise was easily overlooked; people tend to take a scientific hypothesis as an absolute truth rather than a provisional, contingent one. But while science tries to find the best approximation of truth, no discipline can claim to completely capture it.

The speculative nature of scientific thought was brought home to the Dalai Lama most clearly through hearing about the work of Thomas Kuhn, who wrote about how paradigms shift in science. The classic underpinnings of Newtonian physics, for instance, were utterly recast by the new paradigm of quantum physics. From this, the Dalai Lama saw, we must take scientific truths not as absolute and unchanging, but as theories that can become outdated if they do not fit new facts.

This powerful mechanism for truth seeking in science has great appeal for him. The self-correcting process through which science continues to sharpen its pursuit of truth parallels the very spirit of Buddhist logic in which the Dalai Lama is steeped: "In a way, the methodologies of Buddhist thought and science are essentially similar."

The Roots of Mind and Life

Not all of the Dalai Lama's early encounters with scientists proved fruitful. In 1979 he met with a group of scientists in Russia to discuss the nature of consciousness. The Dalai Lama was explaining to them the Buddhist view of consciousness articulated in an Abhidharma theory, a sophisticated science of mind that offers a fine-grained explanation of the links between sensory perception and cognition. "One of the Russian scientists was immediately dismissive, expressing his disapproval," the Dalai Lama recalls, a bit bemused. "He thought I was talking about some religious idea of soul."

At another meeting, hastily set up by his hosts in a European country, the scientists who came seemed to have a condescending attitude, as though they were begrudgingly granting some great favor by talking with the Dalai Lama. They appeared utterly closed to any possibility that some kind of insight might come from the Dalai Lama's direction.

And at a conference on religion and science, one of the scientists stood up to introduce himself, stridently proclaiming, "I am here to defend science against religion!" The scientist seemed to assume the meeting would herald religious attacks against science, rather than seek common ground. But when the Dalai Lama asked, during a discussion at that same meeting, for a scientific answer to his question, "What is mind?" he was met with baffled silence.

The need for a meeting with scientists who were better prepared—and who were open to engaging Buddhist thought—was all too obvious. So when Adam Engle, an American businessman, and Francisco Varela, a Harvard-trained biologist working in Paris, first proposed just such a series of weeklong meetings with top-level scientists, each focusing in depth on a single scientific subject, the Dalai Lama was more than receptive. He was quite happy that his meetings with scientists would no longer have to be sporadic, nor due to his initiative alone.

The first Mind and Life meeting, in October 1987, started on an auspicious footing. Jeremy Hayward, a physicist and philosopher with an Oxford degree, gave an extensive basic introduction to the metaphysics of science, from its logical positivist underpinnings through Kuhn's notion of paradigm shifts. It was Hayward who detailed the paradigm shift that occurred when classical Newtonian physics was challenged by quantum theory.

Hayward's presentation filled in some missing pieces in the Dalai Lama's understanding of the philosophical premises underlying the scientific method. And it began what has since become tradition at these meetings: Whatever the scientific topic, a philosopher is invited to bring a larger perspective to the table.

That first meeting also set the format followed in all others: a presentation by a scientist or philosopher in the morning, with afternoons devoted to an open discussion. To minimize confusions that inevitably arise in a dialogue between vastly different traditions, cultures, and languages, there are two interpreters at the Dalai Lama's side (rather than the standard one), for crucial in-the-moment clarifications. And to promote a sense of intimacy and spontaneous openness, the meetings are private, with no press and just a handful of invited guests as onlookers.

The topics covered reflect the Dalai Lama's wide-ranging scientific interests. They have included scientific method and the philosophy of science, neurobiology and cognitive science, psychoneuroimmunology and behavioral medicine. One meeting explored dreams, death, and dying from perspectives ranging from psychoanalysis to neurology. Another meeting reviewed the social psychology of altruism and compassion. Still another focused on quantum physics and cosmology.

Gathering Ammunition

What have been the benefits of these dialogues with scientists? "Now when I look back at my contact with scientists over the years, I think it's been very fruitful, very useful," the Dalai Lama says. "I've gained a lot of new views and understanding, of course. But even more, I think many of the scientists have had their first opportunity to hear the perspectives of Buddhist thought."

Buddhist insights, he has found in these dialogues, often have led scientists to a fresh perspective on their own assumptions, particularly in understanding the nuances of human consciousness, where Buddhism has a particular strength. For some scientists, that first brush with Buddhist ideas has reshaped not just how they think about their own scientific explorations, but their notion of what to look for in their research. They come away thinking differently about their own field.

For the Dalai Lama, this spread of the influence of Buddhist thought in several scientific circles represents one payoff of what is, from the perspective of Buddhist history, a pioneering move on his part. In these dialogues with science, the Dalai Lama has been not just a student of science but, to a meaningful degree, a teacher to science. To the extent that Buddhism harbors unique—and potentially helpful—insights into the human condition, he believes, they should be shared, to become part of a wider body of knowledge.

The Dalai Lama feels particularly pleased by the new perspective scientists have gained on Buddhism itself. As he puts it, "Some are beginning to see how relevant Buddhism actually can be to science. I think as time passes, it seems that now some scientists, compared to what they thought earlier, have a new recognition of the usefulness of these discussions with Buddhist thought"—a marked shift from that scientist in an early encounter who felt he had to defend science against religion.

The Mind and Life dialogues have also been useful in another way: giving the Dalai Lama what he calls "ammunition" for his public talks around the world. Though he does not take notes during the hours of scientific discussion, certain key points have stayed with him, which he often mentions in talks. For instance, he heard long ago that when newborns are held and touched more, they have better neural development—and he's repeated this scientific finding hundreds of times in public lectures about compassion and people's innate need for love and caring. He does the same with data on how chronic hostility heightens the risk that people will die from disease.

"Time and again he takes nuggets of empirical evidence and theories from science," says Alan Wallace, who often translates at the Dalai Lama's meetings with scientists, "and disseminates them throughout his own monastic communities. And when he travels worldwide he repeatedly cites what he hears at meetings like Mind and Life."

Finally, an underlying motif in all his talks with scientists has been his desire to have a Buddhism that is current and contemporary, in keeping with scientific evidence. Where there is evidence that clearly refutes Buddhist assertions, he wants to know about it—and to change accordingly. That way the Buddhist tradition as a whole will maintain its credibility in the modern world, rather than fitting what some detractors dismiss out of hand as "superstition."

Even so, when it comes to the central doctrines of Buddhism, during his decades of dialogue with scientists, the Dalai Lama has found far more agreement than disagreement with modern scientific findings.

A Natural Feel for Science

To all of these meetings, the Dalai Lama brings to the table a unique combination of spiritual and philosophical training, the mind of a debater, and an openness to dialogue. Looking back over his own background, the Dalai Lama cites some general Buddhist principles that guide him in these encounters with science. For one, Buddhism has its own detailed explanations of the nature of mind and the relationship between mind and body. For another, there's the Buddhist attitude that experiment and investigation are more important than simply taking the Buddha's word for it—and in that spirit, the Dalai Lama finds it helpful to listen to the findings of science.

While those unfamiliar with Buddhism may think of it as a single benign viewpoint, it actually offers a huge variety of diverse teachings. Just as modern science represents an abundant assortment of schools of thought, Buddhism too offers innumerable perspectives on the human condition. In this engagement with science, the Dalai Lama draws on insights not just from the extensive array of texts within Vajrayana, the school most common in Tibet, but from diverse sources among many other branches and schools of thought in Buddhism.

Then there's his debate training. Often when he listens to presentations by scientists where they draw correlations between phenomena to show a given correspondence, his debater's ear listens with a critical perspective. As happened over and over in our own dialogues, the Dalai Lama points out that the characteristics under discussion can be seen in many different perspectives. A correlation or correspondence is not invariable—it may hold in some cases but not others. And so he offers challenging counterexamples or questions. Combined with his expertise in what Buddhist scholar Robert

Thurman has called the "inner sciences," that makes him an apt collaborator for those seeking to do research on the mind.

The Dalai Lama's natural feel for the scientific method becomes very clear when he engages in discussions with scientists about their work. Time and again I have seen him listen with keen attention while a scientist from one field or another described a line of research. His Holiness then pursues a pointed series of methodological queries, suggestions, or challenges that ends with the scientist saying, "Actually, Your Holiness, that is exactly the experiment we want to do next."

Getting the personal chemistry right has been a key to these meetings. No matter how famous or successful scientists may be, the dogmatic, the pompous, or the self-infatuated disqualify themselves from the start. Those who sit with the Dalai Lama for this five-day meeting need to come with an attitude much like that of those spirited monastic debates, where new insights emerge through the back-and-forth of point and counterpoint.

"It's just like when you enter a debate in the courtyard," says Thupten Jinpa, one of the main interpreters for these dialogues. "When you have a meeting where the participants are totally open and receptive and willing to think aloud and play with ideas, it works."

In that sense, our meeting—the eighth Mind and Life conference, "Destructive Emotions"—worked unexpectedly well. This meeting, more than any of the others, bore scientific fruit through, for one, the collaboration that resulted in the Madison studies. But that research represents just one among many scientific payoffs from our meeting. And all these were natural by-products of a unique open exchange of ideas and findings. What follows offers a window into that dialogue, a scientific exploration at the cutting edge.

Day One:
What Are
Destructive Emotions?

Dharamsala, India
March 20, 2000

3

The Western Perspective

Jet-lagged, we trickled into the Imperial Hotel, an elegant vestige of the British Raj, just a few blocks from Connaught Circle, New Delhi's Times Square. We had arrived from a handful of countries—the United States, France, Thailand, Canada, Nepal. All told, we were ten: two neuroscientists, three psychologists, two Buddhist monks (one Tibetan and one Theravadan), a philosopher of mind, and two expert Tibetan translators proficient in philosophy and science.

Our topic for a week's discussion with the Dalai Lama was to be destructive emotions. But apart from fatigue, the emotions we felt most strongly were an eagerness and sense of quiet elation in anticipation of the days to come.

This would be my second time as moderator for a week of discussions between the Dalai Lama and a group of scientists; I had led a previous round of the Mind and Life meetings, on emotions and health, in 1990. The most seasoned among us was Francisco Varela, a cognitive neuroscientist from a research institute in Paris, who had not only cofounded these dialogues but participated in three before this and was personally close to the Dalai Lama. Francisco's health was a concern to many of us, who were his friends. He had been fighting liver cancer for the last few years, and just months before had gotten a liver transplant. We knew his health was fragile, though his spirits were high.

Another old hand was Richard Davidson, head of a laboratory for affective neuroscience at the University of Wisconsin; he had led the previous

Mind and Life meeting two years before, on altruism and compassion. Then there were the two translators. Thupten Jinpa, a former monk and now head of a project to translate classic Tibetan texts, is the Dalai Lama's main English-language interpreter on his worldwide trips. Alan Wallace, also a former Tibetan monk, was at the time a professor at the University of California at Santa Barbara; his science background and fluency in Tibetan made him uniquely qualified to interpret at these meetings, as he had done many times before. There was Matthieu Ricard, a Parisian turned Buddhist monk, who now lives in a monastery in Nepal and interprets for the Dalai Lama in French-speaking countries.

Then there were the newcomers, who would be meeting the Dalai Lama for the first time: Owen Flanagan, a philosopher of mind at Duke University; Jeanne Tsai, a psychologist who is an expert on cultural influences on emotion, then at the University of Minnesota; her mentor Paul Ekman, a world-renowned expert on emotions, from the University of California at San Francisco; and Mark Greenberg, a pioneer in social and emotional learning programs for schools, whose base is Pennsylvania State University. Finally, there was the Venerable Somchai Kusalacitto, a Buddhist monk from Thailand, who had been invited at the Dalai Lama's special request.

As moderator and coplanner, with Alan Wallace, I had been responsible for choosing and inviting the participants. As with planning a great dinner party, the trick was partly in balancing the right mix of old friends and new acquaintances, as well as being sure the right scientific bases were covered for a lively dialogue. We had gathered several months before for a two-day preliminary meeting at Harvard, but now we were thrown together for the week, when friendships could be forged.

The next morning we were aboard a bus, beginning our pilgrimage to Dharamsala, the Himalayan hill town where the Dalai Lama lives. The route to the Delhi airport had had a face-lift for the arrival of President Clinton, who toured India during the week of our meeting with the Dalai Lama. For the occasion New Delhi had a Potemkin-village quality: main thoroughfares lined with colorful satin flags, piles of fresh red earth ready to be spread on the streets. The tin-and-cardboard or tent encampments for the poor that spread over so many of the open spaces of the city had been masked with decorative colored cloths.

India in springtime was gentler than usual in its assault on the senses. The heat in Delhi was still tolerable, even balmy in the early morning. But by the time our flight for Jammu took off, a blanket of smog covered the gray-brown sprawl of Delhi below.

As we emerged from the Jammu airport into the parking lot, where we boarded another bus, soldiers in camouflage fatigues lounged under the dusty trees. The day was heating up. Despite the fierce traffic, the sweep of countryside and rhythm of the road caught us up. Finally, mountains materialized in the distance—our first clear view of the snow-covered Himalayas. The foothills of the Himalayas rose sharply above the plains below, making visible the upthrust from the collision of the Indian subcontinent into the Asian landmass. The fields became greener and less dusty, the rivers broader, faster. The air cooled, and then slowly, almost imperceptibly at first, we started to climb. The land became hilly, with patches of terraced fields and houses tucked into the folds of the land. The road started to wind, and we began a serious climb.

By the time darkness closed in completely, there was still at least an hour to go until we reached Dharamsala, and seven hours behind us. At the prospect of driving at night on these mountain roads, nervous camaraderie reached new levels. "In a few minutes we'll be singing," someone commented, but instead we competed with horror stories of other road trips. Matthieu won hands down with his tale of a horrific three-day-and-night bus trip from Kathmandu to Delhi with one frazzled driver.

Finally we reached McLeod Ganj, the small town in Dharamsala district where the Dalai Lama lives. The hamlet was founded as a hill station where the British colonial government (hence the "McLeod") could summer out of the fiery, draining heat of the plains below. McLeod Ganj clings to a steep ridge, with snow peaks behind and the broad, perpetually smoggy plains of India below. Even at night the streets are thronged with people wending their way by the small shops and restaurants that line the single main street. Older Tibetans in their native *chubas* expertly wield prayer wheels and mumble mantras; younger Tibetans in Western garb wield briefcases and cell phones.

Our nonarrival was the final joke: The bus became inextricably stuck in a narrow lane, hemmed in by parked taxis and unable to move forward or turn around. Loud negotiations between the driver and various voices in the dark continued for another twenty minutes before it became clear that we were a two-minute walk from our final destination, Chonor House, the pleasant guest house operated by the Tibetan government in exile, where we would stay the week. We unloaded and distributed the luggage in the dark, muddy lane and trekked the last few feet to a day's rest before Monday, when our meeting would start.

Dharamsala is Lhasa in miniature; here the Tibetan government has set up its headquarters in exile. On the edge of town, atop a small hill, the Dalai Lama lives in a walled compound guarded by soldiers from the Indian army. No one enters without going through a security check. Within the several acres of that compound the Dalai Lama has his office, his simple home (which he shares with a favorite cat), and his garden. Close by there are government office buildings in squat bungalows, a Buddhist temple, and a large meeting room, where we would have our dialogues.

The Meeting Begins

Monday morning a nervous anticipation filled the air in the large hall as we awaited the arrival of the Dalai Lama. A few rows of chairs for onlookers ringed the space where our discussions would take place. A large coffee table filled the middle of an oval formed by two long couches, on which the participants sat, with armchairs completing the ring at each end. A film crew manned strategically placed TV cameras, taping an archival record of our talk. A rainbow of *thangkas,* the Tibetan scroll paintings, ringed the room, along with rows of flowering plants and two large vases filled with roses in full bloom.

One of the monks who attend the Dalai Lama scurried around the room making last-minute adjustments. The hall, at other times used for religious rituals and teachings, has a small raised stage at the front with a large painted scroll depicting Sakyamuni Buddha centered behind a high, colorful seat where the Dalai Lama ordinarily would sit if conducting a ritual. But today he would sit in an armchair at one end of our casual, cozy setting for dialogue.

A murmur swept the room, as it would each day when the Dalai Lama entered the hall. Everyone stood while he briskly approached the large *thangka* of Sakyamuni and made three prostrations, touching his head to the floor, pausing to say a short, silent prayer. Then he came down from the small stage to the area where our conversations would take place.

Adam Engle, the chairman of the Mind and Life Institute, had escorted the Dalai Lama into the room; Adam held a long white scarf, the traditional Tibetan *khata,* which he had presented to His Holiness and which, as is customary, was immediately given back to him. Adam accompanied the Dalai Lama down the stairs to me so that I could introduce him to each of the presenters in turn.

He shook hands with the Westerners, but when he met the Venerable Kusalacitto they both bowed, palms together, in the traditional monks' greeting; the Dalai Lama took Kusalacitto's hands in his as they bowed, their shaved heads almost touching, and they exchanged a few words. He greeted Francisco Varela with a hug, then touched their foreheads together and, with a big smile, patted his cheek affectionately. On seeing the lamas who would sit behind him during the week, he again paused for a few words of greeting in Tibetan. Then, as he so often does when he enters a room, he looked around for other familiar faces, waving at old friends he spotted.

As the Dalai Lama took his seat everyone else sat down to begin the day's discussion. The Dalai Lama sat in a large armchair with Alan Wallace and Thupten Jinpa, his two interpreters for the occasion, seated just to his left. He immediately took off his shoes to sit cross-legged. On his right was another large armchair in which each presenter would take a turn; for the first morning, as cochair for the week, I sat there to begin our session.

A Compelling Topic

The day, though sunny, brought an unseasonal chill for Dharamsala at the end of March. Though he did not mention it until the next day, the Dalai Lama had a bit of fever that first day. The main sign of his cold was a cough.

As the Dalai Lama settled into his chair, I began the session. "Your Holiness, I am so happy to welcome you to this eighth Mind and Life conference. As you requested, the topic this time is destructive emotions.

"This is a compelling topic, always relevant," I continued. "As we were leaving the United States to come here, the cover story of a major newsmagazine was about a six-year-old boy who had shot and killed a classmate. When I arrived in New Delhi, I saw in the *Times of India* a similar front-page story: Two cousins were arguing over some land, and one shot the other. There is no question that destructive emotions are a great cause of suffering, not just at this gross level but in subtle ways for all of us. Our purpose here this week is to explore the nature of those emotions, why they become destructive, and what we can do about it.

"We have three goals. One is to inform. In a sense, these conferences really began as a tutorial for you, because of your own interest in science. We have assembled a scientific feast, and we present it to you as an offering. The second goal is that of a dialogue. We understand that Buddhism has really thought about these issues far longer and more deeply than the West, and we have much to learn about them from Buddhism. The third goal is to collaborate: to engage intellectually and see together where our ideas will bring us. We have designed the week, as you will see, to find ways of putting these ideas into action."

The Week Ahead

"The week begins today with a philosophical overview. Professor Owen Flanagan will give a Western perspective on what we mean by destructive emotions. Matthieu Ricard will give a Buddhist point of view; in the afternoon the Venerable Kusalacitto will contribute to the discussion from a

Theravadan perspective, and Alan Wallace will moderate. Tomorrow Paul Ekman will discuss the nature of emotion from a scientific point of view and explain more deeply what Western science understands about emotion, particularly destructive emotion, and the extent to which people's emotional responses can be altered.

"The next day Richard Davidson will present a review of the brain basis of destructive emotions, particularly," I said, using a term from Buddhism, "the Three Poisons: aggression, clinging, and delusion. He will also explore the very important theme that we call neural plasticity, the extent to which the brain's responses can be altered by experience.

"That theme will be picked up on the fourth day by Professor Jeanne Tsai, who will explore how different cultures uniquely shape the way people experience and express emotion. That same day, Mark Greenberg will explore more deeply how childhood experiences shape individual responses and also tell about some new educational programs that teach children beneficial emotional responses from the earliest school years.

"Finally, on the last day, Richard Davidson will return briefly to show us some very exciting new findings about the brain and the health effects of mindfulness meditation. The main presentation that day will be by Francisco Varela, on innovative methods for merging the experiential knowledge of Buddhism with Western scientific methodologies to explore consciousness and emotions, and to think through with you some ways of putting all of this information into a scientific agenda for action."

I ended my overview in the Tibetan tradition of dedicating a virtuous effort to the well-being of others: "Of course, our hope is that this will be of benefit not just to the people in this room but to the world at large."

I then turned the day—and my chair at the Dalai Lama's side—over to Alan Wallace, who on this occasion was wearing two hats: that of philosophical coordinator as well as of interpreter.

An Unlikely Interpreter: The Monk on a BMW

How did Alan Wallace, the son of a Protestant theologian, become a Tibetan Buddhist monk—one uniquely prepared to be the translator His Holiness relies on when engaging with scientists?

Although Alan hails from Pasadena, his childhood was anything but a southern California stereotype. His father, David H. Wallace, is a scholar of biblical Greek and New Testament theology, and as a child Alan went along on trips to Edinburgh, Israel, and Switzerland, where his father studied with some of the great Protestant theologians of the day. Despite his religious legacy—aside from his theologian father, Christian missionaries and Bible school teachers were scattered through both sides of his family tree—Alan was drawn quite early to science and planned a career in it. He started at the University of California at San Diego in environmental science, and the summer of 1970 found Alan hitchhiking through Europe on his way to a junior year at a German university.

At a youth hostel in a small town in the Swiss Alps, Alan chanced upon the translation by Walter Yeeling Evans-Wentz of *The Tibetan Book of the Great Liberation,* one of the very few Tibetan texts available in English at that point (*The Tibetan Book of the Dead* being another). It was Alan's first encounter with Tibetan Buddhism, other than a superficial treatment of Buddhism in a course on Indian civilization. While that first gloss had not rung any bells for Alan, Evan-Wentz's translation set off a carillon.

When Alan arrived at the University of Göttingen, he found to his great delight that there was a Tibetan lama on the faculty in the university—very unusual at the time. He wound up dropping all of his classes except for Tibetan. The following summer, while studying in a Tibetan Buddhist monastery in Switzerland, he happened upon a bulletin from the Library of Tibetan Works and Archives in Dharamsala saying that they would be holding classes for Westerners on Tibetan Buddhism—and the Dalai Lama would be teaching. Alan sold or gave away virtually everything he had, and bought a one-way ticket to India.

In October 1971 Alan arrived in McLeod Ganj and immediately joined the one-year class on Tibetan Buddhism given to a group of eight Westerners—the class advertised in the bulletin. Of the eight, seven had already been living in Dharamsala. Alan, it turned out, was the only person in the world beyond who had responded to the bulletin announcing the classes.

After a year's study, Alan entered the first class of the Institute of Buddhist Dialectics—along with thirty or so Tibetan monks—which was just being started in Dharamsala in 1973. He ended up becoming a novice monk, and stayed there almost four years.

After Alan had spent fourteen months in that monastery, he attended a ten-day retreat in *vipashyana* meditation taught in Dharamsala by a visiting Burmese teacher, S. N. Goenka. This experience inspired Alan to put into practice what the theory pointed to—he wanted to meditate. And so he moved into a small hut up the mountain and continued his meditation practice for the next year, during which time he did some of his first translations, mainly of Tibetan medical texts. In 1979, when the Dalai Lama made one of his first visits to Europe, Alan was asked to be his interpreter—a role he has played on and off since then.

Another turning point in Alan's life came in 1984, when his reputation as a translator got him invited to an institute set up by Robert Thurman, then a professor at Amherst College. Once there, Alan decided to return to college to finish his undergraduate studies, and soon was admitted to Amherst. There, studying with Arthur Zajonc, a quantum physicist, Alan wrote a senior thesis comparing the underpinnings of quantum mechanics to the Dalai Lama's commentary on the "Wisdom" chapter of Shantideva's classic work *A Guide to the Bodhisattva Way of Life*. Later the thesis was published in two volumes, among the first of his more than twenty books.[1] By the time Alan graduated (summa cum laude), he was thirty-six—and still a monk.

Setting off across the country on a BMW motorcycle, his monk's robe in his saddlebag, Alan stumbled across a remote retreat center in the parched Owens Valley, high in the semiarid hills of California's Sierra Nevada range. There, after his graduation from Amherst, Alan settled in for a nine-month solitary retreat. While there he went through the age-old procedure for formally returning to lay life—not unusual in Asian cultures, where many people spend a period as monks or nuns—and continued on his retreat.

It was also during this retreat that Alan got a message from Adam Engle, asking him to translate for the first Mind and Life conference. Alan was the only person whose scientific background matched his ease in the Tibetan language and Buddhism. Alan at first said no, intent on honoring his retreat. But Engle persisted, even securing a letter from the Dalai Lama requesting his presence. Alan has missed only one Mind and Life conference since.

In the meantime, Alan went on to do a doctorate in religious studies at Stanford, where his dissertation on attention drew heavily on the early-twentieth-century American philosopher and psychologist William James, making links to Buddhist philosophy and practice.[2] By now married to Vesna Acimovic, an Asian studies scholar, Alan went on to teach at the University of California at Santa Barbara, where he established a program in Tibetan culture, religion, and language, which eventually led to an endowed chair now called the XIV Dalai Lama Professorship of Tibetan Buddhism and Cultural Studies. After teaching at UC Santa Barbara for four years, he returned to the high desert of California for a six-month solitary retreat. To this day, Alan continues to write on the potential for collaboration between modern science and Buddhism—a central theme in his own life—and is now hoping to establish an institute where experimental and theoretical research in contemplative training will be conducted.

A Philosophical Beginning

"Good morning," Alan began. "We are starting today in the same way we have started each of the Mind and Life conferences since the first in 1987. Although the theme of these conferences is an engagement between Buddhism and science, we have thought from the beginning that it would be very important to include a philosopher in every meeting: someone who would raise issues that might not be raised explicitly within the scientific domain.

"There are various reasons for this. Science is not an autonomous discipline even within our own civilization, although it appears nowadays to stand on its own as if it were independent of philosophy or religion. But in reality, any critical survey of the history and development of science demonstrates that this is clearly not true. It grows out of our civilization and is deeply embedded in Western philosophy, going back to Plato, Aristotle, and even earlier. Science is embedded also in our theological traditions, Judaism and Christianity. It has always been so, although less explicitly so in the twentieth century. That is one rationale for bringing in philosophy explicitly.

"There is another rationale, too, which becomes clear as we try to understand the relationship between scientific theory, scientific exploration, and reality itself. When we in the West first engage with Buddhism, it is almost inevitable that we bring out one of our familiar stereotypes and apply it to Buddhism, calling it simply a 'religion.' It looks then as if we are engaging a science with a religion, and a lot of people would think that's a mismatch. But Buddhism has never been simply a religion as we define it in the West. From the very beginning it has also had philosophical elements, as well as empirical and rational elements that may invite the term 'science.'

"So we have a rationale from both the Western and Buddhist sides to have a philosopher here, and this morning we have not just one philosopher but representatives of each of these traditions, Professor Flanagan representing the Western philosophical tradition and Matthieu Ricard the Buddhist."

What Is a Destructive Emotion?

"I was invited to define the topic of destructive emotions, and I can do so with a one-liner: Destructive emotions are those emotions that are harmful to oneself or others." That simple definition had been arrived at by our group as a whole during two days of heated discussion at our preliminary meeting at Harvard several months before.

"But what exactly do we mean by 'harmful'? What are the nuances, the degrees, the manner in which something might appear to be harmful but in fact not be harmful? These are the questions we will be talking about in the coming days. We are interested not only in the nature of destructive emotions, but in the factors that catalyze destructive emotions: events, genetic background, brain function, and whatever other factors may be involved. What is the source of destructive emotions; from what do they actually arise?

"These are seen as very interesting issues in Buddhism. What are the effects of destructive emotions on oneself, on the environment, on other people? Once we have identified the destructive emotions and seen their causes and their detrimental effects, then we can ask what the antidote is for these afflictions. What is the medicine? How can we counteract them? Should we look to drugs, to surgery, to gene therapy, or to psychological therapy, or should we look to meditation?

"Finally, an issue that is utterly central to Buddhism from the very beginning is whether it is possible to be completely and irreversibly free of any or all of the destructive emotions. That is an extraordinarily fruitful question for all of us to attend to.

"These questions are equally pertinent to the Western and the Buddhist traditions. We have been raising these questions in the West as far back as our ancient heritage: the Bible, Plato, Aristotle. In Buddhism they have always been a central concern. The common ground of shared issues shows the importance of the topic, but there are some very, very important differences in terms of the ways each tradition explores these issues. I think we will find both the common ground and the differences equally fascinating, and we need to understand the reasons for both."

A New Breed in Philosophy

"Having said that," Alan began his introduction to the first presenter, "I would like very briefly to introduce Professor Owen Flanagan, the James B. Duke Professor of Philosophy at Duke University. But to illustrate my point, he is not simply a professor of philosophy, as if philosophy were an autonomous discipline, but also professor of neurobiology, professor of experimental psychology, professor of cognitive neuroscience, and—as a grace note, perhaps—professor of literature."

Indeed, Owen Flanagan represents a new breed of philosopher. While steeped in the traditions of his field, he also stays current in any and all scholarly fields that might inform his own. With his special focus in philosophy of mind, this means Owen keeps up with findings in psychology, cognitive science, and neuroscience—making him particularly suited for this dialogue on emotions.

During his college years at Fordham it was a toss-up whether Owen would gravitate to psychology or philosophy. In that respect, he sees himself as similar to an idol of his, William James, who never could decide whether he was a psychologist or a philosopher—and so became a founder of both fields in America.

As it turned out for Owen, the reigning psychology of the day, behaviorism—with its emphasis on the methodical study of stimulus and response in rats—was repellant enough, and the freedom and rigor of the intellect in philosophy appealing enough, that he went on to graduate work in philosophy at Boston University.

Owen's interest in the role of emotions in the life of the mind crystallized in 1980, when he decided to teach a unit on emotions in his philosophy of mind course at Wellesley College. He discovered a scientific paper by Paul Ekman and his colleagues on expression of emotion in the human face—one of the first empirical studies in what has by now become a major field of research. That paper fascinated him because it offered the first hard evidence that human emotions were universal. That finding spoke to a philosophical question about human nature: Are humans inherently loving and compassionate or inherently selfish—or do they operate on a spectrum that includes both?

Emotions figure prominently in the book Owen considers his most important. Published in 1991, *Varieties of Moral Personality* explores the role of emotions in human nature, the importance of ethics, and moral relativity. A key chapter addresses the connections among virtue, happiness, and mental health. In the best of all possible worlds, Flanagan points out, being good—virtuous—would mean both happiness and mental well-being. In the worst case, one's ethics and emotions are at odds. The question is, to what extent do they in fact coincide?

Making a Good Life

Wearing a knee-length beige Indian *kurta,* Owen took the presenter's chair next to His Holiness. He'd confided to me that he felt a bit apprehensive, if only because he is by habit a pacer and a fast, New York–style talker when lecturing; here he would be sitting, and speaking slowly and deliberately, so that His Holiness could follow his English.

"It's a great honor to be here and to have the opportunity to speak with Your Holiness, the other monks here, and fellow Westerners," Owen began. "I have a lot to learn. I'll try in my conversation today to lay out a very general picture of how those of us in the West, philosophers in particular, have thought about the role of the emotions—the role of virtues—in making a good life.

"In thinking about my presentation, I realized that there is no part of philosophy, at least not in the West, where we talk about the emotions in isolation. Within philosophy we talk about emotions in terms of what makes for a good life. How do the emotions either aid or harm the process of being a good person?

"I will try today to set out some topics that I know the other speakers will raise—about the relationship between descriptive or explanatory science and ethics, and how ethics use the emotions. Just as within the different varieties of Buddhism there are many different views, we have many different traditions in the West, some of which see the emotions as terrible things and some of which treat them as positive. Part of what I will talk about today will be an attempt to present some of the main views and attitudes that we have about the emotions, and to describe to you, from this philosopher's armchair, the mental states that we rank very highly in the West.

"From my conversations with Matthieu, I think there are some real differences here between Buddhism and the Western view. We rank certain kinds of self-respect and self-esteem, self-worth and self-accomplishment, very, very highly. We also have certain conceptions about the importance of love, including romantic love and friendship, that I suspect are different."

An Ethics Without Religion

"I thought it would be useful to start by saying a little about my life's work. I am hesitant to put it in those terms because it sounds like my life's work is over, but I have been working on these problems since I was a thirteen- or fourteen-year-old boy. It may sound grandiose, but these are the problems of the nature of the mind, the nature of morality, and what makes life meaningful. Some of my interest in these questions came from the fact that I lost my faith in Roman Catholicism at a certain point and became very concerned about questions such as why be moral, if there is no God?"

Raised in a traditional Roman Catholic family in Westchester County, outside New York City, Owen recalls his father as a "hellfire-and-brimstone" Catholic. For the young Owen, who started being taught by nuns in parochial school at five, there was a lot of scary talk about sin and heaven and hell—powerful beliefs in the life of a shy and anxious young boy. Owen's philosophical bent took the form of a precocious theological curiosity—mainly because he was constantly scared he might do the wrong thing and end up in hell.

His first open revolt against the strictures of organized religion came when he was still quite young. A favorite uncle—his mother's brother—was a lapsed Catholic. When the uncle was about to get married in an Episcopal church, Owen's mother, a faithful Roman Catholic, naturally wanted to go to her brother's wedding.

But one night Owen overheard his mother telling her father that she'd spoken to the parish priest about going, and the priest had forbidden it because it would mean worshiping in a different church. On hearing that, Owen yelled from the next room, "Father O'Connor is a horse's ass!"

By the time Owen was thirteen, he was sneaking out of Sunday mass to go to the diner for pancakes with friends. His father, fearing Owen might go the way of his favorite uncle, gave him the Penguin abridged version of St. Thomas Aquinas's *Summa Theologica,* with its five proofs of the existence of God. Owen read the book with immense fascination, testing his own analytic sensibility against Aquinas's arguments. Though he immediately saw logical holes in some of the arguments, he was thrilled nonetheless by the play of intelligence.

Owen's epiphany came the first day of his philosophy course freshman year at Fordham. His instructor, a young philosopher from Yale, said, "Plato posits the Good..." and Owen was completely enthralled. He had a vague idea of what positing was, but he had never heard of anyone doing it before. Then there was that definite article, *the,* appearing before *Good.* It took his breath away; he was smitten. That year of Plato, Aristotle, Nietzsche, and Kant—whose works Owen found incomprehensible—sealed his fate as a philosopher. But Owen also loved some of the psychology courses he took, particularly one on the history of psychology, taught by a Hungarian priest who explored the philosophical assumptions underlying the various theories. In this nexus of a scientific and philosophic exploration of fundamental issues, Owen found his intellectual passion. From that time on, Owen's intellectual mission has been, in part, to answer the great ethical questions without recourse to religious doctrine.

Owen continued his introductory remarks by noting that the book the Dalai Lama had just published, *Ethics for the New Millennium,* was written from the same perspective. "I know His Holiness has said in many of his books that his project is to help us see a way of life that can be accepted by people who come from different religious traditions, or from no religious tradition at all, and I think that this is exactly right."

Facts Versus Values

Owen then addressed the issue of how emotions are viewed in Western philosophy and Buddhism—a question that was to guide most of the day's discussion. "A final preliminary observation: When Matthieu and I were talking, and when I was reading Your Holiness's books, I began to see a difference in the way we think about emotions. In the West, we make a big distinction between saying, 'There are flowers in this room' and saying 'There are beautiful flowers in this room.' We think of the first statement as a fact—it involves a description—whereas the second involves a value judgment or a norm, in this case regarding aesthetics.

"Scientists will teach us how an emotion like anger or fear runs through the brain. Whether anger or fear is good or bad, we think of as a different question, one that has to do with philosophy in some sense. Or to decide that saying 'There's a beautiful flower in the room' in addition to 'There's a flower in the room' involves a separate judgment, an aesthetic one."

This provoked a long discussion in Tibetan about the fact/value distinction in philosophy, and how in the West the sides of that split are associated with objectivity and subjectivity, respectively. As would be true throughout the dialogue, the Dalai Lama then asked a question in Tibetan, which Jinpa translated into English: "Are you implying that this distinction is fundamentally different from the Buddhist understanding?"

"Yes, I do think there is a difference," Owen replied. "We will find out this week how much of a difference it is. But, for example, in both your book *The Art of Happiness* and *Ethics for the New Millennium,* when I read you saying, 'I truly believe we are compassionate deep in our nature,' my reaction to that is that you are correct in thinking that we *can be* compassionate."

His Holiness laughed in appreciation of the point.

"But," Owen added, "whether we are compassionate deep down inside, the Western philosophical tradition would say, is not so obvious. You'll see why in a moment when I tell you how we have usually thought about human nature."

Three Questions for Philosophy

Projecting a slide showing the interconnection of academic disciplines, with arrows linking them, Owen continued. "This is just to say a little about how I work, and how I hope to contribute. Whenever I approach a problem, whether about the nature of consciousness or about the good life, I am first of all very interested in what people say about their experience introspectively—what Western scientists and philosophers call phenomenology. Then I usually take what is said introspectively and read what neuroscientists say about what's really going on in the brain.

"I am also very interested, as are several of my colleagues here, in evolutionary biology. Like most people in the West, we begin our discussions of emotions by thinking first in Darwinian terms. We think of emotions as having been handed to us, perhaps by ancestral species of hominids that existed before *Homo sapiens.* The first question I will address is: How do we in the West think about what humans are like—if anything—deep down inside, beneath the clothes of culture and history? I say 'if anything' because some think that humans cannot be described independently of culture. But those of us who are influenced by Darwin's theory of evolution believe that there must be some universal human traits that come with the equipment.

"The second question is one that was raised from my readings in Tibetan Buddhism and in His Holiness's work: Is there some goal all humans seek? This is a very basic question in Western ethics, and, as we'll see, there is much overlap here with Buddhism. I also want to talk about the relationship between virtue and happiness because I think this has concerned everyone.

"The third question is: What makes a good person? This will go more deeply into the question of how a soul should be structured. How should the emotions be modified, moderated, or suppressed? Using meditation? Or drugs?

"To address these topics, I also need to speak about destructive and constructive emotions. I will give my own list of the states of mind that we in the West think are destructive and constructive, and this will lead to discussion—I'm not convinced I'm right."

The Western View: Essential Compassion Is Not Included

"When I ask what humans are like deep down inside, I am asking what comes with our kind of body, or our kind of animal—I do think of us as animals. In the Western philosophical tradition there have been three main answers, views that one sees again and again in the West."

Owen projected an overhead that read:

1. Rational egoists
2. Selfish and compassionate
3. Compassionate and selfish

"One is that we are rational egoists: Each person watches out only for his or her own good, but sees rationally that only by being nice to others is it possible to get what he or she wants. This is a very widespread view. In economics as well as in philosophy, many people think that things work smoothly only because each of us is smart enough to see that our own good depends on treating others well.

"By the way, Your Holiness, you will see that your own answer—that we are essentially compassionate—is not included in the three main answers that Western philosophy offers. You do, however, find a Western tradition that says humans are both selfish *and* compassionate. If you think about how fragile human infants are, there is no way they could survive unless there was compassion or sympathy on the part of their caretakers. So it seems pretty clear that whether you put compassion before or after selfishness, it's necessary for survival.

"Notice that the only difference between the second and third answers is the order. Philosophers who believe that people are selfish and compassionate think that once we have taken care of our own basic needs, then there is time left over to be loving and compassionate of others.

"The people who take the third position—that we're compassionate and selfish—say that we are basically compassionate, loving creatures, but if there is scarcity of resources such as food, clothing, and shelter, then compassion will drop out and our selfish side will emerge."

Compassion: Only for Others?

That distinction triggered another heated discussion in Tibetan, about how in English—and in Western culture—the notion of compassion seems only to apply to others. His Holiness asked Owen: "The Tibetan term for caring or compassion, *tsewa,* includes both self and others. So when you speak of compassion, can it apply to oneself as well as others?"

"I'm not sure how to answer that," Owen replied. "The text that comes to mind—Aristotle in *The Nicomachean Ethics*—says that self-love is not always egotistical. It involves respecting yourself."

"The question was really," the Dalai Lama said, "is the word 'compassion' used purely in the altruistic sense?" This was a key point of difference, and there were very animated discussions between His Holiness and the translators concerning various concepts in Buddhism that may be translated by the single word "compassion" in English.

The Dalai Lama pressed his point: "In the Tibetan term *tsewa* the connotation is the wish 'May I be free of suffering, and free of the sources of suffering.' And then there is empathy, on the basis of which one can recognize the kinship of self and others, and then feel compassion for others. But it all comes under the rubric of one term, 'compassion.' Is there a significant difference between this and the Western view?"

"My first reaction," said Owen, "is that there is a significant difference, but I will think more about it as the day goes on. We certainly have a view in the West that you can love others only if you love yourself—that if you have low self-esteem, self-hatred, or lack of self-respect, then you are in no position to love other people."

At that, the Dalai Lama gave a nod of understanding. This point about low self-esteem had come up in the 1990 Mind and Life meeting on health and emotions, which I had also moderated.[3] Sharon Salzberg, an American Buddhist teacher, had described teaching a meditation that starts with developing lovingkindness toward oneself before going on to others. One reason for this emphasis, she explained, was that so many people in the West nowadays have very low self-esteem—even self-contempt. On first hearing this, the Dalai Lama had been somewhat incredulous; the very concept of self-loathing was foreign to him.

Now he made a long point in Tibetan about how in his view caring for oneself and others is fundamental to human existence, and that to leave out the self in the Western view of compassion is a drastic omission. In essence, compassion is more than simply feeling for another—empathy—but a concerned, heartfelt caring, wanting to do something to relieve the person's suffering. And that holds whether the being involved is oneself, someone else, or an animal.

He then turned to the Venerable Kusalacitto for the viewpoint from his branch of Buddhism: "In the Pali tradition," the Venerable Kusalacitto responded, "the term for compassion applies both to oneself and to others. This is true of both *karuna* and *metta,* compassion and lovingkindness," he noted, citing the terms in the Pali language, a tongue the Buddha used, which continues as the language of scriptures in the Theravadan Buddhist tradition in Thailand, Burma, and Sri Lanka, among other countries.

"So there is homogeneity here both in the Pali tradition as well as the Sanskrit that comes into Tibetan Buddhism," Alan Wallace summed up. "The terms for both lovingkindness and compassion apply both to oneself and to others. But if, in the Western context, compassion pertains only to others, then the mental state that is directed to yourself might be in opposition to compassion for others. The connotations of the terms may have very big implications."

The One Word English Sorely Needs

"We certainly have a concept in the West of feeling sorry for yourself," replied Owen, "and we do not think of it as very positive. It is an excessive feeling that things aren't going well for you. Again, it is selfish."

The Dalai Lama clarified further, "When I make the point that human nature deep down is compassionate, I am using a term that includes compassion for oneself as well as others. But there are other terms in Buddhism that would set compassion for oneself in opposition to compassion for others. There is a term that is usually translated as 'self-cherishing,' which implies a me-first attitude, setting one's own well-being as the highest priority—as opposed to cherishing others, holding a very sincere concern for the welfare of others as an end in itself, and not because of how it filters back for one's own benefit. If you set these in opposition to each other and then ask, 'Is human nature one of cherishing others?' we'd have to come to the conclusion that no, it is not."

The Dalai Lama pointed out that they were now in the arena of linguistics, one of many disciplines that informed Owen's views in philosophy. Semantics can have real consequences for how people experience their world. Some anthropologists have argued that in a sense, a people's language creates their reality: We may be blind to phenomena or concepts for which we have no words. That was implicit in the Dalai Lama's next point.

"There should be, English being the rich language that it is, some term that corresponds to the Tibetan word for compassion that applies both to oneself and others. If there isn't one, you have to make one up."

The Dalai Lama, laughing now, then turned to Matthieu Ricard, asking in Tibetan, "Is the French language better on this point?" Matthieu responded that it is about the same in French.

"They're better on romantic love," Owen wisecracked, and again His Holiness laughed.

A Social Harmony, but Not an Inner One

Returning to his presentation, Owen next addressed the question of which emotions contribute to virtue—that is, which emotions the Western philosophical tradition has considered important for moral life. He started with those that are seen as basic to human nature. "These are the ones they would say come with the kind of creature we are: anger, contempt, indignation, fear, happiness, sadness, love, friendship, forgiveness, gratitude, regret (or remorse for having done something wrong), shame.

"Then there's—possibly—guilt. I know that guilt is absent in the similar list from the Buddhist tradition. This could be a matter of semantics, or it could be that Buddhists really don't feel very guilty (which I think is good). But in the West, guilt is an important emotion, related to shame.

"And then there's compassion. This is a list of what most moral philosophers who have thought about the nature of goodness would consider. But these are simply emotions that exist in people. I haven't said a word yet about which ones are good or bad, which ones are worth moderating or modifying."

"But you have labeled them all as 'moral' emotions," the Dalai Lama said with a smile, in a subtle allusion to Owen's earlier fact/value distinction. "Isn't that an evaluative judgment?"

"That's why I put it in quotes, in case you asked that," Owen said, laughing. "But you're absolutely right. We have views about whether feelings of anger, contempt, or indignation are sometimes appropriate and sometimes inappropriate."

Owen continued, "The basic rationale for including these emotions on the list ties in with the way we think about evolution. We think that humans evolved as social animals—we need each other. Social interaction involves opportunities for being treated well or being treated badly. Each of these emotions arises in response to social situations. For example, I become fearful if a person is threatening to harm me. I feel love when someone has treated me well, possibly in response to my treating him or her well. So the unifying idea behind the so-called moral emotions is that they are used to structure our social life to go as smoothly as possible. It's less important in our tradition to think about how to structure your own soul."

The interpreter Thupten Jinpa restated this difference between Western and Buddhist perspectives: "Is the point that philosophers in the West understand these emotions more in terms of how they facilitate interpersonal relationships than how we can perfect our inner nature?"

"That's exactly right," said Owen. "We have so much focus on the self—self-worth and self-esteem—but much less of a tradition of trying to harmonize yourself internally. These emotions and moral principles governing them all involve social relations."

A Dissatisfied Socrates or a Happy Pig?

Next Owen addressed a point the Dalai Lama has made in his writings, particularly in *Ethics for the New Millennium:* that the goal that all humans seek is happiness. "There is general agreement in the West that this is right," Owen commented. "But there is one worry. This comes from the philosopher Immanuel Kant, who said that it is one thing to be happy; it is another thing to be good." Owen added wryly, "I just throw that out there to make us all nervous."

The Dalai Lama asked, "From the Kantian perspective, where the sharp distinction is drawn between happiness on one side and goodness on the other, how would goodness be defined?"

Owen answered by showing his next slide, which asked: "What is happiness? Pleasure? Higher pleasures? Flourishing? Virtue?"

"Just as in Buddhism, everybody agrees that happiness is the goal,"

Owen explained. "But there are lots of disagreements about how to define happiness. For example, is it simple sensual pleasure, or is it only excellent higher pleasures?"

The Dalai Lama asked, "In the Western tradition, do they make the distinction between physical and mental well-being or happiness? This is a very important distinction in Buddhism."

"Yes, in fact they do," said Owen. "Almost all the philosophers who agree that happiness is the goal of life immediately see they have to make distinctions among the so-called higher and lower pleasures, or types of happiness. Take Aristotle's term *eudaimonia,* which for years was translated as 'happiness' and is now generally translated as 'flourishing.' It's a plant metaphor—the idea is that the plant doesn't actually have to feel happy to be flourishing."

Alan asked, "Owen, will you be unpacking the concepts of higher and lower happiness? Those are pretty vague."

Owen gave a pithy reply. "One philosopher—John Stuart Mill in *Utilitarianism*—said, 'Every human would seek to be Socrates dissatisfied rather than a pig satisfied.' There's something about the capacities that Socrates has that are the kinds that people naturally and appropriately want to realize. That's one way of thinking about higher and lower ones."

Better Good than Happy

"Maybe the best way to think about Kant's distinction between happiness and goodness, or virtue," Owen continued, "is to ask whether happiness involves just *feeling* a certain way or *being* a certain way. Plato says that the good person is happy and the happy person is good. They necessarily go together. But people who read Plato realize that his happy person doesn't sound happy in the sense of a child getting presents. It's a very calm state of being.

"I think when Kant said that it's one thing to be happy but another thing to be good, he thought first of all that the demands of being a good person are so hard—that there are always temptations. The demands of living a morally good life are such that you might have to sacrifice all the things that would bring you happiness. You might have to give up your life. You might have to ask your children to give up their lives for some important cause.

"Kant went so far as to think that if you performed a moral action because you were emotionally pushed to do it, it had no moral worth. For example, he thought that although the love between parents and children is natural, it has no moral worth—because morality has to involve struggle against the self."

Alan interjected, "Is it true that Kant came to the conclusion that it is better to be good than to be happy?"

Owen replied, "Yes. He thought that if there is a kind of happiness you have to give up when you stand by an important moral cause, that is a price you should be willing to pay."

To Flourish Is to Be Happy

Owen's next topic was how the emotions themselves have been characterized in the West. "One model goes back to Plato. He uses the metaphor that reason is a chariot driver with two wild horses, emotion and temperament, that are always trying to get out of control. It's a simplistic characterization, but certainly among Greek philosophers, there is a tradition that reason must conquer the emotions—moods and temperament—which are the cause of all trouble.

"Temperament is a certain emotional style, like being a shy or a moody person—it's a trait. Anger is an emotion; a person with an irritable temperament is constantly prone to being angry. Plato argued that the emotions, temperament, and appetites for sex or food are all causes of trouble, and human reason needs to take control.

"Plato's student Aristotle took a different view. He had the idea of happiness as a kind of flourishing, and he articulated the Doctrine of the Mean, which is very, very close to Buddhist doctrine. Aristotle thought that there was a set of virtues—including courage, friendship, and compassion—that should be in a harmonious relation inside each person. This comes about through being exposed to wise elders who display those characteristics.

"Aristotle also thought that every virtue involves an emotional component. For example, there is a time when it is appropriate to show anger, but you need to express just the right amount of anger in just the right way, to the right person at the right time. It's no easy task."

His Holiness chuckled at that.

Owen continued, "Aristotle thought that the virtuous response generally came from learning through imitating elders, or through *phronesis,* which means 'practical wisdom.' If you were confronted with a new situation, you would need to think more about it. But usually, knowing how to moderate your emotions so that they lead to positive action and good feeling will come naturally, automatically. Hopefully you won't always have to use your powers of discernment."

This led to a discussion in Tibetan among the Dalai Lama, his translators, and the row of Tibetan lamas behind him, trying to find the term in

Tibetan that corresponds to *phronesis*. They agreed that *so sor togpa*, meaning "discerning intelligence," comes quite close.

An Enlightenment Without Religion

Owen returned to one of his central themes: Can there be a philosophy of the good life without the underpinnings of religion? For centuries in the West, of course, thinking about virtue was inseparable from religion. Owen picked up his account: "In the West during the eighteenth and nineteenth centuries, we had our own Age of Enlightenment (although what we mean by *enlightenment* is very different than in Buddhism). It's sometimes called the Age of Reason; philosophers started to realize that the good life need not be based on any particular religious view. In our Enlightenment, philosophers tried to defend different principles that would govern moral action.

"Most Westerners, especially if they are not religious, will fall into either the utilitarian camp or the Kantian camp. Although we philosophers can argue for weeks, months, years, and centuries about the differences between the two, they have a huge amount in common."

The Dalai Lama asked Jinpa to clarify the distinction between utilitarian and Kantian notions of virtue, and Jinpa briefly did so in Tibetan. Jinpa checked his summary with Owen: "Could you characterize the principal difference between the two in this way: that the utilitarians would engage in moral actions because they lead to higher goodness, whereas the Kantians argue that you must engage in moral actions regardless of the related effects? Is there also an ontological difference between the two regarding the status of goodness—that from the utilitarian point of view, goodness is in some sense relative and contextual, and from the Kantian perspective, goodness has a certain degree of absoluteness?"

"That's right," Owen responded. "On the other hand—"

The Dalai Lama broke in, pursuing the point: "So how can one defend an absolute good without recourse to some theological condition?"

Owen conceded, "Well, in Kant's case, there *was* a theology. He was a pietistic Lutheran."

The Dalai Lama gave a satisfied smile. His point had been made—Kant's ethical philosophy is not unrelated to a religious perspective.

The Hundred Versus the One

Owen continued, "The utilitarians claimed that it might be morally justified, for example, if a hundred people gained pleasure out of doing something harmful to one person. But then, some would argue, that shows disrespect for the person, which is a higher value, a higher good."

Noticing that the morning tea break was fast approaching, Alan said, "We need to bring this to a close, but before we do, we don't want to let you off the hook. We have those hundred people waiting in the offing and the one person—what do we do as a utilitarian?"

"Utilitarians would say that logical consistency requires you to act for the greatest amount of happiness for the greatest number of people in the long run," Owen replied. "How long is the long run? Forever. It is very hard to put into effect. The usual objection to utilitarianism (though some people think it is a good thing about it) says that if you have to sacrifice one person to save the lives of a hundred people, you ought to do that. A Kantian will put a restriction on that and say that even if a hundred people will die as a result of your decision, you ought never to violate the principle of not killing. Neither principle involves worrying about how you feel emotionally about anybody; they are both based on the idea that you must be consistent."

Now Owen spoke to the Dalai Lama's earlier point connecting religious belief and philosophy: "The main point I want to emphasize is that our moral conception in the West now acknowledges that you don't need to go to church to learn these principles. You need to study moral philosophy and then you should go out and be a good utilitarian or a good Kantian. In most cases they are close, because they both involve respecting all persons equally—no one counts more than any other person."

Destructive and Constructive States of Mind

Mindful of Alan's hint that the morning tea break was near, I asked Owen to get to a key point—his list of constructive and destructive states of mind. They popped up on his overhead:

Destructive states of mind

Low self-esteem
Overconfidence
Harboring negative emotions
Jealousy and envy

Lack of compassion
Inability to have close interpersonal relations

Constructive states of mind

Self-respect
Self-esteem (if deserved)
Feelings of integrity
Compassion
Benevolence
Generosity
Seeing the true, the good, the right
Love*
Friendship*

"I am not defending this list," said Owen, "but just trying to describe the Western view from the philosopher's armchair."

Reading through the list of destructive mental states, Owen noted that the last item, the inability to have close personal relationships, may reveal further differences between the Western and Buddhist views. "I starred love and friendship in the second list because I am particularly interested in talking about them this week. Just as we would think it was destructive not to be able to have close intimate personal relations, we think it is constructive to be able to have deep loves and friendships.

"Integrity," Owen elaborated, "means that you follow your principles; you live your life according to your beliefs." While there are several terms in Tibetan for honesty and lack of guile or pretense, none of them seems to have the precise array of connotations of "integrity," Alan noted as he explained to the Dalai Lama the difficulty of translating the term into Tibetan.

"About self-esteem, I've written up there in parentheses 'if deserved.' There are a lot of people walking around who have excessive self-esteem. They think they're people of integrity—and they're not. So these feelings of self-esteem are constructive only if they're deserved. I think that things like compassion, benevolence, and generosity would appear on both the Buddhist list and our list. Also, the ability to see things truly—direct perception.

"The list could get longer if we include other, less important constructive states of mind, such as appropriate confidence and humility. But I will stop at this point and thank Your Holiness, and the audience, very much."

As Owen finished his review of the list, the Dalai Lama asked, "Did you make a distinction between negative and destructive?" Owen replied that he had not—though that point would be a major focus of differences between Buddhist and Western views of emotion in days to come.

The Yeti and the Marmots

During the tea break, Francisco Varela, looking thin but happy, came up to say hello to His Holiness, who greeted him with special affection, saying warmly, "One of my oldest friends—a great scientist."

With moral support and encouragement from the Dalai Lama, Francisco had in the previous year undergone a liver transplant, the only medical hope after hepatitis ravaged his liver. For Francisco, it seemed like a miracle to be there at all, for the time being no longer in a constant state of medical emergency, though he still survived on a complicated daily cocktail of medications. He felt tremendous gratitude to the Dalai Lama for an almost intimate sense of personal caring.

"It felt like a reunion," Francisco said later of these moments with the Dalai Lama. "Being out of a life-threatening situation finally—to me it really felt like a tremendous sense of celebration. It was truly like a gift. A gift of life . . . of caring."

During the tea break there was a more relaxed flow of activity in the room. Owen brought his son over to pose for a picture with the Dalai Lama; a few observers came up one by one to have a few words. Then Bhikku Kusalacitto approached, presenting the Dalai Lama with some Pali scriptures.

The Venerable Somchai Kusalacitto was born into a farming family in the far north of Thailand in 1947; his father was Chinese and his mother Thai. Drawn to Buddhist study early in life, he ordained as a monk at twenty. Academically gifted, he excelled in the traditional monk's curriculum of scriptures in the Pali language, and went on to get a B.A. in Buddhist studies in Thailand and a Ph.D. in Indian philosophy at the University of Madras.

The Venerable Kusalacitto's career as a scholar began with an appointment as dean at Mahachulalongkornrajavidyalaya Buddhist University in Bangkok, where he now holds the post of deputy rector for foreign affairs and lectures on Buddhist topics and comparative religion. While living as a monk and serving as assistant abbot at the Chandaram Buddhist monastery, he also makes frequent appearances on Thai radio and television and writes for newspapers and magazines on Buddhist topics. He is a cofounder of an international society for Buddhists engaged in social issues, of a group advocating an alternative educational system in Thailand, and of yet another group of Thai monks dedicated to preserving the simple life of the forest monastic tradition. And he continues to publish scholarly works on Buddhism.

For the Dalai Lama, bringing this scholarly monk from Thailand to our meeting was of special importance—not just for our scientific agenda, but for his own interest in opening dialogue between the many schools of Buddhism. Such dialogues in the early centuries of Buddhism in India, when numerous schools regularly discussed and disputed their differing viewpoints, reflected a golden age. But as Buddhism spread throughout Asia and evolved into its present branches and subbranches, those dialogues dwindled; in isolated Tibet they virtually vanished.

As we were arranging this meeting, the Dalai Lama had specifically requested that scholars representing other branches of Buddhism be invited. He had laughingly complained that he has had more dialogues with Christian monks than monks from other branches of Buddhism. As a representative of the Vajrayana school of Buddhism, which came to Tibet from India in the tenth through twelfth centuries, the Dalai Lama was eager to engage those from the Mahayana branch—most common in East Asia—and from the Theravadan arm, prevalent in Southeast Asian countries such as Thailand, the Venerable Kusalacitto's home.

So the Dalai Lama accepted the Pali texts from the *bhikku* and said in appreciation, "A monk from Theravada—that's very good. So far my serious discussions have been more with Western traditions than with our own Buddhist brothers, especially our elder monks in Theravada. I'm very happy to be going to Thailand. I'm looking forward to the visit . . . unless some lightning strikes!"

"My university plans to present you with an honorary degree," Bhikku Kusalacitto said.

And Alan joked, "Then Your Holiness will become a Ph.D.—Dr. His Holiness!"

Before we started the session again, I asked the Dalai Lama, "Are there any points you want to raise or speak to?"

"There's one area," he said thoughtfully. "Exactly how the mind functions in the arising of these emotions, in terms of conceptual and nonconceptual states of cognition."

Alan clarified, "It's a characteristically Buddhist view, something he'd like to present from his own side. There's no hurry, but it will come up. This afternoon will be an optimal time for that."

The Dalai Lama was keen to show the complexity of the Buddhist understanding of the nature of cognition, and to make clear that this framework does not make the sharp distinction between emotion and cognition (or reason) found in Western psychology. The Tibetan term *shepa,* often translated as "consciousness" or "cognition," actually subsumes them both—its meaning is closer to "mental event." The mental events that Buddhism calls "afflictions" are seen as "conceptual"—a broader term that includes what in English are called thoughts, mental images, and emotions.

The Dalai Lama hoped to make some of these points after lunch—"not a formal presentation—just a few words of explanation," as he put it.

"You've been preparing forty years for that presentation," someone said to the Dalai Lama, to which he replied with an old Tibetan story.

"A yeti stands by a marmot hole, waits for one to come out, grabs it, and stuffs it underneath him to wait for the next one—he wants to catch a bunch. Another marmot comes out, and the yeti lunges, grabs it, and sits on it—while the first marmot runs off. The next marmot comes out, and the yeti lunges for it, grabs it—and the marmot he's sitting on runs off.

"Just like that," said His Holiness merrily, "I've caught lots of marmots—but I've lost lots of them, too, over the last forty years. So, finally, there aren't many left!"

4

A Buddhist Psychology

I remember meeting the Tibetan teacher Chogyam Trungpa in 1974, while I was at Harvard teaching in the psychology department. "Buddhism," he declared, "will come to the West as a psychology."

The very idea that Buddhism had anything to do with psychology was at the time for most of us in the field patently absurd. But that attitude reflected more our own naivete than anything to do with Buddhism. It was news that Buddhism—like many of the world's great spiritual traditions—harbored a theory of mind and its workings.

Indeed, there was nothing in my training as a psychologist to suggest that modern psychology is just a more recent version of a project to understand the human mind that goes back two millennia. Modern psychological theories have their roots in European and American science and culture, and the field of psychology itself can be seen as culture-bound—myopic, almost solipsistic, in its ignorance of psychological systems from other places and times.

As it turns out, most Asian religions have at their core a psychology, though this is usually the provenance of scholars and little known to the mass of lay adherents. These psychologies are both theoretical and applied, setting forth practical methods to help the appropriate "professionals"—be they yogis or monks—discipline and regulate their minds and hearts to achieve a more ideal state.

Perhaps the richest of these "alternative" psychologies is to be found within Buddhism. Since the time of Gautama Buddha in the fifth century

BC, an analysis of the mind and its workings has been central to the practices of his followers. This analysis was codified during the first millennium after his death within the system called, in the Pali language of Buddha's day, Abhidhamma (or Abhidharma in Sanskrit), which means "ultimate doctrine."

Every branch of Buddhism today has a version of these basic psychological teachings on the mind, as well as its own refinements. That day we were to hear a Tibetan view, with a focus on emotion.

A Scholar and a Monk

After the tea break, Matthieu Ricard, wearing maroon and saffron monk's robes like the Dalai Lama's, took the presenter's chair next to His Holiness.

"From the translator's seat," said Alan, donning his moderator's hat, "I will very briefly introduce Matthieu, who came first to Asia in 1967 and has been living there since 1972."

Born into a privileged circle of the French intelligentsia, Matthieu Ricard had a childhood rich in encounters with remarkable people. His mother, an artist, was a close friend of André Breton, one of the fathers of Surrealistic painting. An uncle was one of the first adventurers ever to circle the world in a one-man engineless sailboat, taking three years. And his godfather was G. I. Gurdjieff, the Russian mystic, who had a significant following among French intellectuals in the middle decades of the twentieth century (though his mother was an enthusiast at the time, Matthieu himself has had no particular connection with his followers).

Notable philosophers and artists were among the dinner guests at the Ricard home—friends of Matthieu's father, who under the pen name Jean-François Revel is one of France's most influential living philosophers and political theorists. Author of twenty-five books—the best-known, *Without Marx or Jesus,* was an international best-seller—Revel holds La Fontaine's seat, one of just forty "Seats of the Immortals" in the Académie Française, among the country's most prestigious honors for intellectuals. A dialogue between Matthieu and his father on science and spirituality, published as *The Monk and the Philosopher,* became an international best-seller.

It was one of his mother's friends, the documentary filmmaker Arnaud Desjardins, who spurred Matthieu Ricard's first trip to find a Tibetan teacher. Desjardins had made a four-hour film for French TV, *The Message of the Tibetans.* Done in 1966, within a few years of the great exodus from Tibet of many great teachers following the Chinese takeover, the film concludes with a five-minute sequence of the faces of dozens of the great meditation masters of Tibet resting in a transcendent state as they gaze silently at the camera, one after another. Seeing those faces, Matthieu was transfixed.

So without knowing more than a few words of English (having studied instead German, Greek, and Latin in school)—and none of Tibetan—Matthieu set off for India. There he was guided to a lama by a friend who had come a few months earlier—Dr. Frédérick Leboyer, whose method of delivering babies "without violence"—in soft light, and placing the baby in lukewarm water—had a vogue a decade later.

As Matthieu tells it, his life really started on June 2, 1967, the day when he first encountered one of those great Tibetan masters in the Desjardins film, Kangyur Rinpoche—his root teacher in Tibetan Buddhism. In the Tibetan tradition of wandering yogis, the *rinpoche* had spent most of his life in retreats. But as is true of many lamas in the Nyingma tradition, Kangyur Rinpoche was married and had a family; he lived in a two-room hut near the Himalayan hill town of Darjeeling.

Matthieu Ricard felt overwhelmed by the master's peaceful compassion, wisdom, and mountain-like inner strength. Just twenty-one, Matthieu lived there with the *rinpoche* for three weeks—and though he did not know it yet, his life's direction had changed forever. Returning to his studies in France, he found his mind going back again and again to that encounter. And so he spent spare weeks of his summer holiday back in India with lamas, even as he completed studies for his doctorate in biology at the Pasteur Institute in Paris.

While a graduate student, Matthieu worked with a Nobel laureate, François Jacob, making discoveries of his own in genetics. And while still in graduate school, he wrote his first book—a definitive account of migration in animals of all kinds, ethology being one of his hobbies (along with music, astronomy, and nature photography). But finally the pull of the spiritual quest became so strong that Matthieu dropped his scientific career and settled into the life of a Tibetan practitioner under the tutelage of Kangyur Rinpoche. Once Kangyur passed away, Matthieu became a monk and the personal attendant of Dilgo Khyentse Rinpoche, spending twelve years with him, day and night—writing a book about his teacher after he died.[1]

Alan finished Matthieu's introduction. "He has been a monk for close to two decades now, and is one of the most senior of all Western Buddhist scholars of Buddhism, especially in the Nyingma tradition. He is a long-time interpreter for His Holiness into French. And, with no further ado, Matthieu, please..."

Although in his capacity as translator he has worked closely with the Dalai Lama, that morning Matthieu was in what could be an awkward position for any Tibetan Buddhist monk, as he was quick to acknowledge.

"It's a bit odd for me to explain anything about Buddhism in the presence of His Holiness," Matthieu began. "I feel like a small schoolboy taking an exam. And, as an ex-scientist, I feel the same way also in front of so many learned persons. Anyway, we have to pass exams from time to time," Matthieu said with a good-humored smile.

The first task Matthieu set himself was to address the gap between the Buddhist and English terms for *emotion.* As he pointed out, "emotion" is a very general term. "The English word 'emotion' comes from the Latin root *emovere*—something that sets the mind in motion, whether toward harmful, neutral, or positive action.

"In Buddhist terms, on the other hand, one would call emotion something that conditions the mind and makes it adopt a certain perspective or vision of things. It doesn't refer necessarily to an emotional burst arising all of a sudden in the mind—which may be closest to what scientists would study as an emotion. In Buddhist terms, such an event would be called a gross emotion—when, for example, it's clear you are either angry, or sad, or obsessed."

The Gap Between How Things Appear and How They Are

To elucidate this key distinction in how emotions are conceived in Buddhist and Western thought, Matthieu then launched into a remarkably concise overview of the perspective from Buddhist psychology. He began by describing a standard very different from that used in the West for marking an emotion as destructive: not just whether it results in obvious harm, but whether it causes a more subtle harm—distorting our perception of reality.

"How from the Buddhist point of view," he continued, "does one distinguish between constructive and destructive emotions? Fundamentally, a destructive emotion—which is also referred to as an 'obscuring' or 'afflictive' mental factor—is something that prevents the mind from ascertaining reality as it is. With a destructive emotion, there will always be a gap between the way things appear and the ways things are.

"Excessive attachment—desire, for instance—will not let us see a balance between the pleasant and unpleasant, constructive and destructive, qualities in something or someone, and causes us to see it for a while as being one hundred percent attractive—and therefore makes us want it. Aversion will blind us to some positive qualities of the object, making us one hundred percent negative toward that object, wishing to repel, destroy, or run away from it.

"Such emotional states impair one's judgment, the ability to make a correct assessment of the nature of things. That is why we say it's obscuring:

It obscures the way things are. Eventually it also obscures a deeper assessment of the nature of things as being permanent or impermanent, as having intrinsic properties or not. And so at all levels it will be obscuring.

"Thus, obscuring emotions impair one's freedom by chaining thoughts in a way that compels us to think, speak, and act in a biased way. By contrast, constructive emotions go with a more correct appreciation of the nature of what one is perceiving—they are grounded on sound reasoning."

The Dalai Lama sat quite still, listening intently, rarely asking for a clarification or interrupting Matthieu. The scientists, by contrast, took notes throughout his presentation—this was the first articulation of the Buddhist side of this dialogue.

The Question of Harm

While Alan's original criterion for destructive emotions rested on their harmful nature, Matthieu showed that there are more nuanced considerations in Buddhism. "Then we come to the description of destructive emotions as something that brings harm to someone else or yourself. Actions are not in themselves good or bad because someone decided they should be so. There is no such thing as good and bad in an absolute sense. There is only the good and bad—the harm in terms of happiness or suffering—that our thoughts and actions do to ourselves or to others.

"Destructive and constructive emotions can also be distinguished according to the motivation that inspires them: egocentric or altruistic, malevolent or benevolent. So both the motivation and the consequences of one's emotions have to be considered.

"One can also distinguish between constructive and destructive emotions by examining the ways they relate to each other in terms of antidotes. Consider, for example, hatred and altruism. Hatred can be defined as the wish to harm others or to ruin something that belongs to or is dear to others. The opposite emotion for that is something that acts directly as an antidote to that wish to harm: altruistic love. It acts as a direct antidote to animosity because, although one can alternate between love and hatred, one cannot feel, at the very same moment, both love and hatred toward the same person or the same object. Therefore, the more one cultivates lovingkindness, compassion, altruism—the more they pervade your mind—the more their opposite, the wish to harm, is forced to diminish and, possibly, disappear.

"Also, when we say an emotion is negative, it's not so much that we are repudiating something, but that it's negative in the sense of less happiness, less well-being, less lucidity and freedom, more distortion."

Alan interjected a question about hatred. "You define hatred as a wish to destroy or repel someone else, what belongs to them, or what is dear to them. Earlier His Holiness talked about whether it is possible to feel compassion for oneself, and I would like to ask a parallel question. Is it not possible to feel hatred for oneself? You seem to define it as only toward others."

Matthieu's reply was a bit surprising: "When one speaks of hating oneself, hate is not really at the core of the feeling. You might be upset with yourself, but this could be a form of pride, a sense of frustration arising from the realization that you don't live up to your expectations. But you can't truly hate yourself."

Alan pursued the issue. "So there's no such thing as self-loathing in Buddhism?"

Matthieu held his ground. "Probably not, because that would be against the basic wish of any living being to avoid suffering. You may feel you hate yourself because you want to be so much better than you are. You may be disappointed at yourself for not being what you want to be, or impatient for not becoming so fast enough. Self-loathing actually includes a lot of attachment to the ego. Even someone who commits suicide does so not out of self-hatred but because of thinking that it's a way of escaping a greater suffering."

Matthieu added a Buddhist perspective on suicide: "One is not escaping anything, because death is just a transition to another state of existence. So it would be better to try to avoid the suffering either by endeavoring to solve the problem in the here and now or, when that is not possible, by changing one's attitude toward this same problem."

The Eighty-four Thousand Negative Emotions

Getting back to his main point, Matthieu continued, "According to Buddhist teaching and practice, where do those destructive emotions come from? Basically, we all know that from childhood to old age, we change all the time. Our bodies are never the same and our minds acquire new experiences with every instant that passes. We are a flux, in constant transformation. Yet we also have the notion that at the center of all that, there is something that defines us, something that has remained constant from childhood that defines 'me.'

"This 'I'—let's call it 'ego clinging'—that constitutes our identity is not simply the thought of 'me' that comes to our mind when we wake up, when we say 'I feel hot' or 'I feel cold,' or when someone calls us. Ego clinging refers to a deeply ingrained grasping to an unchanging entity that seems to be at the very core of our being and defines us as a particular person.

"We also feel that this 'I' is vulnerable and that we need to protect it and please it. From that come aversion and attraction: aversion to whatever might threaten this 'I,' and attraction toward whatever pleases or reassures this 'I' and makes it feel secure, happy. From these two basic emotions, attraction and repulsion, a host of diverse emotions will come.

"In the Buddhist scriptures, one speaks of eighty-four thousand kinds of negative emotions. These are not all identified in detail, but this vast figurative number reflects the complexity of the human mind and gives one to understand that methods to transform this mind need to be adapted to the great variety of mental dispositions. This is why one speaks of eighty-four thousand entrance doors to the Buddhist path of inner transformation. Anyway, these multifaceted emotions boil down to five main ones: hatred, desire, confusion, pride, and jealousy.

"Hatred is the deeply felt wish to harm someone else, to destroy their happiness. It is not necessarily expressed in a burst of anger. It's not expressed all the time, but it will manifest when meeting with circumstances that trigger one's animosity. It is also connected with many other related emotions, such as resentment, bearing grudges, contempt, animosity, and so on.

"Then the opposite is attachment, which also has many aspects. There is the plain desire for sensual pleasures or for an object we want to possess. But there is also the subtle aspect of attachment to the notion of 'I,' to the person, and to the solid reality of phenomena. Essentially, attachment has to do with a kind of grasping that makes you see things in a way that they are not. It will make you think, for instance, that things are permanent—that friendship, human beings, love, possessions, will last—although it is clear that they will not. So attachment means clinging to one's way of perceiving things.

"Then there is ignorance, the lack of discernment between what needs to be accomplished or avoided in order to achieve happiness and avoid suffering. Of course, ignorance is not normally regarded as an emotion in Western culture, but it is clearly a mental factor that prevents a lucid and true ascertaining of reality. It is thus a mental state that obscures ultimate wisdom or knowledge. Therefore it is considered to be an afflictive aspect of mind.

"Pride, too, has many aspects: being proud of one's achievements, feeling superior to others or holding them in contempt, wrong assessments of one's own qualities, or not recognizing others' good qualities. It often goes with not recognizing one's own defects.

"Jealousy can be seen as an inability to rejoice in others' happiness. One is never jealous of someone's suffering, but of their happiness and good qualities. From a Buddhist perspective, it is a negative emotion. If our goal is precisely to bring well-being to others, we should be happy if they find happiness by themselves. Why should we be jealous? Part of our work is already done—there is that much less to do."

The Illusory "I"

"Why are all these basic emotions so closely related to the notion of 'I'? Let's imagine that you suddenly tell somebody, 'Could you please get angry, very angry, right now?' Nobody will get completely angry—no one can do that, except maybe a really good actor who can mimic anger at will for a relatively short time.

"But if you say to the same person, 'You are a scoundrel; you are such a disgusting person,' then you don't have to wait for very long. That person will immediately get angry. Why this difference? Because you have targeted the 'I.' Since this notion of there being a self seems to be at the source of all emotions, it follows that if one wants to work with emotions, one has to investigate in depth this notion of 'I.' Does it really stand up to analysis as a truly existing entity?

"So there is a very deep approach in Buddhist philosophy and practice to try to examine if that 'I' is just an illusion, just a name we attach to that stream and flux in continuous transformation. We cannot find the 'I' in any part of the body, or as something that would pervade the body in its entirety. We might think that it lies in the consciousness. But consciousness is also a stream in continuous transformation. The past thought is gone, the future one has not yet arisen. How can the present 'I' truly exist, hanging between something that has passed and something else that has yet to arise?

"And if the self cannot be identified in the mind or the body, nor in both together, nor as something distinct from them, it is evident that there is nothing we can point to that can justify our having such a strong feeling of 'I.' It is just a name one gives to a continuum, just as one can point to a river and call it Ganges or Mississippi. That's all.

"But yet when we cling to it, when we think there is a boat on that river, that is when all the troubles come—when we begin clinging to this notion of 'I' as something truly existing, that needs to be protected and pleased. Aversion, repulsion, the five afflictions, the twenty secondary ones, and eventually the eighty-four thousand aspects of afflicting emotions will unfold."

Three Levels of Consciousness

"The next question is: Are these negative emotions inherent in the basic nature of mind or not? To answer this, we need to distinguish different levels of consciousness. According to Buddhism, there are three levels of consciousness: gross, subtle, and very subtle.

"At the gross level we have all the kinds of emotions. The gross level corresponds to the functioning of the brain and the interaction of the body with its environment. The subtle level corresponds to the notion of the 'I' and to the introspective faculty with which the mind examines its own nature. It is also the mind stream that carries on tendencies and habitual patterns.

"The very subtle level is the most fundamental aspect of consciousness, the mere fact that there is a cognitive faculty rather than not.[2] It is sheer consciousness or awareness, without a particular object upon which consciousness is focused. Of course, we generally do not perceive consciousness in such a way; this takes contemplative training.

"When we say various levels of consciousness, it's not like three streams running in parallel—it's more like the ocean with its different depths. Emotions concern the gross and the subtle level but do not affect the most subtle one. They could be compared to waves on the surface of the ocean while the fundamental nature of mind corresponds to the ocean's depth.

"The very subtle level is sometimes referred to as 'luminous,' but when we speak of the luminous aspect of mind, it does not mean that there is something glowing somewhere. The adjective 'luminous' refers simply to the basic faculty of being aware, without any coloration from mental constructs or emotions. When this basic awareness, sometimes called 'the ultimate nature of mind,' is fully and directly realized, without veils, this is also considered to be the nature of Buddhahood."

Throughout Matthieu's talk, the Dalai Lama was listening intently, sometimes nodding slightly. This was familiar territory, and he did not interrupt for clarification or to challenge an idea.

Freedom from Destructive Emotions

"The next step is to determine whether it is possible to free oneself entirely from destructive emotions. This is possible only if negative emotions are not inherent in the ultimate nature of mind. If negative emotions, like hatred, were inherent in the most subtle aspect of mind, they would be present at all times. We should be able to look at the depth of consciousness and find in it hatred, craving, jealousy, pride, and so on.

"Yet just our ordinary experience tells us these negative emotions are intermittent. And contemplatives tell us that as they go deeper toward realizing the fundamental aspects of consciousness, they do not find negative emotions in the luminous continuum at the very subtle level. It is rather a state that is free from all destructive emotions and negativity.

"Even though the vast majority of people experience negative emotions at various times, that does not mean that such emotions are inherent in the nature of mind. To give an example, when a hundred pieces of gold lie in a dusty place, all of them might be covered with dust, but that does not change the nature of gold itself. The belief, based on contemplative experiences, is that destructive emotions are not embedded in the basic nature of consciousness. Rather, they arise depending on circumstances and various habits and tendencies that express themselves from the outer core of consciousness.

"This opens the possibility for working with those ephemeral emotions and the tendencies that breed them. If destructive emotions were inherent in the mind, there would be no point in trying to gain freedom from them. It would be like washing a piece of charcoal, which can never become white. To recognize the possibility of being free is the starting point of the path of inner transformation. One can drive away the clouds and find that, behind them, the sun has always been there and the sky has always been clear.

"To consider whether those destructive emotions are part of the basic nature of mind, we need to examine them. Take anger, for example. A strong burst of anger seems irresistible, very compelling. We feel almost powerless not to feel angry; it is as if one has no choice but to experience it. This is because we don't really look at the nature of anger itself. What is anger? When you look from the distance at a large summer cloud, it seems so massive that one could sit on it. Yet if one goes into it, there is nothing to grasp, nothing but steam and wind. At the same time, it obscures the sun, so it has an effect.

"So with anger. One classical approach in Buddhist practice is for the meditator to look straight into the anger and ask: 'Is anger like an army commander, like a burning fire, like a heavy stone? Does it carry a weapon in its hand? Is it somewhere we can find, in the chest, the heart, the head? Does it have any shape or color?' Of course one does not expect to find someone thrusting a spear into one's stomach! Yet that's how we conceive of anger, as something very strong and compelling.

"But the experiment will show that the more you look at anger, the more it disappears beneath one's very eyes, like the frost melting under the morning sun. When one genuinely looks at it, it suddenly loses its strength.

"One discovers as well that anger was not what one had originally thought. It is a collection of different events. There is, for instance, an aspect of clarity, of brilliance, that is at the very core of anger and is not yet malevolent. Indeed, at the very source of destructive emotions there is something that is not yet harmful.

"Thus," Matthieu explained, "the negative qualities of emotions are not even intrinsic to the emotions themselves. It is the grasping associated with one's tendencies that leads to a chain reaction in which the initial thought develops into anger, hatred, and malevolence. If anger itself is not something that is solid, it means anger is not a property that belongs to the fundamental nature of mind."

A Universal Antidote

"That leads to how to deal with negative emotions, not just by observation, but in terms of inner transformation. As negative emotions creep continually into the mind, they transform into moods and eventually into traits of temperament. Therefore one needs to begin by working with emotions themselves. One can do so in several ways and at various levels—beginning, intermediate, and advanced.

"The first way, when we try to avoid the negative consequences of the destructive emotions that bring unhappiness to self and others, is to use antidotes. There is a specific antidote for each emotion. As I mentioned earlier, we cannot feel hatred and love simultaneously for the same object. Thus love is a direct antidote to hatred. Likewise, one can contemplate the unpleasant aspects of an object of compulsive desire, or try to have a more objective assessment. For ignorance, or lack of discernment, we try to refine our understanding of what needs to be accomplished and what avoided. In the case of jealousy, one can try to rejoice in others' qualities. For pride, we try to appreciate others' achievements and open our eyes to our own defects to cultivate humility.

"This process implies having as many antidotes as there are negative emotions. So the next step—in the intermediate level—is to find if there is an antidote that could work for all of them. This antidote is to be found in meditation, in the investigation of the ultimate nature of all negative emotions. One finds that they don't have an inherent solidity—that they exhibit what Buddhism calls emptiness. It's not that suddenly they all vanish into the sky, but that they are not as solid as they seem.

"Doing so enables one to demolish the apparent solidity of negative emotions. This antidote—the realization of their empty nature—acts on all emotions, because although emotions manifest in various ways, they are identical in not having a solid existence.

"The last way, which is also the most risky, consists not in neutralizing emotions or in looking at their void nature, but in transforming them, using them as catalysts for swiftly freeing oneself from their influence. It is like someone who falls into the sea and takes support from the water itself to swim and reach the shore.

"These methods are sometimes compared with three possible ways of dealing with a poisonous plant. One alternative is to uproot the plant carefully and remove it from the ground completely. This corresponds to the use of antidotes. A second alternative is like pouring boiling water onto the plant. This is like meditating on emptiness. The third alternative is that of the peacock, which was traditionally thought to be able to feed on poisonous substances. The peacock comes along and eats the plant. Not only is the peacock not poisoned, when other animals might die, but its feathers become even more beautiful. This corresponds to the practice of using and transforming the emotions as a means of enhancing one's spiritual practice. However, this last method is risky. It only works for peacocks—lesser animals would get into serious trouble!

"In all three cases, the results are the same, a common goal is achieved: We are no longer enslaved by negative emotions, and we progress toward freedom. It does not really matter which method is 'higher' than the others. They are like a key. The purpose of the key is to open the door. It does not matter whether it is made of iron, silver, or gold as long as it opens the door. In practical terms, whichever method works best for the inner transformation of each individual is the most suitable and the one that needs to be applied.

"Let's remember, however, that the last one, however tempting it may seem, is like trying to take a jewel from the top of a snake's head. If, while trying to use emotions as catalysts, one does not truly transform them but instead experiences them in ordinary ways, one will become more enslaved than ever!"

Before, During, or After?

Matthieu then turned to a related theme, the timing of an intervention with a destructive emotion. Does one deal with such emotions after they arise, at the time they arise, or before they arise?

"The first intervention—after they arise—is the beginner's approach, because usually one realizes the negative or destructive aspects of some emotions only after having experienced them. You then use reason to investigate their consequences—seeing, for example, that a strong burst of hatred, which makes one perceive someone as entirely evil, can cause much suffering to others and certainly does not make us happy either. In this way, we can distinguish the emotions that bring happiness from those that cause suffering. It will then become clear that the next time such emotions are ready to arise, it is best not to give them free rein.

"When one has gained some experience in this practice, the next stage is to deal with emotions as they arise. The crucial point here is to free emotions at the moment they surge in one's mind, so that they don't trigger a chain of thoughts that proliferate and take over the mind, thus compelling one to act—to harm somebody else, for instance. For this, one stares at the newly born thought, in the way we described earlier, asking whether it has a shape, location, color, and so on, in order to discover that its true nature is emptiness. If we become experienced in this process, thoughts and emotions come and go without giving birth to a host of binding thoughts, just as a bird flying through the sky does not leave any trace, or like a drawing made on water—as you draw it, it disappears at once.

"Of course, this is something that requires long practice, but with training it can certainly become a perfectly natural response. The Tibetan word for meditation means, in fact, 'familiarization.' One becomes familiar, through practice, with this way of seeing thoughts come and go. You get used to it.

"Then, when you are quite experienced, the final step comes: Even before an emotion might arise, you are ready in such a way that it will not arise with the same compelling, enslaving power. This step is linked to realization, a state of achieved transformation, where the destructive emotions don't arise with nearly the same strength.

"To give an example, a very trivial one: If you have a stomach with a lot of gas, it's hard to repress it all the time—that can be painful. But it's not really good manners to let it go as it comes. Both repression and just letting loose—those are not good answers. So the best is to cure the problem so that you don't have to either fart or suffer!

"Emotions are a bit like that. There is a point, with experience, when practitioners have had lovingkindness soak their mind. It becomes second nature, so hatred is expelled from one's mind stream and there is no way that one would harm someone willingly. Hatred no longer arises, and there is nothing to be repressed. This marks a validation of one's spiritual practice."

Deep Fulfillment

"It might be thought that if one gets rid of all emotions, one will become as torpid and unresponsive as a log. But this is completely false. When the mind is free, it is lucid and clear. The sage who is completely at peace and free from disturbing emotions has a much greater sensitivity and concern toward others' happiness and suffering—whereas a distracted and confused person is unaware, just as one does not feel a hair in the palm of one's hand. By contrast, the sage, completely at peace and free from those disturbing emotions, has an acute perception of others' suffering and the law of cause and effect; he feels them as keenly as if he had a hair in his eye. He has a much finer sense of judgment and a wider compassion.

"People might say that if you don't express emotion, it might lead to unhealthy states of mind. But emotions can be expressed in many different ways. For example, anger can be expressed not by letting it burst out in rage and insults, but by confronting it with our own intelligence. We don't have to repress our emotions. We can channel them into a dialogue with our intelligence, using them to understand the nature of our mind, watching how they subside of their own accord without creating more seeds for their future arising. For the moment, one thus avoids the harmful consequences of hatred, and in the long term it will have no cause for reappearing in such violent ways.

"The final question is whether it is possible to rid oneself completely of negative emotions. The answer has to do with wisdom and freedom. If you consider that destructive emotions restrain our inner freedom and impair our judgment, then as we get more free from them, they will not have the same strength. We will have more freedom and happiness.

"We should distinguish pleasure from happiness. Happiness is understood here to refer to a deep sense of fulfillment, accompanied by a sense of peace and a host of positive qualities such as altruism. Pleasure depends upon the place, the circumstances, and the object of its enjoyment. One can get pleasure at certain times and not at others. It is bound to change. Something that is pleasurable at one point might soon give rise to indifference, then to displeasure and suffering. Pleasure exhausts itself in the enjoying, just like a candle that burns down and disappears.

"By contrast, a deep sense of fulfillment does not depend upon time, location, or objects. It is a state of mind that grows the more one experiences it. It is different from pleasure in almost every way. What we seek by disentangling ourselves from the influence of destructive emotions is the kind of inner stability, clarity, and fulfillment that we are referring to here as happiness."

Original Goodness, Not Original Sin

Matthieu concluded: "In one of his articles, Owen mentioned a philosopher who said that throughout human history, there has probably been no one who has been truly happy and truly good. Buddhism offers a different perspective. The Tibetan word for Buddhahood has two syllables: *sang,* which refers to someone who has cleared away all obscurations, and *gyey,* which refers to one who has developed every possible excellence, like light replacing darkness. Buddhahood is conceived as ultimate goodness, the actualization of the goodness at the fundamental core of consciousness.

"Since the potential for actualizing Buddhahood is present in every sentient being, the Buddhist approach is therefore closer to the idea of original goodness than to that of original sin. This primordial goodness, the Buddha nature, is the ultimate nature of the mind. This state of realization is said to be utterly devoid of negative emotions and, consequently, of suffering. Is such a realization possible? In answer to this, one has to rely on the testimonies of the Buddha and other enlightened beings.

"As I mentioned earlier, the possibility of enlightenment is based on the notion that obscuring emotions are not inherently part of the fundamental nature of the mind. Even though a piece of gold may be buried in the mud for centuries, in itself it never changes. All one needs is to remove the various layers that cover the gold and reveal it as it is and has always been. Attaining Buddhahood is therefore a process of purification, of the gradual accumulation of positive qualities and wisdom. Ultimately, one comes to a state of full awareness in which obscuring or destructive emotions have no reason to arise anymore.

"One may wonder how an enlightened being can function without emotion. It seems to be the wrong question, since destructive emotions are precisely what prevent one from seeing things as they are, and so functioning properly. Obscuring emotions get in the way of a correct ascertainment of the nature of reality and of the nature of one's mind. When one sees things as they are, it becomes easier to rid oneself of negative emotion and to develop positive emotions, which are grounded in sound reason—including a much more spontaneous and natural compassion.

"Everything must be based on direct experience. Otherwise it would be like someone building a beautiful castle on the frozen surface of a lake; it is bound to sink when the ice melts. As the Buddha said, 'I have shown you the path. It is up to you to travel the path.' It's not something that comes easily. Experience requires perseverance, diligence, and constant effort. As the great Tibetan hermit Milarepa said, 'In the beginning nothing comes, in the middle nothing stays, in the end nothing goes.' So it takes time. But what is encouraging is that if you progress to the best of your capacity, you can definitely check that it works."

As Matthieu concluded, the Dalai Lama bowed his head to him in appreciation, saying with a smile, "In addition to his title of *gelong*"—that is, monk—"Matthieu should also now have the title of *geshe*"—the equivalent of a Ph.D. in Tibetan spiritual studies.

5

The Anatomy of Mental Afflictions

When a political event triggers a sense of moral outrage in us, can we act forcefully, yet stay free from the distorting sway of rage? More to the point, can our political leaders do so, since their actions reverberate through the lives of so many people?

Given that people in the grip of rage readily make flawed decisions and act out impulses they later regret, the answer is more than academic. I remember a conversation about anger in world leaders with Ronald Heifetz, founding director of Harvard's Center for Public Leadership at the John F. Kennedy School of Government. He observed that anger in a leader can take on a special amplifying power among those led, simply because people pay so much attention to what they say and do—and so skilled leaders have learned to carefully calibrate how they display their dismay and anger. But beyond that, leaders must know how to cool their own rage if they are to make the best political decisions.

For instance, in 1963, when John F. Kennedy learned that the Soviets had brought nuclear missiles to Cuba, he became enraged, taking it as a personal affront—after all, the Soviet ambassador had assured him just months before that such a thing would never happen. But Kennedy's closest advisors deliberately made the effort to help him calm down before deciding what steps to take—and so may have averted a world war.

Of course, moral outrage in the political arena can mobilize grand actions that right injustices—as with Gandhi's protests of British colonialism and Martin Luther King Jr.'s leadership of the American civil rights movement. But, as Heifetz pointed out, in such movements leaders play the role of transforming rage into effective action. One way is by giving words to what people are feeling, and so letting them know the leader understands. But then the leader goes another step: absorbing their anger rather than letting it drive them to impulsive, destructive acts.

At the personal level, just such a transformation of raw anger into effective action was one of the topics that emerged over the course of our afternoon discussions. Buddhist psychology, it turned out, draws a distinction between anger fueled by biased perception, on one hand, and clear, forceful—even wrathful—action against evil, on the other. And it offers not only a model for mobilizing the energy of moral outrage in the service of compassion, but practical methods for doing so. What would the world be like if more leaders applied such methods to themselves?

A Buddhist Framework

After our lunch break, we gathered again. As at the start of each session, there was a buzz of conversation in the room, which abruptly drew to a close as the Dalai Lama entered and was seated. Alan Wallace began our afternoon session with an important caveat: "We were all very fortunate this morning to have two sterling representatives of their respective traditions, Western and Buddhist. In my conversation last night with Owen and Matthieu they both suggested that I point out what is perhaps obvious, that is there is no such thing as 'the Western tradition' in the sense of one monolithic entity that has cruised through time for the last twenty-five hundred years, any more than there is one monolithic entity that is Buddhism.

"In fact, as soon as one penetrates through the surface, you find multiple strands, many of which are internally incompatible to varying extents and in various ways. At the same time, it is still viable, as we have seen this morning, to make some valid generalizations that are clearly and distinctly Western, and others that are clearly and distinctly Buddhist. So this duet has begun. His Holiness commented to Jinpa and myself this morning that he already had some thoughts that were percolating in his own mind. So now I would like to invite His Holiness to respond."

The Dalai Lama wished to explain some basic premises underlying the Buddhist concept of destructive emotions. His explanations drew on the Abhidharma, a foundational text for Buddhism's highly sophisticated epistemology, which includes not just a phenomenology of mind but a theory of how we know. This theoretical discussion offered a glimpse—rarely seen by Westerners who do not go to his religious teachings—of the Dalai Lama's scholarly training; as a *geshe* of the highest rank, he was drawn to subtle levels of issues raised by our discussion. No doubt many of his comments went over the head of some of those present; in effect it was a graduate-level presentation for those who had barely achieved a grade-school grasp of Buddhist thought. As usual, while making more theoretical comments, this afternoon he spoke in Tibetan, with his remarks interpreted into English.

The Dalai Lama paused with palms together in greeting to the Venerable Kusalacitto, the Thai monk, who was coming in a bit late, and then began. "After listening to the morning's presentation, it occurred to me that—regardless of whether it has any direct bearing on what we discussed this morning—it might be helpful to bear in mind the Buddhist distinction between two principal categories of experience. On the one side are those that are related to and contingent upon our senses. On the other hand there are experiences that are not so directly contingent upon sensory faculties, which the Buddhist framework describes as 'mental.'

"The Buddhist understanding of what we call 'feeling' pervades both of these realms, sensory and mental. What is meant here by 'feeling' is not as broad as the term in English, but simply feelings of pleasure, pain, and indifference. In comparison to the feeling or sensation in the realm of the senses, the feeling in the realm of the mental is thought to be of greater significance from the Buddhist point of view. Evaluative judgments—between right and wrong, beneficial and harmful, desirable and undesirable—take place at the mental, conceptual level as opposed to the sensory. When we talk about the application of reason, about the ability to judge long-term consequences, the process of analysis, we are talking about activity in the realm Buddhists call discursive thought."

He then made a key distinction between conceptual as opposed to nonconceptual cognitions. "Sensory cognitions are considered to be nonconceptual; their engagement with the object is unmediated by language or concepts. They are also said to be more direct and nondiscriminatory. Take seeing a flower in front of you. Visual cognition is very direct—it only apprehends the flower present there as colors and shapes. But when you have a thought of a flower—a conceptual cognition—that expands time to include the flower that you saw yesterday and the flower you saw today.

"However, this mental realm of cognition is not necessarily conceptual all the time. For example, if you think of a flower, and constantly reaffirm the thought of the flower and focus on it, you can directly engage with an object that is a construct of your mind—not a physical object, a flower out there, but rather a mental construct, an imagined form of the flower. Your engagement with it in the first moment is unmediated; at which point it is in a nonconceptual mode.

"In short, sensory perception is only nonconceptual, while mental cognition—like visual memory—can be of two types: conceptual and nonconceptual."

Forms: Tangible, Intangible, and Imagined

The scientists were taking notes again—this was a framework of analysis completely different from those they had been schooled in. The Dalai Lama continued by noting how difficult it could be to understand that the idea of a thing can get mixed with its mental image. "Many of the afflictions, such as attachment or desire, can increase to such a point that the image does not correspond to reality outside the mind."

This is a key point in Buddhist psychology: the process by which desire (or aversion) creates what amounts to a "form" in the mind, the imagined image of the object of desire.[1]

"In fact, there are said to be five types of imaginary forms."[2] Here, as he approached even more rarified territory, the Dalai Lama paused to consult with Alan, Jinpa, and Amchok Rinpoche, director of the Library of Tibetan Works and Archives, who was in the row of four lamas sitting just behind him.

After a brief consultation in Tibetan, he explained that one of the types of imaginary forms "arises in the context of a meditation, such as a visualization," an intentionally evoked, intangible image that exists in the mind's eye.[3] A second is "the type of mental image that arises in the context of afflictions." These, sometimes called imaginary forms, might include what the West would call projections, fantasies, or otherwise imagined ideas about something or someone. They represent the distorted nature of afflictive emotions.

The mental picture we hold of someone we are attracted to, for instance, will be an idealized version of the actual person. That image, a projection of the mind, is innately afflicted, since it invariably distorts the reality. This distortion pertains not just in fantasies and daydreams but also during ordinary thinking.

Mental Afflictions: The Two Types

"So," the Dalai Lama continued, "when we talk about afflictions, we refer to specific kinds of conceptual modes of cognition. Some of the antidotes for these afflictions may at the initial stage be conceptual, but later they can develop into nonconceptual states." In other words, the means for neutralizing destructive emotions include meditation practices involving thoughts—the conceptual—and those that transcend thought—the nonconceptual.

The Dalai Lama noted, "Mental afflictions—called *kleshas* in Sanskrit—by definition are considered distorted. The term 'mental afflictions' overlaps with 'destructive emotions,' though not exactly. As the closest parallel concept in Buddhism, it would play a major role in our discussion.

"There are two principal types of mental afflictions," the Dalai Lama continued. "One type is an afflictive view of reality, and the other is not." Here he was referring to a distinction between afflicted intelligence, which is more cognitive, and emotional afflictions such as attachment, anger, and jealousy. The distinction depends on whether the distortion stems mainly from a skew in thoughts and ideas or from emotional biases. The distinction also affects how the particular distortion may be corrected or countered.

Afflictive intelligence distorts reality. The Dalai Lama cited two views that Buddhist thought classically regards as afflicted: substantialism and nihilism. Put simply, these are philosophical polarities: A nihilistic view denies the existence of something that *does* exist, while a substantialist view asserts or reifies the existence of something that does *not* exist.

"Let's imagine that one holds a nihilistic view and asserts the utter cessation of something that in reality has an ongoing continuity. This is a distorted view, an expression of afflictive intelligence. If one simply responds to that affliction by saying, 'That's bad, I don't like it,' that doesn't make a distorted view go away. One can't make a distortion go away simply by reprimanding it. Rather, one needs to bring in reason; to counteract a distorted view, one has to bring in unafflicted intelligence to counteract afflicted intelligence.

"You need to counteract it with something that ascertains the nature of reality—not simply with an impression, a desire, or a prayer. These afflicted views have arisen through a process of thinking, and so you may be quite confident they are true. Therefore, they need to be counteracted by the application of right insight so that the certainty you were holding previously can be undermined and shattered. So the Buddhist would say distorted views need to be undermined by undistorted views."

Countering Afflictions

Now the Dalai Lama brought the discussion around to the topic at hand: countering destructive mental states, including emotions. "Generally speaking, when we adopt a specific antidote for mental afflictions, the antidotes tend to reflect the nature of the afflictions themselves. For example, to counter attachment, there are meditations designed to bring to mind the unattractive characteristics of the object of your attachment. Whatever you're craving or clinging to, you attend to its unattractive qualities to counteract that obsessive craving for it. Or, for anger or aversion, you cultivate lovingkindness.

"As Matthieu was saying earlier, these antidotes directly counteract the respective afflictions. These are not factors of intelligence or realization. But as you arouse lovingkindness or compassion, intelligence will certainly play a role in that process.

"And so the meditative cultivation of lovingkindness and compassion in the Buddhist context depends on attending to those aspects of reality that arouse lovingkindness. It doesn't come out of nowhere, or out of prayer or something like that. It comes from attending to certain facets of reality that themselves ignite or arouse compassion and lovingkindness.

"Let's take this Western term, 'emotion,' and draw on its Latin etymology of 'that which sets in motion.' In Buddhist understanding there are two ways in which the mind is set in motion or aroused. One is cognitive, using reasoning and taking evidence into account." This more thoughtful mode, he added, tends to give rise to positive emotion, as in arousing lovingkindness.

"There is another way in which the mind is set in motion that is much more spontaneous. There may be a little bit of reasoning that goes on in this process, as when one looks at an object and says, 'That's attractive,' but the reasoning is pretty flimsy. A lot of the negative or destructive emotions arise from that more spontaneous category."

By now the Dalai Lama had become quite animated in making his points, emphasizing each with gestures almost reminiscent of a Tibetan-style debate. He concluded, "Therefore, from the Buddhist point of view, even in dealing with the afflictions, understanding the nature of reality becomes very important because lack of understanding leads to either reification, some kind of nihilism, or false denial. For that reason, valid, verifying cognition is very important."[4]

Some Questions

I could see by his body language that Francisco Varela wanted to ask a question, and, nodding to give him a go-ahead, said "Francisco," to alert His Holiness.

The points the Dalai Lama had made about reification and nihilism, while seemingly abstruse, are quite familiar to most practitioners of Tibetan Buddhism, including Francisco. Buddhism encourages us to look at reality on two levels. At the ultimate level, one realizes the emptiness of one's mind and of nature; at that level, seeming entities break down into their constituent processes. Yet at the conventional level of everyday reality, we all function as though the self or the objects around us were the fixed entities they seem to be.

For Francisco the scientist, the Buddhist view of an "empty self" fit well with models of the "virtual self" that are being developed in his own fields, biology and cognitive science, as well in the philosophy of mind. In this view, the self can be seen as an emergent property at the mind's interface with the world. Like the mind, the self has no substantial existence. It cannot be located anywhere, but rather is produced by an underlying network of biological and cognitive systems. However, through something like an optical illusion of the mind, we reify the self, attributing to it a solidity that under more systematic scrutiny proves illusory.

Drawing on this background, Francisco asked the Dalai Lama to clarify the level he was addressing. "When you speak of reifying reality, are you talking about not understanding the empty nature of reality, or are you talking of a more relative nature?"

"Both levels," the Dalai Lama responded. "The phenomenological nature of reality as well as its ontological nature. In every way, reality must be understood." In other words, in the Buddhist framework, the everyday, relative reality reflects the phenomenology of our ordinary experiences; the ultimate level reveals its true qualities—its ontology.

Francisco pursued the point about truth: "What do you do with the assessment of a situation where there are multiple opinions? How can there be one, and only one, correct perception?"

The Dalai Lama responded, "In terms of what is being presented to the senses, there are some perceptions that are just wrong. This is very pertinent for science. If something is white, it's not black; if it's black, it's not white. It is not a matter of opinion or perspective; it's true or false.

"But if we consider conceptual cognition, it is said there are an infinite number of perspectives on whatever is being presented to the mind. This is because mental cognition selects specific features of the object in question, whereas sensory perception does not. Whatever you filter out or select determines what is true from that perspective. One person filters out this, and this cognition is true from his perspective, while another person filters out something else, and that cognition is true from his perspective. Owen brought up the issue of beauty, the difference between facts and values that are in the realm of conceptualization."

"In that case," Francisco said, "understanding the true nature of the world involves understanding that it is underdetermined, understanding its multiplicity or possibility. Now, the reason I make this footnote is because the empiricist tradition is very dominant in the Western mind. Empiricists would immediately translate your statement concerning the true nature of reality into an objective, verifying mode that is much less subtle than what is being talked about here."

The Fragility of Afflictions

The Dalai Lama saw that Owen Flanagan had a question, and gestured for him to go ahead. "I'm very confused now," Owen said. "I would ask a clarification of His Holiness and of Matthieu."

Owen began on a note of agreement. "Matthieu made the claim, and I think Western philosophers now understand this, that there is a problem with reifying the self. Still, there was a very long tradition of believing that there must be an ego, an 'I' or self.

"The argument that you have given in your writings," Owen said, gesturing to the Dalai Lama, "the argument that Matthieu gave this morning, and the philosophical arguments that my friends and I put forward in America converge on the conclusion that—whether you look at the human body or the way the mind works, the way it interacts with the world—it is a mistake to think there is a permanent ego or self. That is a form of argument we are used to in Western cognitive science and philosophy of mind."

Then he went on to challenge Matthieu's leap from premises about advanced meditation techniques to statements about basic human nature. "There was a second argument that Matthieu put forward in talking about luminous consciousness, that once one learns certain meditative practices or techniques, one realizes that one can void one's mind of all the afflictive emotional states. Then he concluded that this shows that the afflictive or destructive emotions are not inherent parts of the mind.

"Here is my problem with the logic of that argument. I certainly accept that there are meditative practices that are self-verifying in the sense that if my mind is voided of all content, then that's true of me. But basing any claim about inherent parts of the mind on this technique is a problem. If I could void my mind of destructive emotions, of positive emotions, of any particular thought and sensation, then this logic would allow the conclusion that none of those things is an inherent part of the mind. I'm curious whether His Holiness or Matthieu is going to accept that."

The Dalai Lama was smiling, waiting to jump in. His reply: "The problem that we are confronting here may have to do with semantics. When Buddhists talk about afflictions of mind not being an inherent part of the mind, certainly they are not claiming that these afflictions are not natural. Just like any other qualities of the mind, these afflictions are also innate aspects of the mind. Rather, the claim is that the afflictions have not penetrated into what is called the luminous nature of mind, which is seen as its most fundamental aspect.

"This claim is made on several premises. One is that the fundamental nature of the mind is luminous. The second is that all the afflictions we experience are rooted in a fundamentally distorted way of perceiving the world. In some sense they don't have a solid, stable support—they are not based on reality, so that makes them fragile.

"Another premise is that powerful antidotes exist that allow us to counter these afflictions and their underlying basis. These antidotes engage with reality in valid ways. And then, finally, these powerful antidotes are qualities of mind, which implies that if you enhance and cultivate them, you can develop them further. So if you take these premises collectively, the argument is that in principle these afflictions are removable."

Owen was now satisfied. "That's what I wanted to clear up. This is extremely helpful because a lot of us will be talking about natural characteristics of the mind. The big question for both groups is how modifiable, plastic, and changeable they are. There are a slew of techniques that we may learn from each other."

Barnacles of the Mind

The Dalai Lama continued, "There are also two broad classifications of mental afflictions. One is better translated as *connate* rather than *innate.* It means 'arising with' or 'coemergent.' In the Buddhist view, since beginningless time, the mind has been encumbered with these coemergent mental afflictions. But there is another class of mental afflictions that are acquired; these you pick up over the course of a life, like barnacles on a boat traveling in the ocean. You may pick up a lot, or you may pick up a few."

As I understood his point, these acquired mental afflictions include not just what psychology sees as neurotic habits but any learned, distorted belief. These might include, for instance, the belief in the natural superiority of one's own group.

"But both types," the Dalai Lama continued, "whether connate or acquired, are separable from the very nature of the mind. This luminous nature of the mind is not some high state, not something that you accomplish, but something that is primordial, fundamental, and essential. If we look at the very nature of cognition or of the mind, it has two salient features. One is the sheer event of knowing, the cognizant event itself, called *rigpa,* simply knowing. The other is the luminous or clear aspect, the factor of awareness that allows for appearances to arise; it's the 'appearance maker.'

"The fundamental nature of cognition, *rigpa,* is that sheer event of knowing. But this fundamental luminosity is veiled by mental afflictions, which by their very nature are mistaken and obscuring—a distorted knowing. And so they are incongruent with the nature of cognition itself, which suggests that cognition and the mental afflictions could possibly be separated."

Perhaps thinking of the three teachers of Dzogchen meditation sitting right behind him—Mingyur Rinpoche, Tsoknyi Rinpoche, and Sogyal Rinpoche—as well as the several Westerners in attendance who had studied with them, the Dalai Lama added, in an aside, "In case any of you have had an introduction to Dzogchen, we are not referring to *rigpa* in the sense used in Dzogchen, of primordial, pristine awareness. This is straight Buddhist psychology, where *rigpa* simply means 'cognition.'"

Varied Afflictions, Various Antidotes

This analysis of the workings of the mind leads to a range of strategies for handling the variety of afflictive emotions, as the Dalai Lama went on to explain. "So there are different types of antidotes for different mental afflictions. Some antidotes entail imagination, where you are superimposing something as a skillful means to counter a mental affliction. Such imaginative meditation does not entail an apprehension of reality.

"But a wide range of other meditative procedures precisely counteract mental afflictions by close engagement with reality itself. By closely engaging with reality correctly, you then diametrically oppose and overwhelm the mental afflictions that, by nature, falsely apprehend the nature of reality.

"In terms of degrees of maturation, or ripeness, of one's mental state—for example, excessive anger—the countermeasures that use some form of imagination to override it are very gross. But it is just a temporary device; it only deals with the symptoms. If you really want to eradicate that mental affliction altogether, there is no way except to engage with reality itself, because the underlying problem lies in a misengagement, or a misapprehension, of reality."

Matthieu jumped in, to clarify: "When we speak of freedom from negative emotion, the point is not so much to get rid of something but to dispel a mistake. To be free from an erroneous way of dealing with the arising of thought, free of an erroneous way of perceiving reality, we are not just blanking out our mind. There is not 'something' to get rid of. We are getting rid of unknowing, and of wrong perception."

The Dalai Lama added, "It's a bit like the stages in education that children go through. As they acquire more and more knowledge, they dispel degrees of ignorance about different subjects. But that doesn't imply that there is a tangible entity called ignorance that is chipped away bit by bit."

Matthieu brought up the classic example of distorted perception: "If you mistake a rope for a snake, when you recognize that it's a rope and not a snake, there is no snake that has gone somewhere."

Paul Ekman, the emotions researcher, had been listening attentively and now spoke up for the first time. His comment was based on his view that emotions have served a positive purpose in evolution, helping us survive. He countered, "The mistake itself would be very useful, it seems to me. You may save your own life—because sometimes it isn't the rope, it *is* the snake. The very mechanism that initially alerts you is useful. So much of the discussion seems to assume that emotions always mislead us, but we wouldn't have them if they were always misleading us. But I can't see how to take my psychological framework and adjust it to the Buddhist framework when it comes to distinguishing when emotions are operating in our service and when they are not."

Jinpa, clarifying the gist of the discussion for the Dalai Lama, suggested to Paul, "You are saying that from the evolutionary point of view, if they are not useful they wouldn't exist . . . so why should they exist?"

The Dalai Lama, after pondering a moment, asked Paul, "From that point of view, how would you regard death? Is there some benefit to death?"

"That's a giant step, isn't it?" Paul asked, surprised by this turn.

"The point is that death is something that nobody aspires to," the Dalai Lama replied, "but the very fact that we were born means death is unavoidable. Yet birth has its benefit—we have to use it well.

"Emotion is like death in that it is part of our mind, part of our life, part of our nature," the Dalai Lama continued. "However, within the realm of emotions, some are destructive, some are positive. So it is worthwhile, or at least there is no harm, in analyzing what kinds of emotion are destructive, and which are constructive or beneficial. So then, with this awareness, let us try to minimize these destructive emotions, and let us try to increase these positive emotions, because we want a happier society. So that's a simple answer."

This exchange—with Paul rather nonplussed by the Dalai Lama's leap to using death as a counterexample—bespoke a collision of cultures. The Dalai Lama, in debate mode, had evoked death as the contrary case to the evolutionary assertion that since we have emotions, they must necessarily serve us well, having value for survival. From the perspective of Buddhist dialectics, this line of argument seemed absurd, and invoking death as the example was meant to make that absurdity clear.

In making this counterargument, the Dalai Lama had skipped over several steps in a logical sequence, which—had this been a debate in a monastery courtyard—might have gone: "Well, if you believe emotions serve us well because of evolution, what about anger? What about rage? What about the human cruelty they cause? How about child abuse?" And that sequence could have ended with his question about the evolutionary usefulness of death. All that to make the point that simply because we have a fact of life, it does not ipso facto make it utilitarian—a point argued similarly by thinkers such as Stephen Jay Gould, who says not all traits produced by evolution are adaptive.[5]

Back to the Everyday

Now His Holiness brought us back to common ground, to the level of everyday concerns. "The framework in which our discussion on the destructive nature of emotion should take place is understanding how emotions affect us within the confines of one human lifetime. Matthieu gave us the standard presentation of the Buddhist view, an account of emotions in terms of spiritual aspiration, the possibility of attaining total freedom from these destructive emotions—what Buddhists call enlightenment or nirvana. Within that view, certain kinds of afflictions—such as grasping at the inherent nature of reality—give rise to negative emotions.

"But that is not really the context in which we are having our discussion—the framework here is a secular one. Within the secular framework, that grasping at the inherent nature of reality need not be afflictive. In fact, it could have positive effects. So there is no need to talk about how to get rid of the belief in the inherent nature of reality."

Paul Ekman was pleased. "I completely agree," he said. "The issue for me is how we identify when emotions are destructive and when they aren't, why sometimes they are and sometimes they're not, as well as how to change that. We can get caught in the words themselves—like 'negative'—because what we generally think of as negative emotions, like fear, can be very positive in some instances."

"Quite true," the Dalai Lama agreed. "In Buddhism also."

From Comic Books to Cambridge

The afternoon's discussion so far had been a heady, somewhat rarified excursion through fine points of Buddhist psychology and philosophy. The Dalai Lama had conducted this excursion with great brio, taking pleasure in exploring such subtleties. The remainder of the day would be taken up with a more specific response from the Buddhist side to Owen's presentation.

Like the Dalai Lama, Thupten Jinpa, a highly regarded Buddhist scholar, had been feeling the need to make clearer the Buddhist position on which particular emotions are seen as destructive. Jinpa, by popular consensus, had been tapped to elucidate the concept of afflictive mental faculties, the nearest Buddhist equivalent to the idea of destructive emotions. Working with Alan during our lunch break, he had prepared a summary based on the classic Abhidharma texts. Alan would, once again, step out of his role as interpreter to present Jinpa's analysis, leaving Jinpa free to serve the Dalai Lama as interpreter should questions come up.

The thousands of people who have seen Jinpa (as his friends call him) interpreting have little idea of the unlikely path his life's journey took on the way to his becoming the Dalai Lama's principal English-language interpreter. Born in western Tibet near Nepal's border, Jinpa was brought to India as an infant when his entire family left in 1960, just after the Dalai Lama had fled the country. He was only five or six the first time he met the Dalai Lama, who was visiting a nursery for Tibetan children in Simla, India. Jinpa, who ended up walking by the Dalai Lama's side holding his hand, asked one question: "When can I become a monk?"

By the time he was eleven, Jinpa had indeed joined a monastery. Always a quick learner, he started practicing English during his spare time after finishing each day's required memorizations and lessons. His early school years had included a smattering of English, and now he continued studying on his own, at first using Indian comic books (English-language renditions of the Ramayana and other great epics of Indian mythology), then graduating to detective stories like the Perry Mason series. On an old transistor radio he had managed to buy he listened avidly to the BBC, picking up the elocution he retains to this day, with its cultured intonation hinting of Oxbridge.

Also helpful were Voice of America broadcasts, whose announcers purposely used a simple vocabulary, spoke slowly, and repeated each sentence. While at a monastery in Dharamsala in the early 1970s, he would hang out with the hippies who had flooded there in those days, to practice his English. Along the way, Jinpa picked up old copies of *Time* magazine, sometimes spending a day deciphering a page word by word, using a pocket dictionary. By the time he was seventeen, he was polishing off Victorian novels.

By then his language abilities—he was the only monk in his monastery who spoke English—singled him out for helping with the businesses that supported the monastic community. He had been living in a monastery in the south of India, but he spent two years "in trousers," working in the silk jute business in Bangalore; after returning to the monastery—and his monk's robes—he was put in charge of running a carpet factory. But his yearning for studies led him to seek out a teacher, a scholar who lived nearby in semi-retreat. In order to continue under his tutelage, Jinpa left his first monastery, joining the Ganden monastery near the Indian town where his teacher lived.

There, at age twenty, Jinpa began studies for the *geshe* degree, a course of study that typically takes twenty to thirty years. But Jinpa's quickness as a student had meant that all through his education, whether at school or the monastery, the gap between him and the next best was large. He completed his studies for the *geshe* degree in just eleven years, an extraordinarily short time. He was awarded the *geshe lharampa* degree, the equivalent of a doctorate in divinity, from Shartse College of the Ganden monastic university, where he went on to teach Buddhist philosophy for several years.

Then, quite by accident, came an opportunity to interpret for the Dalai Lama. In Dharamsala to visit his brother and sister in school there, Jinpa heard the Dalai Lama was scheduled to give some Dharma teachings the next day. Deciding to stay for these, he was approached by one of the organizers, who had heard that Jinpa spoke English well. The scheduled interpreter was delayed a day. Could Jinpa pinch-hit until he showed up?

Rather reluctant, and not a little nervous, Jinpa found himself translating what turned out to be a text he had learned by heart, and so was easy to translate. And his translation was broadcast over a short-range FM frequency that the English-speakers in the large audience tuned to, giving Jinpa the added pleasure of feeling like one of the announcers on the sporting matches he so enjoyed hearing on the BBC. He ended up doing most of the translation for the remaining days of the teaching.

That led to a meeting with the Dalai Lama, who asked Jinpa if he'd be willing to travel with him as an interpreter—an honor Jinpa was more than happy to accept. He has been the Dalai Lama's main English-language interpreter since 1986, especially for overseas trips and on numerous books.

It was during meetings between the Dalai Lama and philosophers or scientists from the West that Jinpa became struck by how little most Western intellectuals knew or appreciated the rich philosophical traditions of Buddhism. There was academic scholarship about Buddhism, but virtually no dialogue between Western and Buddhist philosophy as equal partners. With a view partly toward remedying that intellectual imbalance, and to expand his own intellectual horizons, Jinpa entered Cambridge University in 1989 to study Western philosophy—still juggling his studies with trips to interpret for the Dalai Lama. There his dissertation was on the philosophy of the great fourteenth-century Tibetan thinker Tsongkhapa.[6]

After getting his B.A. in philosophy and Ph.D. in religious studies from Cambridge, Jinpa stayed on there as a research fellow in Eastern religion at Girton College. While at Cambridge, he gave back his robes to live the freer life of a layperson. Now married (to Sophie Boyer, whom he met on a trip to Canada), Jinpa is the father of two children and lives in Montreal. There he works on the editing and translations of Tibetan texts and directs the Institute of Tibetan Classics, a program dedicated to making the key Tibetan classics part of the global intellectual and literary heritage. And, in keeping with his intellectual quest in the West, he has written the entry on Tibetan Buddhist philosophy for the *Encyclopedia of Asian Philosophy.*[7]

During his years of *geshe* studies, Jinpa had distinguished himself in the central skill of Tibetan intellectual discourse, debate—a skill that has become almost second nature to him. Even today, as he interprets for the Dalai Lama, he spontaneously finds himself raising questions in an echo of the debating style, acting as an intellectual sparring partner for His Holiness. Sometimes he will make a subtle motion that signifies his uneasiness, a shift in body language unnoticed by the audience but which the Dalai Lama picks up. Then Jinpa will politely make his objection.

Though he seldom gives in to this temptation during his ordinary interpreting duties—and never at a religious teaching—throughout our meeting we saw Jinpa's debating skills more openly displayed, almost as if by reflex, though usually in discreet conversations in Tibetan where he would challenge points about Buddhist philosophy. These microdebates led to much animated discussion in the Tibetan circle—giving our conversation a backdrop of the monastic intellectual dialectic.

Destructive Emotions: The Buddhist List

By way of introducing Jinpa's contribution, Alan said, "Owen very usefully set up a list of a variety of different emotions—quite a heterogeneous group from the Buddhist perspective. We thought it might be useful to take just a few minutes to set up a Buddhist list. As many of you may know, there isn't a Buddhist term in Tibetan or Sanskrit that translates very nicely and neatly as 'emotion.' "[8]

As Matthieu had pointed out, Buddhism has as a pivotal assumption the need to overcome the destructive pull of what Western psychology calls emotion. But the Buddhist analysis draws the boundary around these harmful emotions differently than does Western thought, seeing them as afflictive states of mind that obstruct clarity and emotional equilibrium. As would soon become apparent, this analysis has led to a much greater specificity and more careful reasoning in Buddhism than in the West regarding just which mental states belong in this category—and why.

Alan went on, "What terms do we have in Buddhist psychology that overlap with Western categories of destructive and constructive emotions? Thupten Jinpa has drawn, from a classic list, six primary mental afflictions, some of which we'll easily identify as emotions, and others not. There is another list of twenty derivative mental afflictions. Again, some are emotions and some not."

The title "Six Main Mental Afflictions" appeared on an overhead, with this list:

1. Attachment or craving
2. Anger (which includes hostility and hatred)
3. Pridefulness
4. Ignorance and delusion
5. Afflictive doubt
6. Afflictive views

"The two mental afflictions of attachment or craving, and hostility or anger," the Dalai Lama pointed out, "are both fixated upon something. One is grasping with attachment, going toward the object, and the other is grasping with repulsion, removing oneself from the object—a sense of impatience."

He continued, "Afflictive doubt is a specific type that leads one toward a misapprehension of reality. It's not merely a vacillation but a doubt that involves veering away from reality."

Alan elaborated, "There are wholesome forms of doubt. In fact, doubt is very important for cultivating deeper insight and understanding. In Buddhism, as in the scientific tradition, you must be skeptical, otherwise you will not progress. The terms here are defined as mental afflictions, but that is not to say that any term that appears in this list is invariably in all cases afflictive."

"In the same way that not all doubts are afflictive?" Paul Ekman asked. "In Your Holiness's writings, you say that not all anger is afflictive. Why don't you specify afflictive anger, so we don't think it's all the kinds of anger?"

Can Anger Be a Virtue?

"There is a distinction," the Dalai Lama said. "There are two very closely related terms in Tibetan, *khongdro* and *shedang. Shedang* is most often translated as 'hatred.' *Khongdro* is often translated as 'anger.' There are indeed types of anger that are aroused by compassion, in which case the anger is a rough state of mind, but I believe it is not hatred, or *shedang*. Compassion is the motivator, though it expresses itself as a type of anger."

"It is therefore accurate anger, seeing reality as it is," Francisco Varela commented.

Alan turned to the Dalai Lama and translated this comment back into Tibetan as "a type of valid anger that is aroused by compassion that is correctly apprehending reality." He then asked, "Does such a thing exist?"

At that the Dalai Lama looked up at the ceiling thoughtfully, finally commenting, "I'm not sure we can say that. But there is certainly something called 'afflictive compassion.' " This elicited a gasp of shock from someone in the room. "Compassion is one of the classic virtues, but it is possible for even that to be afflictive."

"Under what circumstances?" I asked, surprised.

"I have encountered this in the Pramanavarttika, a classical primary text on the epistemology of the Indo-Tibetan Buddhist tradition, but it doesn't give any instances.[9] It just says that there is such a thing. Normally, compassion is regarded as a virtuous, or wholesome, state of mind. Likewise, it is possible for affection to be mixed with attachment." This same mixture of compassion and attachment, presumably, was what would make compassion become afflictive.

"But since there are definitely references to afflictive compassion, maybe it's possible for there to be virtuous anger!" The Dalai Lama proposed this with a burst of laughter, for the very notion of "virtuous anger" is an oxymoron in Buddhist thought.

The Dalai Lama then suggested, "My solution might be that instead of using anger on the list, let's use hatred, *shedang*."

"It all depends upon our motivation," Matthieu Ricard suggested. "If someone is walking toward a cliff, about to fall off, and is not listening to you when you say, 'Stop!' you might get angry and say, 'Hey you, stupid, stop!' Your motivation is completely altruistic. You are getting angry because quiet ways have not been efficient in stopping that person in her course to harming herself."

As is often the case when learned Tibetans debate points in Buddhist philosophy, a long, impassioned discussion ensued among the lamas present. The Dalai Lama was uncomfortable with Matthieu's suggestion that there could be a virtuous anger from a Buddhist point of view—that is, an instance of anger that is not afflictive. His view was that if it is genuinely anger, then by definition it would be afflictive—even if it manifests in compassionate action. On the other hand, it might be possible to *seem* to act in anger without actually having the inner experience of anger. Such seeming anger could be grounded in compassion, as in Matthieu's example. But the Dalai Lama did not want to give an impression that would undermine the basic Buddhist characterization of anger as afflictive.

Alan finally reported: "Matthieu pointed out that sometimes a kind of wrathful behavior or harsh words—'Stop it, you fool!'—may be the most skillful means, or even the only means, to stop a person from going over the cliff. But the question is, must you have the inner mental affliction of anger in order to give that outer display?"

The Dalai Lama suggested, "If you follow the continuum of cognition, at a prior moment in this sequence you could have compassion arise as a motivation. Then, in a later moment of awareness, there could be an arousal of anger that was instigated by compassion. That could happen."

The Dalai Lama went on to point out that in the Vajrayana branch of Buddhism, which predominates in Tibet, there are spiritual practices that explicitly aim to transform hatred and aggression (as well as craving and attachment) rather than simply countering or suppressing them, as is the case in other branches of Buddhist practice. The mental afflictions themselves are worked with directly in ways that, finally, free the practitioner from their hold. For someone who had achieved freedom from the afflictions in this way, he concluded, "there are times when the most effective procedure, the most skillful means, would be a wrathful demeanor—wrathful speech, wrathful activities"—but the person would be free of any feeling of anger despite the external display.[10]

The Value of Moral Outrage

Owen leaned forward to enter the fray. "His Holiness was cautious about saying there could be anger born of compassion, anger that is nonafflictive. I think there is a difference, maybe, between Buddhist views in these areas and Western ones. I think this relates to Paul's views about positive emotions. I think we value moral indignation or moral outrage not just because it might be useful in practice. But in fact we value deeply feeling outrage in the face of Pol Pot or Hitler, or Stalin, or Milosevic—pick your favorite. Is there a difference here?"

"There is definitely a concept of moral outrage against injustices," the

Dalai Lama replied, "but in the Buddhist context it occurs in Vajrayana, which is not really mainstream Buddhist psychology. For example, there is the idea that the symbolic significance of a wrathful deity is to display wrath or ferocity against some form of evil.

"In the incident that Matthieu mentioned," he continued, "of anger toward a person about to walk over a cliff, there are two things going on. There is compassion toward the person who is about to go over the cliff, and there is anger at the stupid behavior this person is involved in. Those two arise very closely together.

"In the meditative cultivation of patience and forbearance, one may attend to a person who is engaging in some terribly vile behavior. As you cultivate patience for that person, you do not have any anger or hostility or aggression toward the person; rather, perhaps, compassion. But there is clearly an attitude that wants to stop, to repulse, and to annihilate that deplorable behavior. And the powerful wish to stop the behavior is completely compatible with the lack of anger toward the person. One is patient toward the person but not patient toward the terrible activity, and those need to be cultivated together so that patience is not conflated with apathy."

The notion that people could radically transform anger into a mix of compassion and patience appealed immediately to Paul Ekman, who had been giving long thought to how to facilitate this change. "I think that is an extraordinarily useful idea," Paul said to the Dalai Lama. "At the same time I read about it in one of your books, I also read exactly the same idea in the latest book by Richard Lazarus, an American psychologist who didn't know His Holiness's work at all.[11] Lazarus pointed out, I think correctly, that this is difficult to achieve, but it is possible. I hope that one of the issues we will get into is how those who haven't spent years and years in meditative practice can try to achieve this. I think there are intermediate steps.

"By the way, it seems to me we have been mixing together two different issues," Paul added. "One is what human beings might be able to achieve with enormous effort and focus, like never to be vulnerable to anger—that might be one of the things we can learn in the West from understanding the theory and practice of Buddhism. The other issue is, can there be instances in ordinary life, as Matthieu was suggesting, where we would agree that anger is not harmful or destructive?"

"I think this is something we can return to repeatedly over the coming days," Alan replied. That would prove an understatement. In fact, the transformation of anger would become one of the more profound themes of the entire encounter, not just in theory, but in the lives of some of us in the room—including Paul himself.

More Afflictions

Alan was clearly eager to further elaborate on the list of destructive emotions prepared by Jinpa. He pushed on. "We have had so much fun with the first six primary mental afflictions, I think you'll have a ball with the next twenty derivative mental afflictions—so why don't we move to those quickly? All of them stem from the primary afflictions of craving or attachment, anger, and ignorance"—the Three Poisons, as they are called in Buddhist literature.

A new list appeared on the screen:

Twenty Derivative Mental Afflictions

Anger

1. Wrath
2. Resentment
3. Spite
4. Envy/jealousy
5. Cruelty

Attachment

6. Avarice
7. Inflated self-esteem
8. Excitation
9. Concealment of one's own vices
10. Dullness

Ignorance

11. Blind faith
12. Spiritual sloth
13. Forgetfulness
14. Lack of introspective attentiveness

Ignorance + attachment

15. Pretension
16. Deception
17. Shamelessness
18. Inconsideration of others
19. Unconscientiousness
20. Distraction

"Of the twenty derivative afflictions," Alan began, "the first five all stem from anger. Wrath is simply an aggravated outflowing, a burst of anger. Resentment is a more lingering holding of anger. Spite is another derivative—these are all clearly emotions of anger. Envy and jealousy are also said to be a derivative of anger. When Thupten Jinpa and I were discussing this and trying to determine what each was a derivative of, Jinpa was quite persuaded that envy and jealousy are derivative of attachment. I was quite persuaded that they were derivative of both attachment and anger. We looked in the text and it said anger. So it may be open to interpretation. Cruelty is very clearly a derivative of anger.

"Then we move to afflictions that are derivative of attachment. Avarice is also called miserliness. Inflated self-esteem—this taps into what Owen was speaking about this morning, an inflated exaggeration of one's own qualities. 'Excitation' is a technical term that specially pertains to meditation: The mind is agitated because it is drawn away compulsively to some object of desire.

"Concealment of one's own vices is a type of delusion that stems from ignorance. This includes self-concealment. 'Dullness' again is a term that crops up mostly in meditation, although it has much more ubiquitous manifestations: It is a lack of clarity of mind. People who meditate become very familiar with that one."

When Ignorance Afflicts

The next set of afflictions derives from what Buddhism calls delusion or ignorance. The list started with "blind faith," and Alan immediately noted how odd that might seem to Western eyes. "Faith itself is considered to be a virtue, but not blind faith. Intelligent faith is reality based, and the absence of that is said to be a mental affliction.

"The next affliction, called *lelo* in Tibetan, is often translated as 'laziness,' but it is much more specific. If a person is working sixteen hours a day, hell-bent on earning a whole lot of money with absolutely no concern for virtue, from a Buddhist perspective you could say that person is subject to *lelo*. A workaholic is clearly not lazy, but such a person is seen as *lelo* in the sense of being completely lethargic and slothful with regard to the cultivation of virtue and purification of the mind. Our translation of this term is 'spiritual sloth,' which we have taken from the Christian tradition, where it is very comparable to the Buddhist notion.

"'Forgetfulness' is again a term from the meditative literature, where it means a lack of mindfulness, where you simply become disengaged. Inward monitoring is crucial in meditative practice, and the absence of that, where you are deficient in introspective attentiveness, is forgetfulness. I think this taps into some of the things you were talking about, Dan, in *Emotional Intelligence*. If you are deficient in that, you'll be less emotionally intelligent."

"Self-awareness?" I asked, since that was the general term used in my book for this kind of introspective attention.

"Buddhists wouldn't quite use that term," Alan replied (presumably because the notion of self is seen as an illusory reification, as the Dalai Lama had pointed out earlier), "but it's very comparable.

"Now," Alan continued, "we have a final set that are derivative of both attachment and ignorance. Pretension—deception of a very specific type—is where you consciously and intentionally pretend to have good qualities that in fact you do not have, or you are exaggerating your good qualities beyond reality. Deception is the flip side of that, where you are trying to conceal, obscure, or downplay your defective qualities.

"Shamelessness is like having no conscience, where regardless of whether anybody else catches you, you don't even have a sense of your own decency internally. That is considered a mental affliction. It's not a lack of remorse—if you engage in something that is really shameful, do you even care? Do you take account of that, regardless of whether you get caught? Inconsideration for others is the flip side of that, a lack of concern for how others regard your behavior. This does not mean you should get hung up on reputation or the like, but it is an absence of realistic concern for the fact that you are a social creature, engaged with others. If you engage in something unvirtuous or something reprehensible and you simply don't care what anyone thinks about it, then you are suffering from that mental affliction.

"Lack of conscientiousness is a totally blasé attitude toward one's actions of body, speech, and mind, with no restraint concerning whether they are wholesome or unwholesome. Finally, distraction is similar to forgetfulness. It's simply a mind that is incoherent, drawn every which way by things that come up. All of those come out of both ignorance and attachment."

Having a Number Seventeen

These explanations had been based on Tibetan sources. But, as in modern Western psychology, there are several schools of thought in Buddhism. The Venerable Kusalacitto, a monk in the Thai Theravada tradition, had been asked to represent the perspective from the classic Pali scriptures. The *bhante* (as monks are addressed in Thailand) spoke up to comment, "If we could go back to number seventeen, shamelessness, in Pali it is the word *ahirika,* 'no shame.' If you have *ahirika,* you can readily do bad things—not just disturb others, but even kill. You don't care about manners or etiquette, or that you are in a high position in society but use it for evil purposes. That's the sense of *ahirika.*

"But number eighteen in Pali would be *anottopa,* being inconsiderate of others. You have no fear of bad karma. You can also do bad things, but because you never consider the consequences."

"It is a type of utter irresponsibility, and a lack of concern about long-term consequences," Alan summarized.

The *bhante's* comment triggered a debate on the nuances of meaning of these two afflictions, as Alan consulted a book called *The Mind and Its Functions* by Geshe Rabten, one of his first teachers, excerpts of which had been distributed to the participants as part of the preparatory materials for the conference. Such debates reflect, in part, long-standing disputes within strands of Buddhism regarding the phenomenology of consciousness. Jinpa hoped the scientists in the room got a sense from the debate itself of the complexity of the literature in Buddhist psychology, and the diversity of sources.[12]

Owen stepped in to make a point: "In one of Plato's dialogues, there is an interlocutor with Socrates named Thrasymachus who is trying to explain that it is much better to *seem* just than to be just. It is pretty clear from his perspective that it feels really good to just seem good, but not to be good."

"He's having a number seventeen!" said Alan.

"He's having a number seventeen and he's defending it," Owen concurred. "In effect he argues that deep down inside, this is what every person aspires toward. And—at least for him—it is pleasant."

Alan had the last word: "In Buddhism his justification would be called afflicted intelligence."

Afflictions Disrupt the Mind's Equilibrium

"That's a very quick sketch," Alan wound up. "Now you have our list. You'll notice that you might quickly deem some of them to be emotions, and others are not emotions at all. But this is a meaningful categorization for Buddhist purposes. The categorization of emotions per se never came up, because it was not deemed particularly useful."

"There is a very important question," Francisco Varela pointed out. "We agree, for example, that shamelessness is an afflicted mental state, yet it doesn't seem to carry a clear emotion with it. What are mental afflictions if they are not emotions?"

"Mental states, mental processes," Alan suggested, citing the more neutral terms most often used.

"Yes," Francisco said, "but isn't it a little funny that some come with emotions and some don't?"

"His Holiness said earlier that all mental states arise with feelings," Alan reminded him. "Pleasure and pain were in his list of emotions. Sadness and joy, happiness . . ."

"Yes, that's a good point," Francisco acknowledged. "But, for example, shame is an emotion. Shamelessness, however, can be perfectly neutral. What does it tell us about the nature of the mind that one can have a mental affliction that is not based on an emotion?"

Here Francisco was highlighting a fundamental difference in the very paradigms that gave rise to the Western and the Buddhist notions of destructive emotions. For the West, the positive or negative valence of an emotion—pleasant or unpleasant—figures in, along with the question of whether that emotion can lead people to harm themselves or others.

For Buddhism, destructiveness depends on a much more subtle measure of harm: whether a mental state (including an emotion) disquiets the mind and interferes with spiritual progress. As Alan summarized the point: "In Tibetan a mental affliction is defined as a mental process that has the function of disrupting the equilibrium of the mind. They all have that in common, whether or not there is a strong emotional component to it."

At that, Francisco nodded vigorously, seemingly satisfied.

A Broader Context for Affliction

As he had earlier, the Dalai Lama felt the need to give the scientists present a fuller sense of the theoretical context for the Buddhist list of afflictive emotions, which he proceeded to do. "My personal position is that not all the items on the list are necessarily afflictions as such. The inclusion of forgetfulness on the list does not imply that all instances of forgetfulness are afflictive. So it is with doubt. There are wholesome forms of doubt—for instance, to cultivate deeper spiritual insight and understanding. As in the scientific endeavor, you've got to be skeptical—you can't do it without doubt. So the twenty that are listed here are said to be afflictive specifically in the sense that instances are derivatives of any of the root afflictions."

He went on to explain the broader context, that these twenty afflictive mental qualities are part of a larger list. "Many mental factors are not at all related to any of the primary mental afflictions. For example, when one is deeply asleep without dreams, there is no sense of shame. You certainly are not suffering from the mental affliction of shamelessness simply because you're not feeling any sense of shame. It has to be conjoined with one of the primary mental afflictions to be a derivative mental affliction.

"To get a better sense of mental afflictions," he went on, "you have to understand them in the broader context of the Abhidharmakosha, a Sanskrit Buddhist text that lists fifty-one mental faculties, although even this is not a totally complete list. There are five omnipresent mental factors, including feeling, discernment, intention, contact, and attention; five ascertaining mental factors, including aspiration, appreciation, recollection, concentration, and intelligence; four variable mental factors—variable in that they may be virtuous or unvirtuous—namely, drowsiness, regret, general examination, and precise scrutiny; and eleven wholesome mental factors, including faith." He concluded, "The lists of mental afflictions make more sense in this context."

As in cognitive science, then, the model of mind in Buddhism includes the neutral processes of mental life that make perception and thought possible. But unlike the scientific model, the Buddhist analysis has a practical, spiritual agenda. The eleven wholesome factors represent elements of mind essential for spiritual progress. By contrast, the mental afflictions are obstacles to that progress. Derived from the Three Poisons—craving, aversion, and delusion—the afflictive states of mind interfere with training in ethical discipline, in meditation, and in insight. In that light, the sense in which forgetfulness, say, or shamelessness obstructs spiritual progress, and so is afflictive, becomes clearer.

Affliction Without Emotion?

Richard Davidson, whose research on emotions touched on some of these same points, asked a question for the first time in our meeting. "Can I go back to the issue of whether an affliction can be produced without a negative emotion? Many Western scientists who study emotion would agree that emotions involve a positive or negative valence—that if an emotion is present, there will be a positive or negative feeling tone. These afflictions are complex mental processes that seem to involve some emotional component. They appear to involve other things as well, but from the perspective I come from, there does seem to be an emotional component to each of these. I wonder if all afflictions necessarily involve a negative emotion or whether it is possible to have them arise in the absence of any negative emotion."

"I have a point of clarification as an interpreter and as moderator," Alan answered. "His Holiness just a few minutes ago characterized attachment as a kind of compulsive going toward or attraction to an object, whereas aversion or hostility is a moving away from. It is very easy to get the impression from the Western terminology that going toward is positive and pushing away from is negative.

"When you say 'positive' do you mean virtuous, undistorted, and unafflictive?" Alan then asked. "Or by 'positive' do you mean more aligned with attachment, where 'negative' means more aligned with aversion?"

"The use of those terms in the West," Richie (as most everyone calls him) answered, "typically refers to conventional lists of positive and negative emotions. Emotions like happiness and contentment would be considered part of the positive rubric. The notion of attachment is not something that has permeated the Western lexicon of emotion psychology."

"It would probably be deemed positive, wouldn't it?" Alan asked. "For example, in saying 'I really love grapefruit'?"

"It would," Richie replied. "That relates to another issue: whether positive emotions can also lead to distortions in our capacity to apprehend reality, similar to the role of destructive emotions that Matthieu described. In the Buddhist framework the positive emotions that are associated with attachment would also presumably lead to an obscuring of our ability to accurately apprehend reality."

Here Alan and Richie had pinpointed a key difference in the assumptions underlying the Buddhist and Western lists. The Buddhist distinction between wholesome and unwholesome (or positive and negative) mental states is that wholesome states bring us closer to spiritual awakening, whereas the unwholesome ones obstruct such awakening.

By contrast, the Western approach contrasts emotions that are pleasant—positive—with those that are unpleasant—negative. The principle in the West boils down, it would seem, to whether an emotion feels good, while the Buddhist rule of thumb regards the emotion in terms of whether it furthers spiritual progress or holds us back.

When Attachment Can Be Positive

"To respond to your point about whether there could be positive forms of attachment," the Dalai Lama said, "it is important to bear in mind the Buddhist context, where the ultimate spiritual aspiration is the attainment of enlightenment, and attachment is seen as one of the main obstacles that hinders the individual from attaining that state. From that point of view, attachment is seen as one of the root afflictions.

"A subtle level of attachment perpetuates the cycle of rebirth over and over and over again. So from that point of view, attachment of course would be seen as an affliction, an obscuration. However, if we change the framework of our discourse and remove this ultimate aspiration of attaining liberation from the equation—if we talk in the secular context about understanding the nature of emotions, then of course that changes the whole definition.

"Some forms of attachment that from the Buddhist spiritual point of view may be seen as an affliction need not necessarily be destructive. In society, some forms of attachment are in fact positive. But in order to reach nirvana, they would be seen as destructive."

"So 'afflictive' is contextual," I commented.

"'Destructive' may be contextual," Jinpa clarified. "Attachment that may be ultimately destructive from the Buddhist point of view may be helpful when you change the framework to the everyday, where the aspiration is a happier life and happier society."

Who's Responsible?

The next question came from Jeanne Tsai, an emotions researcher now at Stanford University. "From a Buddhist perspective," she asked, "is there any differentiation among individuals who are more or less responsible for their afflictive state? In clinical psychology we have this notion that some individuals have no control over destructive behaviors: individuals who are schizophrenic, or who have psychotic states because of some sort of genetic or biological disorder or perhaps because something happened during birth. What is the Buddhist perspective on a psychopath, or a person who engages in very destructive behaviors toward other people and has no remorse, or who has no control over it?"

"There is definitely a parallel concept in the Buddhist understanding of moral values," the Dalai Lama answered. "Those actions that are committed by people out of ignorance are considered to be less negative than where the individual acts knowingly with full awareness of the consequences and severity of the action, which is considered morally reprehensible. Ignorance is therefore often an excuse. For example, it is possible for a person just walking along to kill ants without even seeing them. In that case, you engage in the action of killing, and you do accumulate karma—but it is pretty lightweight. You didn't even know that it happened.

"Now," the Dalai Lama continued, "take little kids who have fun squashing flies, or giving them to spiders, not even knowing that flies have feelings. That type of killing is motivated by ignorance and delusion. Similarly, people who sacrifice animals thinking this is going to satisfy some god also act out of delusion because they don't know that this is really harmful. It would rarely be the case, I suspect, that they are doing this out of malice or any real wish to injure the creature in question. Rather, they have a notion that this is good, that it is going to please the god.

"That kind of killing arises out of the motivation of delusion. A second level of moral responsibility occurs when killing out of attachment. You want to eat that yak over there. You don't want to hurt it; you just want to eat its flesh. A further level is where you want to inflict injury. You really want to harm, and you go out and kill with that intent of malice.

"In terms of responsibility, the lightest karma is probably that which stems from delusion; somewhat heavier is that which stems from attachment; and the heaviest, and where you bear the greatest responsibility, would be that arising out of malice. People who are psychotic, schizophrenic, and so forth are suffering from an intense form of delusion. So killing out of schizophrenia would be out of a very deep delusion. The responsibility and karmic repercussions would be even less because of the intensity of the delusion."

I asked, "What do you think about the case I mentioned, of the six-year-old boy who got angry, brought a gun to school, and killed a little girl? He is not being charged with murder, by the way."

That set off a long discussion among the Tibetan circle, considering the nuances of the case. "He is angry," the Dalai Lama finally observed. "It certainly is an instance of killing out of anger. It is also killing out of a very strong dose of delusion. Am I right in thinking that this six-year-old boy may have wished to shoot and kill the girl but did not fully grasp the idea that once the act was committed, the girl would never be restored to life?"

"It is unclear whether he understood what death is," I replied.

"How can he think she's not going to die?" Matthieu asked with some skepticism. "Doesn't he understand what death is?"

"That's a developmental question," I pointed out.

Taking up that point, Mark Greenberg, a developmental psychologist, commented, "Under about age seven, we believe that most children don't understand the permanent consequences of an action like that. We assume that what he wanted to do was to hurt her feelings or maybe hurt her physically but in a temporary way, not in a permanent way."

Alan pointed to one of the factors that might, in a young child, contribute to such "magical thinking" that death does not last. "And bear in mind, six-year-old kids watch cartoons in which the cartoon creatures are being killed, falling on their heads, going over cliffs, filled with bullet holes, and then they get up again. It's not so clear in the kind of media they are seeing that death is irreversible."

"Yes," Matthieu agreed. "I read that American teenagers have seen forty thousand such killings on TV by the time they are twenty. Obviously that has an influence."

Alan took that comment as an opportunity to segue into a wrap-up of the day's conversation: "Perhaps the moral of the story is that we all need to get greater clarity and be more responsible, and to notice that it is four o'clock. We should release His Holiness with great gratitude for joining us. Thank you so much—and especially to our two presenters today."

And so we ended the day where we started: reflecting on the role of destructive emotions in the perplexing case of a six-year-old murderer.

Day Two:
Feelings in Everyday Life

March 21, 2000

6

The Universality of Emotion

Is there any value to rage, panic, or depression? Could destructive emotions be evolutionary "spandrels"—accidental by-products of natural selection?

In engineering, spandrels are architectural side effects of dome and arch designs—they have no essential function, so you get them "for free." They are a design element that can have an aesthetic bonus or are simply put up with but are not needed for structural support.

In 1994 Owen Flanagan gave a presidential address to the Society for Philosophy and Psychology called "Deconstructive Dreams: The Spandrels of Sleep." The paper took its theme from a theory by Stephen Jay Gould and Richard Lewontin proposing how spandrels occur in evolution. As in architecture, spandrels in human behavior serve no survival function, but arise as a by-product of something else that does. Flanagan's argument on dreams, influenced by pioneering research done by Alan Hobson at Harvard, was that though sleep has an adaptive purpose, dreaming was not selected for such a purpose by Mother Nature. Dreams are rich and can be used for self-exploration, but they are not, in this view, essential for survival.

In the same way, destructive emotions can be seen as spandrels, as by-products of something useful in human behavior that in themselves serve no survival function and, in fact, at times have negative survival value. This principle might reasonably apply to any of the distressing emotions, particularly craving, anger, fear, or sadness (not to mention envy and jealousy, from the Buddhist list), at the point when they tip over a threshold to become destructive. Indeed, much of the official diagnostic manual of the American Psychiatric Association can be read as a typology of useless, destructive emotions, disorders created by an otherwise useful emotion that has reached a point of excess, is out of place, or is simply out of control.

Not everything that exists in the human repertoire of behavior is an adaptation, though most seem to be. Owen Flanagan agrees with the evolutionary school of thought that asks what the adaptive value of a given human trait is. Paul Ekman does just that with the basic emotions. He thinks that they almost certainly evolved as adaptations in environments in which they were necessary for fitness. But one question that his presentation on our second day raised was whether even though basic emotions have an evolutionary usefulness, might destructive ones be spandrels in the design of human behavior—elements we have to put up with but do not need?

A Somber Tone

Yesterday there had been gorgeous sun; this day storm clouds hovered, and rolling thunder punctuated the proceedings throughout the day. By lunchtime there was an intermittent cold drizzle.

News of a rabid dog loose in town made us apprehensive about walking the roads; we heard that it had attacked seven people. Dick Grace, one of our observers and a man of compassionate action, somehow encountered one of the victims, a small child whose face had been mangled by a nasty bite, and arranged for hospital care.

On this day the Dalai Lama was bothered by a cough; he'd been coming down with a cold, picked up the week before on a five-day trip to south India, where he had given ordinations to hundreds of Tibetans who were becoming monks. The drizzle, the mad dog, and the Dalai Lama's cold all made for a somewhat somber tone—a fitting backdrop, perhaps, to our topic, the destructive emotions.

To open the session, I went back to the metaphor of a tapestry, saying, "Your Holiness, as you know from previous meetings here, this dialogue is a little like weaving a very richly patterned carpet, which emerges as we go on. Yesterday we set down the main strands of the loom, the philosophical understanding. Owen Flanagan presented the diverse issues that are raised by moral philosophy from a Western point of view. Matthieu summarized for us a Buddhist view on the key point of emotions as obscuring seeing clearly, and the notion that we might intercede differently before, during, or after an afflictive emotion. And we saw the list of afflictive emotions that Alan presented, which was very intriguing in juxtaposition with the list that Owen had presented earlier, not just for the many overlaps, but also for the many important differences. These are just some of many ideas that may be picked up again during the day as we go on.

"Your Holiness was kind enough to share with us a glimpse of the very sophisticated understanding that Buddhist psychology has regarding the nature of afflictive emotions and the processes of mental acts. We need such insights: If we are going to intervene effectively in a process, we need to understand it precisely so that the remedies will be appropriate to the problem.

"So those are the lengthwise strands of the loom. Now we begin to weave across them—and from those interconnections, the richness of the pattern will emerge. We start with Paul Ekman, who is professor of psychology and the director of the Human Interaction Laboratory at the University of California Medical School in San Francisco. But what you really should know about him is that he is a master of the face and of reading emotions. He has done more than thirty years of world-class research, and has a very unique personal mastery—almost a *siddhi,*" I said, using the Sanskrit word for an extraordinary human capacity.

"He taught himself to control voluntarily each of the more than eighty muscles in the human face so that he could precisely analyze and scientifically score which muscles were moving in conjunction with which particular emotion. As a result, he has an extraordinary ability to sense very rapid emotions that reveal one's true feelings on the face. He has taught this skill to law enforcement agents, such as the Secret Service."

And, on a lighter note, I added, "I'm just preparing you for the fact that if you have some feeling you are hiding, he'll detect it."

The Emotion Detector

Here's a choice Paul Ekman moment. It was an unseasonably warm early December day in Cambridge, and Paul and I were walking along bumpy brick sidewalks by charming yellow Victorian houses, on our way to a meeting at Harvard Divinity School's Center for Comparative Religions. That morning I was in charge of coordinating the efforts of the seven very disparate scholars who would present their thinking and findings on the topic of destructive emotions to the Dalai Lama the following March. While my mind was partly on the meeting I had to run in a few moments, I was intrigued by what Paul was telling me.

The world's most eminent expert on the way the face expresses emotions, Paul had developed a one-hour videotape that, he assured me, could teach anyone to recognize the tiniest signs of anger or fear—or any major emotion—as they flit across someone's face. People could learn in an hour, he told me, to detect these clues to microemotions, even when they last just a twenty-fifth of a second.

I wasn't just interested, I was fascinated, even excited. I'd been telling audiences in my lectures for years that empathy, the ability to read emotions in someone else, could be learned. And I was often asked how. Now Paul had a more specific answer for me.

But as we approached the center where the meeting was to be held, Paul went off on what seemed to me an irrelevant tangent, telling me about a book he was writing. I was still interested, but also feeling pressured and preoccupied by thoughts about the meeting I had to chair in a few moments. I had the thought that in the minute or so left us, I'd rather have heard more about his videotape. For the briefest moment I started to feel impatient, even a bit irritated with him, though I was sure I didn't show it.

And, at that very moment, he seamlessly wove into what he was telling me this comment: "For example, if someone had gone through the videotape training in detecting emotions, they'd know that right now you're getting a bit irritated with me."

It was a minor miracle: How, I wondered, had he known I was getting irritated for just that split second? But Paul gave not a hint he'd done anything the least bit unusual. He went back to the video, telling me about how he'd been training police to help them be more empathic. He finished just as we got to the room where our meeting was about to start.

That moment typifies Paul's genius: He's not a reader of minds—but he is without doubt the reader of emotions par excellence.

Examining the Unexamined

Paul Ekman's academic career began at fifteen, when—fleeing his dysfunctional family in New Jersey—he found a refuge at the University of Chicago, which had a program that admitted bright students who, like him, had never finished high school. In a sense, it saved his life: He went from bored rebellion at home to great intellectual challenges, one of which, his discovery of Freud, led to his decision to become a psychotherapist.

Paul went on to study clinical psychology at Adelphi University, one of the few graduate programs at the time that focused on clinical practice rather than academic research. Yet he turned out to be the black sheep of his class, becoming a researcher rather than a psychotherapist. The critical moment came while, as a graduate student, he observed psychotherapy sessions from behind a one-way mirror and was impressed by how much of what was going on was not in the words but in nonverbal channels such as tone of voice, facial expression, and gesture.

So Paul set out on what would become his life's task: to examine the unexamined. From Adelphi he went to the Langley Porter Institute, the psychiatric hospital at the University of California Medical School in San Francisco, largely because of the presence of Jürgen Ruesch, one of the few researchers who had published anything about nonverbal behavior.

Drafted into the army straight out of graduate school, Paul became the chief psychologist at the huge training base in Fort Dix, New Jersey. While he was supposed to do psychotherapy, not research, none of the forty thousand soldiers who passed through the base every eight weeks had much time or inclination to see a psychologist. But there Paul was to have two early successes as a researcher.

In one study, he showed that if soldiers were allowed to "deselect" themselves within the first three days of training—that is, declare that they were unfit for the military and be sent home—there would be no change in the overall discharge rate. In other words, soldiers would not take undue advantage of this escape clause, but instead everyone would be spared these same soldiers having a breakdown over the course of boot camp training and being sent home later anyway. Thereafter, the general in charge of Fort Dix changed policy and gave new soldiers the chance to leave the army right at the start of training.

Then Paul turned his attention to the stockade, which was largely populated with soldiers who had gone AWOL. Paul showed that most had turned themselves in after running off, and that those whose punishment was just extra duty with their company rarely went AWOL again. But those who were sent to the stockade repeated 90 percent of the time. This resulted in another policy change, with the standard punishment becoming extra duty rather than the stockade.

These initial successes made Paul feel that the way to change the world was not through psychotherapy but through research.

The Man of Seven Thousand Faces

After returning to do research at Langley Porter in the 1960s, Paul met Sylvan Tomkins, a philosopher turned psychologist whose work on nonverbal expression of emotions became an inspiration for Paul's own. Getting a grant to study gestures and the expression of emotion cross-culturally, Paul went to study a group in New Guinea who were thought to be living much as people lived in the Stone Age. There he discovered that the ways emotions were expressed among this remote tribe were perfectly recognizable anywhere in the world—which became a landmark finding in the understanding of the universal nature of the expression of emotions. That led him to a serious reading of Darwin, who long ago had proposed just that universality.

I first met Paul in the early 1980s when I wrote an article on his research on the facial expression of emotion. Early on, Paul had realized that expressions on the face offered a direct window on a person's emotions—but there was no scientific system for reading emotion from the movements of key muscles on the face. So Paul set out to build that system. To do so, he and fellow researcher Wallace Friesen spent a year or so not just studying facial anatomy but also learning to consciously move every muscle on the face, one by one, so that they could study how each played into the configuration for a given emotion. Facial anatomy allows about seven thousand visually distinct combinations of those muscles.

That work was more than painstaking—it was painful. Paul borrowed a method from Guillaume Duchenne du Boulogne, a nineteenth-century neurologist who had electrically stimulated facial muscles in order to try to describe how they change appearance—except that the person whose face Duchenne used had no sensitivity to pain in his face, and so did not mind the mild shocks. Paul was not so lucky. When he was in doubt about how, precisely, a muscle moved, he would thread a needle through the skin into the muscle and electrically stimulate it. It was, Paul still recalls, not a lot of fun.

But the result, six years later, was a breakthrough in the scientific study of emotions. Each emotion, Paul's research revealed, could be mapped in terms of the movements of underlying muscles—so accurately that the formula for a given emotion could be written in a precise notation. For the first time, scientists could accurately measure a person's emotions, simply by observing the moment-to-moment shifts in their facial muscles.

Today, the Facial Action Coding System is in use by more than four hundred researchers around the world. Two research teams are trying to automate the system, so that someday—probably within the next five years—it will be possible for researchers to get readouts of even the slightest emotional shifts a person goes through, just as an EEG gives a continual reading of brain waves.

The opportunity to come to the meeting also coincided with Paul's work on the book he tried to describe to me during our walk in Cambridge.[1] It would deal with many of the same issues we were discussing, notably the question of when emotions are functional or dysfunctional, and how we can change what we become emotional about. While Paul felt that in his decades of research on emotions he had learned much that would interest the Dalai Lama, he was even more excited about what he might learn himself. The centuries of inner science developed in Tibet, Paul suspected, might offer useful lessons on methods of managing our emotional experience that Western science as yet knew little of.

Paul also had a more personal agenda for our meeting in Dharamsala. Since having had an assignment—in the army during the peak of the Cold War—to analyze the potential casualties in the event of a nuclear bombing, Paul had been active in nuclear disarmament groups. His activist spirit was taken up by his college-age daughter, Eve, who since she was fifteen had been working to help the Tibetan cause. Eve's interests had prodded Paul to come here to Dharamsala, and he brought Eve with him to be a spectator; Paul's nonverbal cues made it very clear that he was proud and delighted to have her at his side during the week.

The Universals

Paul, whose task was to review a scientific framework on emotions, began, "Your Holiness, it is a great honor to be able to speak to you. I have to apologize for the fact that although I have spent forty years studying emotion, I have only spent four months learning anything about Buddhism. All I really know is what I have read in four books of yours, so you will have to forgive my naivete when I try to make connections if I have misunderstood them.

"In my talk I am going to distinguish between scientific facts, for which we have evidence, and theory, for which we don't have evidence but which addresses some of the most interesting questions. I'll try to spend more time on the theory than the facts, but I will begin with the facts.

"Let me begin with the issue of universals. When I began my research in this area, the general belief in the West was that emotions were quite different from one culture to another, like language or values. They were assumed to be learned, and to vary and reflect each culture. This was in contradiction to the view in Charles Darwin's book of 1872, *The Expression of Emotion in Man and Animals.* Darwin held that our emotions have evolved, that we share some of our emotions with other animals, and that they are a unifying force for all humankind."

As Paul showed a series of slides of faces with dramatic expressions, he noted, "In my first research, I showed these very faces and others like them to people in twenty-one different cultures around the world. The viewers were asked to say what emotion was shown. Despite the differences in culture and language, the same emotions were ascribed in each culture. Everyone said the expression of the first picture was happy, though they might have used a different word for it. The next one everyone called disgust or disdain.

"This kind of research, though, left a gap. Because all of the people I had studied had been exposed to the same television and movie films, you could

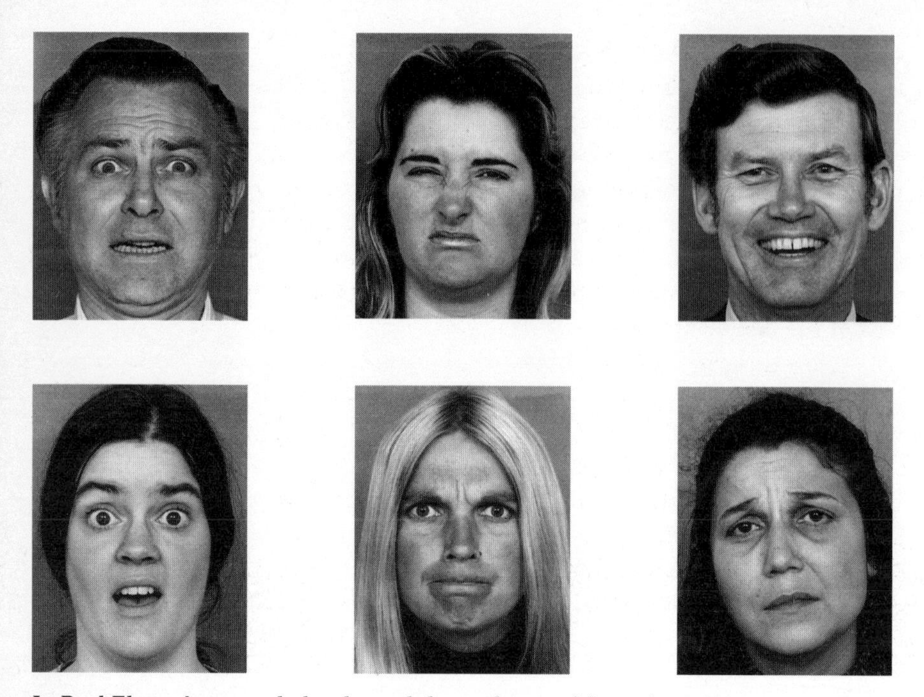

In Paul Ekman's research, he showed these photos of faces depicting a range of emotions to people in different cultures, asking them what emotions were shown.

argue that they were learning these expressions from Charlie Chaplin, John Wayne, or Richard Gere"—an acknowledgment that Gere was sitting just behind Paul, observing the session—"not as a product of evolution. To close that gap, I had to study people who had had no contact with the outside world. There was a scientist at that time who was studying a group of Stone Age people in New Guinea who had a particular disease, and he had taken over a hundred thousand feet of movie film of these people. They were still using stone implements, and had had no prior contact with the outside world.

"I spent six months studying those films. That is when I really made my discovery, because I saw nothing I hadn't seen before. There was nothing unique, nothing new, and I could tell from what happened both before and afterward in the film that my interpretations of their emotions were correct. I didn't need to learn their expressive language—their facial expressions. Their expressive language was my expressive language.

"In 1967, I went to New Guinea to study these people," Paul added as he showed slides of some of the spontaneous expressions his team had photographed. "Here is a young boy showing joy. This woman is showing surprise with raised eyebrows. In the next, the woman in the far back is glaring at me in anger because I had broken a cultural rule by paying attention to her. A man was showing this expression of disgust as he watched me eat the canned food that I had brought with me, and I, of course, showed similar expressions when I ate his food.

"Now, these are nice as examples but not as evidence; I needed to do systematic experiments. In the most interesting experiment, I would tell them a story and ask them to show me what their face would be like in each story." As he continued his narration, Paul showed some frames taken from his own film of the New Guinea tribe.

"They did not know what a camera was, so they were not embarrassed about being filmed during the following scenarios: 'Show me what your face would look like if you were about to fight.' Or 'if someone did something you didn't like but you were not going to fight.' Or 'if you learned your child had died.' Finally, 'if friends come to your village whom you haven't seen in a long time.'

"It should be no surprise that when I showed these pictures to American college students who had no familiarity with these people, they had no problem understanding their emotions. For me, this was decisive in showing the

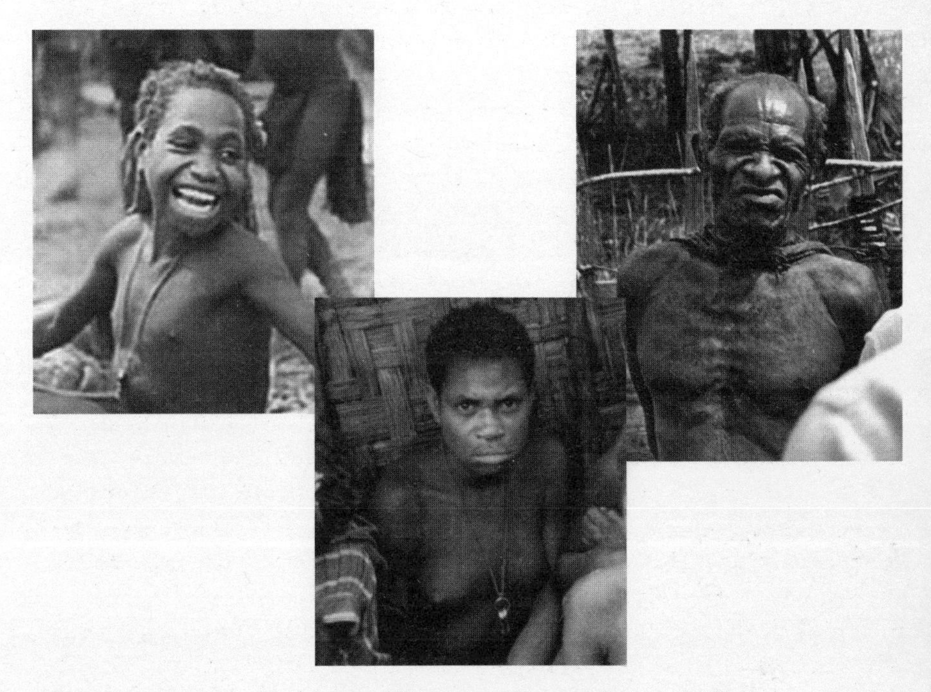

A boy shows joy; a woman, anger. The man is disgusted at seeing Paul eat canned food.

universality of expression. Darwin was right: This is part of the unity of humankind.

"There are universals not only in the expressions of emotion but also in some of the events that bring forth the emotion. We don't have the best evidence for this, but what we do have suggests that it is the same for all people on an abstract level, though the specifics may vary. For sadness or anguish, the common theme is an important loss. What or who that loss may be varies from one individual to another and from one culture to another.

"Just as there are universals in what brings forth an emotion, there are also universals in some of the changes that occur within our body when we feel an emotion. With a colleague, Robert Levenson at the University of California at Berkeley, I looked at the changes in bodily organs with each emotion. Let's take just the examples of anger and fear. In both of these emotions there is an increase in heart rate, and sweating also occurs. But in anger the hands get hot, while in fear the hands get cold. This difference in skin temperature is universal. I say this is universal because we studied this also in a culture in the highlands of western Sumatra, the Minangkabao, and we got exactly the same findings on the physiology."

Eighteen Kinds of Smiles

"Another point is the difference between voluntary and involuntary expression. It was not I who discovered this, but a French neurologist of the last century, Dr. Guillaume Duchenne."

Paul showed an image of Dr. Duchenne with a patient with a simulated smile, and another with a genuine smile. "The patient, on the left, had no pain sensation in his face. Dr. Duchenne applied electrodes to stimulate the muscles. He discovered, for example, which muscle pulls the lips up. But when he looked at the picture, he said, 'He's smiling but he doesn't look happy.' So he told the man a joke and took the second picture. The difference between the two smiles is in the muscle around the eye, which pulls the cheeks up."

Showing photos of himself with a simulated smile and a genuine smile, Paul commented, "That muscle around the eye does not obey the will, Duchenne said. The movement only occurs with genuine emotion. In Duchenne's words, 'Its absence unmasks the false friend.' Your Holiness, in one of your books you talk about your interest in smiling. I have tried to distinguish eighteen different forms of smiling."

This elicited a large smile from the Dalai Lama, one that seemed to engage every muscle of his face. "Eighteen!" the Dalai Lama exclaimed. Then he added wryly, "When will you find the nineteenth one?"

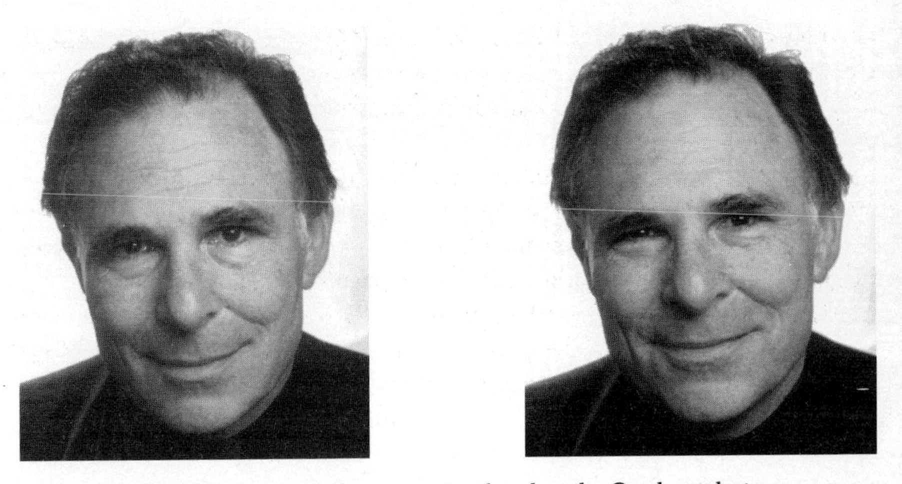

On the left, Paul Ekman demonstrates a simulated smile. On the right is a Duchenne (genuine) smile.

"I am hoping not to, actually," Paul replied. "I have enough trouble convincing people there are eighteen. Let me tell you about some of the research of the last decade. Duchenne's findings were totally ignored up until fifteen years ago, as if they hadn't existed.

"The first real evidence was in our study showing differences in smiling when people lied, claiming to feel good when they were in fact miserable. In two studies I did with Richard Davidson, we found different patterns of brain activity with these two kinds of smiles. Much of the brain activity you find with genuine enjoyment occurs only if the muscle around the eye is engaged."[2]

Lies, Detection, and the Emotional Package

From simulated smiles, Paul moved on to discuss his research on deception and lying. "This I have worked on only in America. Our research has shown that most people are easily misled by deception—even policemen, psychiatrists, lawyers, and customs officials. They are unable to detect lies from simply talking to someone."

"What about politicians?" the Dalai Lama asked, smiling. Though the comment was voiced with lightness, Paul read a poignancy into the question. On the flight over to India, Paul had read the Dalai Lama's autobiography, *Freedom in Exile,* and he had been struck by how often the Dalai Lama described being deceived by the lies of politicians as the Chinese took control of Tibet.

Paul answered, "I have only studied the lies of politicians, not whether they can tell if someone else is lying. But the fact that people cannot tell, in a sense, is surprising, because there are many subtle behavioral clues that reveal whether someone is truthful or lying. These can be seen through measuring the face and the voice. These body and speech measurements are over eighty-five percent accurate in being able to discern truthfulness from lying.

"We have found a very small group of people who are as accurate in their judgment as our objective measurements. They are extremely good at just listening, looking, and immediately knowing. I am working on trying to discover how this ability occurs, because less than one percent of people have it."[3]

Then Paul turned to the close connection between facial expressions of emotions and changes in the body. "In the course of our research we found something that surprised us. If you intentionally make a facial expression, you change your physiology. By making the correct expression, you begin to have the changes in your physiology that accompany the emotion. This was seen in both work on the bodily physiology and some work with Richard Davidson on changes in the brain. The face is not simply a means of display, but also a means of activating emotion."[4]

"Does that include voluntary expressions?" the Dalai Lama asked.

Paul answered, "This is strictly voluntary—but these expressions turn on the involuntary system." In other words, simply putting the face into a smile drives the brain to activity typical of happiness—just as a frown does with sadness, which was another finding of the research Paul did with Richard Davidson.

Paul added, "I would like to mention individual differences in emotion. I started with universals, but for the last ten years I have been working on how each individual differs. People have individual differences in their affective style. Some people's emotions occur much more quickly than others. Some people have a much stronger emotional response. In some people the emotion lasts longer. Some people's signals are very clear, and those of others are hard to see.

"Our findings also show that the emotional system is unified, not fragmented, in most people. It is not, as some earlier scientists had claimed, that you can have a big expression and a small physiological response. The different parts of the emotional package go together. If expressions are big or fast, so are the changes in the bodily systems directed by the autonomic nervous system. We have also shown that, by and large, these differences among individuals are not limited to one emotion. If you have a big anger response, you will have a big fear response too."

These differences suggest one reason people may have emotional misunderstandings: We all—naturally, but incorrectly—assume that others experience emotions exactly as we do. Paul's findings also suggest that some people—those with fast, strong, and long emotional responses—may have particular difficulty managing their emotions. That raises the question of how early in life these differences in how we experience emotions begin. Paul believes that if we knew this, we could intervene developmentally to give people a better chance at managing their emotions. For Paul, this possibility seemed considerably ahead of what we know now. However, Mark Greenberg's presentation two days later would describe programs for children that try to help them in just this way.

Freedom in Expression

Paul later told me that he had been struck by how openly and freely the Dalai Lama expressed his feelings. His face, Paul saw, was unusually expressive, revealing moment-to-moment changes not only in his emotions but in his thoughts: You could sense in his face when he was concentrating, doubting, understanding, agreeing. And then, most prominent of all, there was his extraordinary good humor, a perpetual sense of bemusement and delight that expressed itself as a contagious enjoyment of every nuance of life that presents itself.

That is not to say, Paul noted, that the Dalai Lama fails to experience sadness or other such feelings. Indeed, he seems highly responsive to the suffering of others, his anguish at their pain fully evident on his face—at least for a moment. But Paul was also struck by how quickly he recovered from distressing emotion—and that his more typical mode of response to others was always seeing the potential enjoyment or amusement, the positive side of whatever was occurring.

As a connoisseur of the human face, Paul had found the Dalai Lama's unusual in several other ways. For one, it was unusually large, and its muscles highly articulated. But more striking was how young it seemed—his face had the muscle tone of someone in his twenties, not a man of sixty-four. That, Paul speculated, was a consequence of the Dalai Lama never restraining his emotions, but instead letting them show clearly on his face—which means the muscles are used a lot more than usual. While most people acquire a self-consciousness that leads them to restrain the free expression of their emotions, the Dalai Lama appeared completely unself-conscious about showing them.

This lack of restraint, in turn, bespoke an unusual sense of confidence. Most children by age four or five have come to feel shame about certain feelings, and so begin a lifelong pattern of restraint in that portion of the spectrum of emotion. But the Dalai Lama appeared to Paul never to have learned to be embarrassed about how he feels—something that occurs only in the most fortunate of children.

Gripped by Emotion

Now Paul turned from reviewing these scientific findings on emotional expression to what happens during the moment we experience an emotion. "In the West, one of the things we say that distinguishes emotion from other mental phenomena is that an emotion can occur very quickly. It can begin in a fraction of a second (even though in some people it often takes much longer). A second distinguishing aspect is automatic appraising. The evaluation that turns on an emotion happens so quickly that we are not aware it is occurring. We are not a witness to the process of evaluation that generates the emotion. We typically become aware that we are afraid, or angry, or sad, after the emotion begins, not before.

"The moment we become aware is a half second or a quarter second after the emotion begins, not before. That's what we mean by automatic appraising." In other words, we can be in the grip of an emotion before we have noticed it starting.

The Dalai Lama asked for a clarification. "There seem to be two things here. One is the process of the arrival of emotion; the other is the feeling of the emotion itself. Are you suggesting that you become aware of both of these only after the fact?"

"No," Paul explained, "you typically become aware once the emotion begins. It focuses and commands attention once it starts but not during the process that generates it. Our lives would be enormously different, for good and bad, if we were actually consciously evaluating, becoming responsible for the start of each emotion. Instead, people feel as if emotion happens *to* us. I do not choose to have an emotion, to become afraid, or to become angry. I am suddenly angry. I can usually figure out what someone did that caused the emotion, but I am not aware of the process that evaluates, for example, what Dan did that made me angry.

"This is a critical issue in the Western understanding of emotion, that the beginning moment—a crucial process—is something that we can only wonder about, but we don't know. We only become aware once we're in the emotion. We're not the master at the start."

"I wonder," the Dalai Lama commented, "whether there might be an analogous situation in meditative practice in which you cultivate an introspective ability to monitor your own mental states. You are especially on guard, on one hand, for the occurrence of excitation, when the mind becomes agitated or distracted, or, on the other hand, when the mind succumbs to laxity and starts to fade out and lose its clarity. As you're developing this introspective ability, in the earlier phases when it's not so refined, you are able to ascertain the occurrence of either excitation or laxity only after it has arisen. But as you get more and more adept at this and you cultivate it more and more finely, you are able to discern even when the laxity or excitation is about to arise. It is similar for the arising of attachment or hostility as well."

"This is a very important issue," Paul replied. "It is something we know very little about. But I hope to get to some ideas about how to increase our ability to know the appraising process."

"This may be of interest to Dan," Alan said, translating a point that the Dalai Lama had made a few moments before. "According to Buddhist psychology, this ability—introspection, the monitoring of one's own mental states—is said to be a derivative of intelligence."

Theories of emotional intelligence, about which I have written, posit that self-awareness is one of its four main capacities.[5] So, to make clear that was the connection being made, I asked, "An emotional intelligence?"

"Actually, emotional intelligence is just one aspect of it," Alan answered. "*Prajña* sometimes means 'wisdom,' but in Buddhist psychology it is more accurately rendered as 'intelligence.' "

In the emotional intelligence model, self-awareness—including the ability to monitor our emotions—represents the fundamental skill needed to be intelligent about our emotional life. Ideally, this would include detecting destructive emotions while they were beginning to build—as the Dalai Lama said meditative practice allowed—rather than only after they have captured our minds, which Paul pointed out is the more usual case. If we can become aware of destructive emotions as they are first stirring, we have maximal choice about how we will respond to them.

Private Thoughts, Public Feelings

"The appraising that occurs," Paul continued, "is influenced by two things. It is influenced by the history of our species on this planet. One theorist says that what we respond to reflects the wisdom of the ages. It is also influenced by our own personal history. Both phylogeny and ontogeny—both what has been useful and adaptive to humankind and what has been useful and adaptive in our own growth and development—determine the appraising response.

"Emotions are public, not private. By that I mean that the expression signals to others, in the voice, face, and in the posture, what emotion we feel.

Our thoughts are private; our emotions are not. Others know how we feel—and that is very important for how people get along with each other."

This point prompted a lengthy side discussion in Tibetan, with the Dalai Lama seeking the Tibetan term corresponding to "thought" as Paul had used it. The problem here is a fundamental one in the Dalai Lama's dialogue with psychology: In the Buddhist view, thoughts are considered to be normally laden with emotions, and emotions are invariably laden with thoughts, so the Tibetan term for thought includes its affective tone. The Tibetan system does not hold to the sharp distinction between thought and emotion made in the West, but rather understands them to be intertwined—a view closer to the reality modern neuroscience is discovering in the brain.[6]

"One might have an attitude that blends into an emotion—say, a negative attitude where the next thing that arises is part of hatred," the Dalai Lama pointed out.

"Many thoughts involve emotions," Paul acknowledged, "but not all thoughts. If the thought is connected to an emotion, then you will see a sign of the emotion. Let me give an example that I emphasize a great deal in my work on deception. If you are talking to someone who is suspected of a crime and they look afraid, you don't know whether that is the fear of being caught or the honest, innocent person's fear of being disbelieved. We can't tell what the thought process is. We can see what the emotion about the thought is, but not its content. In both cases you're afraid.

"In Shakespeare's play, Othello killed Desdemona. He was right in seeing that she was afraid, but he was wrong in what he attributed it to. He thought it was a woman afraid because she had been caught in an infidelity. But it was a woman afraid for her life from a jealous husband."

"In the Buddhist context," the Dalai Lama said, "there is often an attempt made to understand the causal relationship between emotions and thoughts. In many cases, we have a powerful emotion that gives rise to a certain intention, so often the emotion precedes the thought or acts as a catalyst for it.

"In Buddhist moral philosophy we speak of three types of unvirtuous mental states, two of which are closely related to emotions. One is covetousness, and another is ill will. Covetousness is generated by a powerful attachment to a given object. That attachment then gives rise to the thought 'I want that.' Covetousness could also be aroused by anger and other emotions. Similarly, anger and hatred often give rise to ill will with their associated thoughts."

"No disagreement," Paul answered.

"The point here," the Dalai Lama clarified, "is that emotion seems to precede thought."

"Sometimes it precedes," Paul replied, "sometimes it is simultaneous, and sometimes it comes after."

Getting Moving Without Thinking

"Two more points: When an emotion begins, it generates changes. It generates changes in our expression, our face, our voice, changes in the way we think, impulses to action. These occur involuntarily, and if we don't go along with them, we experience it as a struggle. We struggle to control, to not show, or to not speak, or to not act. A defining aspect of emotion is the fact that it takes us over for a moment, or sometimes many moments," Paul said.

"Emotions can be very brief. It is possible for an emotion to last no more than a second or two. I can be happy one moment and angry the next, and sad right after that. Or an emotion can continue over some length of time.

"What I have been describing is really an evolutionary view of emotion. There is a statement by Charles Darwin in his autobiography regarding his view that 'all sentient beings developed through natural selection in such a way that pleasant sensations serve as their guide, and especially the pleasure derived from sociability and from loving our families.' I think this statement overlaps with His Holiness's views, although there are some interesting differences."

At that point Paul gave the Dalai Lama a copy of *The Expression of Emotion in Man and Animals,* Darwin's classic book on emotion, which Paul had recently edited with modern scientific commentary. "One of Darwin's principal ideas that has withstood time is the continuity of the species. In other words, emotions are not unique to humans. In Western thought, it had been variously believed that animals had emotions but humans did not, or humans had emotions but animals did not. If we recognized that animals have emotions, we might not treat them the way we do. So there is continuity between species as well as universality across cultures.

"Another of Darwin's ideas is probably the most critical: that our emotions evolved over the course of our history to deal with the most important issues of life—with child rearing, friendship, mating, antagonisms—and the function of emotion is to get us moving very quickly without having to think.

"One example is very vivid in my mind from the journey coming up here," Paul said, recalling our harrowing experiences on India's crowded highways, an unpredictable mix of huge Tata trucks, overpacked buses, taxis, rickshaws, pedestrians, cows sunning themselves—all following the random law of Brownian movement. When one vehicle passes another, there is often still another speeding toward it from the opposite direction. There ensues a daredevil, adrenaline-drenching set of moments when both drivers lean on the horn nonstop until they squeeze by.

With that scene fresh in his mind, Paul continued, "You are driving a car, and suddenly another car moves as if it is going to hit you. Without thought, before you know what's happened, you twist the wheel, you hit the brake. The emotion has saved your life. If you had to think in order to recognize the danger, and think about what to do, you would not survive. Now, those very features get us into trouble also."

The Dalai Lama posed a question: "Wouldn't you say that rapid reaction was a conditioned response, because if the person hadn't learned how to drive, how to hit the brake, he couldn't do it?"

"Absolutely correct," Paul replied. "It's really interesting that this is something we learn, not as a child but as a young adult, and yet it becomes part of the emotion mechanism. It becomes part of a built-in theme: If something is moving fast toward our visual field, we respond. It doesn't matter what it is. The closer a response is to that theme, the easier it is for us to learn it. But most of the things we become emotional about are things we have learned in the course of growing up. The issue I will get to later is, can we unlearn some of them?"

The Basic Families of Emotions

"The last of Darwin's ideas that is relevant to our talk is that there are different emotions. They are not simply positive or negative emotions. Each emotion has its own signal and purpose. The question then becomes, how many emotions are there? So I've listed those for which there is good scientific evidence."

The question of which emotions are basic—those that others derive from—has been a subject of intense debate in this scientific field. There are several schools of thought, and a body of recent research to resolve the question, including cross-cultural studies to see if an emotion is universal and cross-species studies to see if it occurs in primates—both indicators that a given emotion may have been essential in evolution. There are up to ten, according to Paul: anger, fear, sadness, disgust, contempt, surprise, enjoyment, embarrassment, guilt, and shame. "Each of these words stands for a family of emotions—not just one emotion. There is, for example, a family of anger feelings."

The list Paul offered had several similarities to that from Buddhist psychology for mental states. Looking back at the end of the week, the Dalai

Lama found the idea of emotion families intriguing. In the moment, he made some immediate comparisons to the typology he was familiar with in Buddhism, which led to a long discussion in Tibetan with Jinpa, who had gone into his habitual debate mode. Finally His Holiness asked Paul, "Would you say that covetousness is an emotion? There is disagreement here."

"It is closest to envy," Paul replied. "I think of each emotion having a family of related feelings; covetousness is part of the envy family," which was not on the list of emotions essential in evolution.

He continued, "I began to study contempt believing it was a strictly Western—particularly English—emotion. But the evidence for its universality was just as good, and there's evidence for it in other animals, not just humans. Stephen Suomi is the scientist who has observed that when a dominant primate is challenged by a juvenile, it responds with the same muscular display for contempt as in humans."

The Dalai Lama asked, "Are all the emotions on the list there—fear, anger, disgust, and so on—spontaneous? Are those in common with animals? And are you necessarily unaware of how they start—could there be instances of fear, for example, that are the outcome of thought processes?"

"Yes," said Paul, "fear occurs when we have negative expectations. Say, for example, I am waiting to learn the outcome of a medical test to see whether I have cancer. I have to wait for a few days and—not continuously, but often, whenever my mind comes back to it and I think of the consequences—I experience fear. In my view—and not everyone agrees with this—primates may also be capable of that process. Some primates, at least, can be aware of how they feel and may be able to anticipate emotional events and suffer in advance of the pain."

The Dalai Lama went on, "This raises the issue of afflicted intelligence. Clearly we can induce fear using our intelligence by pondering, by anticipation, and so forth. I wonder about the extent to which animals also can arouse emotions such as fear through cogitation. It is probably possible in principle, but rather marginal compared to the extent to which human beings do it."

"I would agree," said Paul, "but I myself worry about the extent to which we may underestimate what happens in other animals. It is so convenient to underestimate." That last point resonated strongly with the Dalai Lama's writings on compassion, which urge that people kill not even an insect.

Seven Types of Happiness

Each of the emotion families, Paul explained, contains a complex of related feelings, as in these seven variations within the happiness family:

Amusement
Fiero (the delight of meeting a challenge)
Relief
Excitement, novelty
Awe, wonder
Sensory pleasures (in each of the senses)
Calm peacefulness

"I believe each of those is an emotion, but the evidence is not as good for some of them. I have added the last possible emotion—a state of calmness or peacefulness—based on what I have been thinking about in the last week. I am not terribly happy with either of those words, but it is in that realm."

"Would you say 'equanimity'?" I suggested, using the term cited in Buddhist literature for a state of balanced contentment.

"That's not a bad word either," Paul agreed. "The fact that we don't have a word doesn't mean it doesn't exist, nor does the fact that we have a word mean that it does exist, as His Holiness has pointed out in one of his books. As an example, I would point to the word *fiero,* which refers to the pleasure that comes when you meet a challenge that has stretched you. In English we don't have a word for that particular emotion, and, as best I can tell from my informants, there is none in German or Russian. But in Italian there is a word specifically for that."

Both Matthieu and Francisco pointed out that French has a similar word, *fierté,* usually translated as "pride," as in a job well done. But, Francisco added, "happiness is not in the equation" for the French term.

"Thank you for that comment," said Paul. "It was the next point and really the last I was going to make before the break. In itself, 'happiness' doesn't tell us what *kind* of happiness. I'm delineating seven kinds of happiness. That doesn't mean there aren't more; the number reflects a limit of my imagination. There is amusement, which can go from very slight to very strong. There is *fiero,* which is different. There is the wonderful feeling of relief: 'Ah! I didn't have cancer.'

"There is a feeling of excitement that comes with novelty. There is a feeling of awe and wonder, a very interesting emotion when we are overwhelmed. It doesn't happen for most of us too often, but it is very important. And there is the feeling of calmness and peacefulness. Those are seven different kinds of happiness I would distinguish."

Alan asked, "Does awe, as intended on this list, only arise with regard to something that is good, lofty, or excellent? If I saw a traffic accident where a body was scattered all over the road, and I responded, 'Wow, is that a mess!'—could I call that a sense of awe?"

Paul replied, "I really don't know the answer to that. But when I have asked people to report experiences of awe, they have only spoken of wonderment."

"Something good, then," Alan concluded.

"So, in the sense that I'm using it," clarified Paul, "let's call it positive awe."

At that, I declared it time for the morning break. During the tea break, His Holiness told me he was very interested in the neural correlates of the mental processes Paul had been discussing. He was pleased when I told him Richard Davidson would address this the next day.

Moods and Their Triggers

After the break, Paul began again: "Moods are not on the list. Moods are related to but different from emotions. The most obvious way they differ is in their duration. Emotions could come and go in a matter of seconds or minutes, but a mood can last a whole day."

"How would you define mood?" the Dalai Lama asked. "Is it an impact left over from an emotional occurrence?"

Paul responded, "That question relates to the second way moods differ from emotions. Usually when we have an emotion we can say what produced it. We can specify the event that triggered it, that brought our emotion forth. Often with a mood we can't. We wake up in an irritable mood or in a very positive mood; we wake up very apprehensive or sad, for no reason that we know. I believe these moods are produced by internal changes that do not relate to what is happening to us on the outside.

"That is one way a mood occurs, but there is a second way: if we have a very dense emotional experience. If we experience amusement again and again in a short period of time, the consequence will be a very euphoric mood. If we are furious again and again, we will then have a long period in which we are irritable. So those are two different routes to a mood."

I asked, "Couldn't there be background thoughts that continually trigger a mood that we're not aware of?" I was thinking of cognitive therapy, which holds that distressing emotions are triggered by subtle thoughts in the mind's background—and that bringing those thoughts into awareness offers a way to free ourselves from their control.

"There certainly could be," Paul agreed. "We don't really know as much about the causes of moods as about the causes of emotions."

The Dalai Lama asked if medical conditions or one's environment—say, dismal weather—could also lead to moods, and Paul acknowledged they might. Alan added the question, "And if one were in an ongoing abusive relationship, couldn't that lead to a mood?"

"That would be a mood produced by the dense emotional experience," Paul answered.

"But it would be an identifiable trigger," the Dalai Lama observed.

"Yes," said Paul. "When a mood is caused by the second path, dense emotional experience, then you know why you're in that mood."

He continued, "When we're in a mood it biases and restricts how we think. It makes us vulnerable in ways that we are normally not. So the negative moods create a lot of problems for us, because they change how we think. If I wake up in an irritable mood, I'm looking for a chance to be angry. Things that ordinarily would not frustrate me, do. The danger of a mood is not only that it biases thinking but that it increases emotions. When I'm in an irritable mood, my anger comes stronger and faster, lasts longer, and is harder to control than usual. It's a terrible state . . . one I would be glad never to have."

That last aside, by the end of the meeting, was to prove prescient for Paul.

There ensued a side discussion in Tibetan among the Dalai Lama, the lamas present, and the translators, at which point Alan commented, "They're looking for the Tibetan equivalent of 'mood.' It's not so easy"—as with the word "emotion," there is no Tibetan word for "mood."

"But I want to remind Your Holiness again of what you have said in your books," said Paul. "If you don't have a name for something, that doesn't mean it doesn't exist."

"We are grappling with how to explain that moods occur spontaneously, inexplicably," Jinpa explained.

Speaking to that point, the Dalai Lama said, "There must be conditions, even though they may not be obvious to us."

Paul replied, "There certainly are conditions that create moods. They are usually opaque to us—they are out of our awareness and so we don't know why we feel the way we do. It is common to say, 'I don't know why I'm so irritable.' That doesn't mean that there isn't a reason; it's just that we don't know the reason."

"Buddhist psychology," the Dalai Lama continued his point, "has concepts for the cause and mechanism of the arising of anger. The term used for what gives rise to anger is literally translated as 'mental unhappiness,' but that's not it really. It's an abiding sense of dissatisfaction. When you have that dissatisfaction, then you can readily become irritable. You are immediately prone to anger. I wonder how close that is to your concept."

"That sounds very close to me," Paul agreed. "Very close."

Buddhist psychology explains the arising in the mind of a given mental state, such as anger, in terms of both immediate and distant causes. These can include external stimuli in the environment, one's physiological state, one's thoughts, and other hidden influences (including what Buddhists see as past life experiences stored in the mind as habitual propensities).

But a fundamental difference is that Buddhists strive to be totally free from anger, while most Westerners view anger, in the proper degree and situation, as perfectly suitable—and few consider whether we can eradicate it altogether.

Paul then delved into the anger family, starting with the emotional cousins hatred and resentment. "I do not use these words in the same way that everyone in the West uses them or as they are used in His Holiness's writings," Paul started. "The exact words don't matter. What matters is to identify whether these are important, separate states.

"Resentment is a long-standing feeling of being treated unfairly and unjustly. When we feel resentment we don't feel it all the time, but when an event occurs that brings it to mind, then the resentment recurs. Resentment can fester like a boil and occupy our mind all the time in the forefront, but it need not. It can be totally out of mind and just called forth when you hear some news."

"When this resentment is not manifesting, not boiling over, would it fit into this large category that comes up so often in Western psychology, the subconscious?" the Dalai Lama asked.

"We can't say where it resides," said Paul. "It is out of consciousness, ready to be reawakened."

"In Buddhist psychology," the Dalai Lama said, "there is an understanding that many of these emotions need not necessarily be manifest. In fact, the emotions themselves may be felt or experienced, but they are also present in the form of habitual propensities that remain unconscious, or dormant, until they are catalyzed."

Here I interjected, "The Pali term is *anusayas,* 'latent tendencies.' " This concept in Buddhist psychology holds that the mind harbors propensities for different emotional states, including the destructive ones, due to past experiences that have built up into mental habits.[7] These latent propensities are seen as why, if strong anger comes on one occasion, it can come later, on another, more easily or strongly—even if in the meantime it fades completely and is replaced by loving compassion or forgiveness. Given the right triggering circumstances, the latent anger can come back full strength. In the Buddhist ideal of eradicating destructive emotions, even these latent tendencies need to be uprooted.

Paul resumed, "Resentment may be easily rearoused, but the key to it is the feeling of unfairness and injustice. Hatred, like resentment, is long-standing. It involves at least three emotions: disgust, anger, and contempt."

"Would you not make a distinction," the Dalai Lama asked, "between resentment that is based on reality and resentment that is conjured up just by thinking thoughts that are unhinged from reality? Would you put them into the same category?"

"Well, they are clearly different kinds of resentment," Paul answered. "Hatred, like resentment, is long-standing. Like resentment, it can be unconscious. Like resentment, it can fester, so it's all you think about all the time. But it differs from resentment in an important way: Although focused on a person, it's not focused on a specific injustice or unfairness. I hope that this afternoon we might discuss whether hatred is necessarily destructive. It depends on the kind of hatred, I'd argue."

Paul gave an example: "My hatred for Hitler could motivate me to dedicate my life to overcoming bigotry and violence. Hatred need not, in my thinking, lead to self-destructive behavior, nor to behavior that is motivated to destroy the other person."

The Subtleties of Love and Compassion

With the list of basic emotions families still on the screen, Paul went on to one of the fifteen or so emotional cousins in the enjoyment family, love. Love, of course, includes but transcends enjoyment alone. While the momentary pangs of love are enjoyable, love refers to a long-term commitment—a complex state of attachment—not just a momentary emotion.

"I try to distinguish the three kinds of love, and I wish we had a different word for each in English. There is parental love. There is loving friendship. And there is romantic love—often the shortest of the three," Paul added, getting a laugh.

"Wouldn't romantic love be a subdivision of loving friendship?" the Dalai Lama asked.

"I don't believe romantic love survives unless loving friendship develops—it provides the structure," Paul answered. "Loving friendship doesn't always develop, and then romantic love doesn't survive. Romantic love has two additional ingredients. One is sexual intimacy, which you don't have in loving friendship, and the other, normatively, is the creation and raising of children in a long-term relationship.

"These types of love are contexts in which many emotions are felt. I love my daughter (who is sitting over there) but that doesn't mean I don't sometimes get angry with her or worry a lot. I rarely feel disgust with her, but I am often surprised or feel pride. I feel many different emotions toward her, but the key is not the emotions. The key is the enduring, unconditional commitment.

"Where does compassion fit? Here I tread on thin ice. Is it an emotional trait? Is it an attitude and not a trait? Compassion certainly seems to be a condition in which you are responsive to the emotions of others. You are able to appreciate and know what they are feeling, but it is more than just empathy. Why is it not easy to acquire? Can anyone become compassionate? Can some people learn compassion more easily than others, and if so, why?"

The Dalai Lama showed keen interest in what Paul was saying, nodding in agreement as he spoke.

"The closest model that I can think of for compassion," Paul noted, "is the absorption and unconditional concern that exists between a mother and infant. It is such a strong state, I don't have the right words for it. It prohibits many negative actions from occurring. That doesn't mean that a mother doesn't sometimes get angry with her infant, but, ideally, she never harms the infant. I know that in the West people would question why I don't say 'caregiver' and infant, but I'm not sure that is as good a model biologically as mother and infant. It is possible. But we are beginning to learn about some of the hormones responsible for biologically mediating that relationship between mother and infant. But I leave that to my friend, Richie"—Richard Davidson, who would speak about the biology of emotions the next day.

"Paul, even in Buddhist texts, that's the model that is used—the mother and infant," said the Dalai Lama. As Alan later elaborated, "In a common Tibetan meditation on compassion, you view all sentient beings as if they were your mother, bearing in mind that in some past life they all must have actually been your mother. This is done to arouse a sense of affection and gratitude by focusing on the person who has shown you the greatest love and compassion."[8]

"The technical definition of compassion," Matthieu clarified from the Buddhist perspective, "is the wish that others may be free from suffering and the causes of suffering, while love is defined as the wish that others be happy and find the causes for happiness."

"There is no question that parents will sacrifice their life for the child, without thought, because of the nature of this engagement," Paul continued. "Before reading your books, I thought that this was unique, that one never felt this except for one's child. You raise the question whether one can feel it for a much wider group of people. I hope we can come back to this issue because I don't have more to say other than to express some of my wonderment about it."

"I wonder whether you make a distinction between afflictive and nonafflictive compassion," commented the Dalai Lama. "An instance of afflictive compassion is a case in which the object of one's compassion is also an object of one's attachment. One sees this as desirable. You see your child as so cute and so adorable that if the child comes in harm's way, there is attachment and compassion together. Whereas in other instances the object of one's compassion is really not at all an object of attachment—it could even be an enemy. That would be nonafflictive compassion."

"That is a very critical distinction that you raise," Paul replied. "I think possessiveness is an aspect of the first type of compassion. I feel, as a parent, the hardest thing for me to learn was to grant autonomy to my children. Just at the point when they got old enough to be able to really harm themselves, I couldn't control them. I had to allow them their freedom, and that is very hard for a parent to do, because you don't want anything bad to happen. But if you don't allow them the freedom to lead their own lives, then something bad has happened. Being a parent means you're committed to worry."

"You are a very good father!" the Dalai Lama said, laughing at first, then nodding with a serious expression, underscoring the sincerity of his remark as the laughter in the room faded. His Holiness later told me he had genuinely found Paul's remarks both eloquent and touching. And this was a moment that Paul was to remember as an emotional high point of the week.

Between Impulse and Action: Leverage Points in the Mind

Paul then turned to a crucial point: how we might better control our destructive emotions. He acknowledged at the outset that science knows little about how emotions are triggered but that it seems to happen automatically, with their initiation occurring out of our awareness. That's why emotions can take us by surprise, coming unbidden into our awareness. The question is whether we can do anything to change the original appraisals that trigger them, so that they become less automatic. That might give us more time between the impulse to act on them and our actual reaction—and therefore more chance to make a more measured response.

"More than forty years ago, when I was a psychotherapist," Paul said, "my teacher said to me, 'Your goal for your patients is to increase the time between impulse and action. If they can spread that time, that is what they will have gained.' What His Holiness is talking about is increasing the appraising time *before* the impulse. It is not the time from impulse to action, but from appraising to impulse. That is an extraordinary and very important difference."

In short, there are two places where consciousness, awareness of what is happening, could make a difference in our ability to regulate destructive emotions. Say, for instance, someone rudely steps in front of us in a line. When that occurs, an appraisal evaluates that person's actions: He's being rude. If we were witness to that appraisal, if we were aware of it as it is happening, we might be able to influence it by talking back and questioning the assumption, noting perhaps that the person didn't see us, or that it doesn't matter enough to become angry. Call this "appraisal awareness." But Paul had little hope that it can be achieved, because appraisals usually happen too quickly, and in areas of the brain that operate out of our awareness.

Moving a moment further in time, Paul continued, the appraisal has already occurred (that person acted rudely and unfairly), and now an impulse to action occurs—say, to curtly object to what the person has done. Here, Paul observed, is the second opportunity for awareness to allow us to make a choice. We might learn to be aware of such impulses and to be able to deliberately evaluate them at this point, and choose whether we wish to proceed and act on the impulse. This "impulse awareness," Paul believed, may be achievable for some of us some of the time—but it isn't easy to achieve and will take practice.

Now, moving a moment or two later, to when we have begun to speak, we hear our voice, we feel the tension in our body, and before more than a word or two get out, we have some awareness of what is happening. At this point the capability to observe ourselves as we are acting allows us a third choice point. Paul called this "action awareness," the ability to monitor our actions and interrupt or modify themes—emotional habits—as they are occurring.

The question is how to educate our awareness so that we strengthen the ability to monitor our appraisals and stretch the time between impulse and action. Here Paul was taken by what he had been learning about mindfulness meditation, a Buddhist practice that trains the ability to monitor what goes on in one's mind. As Paul understood mindfulness meditation, it offers a means of obtaining action awareness and impulse awareness (though he wonders if it can achieve appraisal awareness). Other techniques he believed might be helpful in achieving action awareness include learning to be more sensitive to the feedback from our bodies about what we are feeling and doing. But he thought these would not help with impulse awareness, let alone appraisal awareness.

The issue is choice. He argued that emotions were not designed or did not evolve for us to have choice about how we evaluate and what we do. Although emotions often serve us well, we would all be better off if we could exercise choice when our emotions lead us to acts that are destructive to ourselves or others, when we are misperceiving rather than correctly perceiving what is occurring. In short, Paul pointed out three different choice points: during the appraisal, during the impulse, and during the actions taken.

"Let me now go back to the more general issue of how automatic appraising operates. It doesn't make us respond to just anything; we become emotional about some things but not others. Moreover, we become emotional about some of the same things as other people, and we become emotional about things that others are not emotional about at all."

"Am I right," the Dalai Lama asked, "in thinking that the general stance in Western psychoanalysis and psychology is that it's the physical and verbal manifestation of negative emotions that is undersirable, and one should therefore try to prevent them from occurring? But, so far as the emotions themselves are concerned, there is an understanding that they are natural parts of the human psyche, and there is nothing wrong with them. They are something that cannot actually be changed or fixed." Here he was contrasting the Buddhist goal of eliminating destructive emotions with the psychotherapeutic aim of changing not the emotions themselves but how people respond.

Paul's answer skirted that topic and went to the question of whether there are fundamental, hardwired emotional responses that cannot be eliminated. "It is very unlikely that we could ever learn not to be emotional about certain events. If there is a sudden sense of free fall, such as occurs when you're flying in an airplane and suddenly hit an air pocket, there is a fear response. I've talked to airline pilots, and they still have that fear response even though it happens every day. That is, at least in my view, an emotion theme that is built into us; we're not going to get over it."

The Dalai Lama asked, "Is it actually true that the pilots, regardless of their repeated exposure, still go through the same emotion? I have found that as I become more and more habituated to flying, my fear response has diminished—the more I fly, the less sweat."

"There are two different issues," Paul clarified. "First is whether the fear response becomes smaller. Second, they might not have become airplane pilots unless they were people for whom this was a less threatening event. And of course airplane pilots have not had your experiences, so we may not be able to generalize from your experience."

"If you want to count my experience," the Dalai Lama said, "you should also take into account that when I first started flying I was really scared!"—an admission that drew some laughs. "The point is that the pilot's experience should count—and there shouldn't be a fear right from the beginning."

Freedom from Fear Itself

Paul went on, "There is a very important issue that is being raised now. Can we ask human beings to learn not to fear some of the things they fear? I would say that for most human beings it is probably more than we should ask for them to unlearn the things that are the product of our evolution. But there are a small number of those things. Most of what frightens us or angers us are things that we have learned, and therefore it should be possible for us to unlearn them."

"There is a corollary in Buddhism," the Dalai Lama noted, "in that mental afflictions are aroused in two ways. One is simply by a spontaneous, brief event—an event happens and the mental affliction is aroused. Other mental afflictions come out of a deeper cause than simply adventitious circumstance. They come out of your predilections and habitual propensities. The latter are more difficult to remedy."

This brought to mind a point I had wanted to raise earlier, about what does—and does not—change through psychotherapy. "Your Holiness," I said, "I would like to mention a study by Lester Luborsky at the University of Pennsylvania. In successful psychotherapy he found that what changed was the action people took, not their feelings—they still had the same fear or anger after psychotherapy, though it was weaker. But they were able to change how they responded even though they felt the same emotional impulse."

"That may be a limitation of that therapeutic approach—you may be able to do better," Paul commented. "If I can use a computer metaphor, there is a storage system in which are preserved the events we have learned to be afraid of, or to be angry or sad about. Things enter that storage system throughout our lives. There may be critical periods during which things that enter may be harder to remove than at other periods. The strength the emotional event has when we learn it may also affect how hard it is to remove it.

"I'd like to come back to a point that His Holiness raised: that there is an important difference between the regulation of our response before and during an emotion. There are three different mental processes—or, if you like, three different opportunities. The goal, I believe, is to do better than the psychotherapy patients Dan mentioned. The goal is to not become emotional about things and then say to yourself afterward, 'Why did I get angry about that? Why did that frighten me?' The goal is for that to no longer happen.

"But if you can't achieve that goal, then the second goal is to not act on the emotion, not let it adversely affect others. And if you can't achieve that goal, then the last is to learn from it in the hope that you'll do better the next time. The first step is, I think, the real goal."

"Do these three goals correspond to the three stages before, during, and after an emotion?" the Dalai Lama asked.

"It seemed as if they did," Paul said, "but I would like to explore that with an example. One more abstract point first before the example: One of the reasons we have so much difficulty once we become emotional is that the emotion itself enslaves us. There is what I call a refractory period, in which new information doesn't enter or, if it does, our interpretation is biased and we only regard the world in a way that supports the emotion we are feeling. That refractory period may be only a few seconds or it may be much longer. As long as it is occurring we can't get out of the grip of that emotion. That doesn't mean we have to act on it, but it is still seizing us. When the refractory period ends, the emotion can end.

"The question that I don't have the answer for is what practices can help us shorten that refractory period," Paul said, noting that there were three ways to intervene: not become emotional at all, shorten the refractory period, or better control how we act even during the refractory period.

The Case of Teasable Tim

Now Paul returned to the example he had promised, drawn from the pages of the book he was writing, called *Gripped by Emotion.*

"Suppose a boy whom I'll call Tim was teased by a cruel father whose teases were made as a joke, but their cruel edge was to mock and humiliate. When Tim would get upset when his father teased him, that delighted his father, and he would tease Tim more. Early, perhaps before the age of five, the possibility that a powerful person would humiliate him through teasing became established in Tim's emotional storage system.

"Now, twenty years later, Tim is a grown man. He is well established. Nobody tries to humiliate him, but if anyone teases him, he responds with immediate anger. He cannot accept a good-natured tease or joke. So how is Tim to deal with this? Clearly, he doesn't want to always get angry. Sometimes afterward he feels, 'I shouldn't have done that. I've overreacted. They didn't mean to hurt me,' but it's not in his control.

"So the first step is to identify this trigger—for his conscious self to know that this is a very important trigger for him, and to know its origin. This isn't always easy. He may need loving help from friends who can help him realize what it is that so forcefully arouses his anger. Once equipped with that knowledge, the next step is for him to think about it, considering the fact that teasing can occur for nice reasons, not just bad ones, and to practice in his mind reevaluating what teasing is.

"And then he can begin to practice reshaping his response. He may even sense when a teasing episode is about to occur, and prepare himself before it happens. So, over time, teasing may become a weaker emotion trigger for anger.

"Seven factors, I believe, determine whether you can remove this trigger. The first factor is how close the event is to the evolutionary theme. No one really knows what the evolutionary theme is for anger, but let's just suppose that it is being thwarted by having something or someone interfere with what you're trying to do.

"The closer the triggering event is to that theme, the harder it will be to ignore the trigger. If Tim's father, instead of teasing him, had pinned Tim's arms to his side and held him until he screamed, his anger would be much harder to unlearn, because that trigger is much closer to the experience of being thwarted. Teasing is fairly far removed. We can learn to be angry about anything, but the further it is from the evolutionary theme, the easier it will be to unlearn it.

"Let me take another example. When the chairman of my department found out what I was writing, he said, 'Explain this to me: Why is it that when I'm driving to work and while merging into a single lane someone breaks the unwritten rule to take turns and his car jumps in front of me, I get enraged? What difference does it make? I only get to work three or four seconds later. At work I don't get enraged when someone raises an obstacle to a plan for the department that I spent months working on. That's enormously important but it doesn't make me furious. The other does. Why?'

"I told him, 'I believe that the experience of that other car coming in front of you is very close to the theme of being thwarted, and it happens physically. Therefore, even though it is inconsequential, it's not inconsequential in terms of what has been stored in our brain. It is much harder to deal with.' "

"That's a very good example," the Dalai Lama commented.

"The second factor," Paul continued, "is the time when the trigger was learned. There may well be critical periods for learning that make it harder to remove later. The general belief in the West is that if it's earlier in life, it's harder. Tim is going to have a hard time removing his trigger because it was created quite early in his life.

"The third factor is how much emotional charge was there when it was learned. In this example there is a very strong emotion. His father teased him unmercifully. That's going to be very hard to remove. Repetition may be a fourth factor that also contributes to the strength of the emotion.

"The fifth factor is a more complex one. Some people are going to have a much more difficult time than others. If Tim is someone whose emotions in general happen very quickly rather than slowly, or if his emotions are very strong rather than moderate, he's going to have more trouble than another person might. The very same experience with a different person would have different consequences.

"The sixth factor is whether Tim is in an irritable mood. Even if Tim has really reached the point where he almost never responds to teasing with anger, if he is in an irritable mood he might, because moods make us more vulnerable.

"The last factor is temperament."

"How would you differentiate between mood and temperament?" the Dalai Lama asked. He later told me he found Paul's distinction between mood and temperament quite useful, something that Buddhist psychology had not paid that much attention to.

"The easiest way is time," said Paul. "Moods last for hours, usually not more than a day. But a temperament is often seen over a long period, though not necessarily throughout life. We don't know exactly. It seems that some temperaments are inherited and others are developed through experience. Even the inherited ones are, of course, affected by experience. But they are fairly stable over many years. If Tim has a hostile temperament, if anger is something that occurs easily and often in his life, it is going to be much harder to get over than if Tim basically has a sociable, friendly temperament."

A Phone Call That Didn't Come

"I would like to consider another example. This occurred in my own life just a month ago, at the point when I was writing what I would say at this meeting and thinking about it. It is not one I'm particularly proud of, but it's a good example because I know it very well. My wife, Mary Ann, who teaches at a different university than I do, was away in Washington at a conference. I live in San Francisco. Whenever one of us is away, we call each evening to say hello. When she called me on Friday night, I told her that on Saturday I was going to be meeting with a researcher for dinner and some work. By the time I got home it would be eleven P.M. my time and it would be two in the morning her time, too late for her to call. So she said, 'I'll call you in the morning.'

" 'Wonderful,' I said.

"Now, Mary Ann knows me very well and knows that on a Sunday when she's away, I am sitting at my computer by seven-thirty in the morning. So seven-thirty in the morning is ten-thirty her time. No phone call. Eight-thirty, still no phone call. At nine o'clock it's now twelve o'clock in Washington, and I start to get a little angry. Why hasn't she called me? Even worse, I have the thought that she's not calling me because of something that happened the night before, so I start to feel jealous. Then I get angry at myself because I have gotten jealous, and also at her, because if she had called me I wouldn't be jealous. You can see I am now in the refractory period. During this period I am unable to access information I have that would stop this emotion.

"The next thought I have is that maybe she's had a car accident. I become afraid. Should I call the police in Washington? Then I get angry again. Why do I have to be afraid? If she'd call, I wouldn't be afraid.

"It's now eleven o'clock, two in the afternoon in Washington. Finally at noon my time she calls. By now I'm quite angry, but I do everything I can to not say anything. I don't say, 'Why didn't you call?' I don't say, 'You made me feel all these terrible emotions.' I want to say those things but I don't. But I am unable to keep the edge out of my voice. I don't want it to be there but I can't prevent it, so I know she knows I'm angry.

"She doesn't say to me, 'Are you angry?' The phone call is really quite unsatisfactory. She certainly doesn't respond positively to hearing the anger, and we can't talk about it. I feel if I say anything about it, if I apologize for it, it'll come out. So I have to avoid it. After two or three minutes we hang up, knowing she's coming home the next night, and we say, 'I'll see you then.'

"Then the refractory period is over, and I think, 'I know Mary Ann hates to use the telephone.' In fact, she hates it so much that if she's home and has to call someone, she'll ask me to call for her. I will often say, 'Yes, but only if you'll wash the dishes.' So if I had thought of that, I would have realized she wasn't calling me not because she's unfaithful or inconsiderate, but because she hates to use the telephone.

"I also know about myself, having been abandoned by my mother when I was fourteen, that anger when I'm abandoned by a woman is an emotional script in my life. I never had the opportunity to show that anger toward my mother, so it sits and waits. I'm sensitive to that. I know that, but I did not use the information. I couldn't access it during this refractory period. I also know, after twenty years of marriage, that Mary Ann's very trustworthy. There's no reason to be jealous. All of this information was in my head, but I couldn't get to it during the refractory period because I could only interpret things that supported this emotion.

"Maybe two minutes after the phone call, fortunately, I did all of this reappraising. I called her back and didn't say anything about having been angry, but now we had a very nice conversation. A few days later, I asked her about the episode, and she said, 'I realized you were angry, but I didn't want to say anything about it.'

"I believe now, in this situation, I would not become angry again, because I have learned. I couldn't shorten the refractory period, but I was able to prevent myself from acting and saying anything I would regret. Then I did a lot of analyzing afterward that I think will now prepare me so that this kind of situation will not call forth anger. I won't have to keep repeating mistakes.

"It may be too much to ask that we can always anticipate when an emotion is going to occur, but part of becoming more skilled, more emotionally intelligent, is to learn from emotional episodes."

This account was one of the moments in Paul's presentation that particularly impressed His Holiness. He saw Paul's approach as a sort of contemplation on recognizing the destructive nature of anger—akin to a Buddhist analytic practice for dealing with such emotions, in which a person logically analyzes the costs of acting from them. But Paul was not a Buddhist; for the Dalai Lama Paul's scientific approach resonated with his own conviction that at their heart all major world religions share the goal of strengthening the good qualities of human nature.

There are, of course, specialized methods unique to Buddhism for dealing with destructive emotions.[9] But the Dalai Lama felt that the ability to train one's mind to better understand what's destructive in emotions—and so control them—is something every human being has the capacity to do, as Paul's example suggested.

Anger: Removing What Thwarts Us

Paul wished to continue his exploration of anger "because it is such a troublesome emotion—the emotion during which we are most likely to hurt others. First, I believe that violence is not built into anger—not a necessary or biologically required consequence. I maintain, though I don't have evidence for it, that what is built into the anger response is the impulse to remove the obstacle that is thwarting us. That does not necessarily require violence."

The Dalai Lama asked, "Are you saying that violence or harming others is not really the purpose or goal of anger from the perspective of the evolutionary theme—that, rather, the purpose of anger is to stop whatever is interfering?"

"This is my view," said Paul. "There isn't evidence, nor is there necessarily agreement among all Western scholars or scientists. I have listed here the most common events that precede anger: physical interference, frustration, someone trying to hurt us, another person's anger. One of the most dangerous things about anger is that anger calls forth anger. It requires great effort to be able to not respond to anger with anger."

At this, the Dalai Lama nodded in vigorous agreement.

Paul went on, "Disappointment in another person's beliefs that offend us can also produce anger. Interference is the common theme for all of these."

The Dalai Lama commented, "In Buddhism there is an understanding that tolerance and anger are opposites. Tolerance or patience in the face of harm caused by others is the opposite of actual violence. I am trying to figure out whether that fits into your point that the purpose of anger, from the evolutionary point of view, is not violence."

Paul answered, "I would take it one step further and say that very often the most successful way to remove the obstacle is to take the perspective of the other person. Rather than verbally or physically reacting, you deal with and understand why the person appears to be creating an obstacle. In His Holiness's writings, there is a distinction made between the act and the actor, which I think is really very compatible with the Western viewpoint."

The Varieties of Violence

Paul continued, "I want to emphasize, once again, that 'anger' is a word for a family of feelings. They vary in their strength, for example, from annoyance to fury or wrath. Other members of the anger family are indignation, self-righteous anger, sulking, passive anger, and revenge. I talked earlier about special cases of resentment and hatred that are related to the anger family.

"I have just begun to read the scientific literature on violence. It's not an area that I myself have worked on, and so my account of it will be brief and only partial. Perhaps the most important unanswered question is whether we all have a breaking point. Can all of us be driven to the point of violence? I can't give an answer to that. I can give my own personal belief, which is no. Some people can and some people can't. But we don't know, and it is very important to find out."

Acts of cruelty, Paul felt, were a particularly important case in point. "Unfortunately, it is not an aberration to act with cruelty, given the right kind of encouragement. But the first act of cruelty is the hardest—as with marital infidelity or lying, once someone has crossed that barrier, then it is progressively easier to cross the line again and again. The key to preventing cruelty, then, lies in finding ways to prevent that first act."

Knowing that the Tibetan people have suffered great cruelty at the hands of their oppressors, Paul hoped to explore this topic with the Dalai Lama in greater depth. He felt that cruelty could find an antidote in its opposite, compassion. If those committing cruelty could be made to see that they are hurting someone like themselves, if they could feel for them, it would be harder—if not impossible—to be cruel. But typically the victim is depersonalized long before the acts of cruelty begin, so that the perpetrators are blinded to the humanity of their victims.

Paul continued, "One of the things that we know from the study of warfare is that almost half of American soldiers never fire their weapons during combat. This bit of data from a study in the Korean War worries the army. That suggests to me that even in a situation where you have been prepared to hate the enemy and your own life is in jeopardy, not everyone can kill. Some people can't, and we don't know enough about the characteristics of those who can and those who can't."

"This may be why," the Dalai Lama said, "soldiers are subject to so much indoctrination."

"But it doesn't always work," said Paul. "It is possible that not everybody can kill. I would at least like to think that is true."

"What about mechanized warfare?" the Dalai Lama asked.

"Mechanized warfare is more dangerous—you're farther away," said Paul.

"That's right, that's right—more dangerous," the Dalai Lama agreed. In fact, a U.S. Army historian makes the case that over the history of warfare, the number of deaths has increased in direct proportion to the distance at which killing was possible. In the old days of flintlock rifles the saying was, "Don't fire until you see the whites of their eyes." But many soldiers did not fire *because* they saw their enemy's eyes and recognized what they were about to do.

"We'd be better off with swords than with guns," Paul agreed. "That way you have to be close to the person."

Continuing, Paul said, "Those who study violence distinguish between different kinds. Instrumental violence is engaged in to accomplish a goal. A criminal asks you to give him your money and threatens you with violence; if you don't give him your wallet, then he commits the violent act to get it.

"Instrumental violence is distinguished from crimes of passion, the typical one being when you discover your spouse in the arms of another person and in the heat of that moment commit a violent act. We do know that people who commit crimes of passion rarely ever commit another violent act."

Paul then showed a newspaper photograph of a woman enraged, struggling fiercely to get at a man. "The man she was trying to attack was the man who had killed her daughter. He had just been sentenced in court. He showed no emotion when he was sentenced, and that was her breaking point. Up until then, she had never tried to commit violence against this man. The interesting thing about the picture is that her husband is restraining her, holding her arm. The power of that picture is to show that even with this most terrible offense, not everybody acts violently. Even though we can understand her violence, we can be reassured by the fact that he was not violent. Not everyone is.

"I am not a psychiatrist, but in psychiatry today there is a classification called intermittent explosive disorder, which identifies people who show chronic, impulsive, severe violence that is excessive—inappropriate to any provocation. Much of the most recent research suggests that there are two different paths to this terrible state. One is head injuries that result in a defect in the area of the brain that normally acts to control emotions, and the other is a more genetically based defect in terms of overreaction."

Is Compassion Basic to Human Nature?

"Before I conclude, I would like to just briefly turn to sadness and agony and make one important contrast," Paul said as he showed a slide of a woman with her face contorted in suffering. As he saw the slide, the Dalai Lama's face briefly mirrored her anguished expression.

Paul compared the image of the woman with a newspaper photograph of a group of angry men at a political demonstration. "I ask you first," Paul said, "to be aware of the difference in your reaction to seeing this woman and your reaction to seeing those angry men in the other slide. I don't believe that when we see anger represented in a photograph, it reaches us as it would if we were present. Yet this photograph of a woman we don't know reaches most people: You feel her suffering. She suffers, and it is an important part of the nature of suffering that the signal asks us for help and we feel that request."

"Therefore I would argue that basic human nature is compassionate," the Dalai Lama said.

"I would not disagree," Paul replied.

"It may be a feeble argument," the Dalai Lama said with a laugh.

"No," Paul dissented. "Actually I think it's an important issue. This is one of the lessons we learn from suffering, and it is critically related to the development of compassion. Compassion arises far more easily in response to suffering than in response to anger."

"I am wondering," the Dalai Lama suggested, "whether there really is a valid distinction between seeing an image of an angry person, which doesn't elicit any emotional response in the viewer, and seeing a soulful image that elicits a response."

"Is it valid?" Paul replied. "I would say it is. The power of suffering is so great that it can reach us even through a photograph. Anger is contagious when someone gets angry with us and we get angry back—just as when someone laughs we laugh with them. Fear is not so contagious. It can be, but not nearly as much as anger, mirth, or suffering. To me this is a testament. It's evidence of the great power of suffering to elicit compassion, and it has implications, perhaps, for how we might teach compassion. I'm not prepared to explain the implications, only to mention the possibility.

"In concluding, I want to say that after spending more than thirty-five years studying emotion I am impressed by how little we still know about it. We have only begun. Science has started to pay attention to it in significant ways only in the last ten to fifteen years. I would like to close my formal presentation with a quote from Charles Darwin, of whom I feel a descendant in some sense.

"It is from the last page of his book *The Expression of Emotion in Man and Animals:* 'The free expression by outward signs of an emotion intensifies it.'

"That raises a question about controlling expression. If expression makes the emotion stronger and we don't wish to act on it, then here is a technique that can help us when we are in the grip of an emotion: Do not express it openly.

"To continue now with Darwin. 'On the other hand, the repression, as far as this is possible of all outward signs, softens our emotions. He who gives way to violent gestures will increase his rage. He who does not control the signs of fear will experience fear in a greater degree, and he who remains passive when overwhelmed with grief loses his best chance of recovering elasticity of mind.'

"I do believe that Darwin raises for us some questions that I hope we will continue to discuss. I have read Darwin's book many times, but every time I read it I see things I hadn't seen before. What impressed me particularly in this passage was the concept of the elasticity of mind. And I thank you very much for the opportunity to talk to you."

As Paul ended, he was wondering whether what he had said was useful or interesting to the Dalai Lama—whom Paul regarded as, in a sense, the conscience of the world. For his part, the Dalai Lama had particularly appreciated the robust scientific data for the universality of emotions, which lent support to his own message of a common, shared humanity. The Dalai Lama gave Paul a deep bow, palms of his hands together, in appreciation.

7

Cultivating Emotional Balance

"How do you define mental health?" During the second Mind and Life conference, in 1989, Alan Wallace had posed this question to Dr. Lewis Judd, then the director of the federal psychiatric research center, the National Institute of Mental Health.

Alan was stunned to find that there was no clear answer from the Western perspective. Mental health per se had not been studied in psychiatry. Instead the focus of research had been on mental disorders, and mental health was defined, largely by default, as the absence of psychiatric illness. The tools offered by psychiatry are intended to attack the symptoms of emotional suffering, not to promote emotional flourishing. Freud himself had proclaimed the goal of psychoanalysis as "normal neurosis."

In Buddhism, by contrast, there are many clear criteria for mental and social well-being, as well as a set of practices for achieving it. When it comes not just to understanding mental afflictions and how to grapple with those, but also how to move into exceptional states of mental health, Buddhism has an enormous amount to offer to the West. That would become clear over the course of the afternoon.

When we reconvened after our lunch break, the Dalai Lama returned to the telling difference between the Buddhist and the scientific views: the criteria by which an emotion is judged to be "destructive." While the scientific standard was whether an emotion is harmful to oneself or to others, the Buddhist rule of thumb was far more subtle: Emotions become destructive the moment they disrupt the mind's equilibrium.

"The criterion I am using to distinguish between constructive and destructive emotions," the Dalai Lama explained, "is right there to be observed in the moment when a destructive emotion arises—the calmness, the tranquillity, the balance of the mind are immediately disrupted. Other emotions do not destroy equilibrium or the sense of well-being as soon as they arise, but in fact enhance it—so they would be called constructive.

"Also there are emotions that are aroused by intelligence. For example, compassion can be aroused by pondering people who are suffering. When the compassion is actually experienced, it is true that the mind is somewhat disturbed, but that is more on the surface. Deep down there is a sense of confidence, and so on a deeper level there is no disturbance. A consequence of such compassion, aroused by intelligent reflection, is that the mind becomes calm.

"The consequences of anger—especially its long-term effects—are that the mind is disturbed. Typically, when compassion moves from simply being a mental state to behavior, it tends to manifest in ways that are of service to others, whereas when anger goes to the point of enactment it generally, of course, becomes destructive. Even if it doesn't manifest as violence, if you have the capacity to help, you would refrain from helping. That too would be a kind of destructive emotion."

How Do You Say "Emotion" in Tibetan?

One dilemma posed by Paul's presentation had been that the English term for "emotion" has no direct Tibetan equivalent—the cultures seem to think about the matter in very different ways. The Dalai Lama suggested we clarify this basic issue. The challenge was to find analytic precision in the Tibetan terms corresponding to "emotion" as used in English.

After some back-and-forth we arrived at a working definition: An emotion is a mental state that has a strong feeling component. From that, however, we excluded feelings that are purely sensory, such as a cut finger or exhaustion; the feelings need be tied to an appraisal—that is, thoughts.

But Francisco Varela returned to the underlying point, that in Tibetan there is no word for "emotion": "I'm very surprised, because it seems that thought, whether irrational or intelligent, is so clearly different from emotion. Granted, in the West we are a little obsessed with the idea that emotions are beyond the control of voluntary action and thoughts are somehow rational. Yet how could it be that in the Tibetan language, given this enormous capacity to discriminate mental events, this very gross distinction is not made?"

In his answer to Francisco, the Dalai Lama challenged the philosophical assumption behind his question—that the natural category was the Western contrast between emotion and thought, rather than to see them as integrated, as in the Tibetan system.

The Dalai Lama began with a disarming observation. "Perhaps it's a matter for future research," he noted, suggesting the possibility of finding a Sanskrit equivalent of the word "emotion" in non-Buddhist sources, or in sources that had not reached Tibet.[1] As the Dalai Lama privately pointed out, an adage from the great scholar Tsongkhapa notes that just because an idea was not found in the texts that were translated into Tibetan, that does not mean it cannot be found somewhere in Buddhism.

But then he suggested a different consideration. "Bearing in mind that the fundamental goal of Buddhist practice is the achievement of nirvana, when you study the mind what you're really concerned with is what specific mental states impede the accomplishment of that end. That's what the six primary states and twenty derivative states"—the unwholesome mental factors that Jinpa had reviewed the day before—"all have in common. Some are emotions and some are not, but it doesn't really matter. What's important is they all share that common factor of being impediments.

"In contrast, modern psychology does not have the aim of nirvana," the Dalai Lama pointed out—prompting Richie to pipe up, "We're trying to change that!"

The Dalai Lama continued, "My conjecture, in terms of trying to understand why the West places such a strong emphasis on identifying emotion, is that, going back to the Enlightenment, even as far back as Aquinas, there is an enormous priority placed on reason and intelligence. What can impede reason? Emotion.

"You have two categories that are set in opposition to each other. The fact that there is a specific term for emotion in Western thought does not necessarily imply that there was a special emphasis placed on understanding the nature of emotion. Perhaps initially the motive for labeling something as emotion was to enhance reason by identifying something that is unreasonable, something that is irrational."

Indeed, the Dalai Lama's challenge to the West's separation of emotion and cognition has support in current findings from neuroscience. The brain, it seems, does not make any clean distinction between thought and emotion, as every region in the brain that has been found to play some role in emotion has also been connected with aspects of cognition. The circuitry for emotion and for cognition are intertwined—just as Buddhism posits that these two elements are inseparable.[2]

Meditation as a Window on Subtle Emotions

Paul agreed with the Dalai Lama's historical analysis of why emotion emerged as a strong category in Western thought. But he also felt that the problem extended beyond how languages define emotion to the underlying differences in cultural frameworks. Paul suspected that it was as difficult for the Dalai Lama to fathom the assumptions of the scientific analysis of emotion as it was for Paul to fathom the subtleties of advanced meditative practice, not having had the experience himself nor knowing the theory behind it. Beyond that confusion, this turn of our dialogue was both too rarified and a bit disappointing to Paul, who had hoped we would more directly engage the issues he had raised in the morning.

Still game, Paul said he wanted to ask a question "about what you said a few moments ago, about the difference between destructive and constructive emotions and the disturbance at the surface level and deeper level. I understood your words, or their translation, but I didn't really understand what you were saying. I wonder if there are aspects of emotional experience that you can't comprehend without certain preparation. Might there be ways of experiencing emotion for those who have been practicing Tibetan Buddhism that are not available, and in that sense incomprehensible, to those who have not?"

The Dalai Lama agreed, in principle, "that there might be certain aspects of emotion that are incomprehensible unless you have experienced them yourself. For example, an important aspect of Buddhist meditation practice is reflection on the transient nature of life, on death, on impermanence. It is said that the more you prolong your meditation, the more you deepen your understanding and realization. At first you can understand intellectually that moments are changing, but you do not feel it. Then you familiarize yourself with this through meditation, and eventually a strong feeling develops. That kind of subtle emotion comes through meditation.

"Similarly, there are certain degrees of grasping at the inherent nature of self that are false from the Buddhist point of view. But there are degrees of this, and there are levels so subtle that, unless you have direct experience of their emptiness, you may not even be able to define them as a false state of mind."

I was struck by the radically different perspectives each side brought to our conversation, and said, "When we met in preparation for this dialogue, we came up with a working definition of destructive emotions as those that harm self or others. Your definition of destructive emotions as what disturbs the calm of the mind is extremely subtle by comparison."

"Yes," the Dalai Lama agreed.

I continued, "It is an entirely different way of looking at it—a profound difference. That is one reason we are so interested in how this guiding principle is applied—what you cultivate and maintain in your practice. What emotional states are developed through deep practice that might guide Western psychology in thinking about the possibility for handling destructive emotions?"

A Radical Disillusionment Calms the Mind

Richard Davidson picked up on my theme: "Are there emotions other than compassion that preserve or reinforce the calmness of the mind?"

The Dalai Lama's answer was surprising: "Renunciation is another." Alan immediately clarified, "I usually translate it as 'renunciation,' but the etymology is more literally 'a spirit of emergence.' "

"It is the first step to really, thoroughly determine how vulnerable we are to suffering," the Dalai Lama said. "If we understand how utterly vulnerable we are, and recognize that these mental afflictions make us so vulnerable, then we can see the possibility of the mind becoming free of those mental afflictions.

"You are recognizing the nature of suffering, but you also sense the possibility of emerging from this ubiquitous vulnerability to suffering—this is why it is called a spirit of emergence. This spirit of emergence could also be called an emotion; there is an enormous amount of emotional content to it. It entails a radical disillusionment with the whole of *samsara,*" the worldly realm of suffering, and our vulnerability to it. "And so, whether you call it disgust or disillusionment, it is a profound sadness with respect to the mundane. This is all, theoretically, in anticipation of ascertaining the possibility of nirvana—complete and irreversible freedom from mental afflictions."

Matthieu elaborated: "It's a strong sense of lassitude, being completely tired of worldly preoccupations with pleasure and pain, fame and obscurity, praise and blame. It's an emotion that makes you want to get out of it—a disillusionment and realization of the pointlessness of banking on *samsara.*"

The Dalai Lama concluded, "The disenchantment that arises is primarily focused on the mental afflictions with the recognition 'Here is the source of my problem.' From that arises the attitude of emergence, aspiring for freedom from them. So that is one example of an emotion that would calm the mind."

Wholesome Emotions

Matthieu returned to Richie's question about emotions that lead to peace of mind, cultivated through meditation. "We often speak of a kind of serenity, not only peace but a kind of invulnerability—not joy in the sense of an expressed joy, but a serenity that, like a mountain, cannot be shaken by the wind of circumstances. It is different from passivity or indifference. For instance, if you are confronted with others' suffering, that serenity doesn't prevent you from having full compassion. It increases your courage for doing something, rather than depressing you as if it were a sad event that hurts your own ego. The serenity that is invulnerable to outward circumstances is not at all synonymous with passivity; it is another specific quality that goes with inner calm."

This equanimity, the Dalai Lama added, counters the strong feelings of attraction or attachment that create disequilibrium in the mind. "You recall I mentioned afflictive compassion, which is mixed up with attachment. In fact, afflictive compassion is something we want to get rid of. How do you remove the component of attachment that is making it afflictive? This is the reason that you start with equanimity in the Buddhist cultivation of compassion. You develop an even-mindedness that then counteracts the attachment or craving. Out of that equanimity, compassion then arises. When it arises, it is nonafflictive compassion, and that is what one really seeks to cultivate."

I was reminded of the very precise lists of wholesome and unwholesome mental factors in the ancient Buddhist system of psychology. So I turned to the Venerable Kusalacitto and asked, "The list Jinpa presented yesterday from the Abhidharma of the afflictive—or destructive—emotions has a corresponding list of wholesome opposites for each of the afflictive emotions. What are some of the moods or emotions that are on that positive list?"

The *bhante* answered by going back to Paul Ekman's distinction between thought and emotion. He began by pointing out that in the Buddhist system, it's not the thought that makes a mind state unwholesome, but rather the emotion that accompanies it. "In Pali scripture, when we talk about thought, thought is nothing but mind, *citta,* which is very luminous and pure—and neutral; neither bad nor good. But when we talk about emotion, the equivalent word may be *kiatasecra,* a mental state that can be classified into groups—some neutral, some wholesome, another group unwholesome."

"It's the wholesome ones I'm after," I reminded him.

He replied that the Pali texts offer a list of twenty-five wholesome, constructive emotions, including faith, self-confidence, buoyancy or flexibility of the mind, mindfulness, and wisdom.

Jinpa took up the topic, citing the Abhidharma Samuccaya, the equivalent model used by Tibetans. Among the fifty-one mental states named by the Abhidharma were the afflictions he had listed the day before. Now he translated the list of eleven wholesome states roughly as "faith, an ability to feel a sense of shame, conscience, nonattachment, nonhatred, and the absence of delusion. In addition, there is a mental factor listed as nonviolence, similar to nonhatred."

The Dalai Lama clarified, "When it says nonhatred or nondelusion, it's not the mere absence of these, but rather something that's diametrically opposed to both." Abhidharma scholars, for instance, debate whether compassion is best understood as closer to nonhatred or to nonviolence.

Jinpa continued, "Then there are vigor or zeal, buoyancy, equanimity. And then we have conscientiousness—concern with whether in body, speech, and mind you are falling into nonvirtue or virtue. These are the eleven."

"Whether the system includes fifty-one mental factors or more or less, none of those sets is meant to be all-inclusive, as though nothing is left out," the Dalai Lama commented. "They are only suggestive, indicative of some things that are important."[3]

"As the venerable *bhante* was pointing out, there is a sense that the mind itself is neutral and it is the mental factors that color it in one way or another. When one's unwholesome mental states arise, that automatically also colors the mind, and not only the mind itself, but also all the other accompanying factors, including feelings. So these mental factors can also be characterized as unwholesome or afflictive. The other mental factors that arise together are not all mental afflictions, but as soon as a mental affliction arises, everything that arises together with it is also afflicted."

As the Dalai Lama mentioned to me in our end-of-the-day session, this review of basic points from Buddhist psychology was one he felt had been missing from the previous day's overview. He was glad to have the chance to further explain this Buddhist model of mind to the scientists present, to give them a better sense of the context from which he approached the question of what makes an emotion destructive.

Beyond Theory to Practice

Matthieu pointed out this analysis was not just theoretical. These factors of mind could be used in a practical way, to balance each other over the course of transforming the mind. "We speak of four things to cultivate: love, equanimity, compassion, and rejoicing. Though you may not see a symbiotic relation at first, you do as you continue to practice. If you practice loving-kindness, for instance, your attachment may grow, so at that time you switch to equanimity. If you keep on practicing equanimity, at some point you may risk falling into indifference, so at that time you raise compassion for those who suffer.

"Now, as a beginner, if you excessively bring to mind the sufferings of beings, you might fall into depression. So then you shift again to rejoicing in some positive aspect of the happiness of others. That shows us how those come together in some way, within the scope of practice."

The Dalai Lama commented on the general principle underlying Matthieu's point, "When we speak of the two major aspects of this practice, namely, wisdom and skillful means, they always have to work in conjunction with each other. No problem or mental affliction or destructive emotion can be dispelled by simply one thing. You always have to approach from a multitude of perspectives, a variety of mental factors, a variety of understandings. It is more complex than simply 'There's the problem and here's the antidote.'

"On a very deep level, when you actually have an unmediated realization of emptiness, that does act as an antidote to all mental afflictions. This is not to suggest that with this realization all your problems vanish with one fell swoop, but it does, eventually, counteract all the mental afflictions. But in the meantime, until we reach that level, it's very important to recognize that as we counteract mental afflictions and other unwholesome tendencies, we always need to have this interplay between wisdom and skillful means.

"To give an analogy, imagine you want to build something—say, an airplane. There is nothing you can build where you can just bring one ingredient, like a chunk of metal, and turn that into an airplane. You always need to bring a myriad of factors together and then you can create your product. The same holds true for transforming the mind. Even when it comes to a direct realization of emptiness, there are multiple factors in that realization. There is the factor of mindfulness; the factor of *samadhi* or deep concentration; the factor of zeal or vigor that brings you to it. So even the realization of emptiness is multifaceted, not just one thing."

A Positive Kind of Fear

From his philosopher's perch, Owen Flanagan raised an objection. "Dan suggested, and His Holiness seemed to agree, that the Buddhist definition of destructive emotions was essentially any emotion that sets one into some sort of disequilibrium or disquiet. I'm a little concerned, and I want to use the way Paul put things. Some of the emotions on Paul's list, such as anger, fear, and sadness, do have a negative qualitative feel, and they are disruptive.

"In the best of all possible worlds, one would not want to experience those states. But this isn't the best of all possible worlds. Furthermore, those states almost certainly have an adaptive explanation in terms of our evolution. In the West, most people would bet that the basic emotions are part of the evolved equipment that helped our species survive, reproduce, and be as successful as we are.

"My question is this: Is there a friendly agreement among us to distinguish the emotions that have negative qualitative feel from those that are destructive? I think most of us will want to say, at the end of the day, that there are times when it's appropriate to feel sad about a certain situation and, in fact, it would be inhumane not to. It would be odd not to experience anger or outrage at seeing a child being abused. It would be odd not to have certain things make one go into a state of fear. These negative states or emotions may get destructive. They are states we want to get out of as quickly as possible. But one of the functions of going into, for example, an angry state is to get someone else to stop doing something, so both of you can move on with your lives.

"My point is along the lines of the Aristotelian Doctrine of the Mean I talked about yesterday. I would have thought that what makes a particular emotional state destructive has to do with it being either excessive, too much of it, or deficient, too little of it. A person who does not respond with a certain kind of empathy at seeing another person suffering has a deficiency. A person who can't stop crying for a month over someone's loss in the stock market has a problem in the other direction."

"Some psychologists," Richard Davidson replied, "in line with what Owen is saying, have suggested that emotions are destructive when they are experienced in inappropriate or non-normative contexts. When fear, for example, is experienced in a familiar situation where there is really nothing to be afraid of, then it's destructive. But if we experience fear at the moment a tiger is about to leap, then it's appropriate and it helps us to survive."

"Even from the Buddhist point of view," the Dalai Lama said, "there are instances of fear that are constructive and positive. For example, there's the sense of disillusionment I spoke about earlier—that general wish to emerge out of this unenlightened existence. That aspiration for freedom is actually grounded in a fear of being under the uncontrollable power of negative afflictions. That is a positive kind of fear that gives rise to a spiritual state of aspiration.

"If you look at the list of the fifty-one mental factors, there are some known as the variable or changeable factors, because other conditions make them either positive or negative, constructive or destructive. On that list could be fear, sadness, and many other emotions, which we cannot say categorically are constructive or destructive."

Paul Ekman was not satisfied. "I can't be certain whether there is an agreement or fundamental disagreement, because I see all emotions as disturbing equilibrium. That's what they do. We have had three attempts from the Western point of view to define what makes them destructive. They are excessive, or they are situationally inappropriate, or they harm self or others. These overlap, but they always disturb equilibrium. The fear that you were just talking about disturbs equilibrium. If it disturbs equilibrium, must it be destructive? Or can it disturb equilibrium and be constructive?"

A Call to the Practical

Paul's questions went unanswered, though, as the Dalai Lama refocused our conversation. "It is important to keep in mind," he began, "that the main purpose of our discussion, our seminar, is how to make a contribution to society—not how to aim for nirvana. I'm Buddhist—my ultimate goal is Buddhahood. This is my business. This allows the possibility that I reach enlightenment." Then, gesturing toward Matthieu, he said impishly, "We have some competition—whether you get there first or I get there first."

Getting serious again, he resumed his point: "Our purpose here is to aim for the betterment of society. So far as I am concerned, my agenda here is in the category that I call secular ethics. Therefore, it is important for the participants, all of us, to keep the scientist's cap on. There may be instances where we will have to recall specific Buddhist ideas, in which case we will take off the scientist's cap and put on the Buddhist's cap."

This was a key point for the Dalai Lama, and the focus of his most recent book, *Ethics for the New Millennium.* For our purposes, the working definition of destructive emotion should preclude the Buddhist aspiration for liberation and stay on the relative level of everyday life, with the goal of creating a better society.

Much of the conversation to this point in the afternoon had been a bit rarified, dwelling on fine points of philosophy and Buddhist epistemology. The Dalai Lama later told me that he felt this had been useful to give the scientists a sense that Buddhist statements about the mind and emotions are grounded in a rich history of meditative practice and system of philosophical thinking. And he felt that especially when it came to the subject of mind and emotions, Buddhist knowledge could make a contribution to science.

In previous Mind and Life meetings he had seen scientists start out a bit leery of Buddhist thinking, only to take its concepts more seriously as the discussion went on. Still, he did not want to give the impression that he wanted to use the meeting to propagate Buddhism. And then, too, he was afraid that if the discussion went too far in this direction, it would become boring for some of the scientists. And so he brought us to the tea break with a call for practicality.

An Adult Education in the Emotions

After the tea break, I asked the Dalai Lama if there were any practical issues that he felt we ought to focus on. This question was to initiate a discussion that would take on increasing momentum over the next few days and lead to one of the major projects to come out of the meetings.

The Dalai Lama thought for a moment and then said, "One of my strongest convictions is that a deeper understanding of the nature of our mind, the mental states and emotions, must lead to the development of some kind of educational philosophy. What the specifics are, I cannot say, nor do I have any time to figure this out."

That would be precisely the topic of a report on Thursday, I told him, when Mark Greenberg would talk about school programs for helping children learn to handle their destructive emotions.

"Very good," he said. Then he answered my question in a different way, by returning to a point in the morning's presentation. "Paul Ekman gave us an anecdote from his personal experience of how, in the aftermath of anger, he reflected on all the reasons why he should not have felt that way, which then helped prepare him for future events. This suggests that if, instead, he had paid no attention to his understanding and had savored the experience of that emotion, it would have been more destructive because it would have led to more anger."

"The point that you make," Paul said, "is to educate our emotions. There are two different levels of this. One begins with early development—educating children. But then there are the rest of us—we're no longer children, but adults. How can we educate our emotions? By what means, without becoming Buddhists?"

"That's right—that's the question," the Dalai Lama agreed.

"It's clearly important if we are going to live in a better world," Paul stressed, little realizing that he would one day spearhead just such a program in educating the emotions.

"Your Holiness," I said, picking up on Paul's point, "one reason we want to have this dialogue with you is that even within the secular context, there are things to learn from Buddhist insights and Buddhist practice that could be applied, free of Buddhism, to the same human emotional reality."

"Yes, yes—that's right," the Dalai Lama said, nodding.

As he later told me, the Dalai Lama's deep motivation for these dialogues was in part to make a contribution from Tibetan Buddhism, with its roots in ancient Indian thought, to help with the problems of the modern world. His enthusiasm for these dialogues was the same as in his public talks around the world, where he emphasized our transformation into good-hearted people—for instance, exchanging anger for compassion and a sense of caring. But he felt that when it came to the commitment to transform society, it would come not through some religious teaching but through general education—an education with a scientific basis. And, he felt, groups of scientists such as those gathered here could help in that larger agenda.

An Immune System for the Emotions

Taking up the Dalai Lama's challenge, I went back to Paul's idea of intervening before, during, or after the grip of a destructive emotion. I said, "One idea we were discussing at lunch has to do with when someone is caught up in an emotion, very angry, like Paul was. What can be done to shorten that period or to help people free themselves from it, whether after, during, or even before?"

"My basic stand on the whole issue of dealing with these powerful destructive emotions," the Dalai Lama responded, "is the following. Just as in the physical realm, if you have a very healthy immune system, then even though you may be exposed to instances of illness, such as catching a cold, you have a much better chance of overcoming whatever the illness is. Whereas if your immune system is deficient, then not only are you much more prone to illness, but also the chances of recovering are lessened.

"In a similar way," the Dalai Lama continued, "when it comes to dealing with destructive emotions and ameliorating them, it's very hard for ordinary people to apply an antidote right there at that instant when strong emotion has already occurred.

"For that matter, I'm sorry to say, it's hard even for most practitioners in the heat of anger. Although one may know intellectually that anger is destructive, that one should not let oneself be swayed by the power of anger, that one must cultivate love toward others and so on, in the heat of anger the chances of recalling this are very limited. In fact, thinking of love at that moment seems very impractical—it's farewell to love and compassion.

"What is required is a general preparation so that your basic mental state is like a healthy immune system. Familiarize yourself with these practices—the wisdom side and also skillful means. This familiarization gives you some strength, some experience there. Then when you see anger, attachment, or jealousy about to come, it's much easier to deal with them. If you have that basic preparation, then in an ideal situation you may be able to detect signs of emotions coming on, if your level of realization is high enough. You would have cultivated a temperament that allows you to detect early signs of these emotions so that you can prevent their arising.

"Or, if that is not possible, when strong emotions like anger arise, you might not let yourself be overtaken by them. The emotional states wouldn't last long; they wouldn't overwhelm you. If that was not possible, at least you would be able to ensure that these powerful destructive emotions did not get translated into negative actions that are destructive to others and oneself.

"In fact, in some cases, even though you may experience powerful destructive emotions, if you feel a deep sense of regret afterward with the realization that this was inappropriate and destructive, then you might be able to cultivate a new determination to change. This is a way of learning from the experience of this emotion."

While the Buddhist goal is to be free of anger altogether, it is just an ideal. To be sure, it's an ideal that goes beyond those envisioned by Western philosophers since Aristotle as well as by modern psychology. Still, the Dalai Lama wanted to talk in terms of what's realistic, acknowledging that in the secular context, it's impossible to eliminate negative emotions completely.

From that perspective, the Buddhist view holds that it's not that we should have no angry feelings, but that when we do, we should be able to consider other options to deal with the situation effectively—not just out of anger. Indeed, one of the main reasons we had gathered, the Dalai Lama felt, was to explore methods to help people reduce the grip of anger in their lives.

Mindfulness: A Fort Against Destructive Emotions

This was another moment when the Dalai Lama would draw the Venerable Kusalacitto into the conversation. Gesturing to the Thai monk, the Dalai Lama said, "It would be very good now to go to a practical note on the cultivation of mindfulness and how that pertains to emotion." To that I added that mindfulness could lend itself to a secular approach to destructive emotions, since it can be learned without becoming Buddhist.

For his part, the *bhante* had been feeling that, for all their testing equipment and material means, the scientists still had no clear path for alleviating troubling emotions—and that Buddhism could be of great help here, particularly in its methods for handling unwholesome states such as anger. So, with little prompting, the *bhante* began a short but classic synopsis of the Buddhist view.

"As His Holiness has said, now we should talk in terms of secular ethics—but I think maybe the scientists want to go to nirvana now," he added with a laugh. "They want to know about how to practice this meditation, because it's with this very technique that we learn that emotion is not intrinsic. It's relative, and each day new feelings arise, but they will not stay with us forever; they stay with us for some period of time and go away. Whether an emotion is constructive or destructive, they stay with us temporarily, then go.

"Lord Buddha expounded on the impermanence of things, which is why negative emotions do not harm us. There is a very important moment when we first make contact with the outside world, when we come to perceive color, sound, whatever. According to the Satipatthana Sutta, the Buddha advises that you must be mindful and aware in the moment when you see the image, hear the sound, or come into contact with any tangible object. If you can hone mindfulness and awareness, then you will see the color or the sound as it is—you will not think about whether that something is good or bad, whether it's a beautiful picture or a very ugly picture, a sweet sound or an ugly sound. When you act like this, your mind will stay very calm. No negative emotion that could harm you will come to you."

Then the Venerable Kusalacitto went on to detail another aspect of mindfulness, concentration, in which the focus stays on a neutral object of awareness, typically the natural flow of the breath, and so wards off destructive emotions by blocking them. "We can say that you have selected an alternative object in the mind. Instead of anger, envy, or aggression, now your mind has focused on a neutral object of awareness. For example, you maintain awareness of breathing in and out, in and out, as long as you can."

He summed up, "So in *satipatthana,* you first cultivate mindfulness and awareness, focusing on the body, on breathing in and out, and focusing mindful awareness on your sensations. As long as you live with mindfulness and awareness, you live in a fortress where destructive emotion will not come to you, will not harm you."

The *bhante* then described what happens when that concentrated attention takes the mind itself as the focus—the observing stance of mindfulness. "Then once you focus your mind, your mind itself can become the object of mindfulness. You can know, in that moment, if your mind state is unwholesome or wholesome, whether your mind is associated with anger, jealousy, greed, hatred, or delusion—or not. You're aware of that in the very moment, whatever arises in the mind."

Once this highly precise and focused awareness has been cultivated, there eventually comes a level of equanimity and an invulnerability to destructive emotions. At this point, he said, "the mind is not joyous, not sad, not sorry.

Then—when you know the real nature of the mind—there is no negative emotion that can harm you. Even an obstacle, an unwholesome mental state, a compulsion can be the object of attention with this technique."

At this point in mindfulness, he said, whatever comes into one's awareness is perceived as "just a form and name"; the mind stays neutral no matter what arises in it. "You simply recognize whatever comes up in the mind as a natural process, arising and passing, that stays with you for some period of time and then goes away—it does not stay forever. And then you can enjoy a state of peace and calm."

With that the Venerable Kusalacitto ended his summary of the path of mindfulness, or *satipatthana,* saying, "That's the technique as Buddha described it."

The Tricky Present

The last level of mindfulness, as the *bhante* described it, bespeaks a point at which perception has become so refined that a person can break the link between the initial sensory impression and the mind's moving toward labeling and reacting to it. Instead of seeing the world through the prism of our habitual categories and knee-jerk emotions, the mind can stay in a neutral mode free of automatic habit.

I knew that Francisco Varela had been doing research on these very processes in perception, so I said to the Venerable Kusalacitto, "There are two points you've made that I would like to ask Francisco about, because they relate to our understanding of the mind and emotion. You said that if we're mindful at the moment of first sensory contact, then we needn't go through the cycle of labeling, of having a word, for what we experience. In other words, we short-circuit an arising emotion. We avoid going down the avenue of destructive emotions altogether.

"The other thing you said was that if we do start to get an emotional reaction, we can calm ourselves by focusing on the breath until it leaves. Those are two different strategies. Francisco, does the first strategy make sense in terms of how we understand what happens in information processing?"

"Let's say we were to apply a strategy for learning through mindfulness," Francisco replied, "in terms of what Paul was saying this morning, to catch the impulse before it becomes expressed. Then you have just a very short window of time. From the scientific point of view, there is no notion that tells us we can actually lengthen this moment, to catch the impulse before the expression comes about. That idea has never entered the scientific literature.

"When somebody gets very highly trained to make that kind of fine discrimination, would it be reasonable to say that in fact this process has been slowed down, or is it that the intelligence has become sharpened or more quick to act? And, from a scientific point of view, is there a way we could distinguish that? What would we look for?"

The Dalai Lama responded at once. "There are, in some Buddhist texts, references to yogis with high levels of realization who can stretch an instant into eons and contract eons into an instant—but there is always a caveat. This is so from the perspective of the yogis. So, for example, if there is a yogi somewhere near us who is expanding instants into eons and we are living here, it wouldn't materially impact upon our time—so it is a subjective experience. It is actually a matter of an individual sharpening the faculty of discernment. However, it is possible for the process of the arising of an emotion to be slowed down. There could be some scope here for dealing with mental afflictions."

The Root of Grasping

"Now, I'd like to remind myself and others that I am putting on my Buddhist's cap," the Dalai Lama said. "In Nagarjuna's *Fundamentals of the Middle Way,* he presents a causal mechanism of how afflictions arise in us, at the root of which lies grasping at some kind of intrinsic reality of things, of self and others, and self in the world. Then when you interact with others, or with the world in relation to a given object, you start projecting. The process of projection leads to whether the object is desirable or undesirable, causing an attraction or a repulsion.

"There is a causal mechanism, and so, from the Buddhist point of view, even though the process normally happens very fast, it is conceivable that for a highly trained yogi or meditator it would be possible to discern the cause and the processes of projection.

"Actually, the meditator needn't be so highly trained. If you seriously look into *shunya,* the nature of 'I,' of self, there might be some change, some effect. One could interfere, especially in the second stage, the stage of the projection, and regulate that, so it doesn't lead to afflictions. There is a possibility here that even though grasping at the intrinsic reality of self or the object has arisen, one could prolong the period in the process between that instant of grasping and the actual arising of the affliction. There is a gap in the mental engagement, the projection, and that period could be prolonged.

"Similarly, just because someone apprehends an object does not necessarily mean that the person reifies—grasps at the intrinsic reality of that object."

To that, Francisco responded, "Logically, then, that should be reflected in the way the process happens, physically and in the brain. We should see different changes."

The Dalai Lama noted, "We don't know whether you will actually be able to find a brain correlation for reification as opposed to apprehension because the point here is to apprehend an object. It doesn't necessarily mean that you reify it. Whether you can actually distinguish that in the brain remains to be seen.

"In terms of precise analysis, what takes place in apprehending a flower? In the very first instant you simply apprehend the flower itself, without reification. That is a valid cognition. But normally speaking, in that second instant, there is the reification of the flower, and as soon as that reification takes place, then you're into a false cognition.[4]

"So, Francisco," the Dalai Lama concluded, "it remains to be seen whether you can find the precise neural correlation of the mere apprehension of the flower, versus the very next instant of the reification of the flower."

"Interesting experiment, no?" Francisco commented.

Some Modest Proposals

Ever eager to pursue experimental possibilities, the Dalai Lama went on to propose one even more interesting to him: "to see whether by just studying the brain you could discern the difference between a valid cognition and an invalid cognition. For instance, it would be interesting as an experiment to give a person a photograph of someone who is known to them by name, but whom they have not seen. You say that this is the person whose name he knows, and so he would, from then on, believe that the person he has heard about is in the photograph. But in reality that photo is of someone else. So that is an instance of false cognition from the Buddhist epistemological understanding.

"Then later he is told that actually you were just kidding—this is not a photograph of the person he thought it was, but this other one is. So from that point onward, he has completely given up the previous thought and now has a new understanding that is a valid cognition. What we see here is a continuing cognition in relation to one and the same object, namely, the image in the photograph. In one instance it is a false cognition; in another it is a valid cognition. I wonder if there is a possibility of determining or distinguishing between the two purely on the basis of brain activity."

Richard Davidson replied, "There are experiments that are directly relevant to that. I'll give you one example of a very simple experiment. You have two lights of two different intensities, a bright light and a dim light. You precede the bright light by a tone of one frequency and the dim light by a tone of another frequency, so that when the tone comes on, you know which light is about to occur. You then present a light that is in between in intensity; sometimes you precede it by the first tone and at other times you precede it by the second tone. It turns out that there is a place in the brain that directly tracks the intensity of the light, irrespective of which tone precedes it. But there are other parts of the brain that correspond to the expectation that is created by the tone."

His interest piqued, the Dalai Lama went on to propose another series of experiments. "Perhaps it would be interesting from the neurobiological view to see whether you can detect differences in brain activity when the mind apprehends an object and when it does not—that is, when there is a mere appearance to the mind but one does not register what it is."

Now the ideas for research were tumbling out: "And also, can one detect a difference between direct perception of a physical object and simply having a generic image of that in one's mind? That would be fascinating."

Speaking to the last proposal, Francisco said, "That has been proven already—there's lots of data on that."

On a roll, the Dalai Lama went on, "And likewise, there's the question of whether by studying the brain you could discern the activation of intelligence as opposed to the activation of an emotion that is not conjoined with intelligence."

Then he shifted gears. "If we could put on the Buddhist's cap again, just for a second, there are two major modes of meditation. One is purely concentrated meditation—for example, *shamatha* or *samadhi,* which is simply stabilizing, focusing, concentrating the mind—as opposed to *vipashyana,* or insight meditation, in which you are really probing into the nature of reality. It would be fascinating to see if you can discover brain correlates for those two very distinct modes of Buddhist meditation." This was, in fact, done in Richie Davidson's laboratory at Madison the following year, as we saw in Chapter 1.

Joining in the spirit of generating research proposals, Richie chimed in, "Another relevant issue is that Western scientists could think about ignorance or delusion as emotions influencing our perception, distorting our ability to apprehend nature as it really is. Assuming that's a valid model, we can search in the brain for those areas where the emotional circuitry can influence the perceptual circuitry and distort our ability to apprehend the world as it is. There are actually some experiments we will show you tomorrow that bear directly on that issue."

Back to a Fundamental Difference

Alan Wallace changed the subject, coming back to a very important question that Paul, Owen, and Richie had all raised: "Is there a fundamental difference in the Buddhist attitude toward some of these destructive emotions? Aristotle said that you should find the appropriate degree for anger and other emotions. Richie has suggested that you must find the appropriate context in which to display emotions. Does Buddhism go along with that, or is Buddhism just fundamentally different?

"If we follow what His Holiness said, keeping to the secular context—not the grand aspiration for nirvana—it seems there are still some very significant differences. In something such as romantic love, if you do think about gaining nirvana, you really want to give up the romance because it's mixed with attachment and it will impede your pursuit of nirvana. But within the context of this life, leaving aside nirvana, if you had no romantic love nor affection between people who can mate and produce children, then the human race would be wiped out. So Buddhism would go along with the idea that there are appropriate circumstances, appropriate degrees, for romantic love."

Alan continued, "But then you come to anger. The ideal in Buddhism does seem to differ from the ideal of Aristotle as well as that of modern psychology. Even though, practically speaking, it is very difficult to simply be free of anger, there is the ideal in Buddhism, in this lifetime, to be free of anger even in situations where you might think it is justified and appropriate. The Buddhist would say it's not that you should have no emotion, but rather you should check out other options that would deal with the situation appropriately and effectively, without anger. I think that is a significant difference."

The Dalai Lama added, speaking emphatically in English, "But in the secular context, for ordinary people, through ordinary methods, it is impossible to eliminate all the negative emotions."

Summarizing, I said, "So then the final point is, Your Holiness, we may not be completely free, but there are methods that we can investigate and explore to reduce negative emotions. That's why we're here."

"That's right," the Dalai Lama said, again in English, quite emphatically. "That strategy, at any rate, is really worth trying—it's worthwhile to make the attempt."

On that note we broke for the day.

For Paul, the day had been a bit frustrating, mainly because of the meandering afternoon discussion, which seemed to relate little to his presentation. Though there had been that moment before the tea break where the Dalai

Lama had said, in effect, "Let's drop this talk of nirvana and get down to the realities of daily life," Paul felt that had not happened; we had gotten too theoretical, losing sight of what could be of practical use. As the Dalai Lama had asked, what here could be of use to people who had no interest in pursuing Buddhism but simply sought to find ways to deal more effectively with their destructive emotions?

I shared some of Paul's frustration. But I also knew that these discussions ripen and develop over the course of a meeting. Many of the themes and ideas we had touched upon that day would bear fruit as the discussion evolved.

Day Three:
Windows into the Brain

March 22, 2000

8

The Neuroscience of Emotion

As a field, psychology has been slowly migrating from its origins in philosophy and the humanities to join the brain sciences. That inexorable shift has come about as new generations of methods in brain research make ever more clear the neural basis of our mental and emotional lives.

Freud and those who followed in his footsteps for the next three-quarters of a century had no way to directly study how the brain shaped behavior; in Freud's day the links between the operations of the brain and our behavior were terra incognita, an unmapped continent. To be sure, some pioneering theories—like Freud's notion of the power of unconscious processes to shape what we do—have been borne out by neuroscience. But the utter lack of ways to observe the brain's operation gave theorists in psychology's early days an open license to concoct what now seem fanciful explanations for human behavior that bore no relation at all to what actually was happening in the brain.

That has changed dramatically—a century after Freud, emerging theories in psychology are increasingly driven by new findings in brain research. Where for most of the twentieth century psychology explained everything from schizophrenia to child development with little or no regard to the workings of the brain, now it is unthinkable to do so.

The neurological basis for current psychological thinking became starkly clear in Richard Davidson's presentation on the brain and emotions. Davidson has led the way in searching for the neurological substrates of emotion, and his work draws on a formidable, state-of-the-art arsenal of scientific methods for studying the brain.

For one, Davidson's lab at Madison utilizes a turbocharged version of the EEG, the brain-wave recording device commonplace in hospitals' neurology departments. The limit of the usual EEG, however, is that it only reads waves from brain activity that takes place just beneath the scalp—a bit like trying to determine the weather map of the United States by reading temperatures along the Canadian border. Davidson, however, has state-of-the-art software, combined with a special electrode array that taps far more sites than with the routine EEG. This allows him to pinpoint activity at locations deep within the brain, not just at the surface—akin to making a weather map based on temperature readings from the entire country.

Then there's the functional MRI, which tracks tiny changes in blood flow throughout the brain, and so offers a different measure of the brain's inner workings during mental activity. And unlike the MRI scanners used in most hospitals, which offer snapshots of the brain, the functional MRI offers what amounts to a video rendition, so that researchers can track the changes the brain goes through during a given activity. The functional MRI and the EEG with source localization were, of course, both used in the research done at Madison with Lama Öser.

Finally, Davidson's lab draws on work with positron emission tomography, known as the PET scan, which uses radioactive tracer dyes to assess the activity of neurotransmitters in the brain. This allows researchers to measure which of the brain's several hundred neurochemicals are involved in a given mental activity.

If Freud had had access to the methods Davidson routinely uses in his research, his theories would no doubt have been very different. In his presentation at the next session, Davidson would draw on findings from all these methods.

On this, the third day of our discussion, Davidson's review of the role of the brain in destructive emotions energized a turn toward the practical, as the group saw the genesis of a program to help people not only overcome destructive emotions but also cultivate positive ones. This proved to be a decisive turning point in our meeting.

The weather had grown suddenly colder; the skies were overcast, and thunderstorms would come by afternoon. The Dalai Lama's cold seemed worse that day, too. Despite the atmosphere of gloom, the Dalai Lama surprised us by arriving early for the morning's session. He was looking forward to Richard Davidson's presentation on the brain correlates of destructive emotions; his quick questions and many interruptions during the presentation bespoke his high level of engagement.

As the remaining participants and observers trickled in, I began by reviewing key points that led to that day's topic. "Let's lay out the model that the Venerable Kusalacitto shared with us, that there is a set of wholesome emotions that emerge more strongly as the afflictive emotions become weaker. That model gives us a way of marking progress—and a sense of what's possible in human development—even if we're not talking about the ultimate level of realization.

"There was your call to us, Your Holiness, for more pragmatic applications—for focusing on what people can actually do in the service of secular ethics and of humanity. Then we touched on the role of delusion as the base for afflictive emotions. This will be one theme that Richard Davidson will continue with today as he discusses the brain basis for the afflictive emotions, the Three Poisons: craving, aggression, and delusion.

"You are familiar with Richard Davidson; he moderated the previous Mind and Life meeting. And he is one of the most eminent researchers in the emerging field called affective neuroscience, the brain science of emotion."

An Alternative Education

Davidson's path to eminence began when he first held an electrode in his hand while still a student at Midwood High School, a magnet school in Brooklyn for gifted students with a flair for science. His task with that electrode was mundane: He had volunteered to help out at the sleep laboratory of Maimonides Medical Center, and he had been given the job of cleaning off the electrodes that had been pasted to the heads of people whose brain rhythms were being studied while they slept.

Just such electrodes have been a basic tool of his trade ever since. Now, as the director of the Laboratory for Affective Neuroscience at the University of Wisconsin in Madison, Davidson—called Richie by virtually all who have more than a nodding acquaintance—is at the cutting edge of the transformation of psychology into a brain science.

Richie and I go way back—to the moment in 1972 when he walked into Gary Schwartz's Monday night psychophysiology seminar, his first class as a graduate student at Harvard, and happened to take the seat next to me. I had just returned from fifteen months of study in India on a Harvard predoctoral traveling fellowship, focusing on meditation and traditional Asian psychologies. I was taking the course to learn the methods of psychophysiology I would use in my dissertation research on meditation as a way to help people better handle physical reactions to stress. And, it turned out, I—along with the opportunity to study with Schwartz—was among the reasons Richie had chosen to come to Harvard.

While still in India, I had written a series of articles, published in the obscure and rarified *Journal of Transpersonal Psychology,* on meditation and its effects on mind and body. Richie, then at New York University and already intrigued by Eastern traditions and the study of the mind, had managed to find and read those articles. So he knew me by reputation and, although he'd never seen a picture of me, intuitively picked the right seat.

After class I offered Richie a ride back to his apartment in my fire-engine-red VW bus, its dashboard a gallery of photos of the Hindu yogis, Tibetan lamas, and other spiritual teachers I had studied with or encountered during my pilgrimage through India. For Richie, whose world had until then largely been circumscribed by Brooklyn and the NYU campus in University Heights in the Bronx, getting into that car brought an epiphany of sorts: "It just shattered my mind," he told me years later.

On that ride we had a long talk about my interest in meditation and its effects, and how that merged with his own personal and scientific fascinations. It was one of those moments when Richie knew he had arrived in the right place: He felt a sense of connection and security, knowing that this was "it." That ride symbolized for Richie the beginning of his alternative graduate education, an odyssey that eventually took him to India to study with some of the same meditation teachers I told him about that night—and that eventually led him to this meeting with the Dalai Lama in Dharamsala.

Pushing the Envelope

While we were both at Harvard, Richie and I coauthored a scholarly article arguing that training attention through meditation would create "trait effects," lasting and beneficial psychobiological changes—an early harbinger of the ideas Davidson would later pursue in terms of brain plasticity and emotions.[1] But that would come much later in his career; the ideas were too far ahead of the science that could support them.

As a scientist, Richie has always pushed the envelope, finding reasons and ways to study the mind that others first resist, then embrace. Even as an NYU undergraduate, Davidson had done pioneering work studying mental imagery, working with psychologist Judith Rodin (now president of the University of Pennsylvania). This was in an era when psychology was largely in the grip of behaviorists, who scorned the study of any internal experience and argued that only actions that could be observed should be the subject of scientific investigation. Richie's fascination with mental processes—such as the images we see only in the mind's eye—was decidedly counter to the prevailing orthodoxy.

But Richie was undaunted, forging ahead with research in what was then the newly emerging field of cognitive psychology. Over the next decade, cognitive psychologists, with their inventive methods for studying the mechanics of the mind's operations, were to oust behaviorists from their stranglehold on what research was "proper" for psychology. But they, in turn, established an orthodoxy: that while mental operations such as images and memory could be studied, emotions were out of the picture. Richard Davidson was to lead the way in overturning what had become the new scientific dogma.

Richie remembers a telling conversation, just before leaving graduate school, with our mentor at Harvard, the late psychologist David McClelland. In that conversation McClelland told Richie that if he felt he was on to something, he should trust his scientific intuition, believe in himself, and not worry about what the rest of the world thought—eventually they would catch up.

That advice helped see Richie through the next ten years of his career—lonely years in which the road he followed was not just unexplored and unvalued but virtually off the current scientific map. In the mid-1970s Richie had chosen to study not just emotions but the links between the brain and emotions. Even worse, he focused on the role of the prefrontal lobes in emotion at a time when conventional wisdom in neuroscience held that the emotions were centered deep in the brain, in the limbic system and brain stem, which were among the first parts of the brain to evolve. The prefrontal area, the last part of the brain to emerge in evolution, was seen as devoted exclusively to the "higher functions," notably thought and planning.

But Richie had studied with Norman Geschwind, the great behavioral neurologist at Harvard Medical School, who made astute clinical observations based on how brain injuries skewed patients' emotions. Another inspiration came from studying neuroanatomy at the Massachusetts Institute of Technology with Walle Nauta, among the greatest neuroanatomists of the twentieth century. Nauta's specialty was the frontal area, and from him Richie heard about signs of connections between the prefrontal cortex and the emotional centers deep in the brain. Those links were little known and much doubted; Nauta was defying the conventional wisdom, and he inspired Richie to see that pursuing the connection between the prefrontal areas and emotion would be a fruitful research strategy.

Launching a Field

In those years, as a junior professor at the Purchase campus of the State University of New York, Richie repeatedly found his grant applications rejected, as were some articles he wrote for academic journals. But, slowly, other researchers started to follow Richie's lead. Scientific interest was sparked in part by such fundamental questions as why, under the same amount of stress, one person falls apart and goes downhill physically, while another stays resilient, going on to lead a long and healthy life. Differences in the circuitry of the brain might offer an answer.

Then, too, there was the changing sociology of science: the study of emotions had flourished during the heyday of Freudian psychoanalysis, only to wither under the behaviorists' scientific attack. The behaviorists held sway in universities through the 1960s, only slowly losing influence to the cognitive psychologists. However, the cognitive approach was as cold as behaviorism; the computer was the accepted model for the mind's operations.

But as brain scientists started studying how mental life arises from the workings of the brain, there emerged the new field of cognitive neuroscience. That was eventually to open a door for the scientific study of emotions: There was, they found, an intricate web of neural connections linking thoughts and feelings, cognition and emotion. By this time Richard Davidson was seen as one of those who had launched the field now known as affective neuroscience, the study of the brain and emotions. Research that had once looked wildly speculative became the formative kernel of a scientific field. Richie's stubborn intuition proved right.

By 1985 Richie had moved on to the University of Wisconsin, where the scientific climate was very open to his research interests; with the help of the university, he raised $10 million to build a laboratory where he could pursue research with collaborators ranging from neuroscientists to physicists. He is currently director of the Laboratory for Affective Neuroscience and the W. M. Keck Laboratory for Functional Brain Imaging and Behavior, one of the few laboratories in the world that focus on studies of emotion and the brain. At Wisconsin, he holds professorships both in the medical school and in the psychology department; one of the posts is named after William James, his hero in the field.

From early in his career Richie has had a deep scientific fascination with how the brain underlies the qualities of human experience. He has also had an appreciation that in many ways the currency of modern culture is science, and that if we can address issues in human consciousness scientifically, we can bring them to the forefront of the culture in ways that would not just be acceptable but have great impact.

It is a measure of Richie's eminence that when the U.S. Congress requested the National Institutes of Health to establish five research centers to study mind-body interaction, Davidson received one of these prestigious grants—for $11 million—to study, among other things, the impact of meditation on brain, immune, and endocrine function, and so on health. It was the first time Richie ever included the word "meditation" in an application for federal funding. That 1999 grant represented a sea change in science; just five years earlier it would have been unfathomable.

And now, for the first time in his career, he feels that the methods of science are able to get their arms around questions of the brain and human consciousness with rigor. Using state-of-the-art brain research tools in his laboratory, Davidson has shown beyond doubt how the prefrontal lobes and limbic system allow us to mingle thought and feeling, cognition and emotion. He has vindicated not only Walle Nauta but himself.

The Neuroscience of Afflictive Emotions

Richie seemed quite relaxed as he took the presenter's seat. He had moderated the fifth Mind and Life meeting, on altruism and compassion, and now presented the Dalai Lama with the manuscript of the volume of those proceedings, *Visions of Compassion,* which he had edited with Anne Harrington of Harvard University.[2]

"The scientists who participate in these meetings," he remarked, "have been irrevocably affected by their participation. When we go back into our scientific communities, we go back as different people. From our perspective, these meetings have produced some very important changes."

That would prove to be especially true on this day.

"This morning," he went on, beginning his formal presentation, "I would like to review three major points. The first point covers some of the brain mechanisms that underlie emotion and the regulation of emotion, and considers some of their evolutionary origins. Next I would like to cover some issues that are central to a neuroscientific understanding of afflictive emotional states. Third, I will raise some facts and theories regarding three of the major afflictive emotional states: anger, aggression, and fear as one cluster; craving as a second; and delusion or ignorance as the third."

Richie began by explaining, "One of the most important things that we've learned in neuroscience is that any kind of complex behavior, such as emotion, is not based in a single area of the brain. Rather, many parts of the brain work together to produce complex behavior. There is no one center for emotion, just as there is none for playing tennis—nor for anything complicated. It involves interactions across different brain areas."

Among the important cortical areas he mentioned was the frontal lobe, right behind the forehead, a critical zone for regulating emotion, one that he was to discuss in great detail later. Another was the parietal lobe, an area where representations from the senses—such as vision, hearing, and touch—all come together. The parietal lobe also plays a role in mental representations, such as when we picture something "in the mind's eye."

Ever the attentive host, as Richie began to show a slide the Dalai Lama signaled the monk in attendance to turn the room lights off, and then checked that the camera operator who was videotaping the proceedings for an archive was comfortable with the lower light level.

Richie then focused on areas of the brain relevant to destructive emotions and their regulation. He showed a slide that pictured the brain as though cut in half from front to back, letting us look at the inner surface.

Richie pointed out the frontal lobes, which are the brain's executive center and play a role in regulating emotions. He then called our attention to another key region for emotions, the amygdala, buried within the middle of the brain in the region known as the limbic system. In an adult, the amygdala is about 1.5 cubic centimeters, about the size of a walnut, and in fact there are two of them—they come in matching pairs, one on each side of the brain.

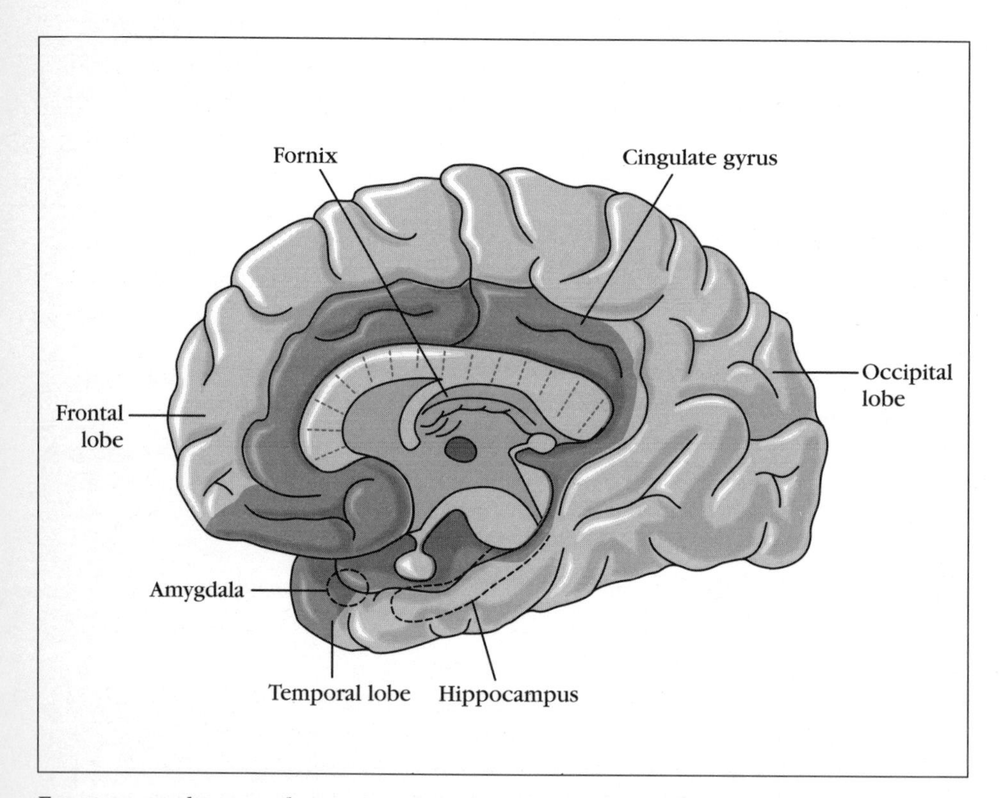

Emotions involve an orchestration of activity in circuits throughout the brain, particularly the frontal lobe, which houses the brain's executive faculties (such as planning); the amygdala, which is particularly active during the experience of negative emotions such as fear; and the hippocampus, which adjusts actions to their context. The areas labeled here are active during the experience of emotion.

"The amygdala," Richie said, "is very critical for certain kinds of negative emotions, particularly fear." We would hear much more about the amygdala—central to the destructive emotions—over the coming days.

The Dalai Lama asked, as he often does, about the implications for animals. His commitment to compassion for all beings includes animals, and throughout this dialogue—as in others—he routinely extended the discussion to include them. He now pointed out that animals show fear-like emotions that are comparable to those in humans, and asked if their brains have the same structures. Richie replied that all mammalian brains do, but that there are important differences in the frontal lobes, which are larger in humans.

Emotions Out of Place

Davidson continued with his neuroanatomy overview by moving on to the hippocampus, a long structure just behind the amygdala that has been linked to memory. As he noted, the hippocampus has an important role in emotion because it is essential for our appreciation of the *context* of events. "I might be in a situation where good things happen to me—for example, my home, where I feel secure and loved by my family—so just the act of going into that physical environment is comforting. The appreciation of that physical environment as a context involves the hippocampus. Some emotional disorders involve abnormalities in the hippocampus, particularly depression and posttraumatic stress disorder."

"I have heard," the Dalai Lama said, "that when a particular part of the brain is damaged, though the mental correlate will be impaired for some time, over the course of time other parts of the brain will start to take over that task in some cases. To what extent does that pertain in these cases? When does substitution occur over time and when, if one part is impaired, is it irreversibly impaired?"

"That's a very important question," Richie replied. "In both depression and posttraumatic stress disorder it has been found that the hippocampus actually shrinks. That can be measured objectively. But there are new findings within the last year indicating that when depression is treated with antidepressant medication, it prevents the atrophy of the hippocampus that typically occurs if the depression goes untreated.[3] So there is considerable plasticity in this structure. To some extent, the functions of the hippocampus and other structures can also be taken over by other parts of the brain, although only to a limited extent, based on what we now know. But that particular issue has not been studied extensively in this area."

"Just to make sure I understand," the Dalai Lama said, "when you're not depressed, the primary functions of the hippocampus are memory and recognition of context? That would imply that when you're depressed, the function of the hippocampus is also impaired?"

"Correct."

"You get over depression and then it's restored to its normal functioning."

"Correct."

Then a joke from the Dalai Lama: "If the hippocampus had the sole function of making you depressed, it would be better just to get rid of it!"

"But that's not its sole function," said Davidson, smiling at the joke. "We need it. But this provides us with a very important insight about one understanding of destructive emotion in the West: the expression of an emotion when it's not appropriate to the situation. For instance, it is natural for a person to experience sadness when a loved one dies. But a depressed person experiences sadness in contexts that are not appropriate. One hypothesis is that such a person's hippocampus is not functioning correctly. The hippocampus provides us with information about context and helps govern emotional responses so that they are appropriate to the context. One problem in emotional disorders, then, is the expression of emotion in inappropriate contexts.

"It's similar for fear and for a phobia, the pathological extreme of fear. It is common to experience fear in response to a threat to our physical survival, but a phobic will experience fear in other contexts, when there is no actual threat at all, let alone to her physical survival. One hypothesis, again, is that there is a problem in the hippocampus.

"In other words, one of the tests of whether or not someone has an emotional disorder is whether the person's emotions are inappropriate to the context—and if so, it may be because of a dysfunction in the hippocampus. Fear and sadness are the emotions that have been studied so far, but it may apply to other emotions, like anger and anxiety, too."

How Experience Changes the Brain

Richie then made a point about changes in brain size over the course of evolution in different species, from primates to humans. "Now, Your Holiness, if we look at the frontal lobe of the brain in relation to the rest of the brain size, in humans there is a higher ratio than in any other species. This tells us that there is something important about the frontal lobe for qualities that are distinctly human. One of the most important human qualities may be our ability to regulate emotion—and here the frontal lobes appear to play a key role. Likewise, the frontal lobes are involved in much emotional dysregulation—destructive emotions."

Again, the Dalai Lama related Davidson's remarks to animals: "You are not suggesting that there is no system of regulating emotions in animals, are you?"

"There is to some extent, but it is not as sophisticated as in humans."

The Dalai Lama nodded, satisfied with that answer.

"One of the most exciting discoveries in neuroscience over the last five years is that the areas of the brain I have been describing, the frontal lobes, the amygdala, and the hippocampus, change in response to experience. They are the parts of the brain dramatically affected by the emotional environment in which we are raised and by repeated experience." This theme of how experience changes the brain—"neural plasticity"—would be a central thread in ensuing discussions.

"What's particularly exciting about these findings is that the impact of environment on brain development has been traced down to the level of actual gene expression. This has only, so far, been done in animals, but we have every reason to believe it applies in humans, too. If you are raised in a nurturing environment, there are actually demonstrable, objective changes in gene expression. For example, there are genes for certain molecules that play an important role in regulating our emotions and which respond to nurturing."

"Are you suggesting," the Dalai Lama wanted to know, "that those who are brought up in a nurturing environment have a greater degree of ability to regulate their emotions?"

"Yes, exactly," Richie replied. "There is evidence for that at the animal level, and Mark Greenberg will be talking about the human side tomorrow when he reports on emotional learning in children. A related point is that neuroscientists believed until very recently—a year or two ago—that we are born with a certain number of neurons, and that's all we have for the rest of our life. They believed that the changes that occur with development are changes only in the connections among those cells and the dying of the cells, but that new cells did not grow, no matter what. Over the last two years we have discovered that to be false. It has now been demonstrated in humans that new neurons do grow throughout the entire life span.[4] That is a fantastic new finding."

The Dalai Lama seemed quite intrigued by this, asking, "When you speak of new neurons forming, you're implying that while some neurons' continuance ceases and they are presumably flushed out as waste, others arise altogether fresh, not as a continuation of earlier neurons?"

Davidson said, "They arise fresh from what we call stem cells, which can become any specific type of cell anywhere in the body. A stem cell can become a kidney cell; it can become a heart cell; it can also become a neuron."

"In a sense it's like a generic cell," the Dalai Lama noted. "And other neurons simply die, they simply cease as neurons—what becomes of them?"

"They disappear, they're reabsorbed into other cells," said Richie.

The Dalai Lama asked, "If some of the neurons in the brain die, some continue, and some of them are freshly produced, what makes some of them carry on? Are there any that continue for the full duration of your life?"

"We don't know the answer to that precisely," Richie told him, "but the new neurons that emerge have been thought to be associated with new learning and memory. These neurons keep growing even in people in their sixties."

"Ah!" said the Dalai Lama—who is in his sixties—sitting up with great interest.

Einstein's Brain

The Dalai Lama then changed the subject. He had been wondering about reports he had read about new analyses of Einstein's brain. He asked Richie, "They said that there were some unusual things about Einstein's brain. What were they precisely?"

"There is an area in the parietal lobe called the angular gyrus, which was larger in Einstein's brain, according to the reports. This is an area where the senses come together, as I was describing previously."

"Is this a legend that has been perpetuated, or is it based on fact?"

"It hasn't been sufficiently studied, but it is interesting. Einstein described that when he engaged in thinking he often had a lot of visual imagery, and what's called synesthesia. Synesthesia is a merging of different sensory modalities in mental content. It is speculated that this area that was enlarged in Einstein's brain may have given rise to his ability to think that way."

"You are probably not able to determine this," the Dalai Lama replied, "but do you think that Einstein was born with this enlarged parietal lobe? Might this account for his exceptional genius—or do you think it developed because of the way he used his mind over the course of his life, and that it actually grew? Which was the chicken and which was the egg?"

"Probably both," said Richie.

"Very safe answer," said the Dalai Lama with a laugh. Then he continued, "I am trying to relate this back to a conversation where the point was raised that every thought process must arise subsequent to brain activity. I'm just putting on for a moment the hat not only of a Buddhist but of everyone who asserts the existence of former and later lives—a theory that holds that a variety of consciousness not dependent on brain activity can be passed on from life to life." The conversation he referred to had occurred during the second Mind and Life conference. The question: Can consciousness in some form continue after death without the brain to support it?

Richie answered by citing an American pioneer in both psychology and philosophy. "In the first chapter of his *Principles of Psychology,* which was written in 1890, William James said that the brain is the one immediate organ underlying the mental operations, and that the whole remainder of the principles of psychology is but a footnote to that single claim."

Francisco Varela countered that in a subsequent book, *The Varieties of Religious Experience,* James contradicts this earlier claim.

"So," said Richie, "James was not consistent himself in that view, and certainly we don't have the requisite evidence upon which to reach a firm conclusion."

Thupten Jinpa commented wryly, "From a Tibetan literary traditional perspective, I think the later writings are considered to be more authoritative."

To which Richie made the rejoinder, "In science the reverse is true."

What Gives Humans Their Distinctive Intelligence?

Getting back to his presentation, Richie put up a slide of the prefrontal cortex on which were labeled key areas: the dorsolateral, orbitofrontal, and ventromedial frontal cortex—this last zone being particularly important for emotion. Richie's slide showed two views of the brain, one from the side, the other from the bottom. "The frontal lobe is divided into a number of different areas. The area known as the ventromedial cortex is very critical for emotion. Patients who have damage to that area of the brain show unregulated, disrupted emotional behavior, such as outbursts.

"The very front part of the frontal lobe has traditionally been thought of as playing an important role in certain types of cognition, particularly planning for the future. Insofar as aspects of emotion also involve anticipation of the future—such as eagerly anticipating meeting a loved one you haven't seen in a long time—this part of the brain would be active in representing that goal in your mind." More generally, motivation hinges in part on the activity of this region of the frontal lobe, which holds in mind the feelings we will have when we reach our goals.[5]

"I want to spend a little more time talking about the frontal cortex, because it is so important to our ability to regulate emotion, and particularly the destructive emotions. The brain areas that are involved in initially activating an emotion are different from the brain areas that are involved in regulating an emotion." The amygdala plays a key role in the circuitry that activates emotion, while the prefrontal cortex does much of the regulation.

"Under most normal circumstances the brain areas that initiate an emotion and those that regulate an emotion are all activated simultaneously—so when an emotion is triggered, the mechanisms involved in regulating that emotion are also triggered. This provides a key to help us understand destructive emotions, because we can examine the brain areas involved in regulating emotion that may not be operating properly."

"One of the unique features of the human species is the capacity for intelligence," the Dalai Lama said. "Can you identify one or more parts of the brain that specifically correlate to our exceptional human intelligence—that which is distinctively human?"

Richie's answer returned to his focus on the frontal lobes. "Earlier I mentioned that any complex behavior involves interactions among different areas of the brain. Intelligence is certainly very complex and will likely involve interactions among different brain areas. That is a safe answer.

"But let me give you a more speculative answer. The frontal lobes clearly are important for unique aspects of human intelligence—not just what we think of in the West as cognitive intelligence but also what we think of as emotional intelligence. The frontal lobes are essential for both."

The fact that some of the same brain areas involved in positive emotions are also associated with the faculty of reasoning piqued the Dalai Lama's interest. He felt it offered a confirmation from neuroscience of what he had always believed: that the constructive, positive emotions can be both grounded in reason and enhanced by it. His debater's habit of raising seemingly disconfirming evidence apparently led to his next question.

"You said earlier that the kind of mental imagery Einstein had seems to be related to a back part of the brain," the Dalai Lama said. "The mental imagery that arises when you think seems to have a correlate in the parietal lobe, right? If we can call that imagination, the power of one's imagination would seem to be very closely linked to the scope of one's intelligence. Therefore, would you think that the parietal lobe, which is not part of the frontal lobe, is also a crucial player in uniquely human intelligence?" The Dalai Lama was rocking back and forth a bit in his absorption.

Richie replied, "Yes. Absolutely. But in the human brain, more than in other species, there are massive connections between the frontal lobe and the parietal lobe. The capacity to imagine, in the sense of Einstein's creative thinking, certainly involved linking the frontal lobe, which was considering some of the more abstract concepts, to the mental visual imagery."

I added, "Einstein reported that he got his insights visually first and then put them into words. He would see equations or physical laws initially as pictures."

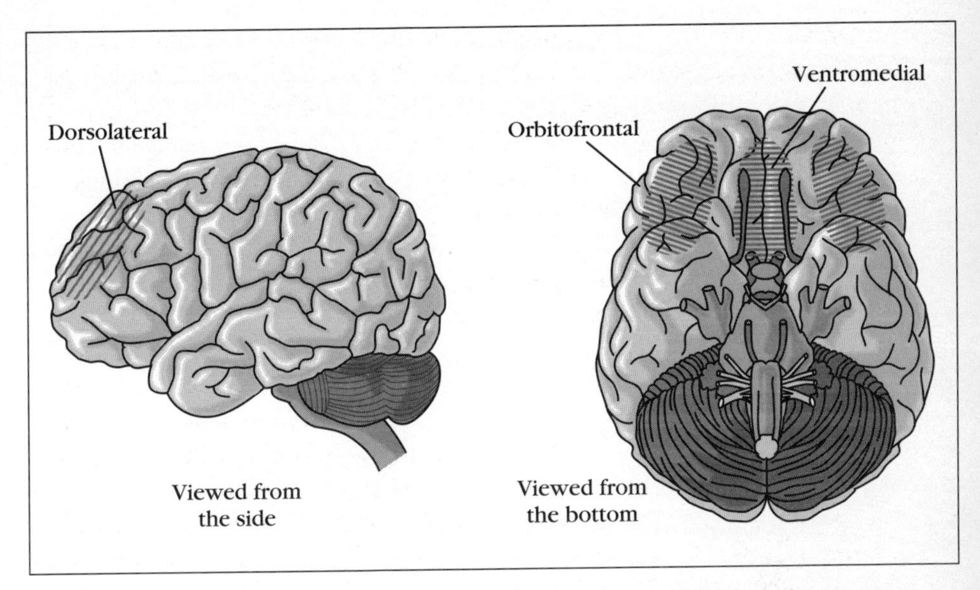

The prefrontal cortex, located just behind the forehead, houses the brain's executive centers for abilities such as planning. The ventromedial zone of the prefrontal cortex is vital for regulating emotions.

The Brain in a Vat

Richie continued, "Your Holiness, there are two other general points. First, the frontal lobes, the amygdala, and the hippocampus are all extensively connected with the body, in particular with the immune system; with the endocrine system, which regulates hormones; and with the autonomic nervous system, which regulates heart rate, blood pressure, and so on. This begins to provide some clue as to how the mind can influence the body, so that we can understand the impact of emotions not just on our mental health but also on our physical health."

This prompted the Dalai Lama to ask a seemingly bizarre question: "Is it theoretically possible (even if it's not mechanically feasible now) to sever the head of a person who is alive and then supply blood and oxygen—whatever it needs—mechanically to the head, and have the brain continue to function as a brain? Is that possible in principle?"

In fact, just such a question has been seriously considered by philosophers of mind. Richie answered, "There is a philosopher by the name of Daniel Dennett who wrote an essay about just that, the brain in a vat, as a metaphor.[6] Just the head—exactly what you're asking. I think that in principle it is possible. One of the interesting questions is whether a brain that is maintained in that way could feel emotions."

At which Alan quipped, "In other words, it might not mind?"

"So in principle," the Dalai Lama said, "the answer is yes, but there is a question about the emotions?"

"Right."

"What about intelligence? Could it be an intelligent brain?" And the Dalai Lama added, with a laugh, "That would be the best—you'd have intelligence with no emotions!"

"I think you would still have emotions," Richie said.

More serious, the Dalai Lama agreed: "As long as there is a sense of 'I am' there are bound to be emotions that go along with it."

The Divided Brain

Richie moved on to another point about the frontal lobes. "The brain in all vertebrate species is divided in two, and extensive research on the functional differences between the two halves suggests that in humans and in other higher primates, regions in the left and right frontal lobes differ in their function for emotion. Evidence suggests regions of the left frontal cortex play an important role in positive emotion, while the right frontal lobe plays that role in certain negative emotions.

"In one experiment, we presented people with pictures designed to activate positive or negative emotions. The positive pictures included, for example, a mother holding her baby in a very loving way. The negative pictures included people who had been injured, such as burn or accident victims."

Jinpa pointed out, "Just for clarity, you're using negative versus positive here in the sense of qualitative experience, rather than destructive versus constructive?"

"Yes. When we present the negative images, designed to evoke emotions like fear, we see an area of activation in the right frontal cortex, reflecting increased metabolism in this region. When we present positive pictures like the mother loving the baby, we see a very different pattern: activation on the left side in areas of the orbital as well as the upper part of the frontal lobe, and some motor areas as well. But these areas are all on the left side, with none on the right side—it's a very different pattern from negative emotions." Richie added a technical aside: that this pattern holds for all right-handed people, and most—but not all—left-handers.

The Dalai Lama's scientific instincts came to the fore. He asked, "Would you hypothesize that if you do this experiment over a certain period of time—maybe repeat it after a couple of weeks, or when the subject is in good health and then possibly in bad health, hungry or not—would such variables make a difference? Or would you always see activation in the same area?"

"Very good question," Richie replied. "We have now done this experiment on the same people three times over the course of two months. We allow several weeks between each time and test them at the same time of day. They may be more or less hungry, they may be more or less tired, but we see, in general, the same pattern of activation each time we test them. It is stable over time."

"Is it still stable if this occurs right after they've had another very strong emotion?" the Dalai Lama asked.

"Another very good question," answered Richie. "We really don't know the answer to that. But we do know that a very strong emotion will, in most people, affect the emotional state in the next moment. Most people don't recover quickly from a strong emotion; it takes some period of time. Some people recover more quickly, while other people take a long time. We think that is a very significant difference among people," underscoring a point Paul had suggested the day before, in discussing the period when people are in the grip of an emotion.

The Woman Who Did Not Know Fear

The Dalai Lama once impishly confessed to me that when he listens to a technical account of brain function he sometimes has what he called a "monkish thought": "What does it really matter for me to know which parts of the brain get activated when positive emotions arise and which parts of the brain when negative emotions arise? It's enough for me that there's some improvement through my own Buddhist practice."

But today he listened attentively.

The amygdala and its role in fear was Richie's next topic. He began by recounting an experiment using images of faces (developed by Paul Ekman) with expressions varying from very happy to very sad. As the study participants saw the faces, the blood flow to their brain was measured.

"Only when the fear face was presented was there activation in the amygdala," said Richie. "When the happy face was presented, there was no amygdala activation. Just the detection of a fearful face is sufficient to activate the amygdala. The amygdala is important both in the detection of signals of fear as well as in the generation of fear itself."

He continued, "There is a skin disorder called Urbach-Weithe disease that involves abnormal mineral deposits that show up as discoloration on the skin. In some cases it has a neurological component restricted to the amygdala: There are mineral deposits in the amygdala that lead to death of the cells. There is one patient who had Urbach-Weithe disease who has provided some wonderful evidence about the role of the amygdala. She was asked to draw pictures of how it would look when she was experiencing different emotions.

"The drawings depict faces that are happy, sad, surprised, disgusted, and angry—all appropriate expressions. But the image that is supposed to represent someone who is afraid shows a baby crawling."

The Dalai Lama asked, "Is the implication that she can't relate to the expression of the actual emotion of fear? Or is it that this woman cannot experience fear? What if you threaten her with a sharp needle? Wouldn't she be afraid?"

"No," said Richie. "If you poked her with the needle, she would show a reaction: pain. But if you threatened her with something aversive—and this has been done with shock—she does not show the increased sweating on the skin that most people would show."

"Would you say she has more courage?" the Dalai Lama asked.

"No, not necessarily. She has been put in risk-taking situations and she will choose riskier options, but I doubt we want to say that's the equivalent of courage. I would call it irresponsibility, not courage."

"Does that mean she would not be afraid of death as well?"

"Quite possibly. I don't know."

"That can't be true," the Dalai Lama said. "So long as there is this natural sense of 'I am,' there are going to be emotions bound to death, and also a fear, to whatever degree it may be."

Richie conceded, "Other research on the amygdala is consistent with Your Holiness's intuition that it involves certain kinds of fear, but not all fear."

"That seems right."

"It's typically the fear of discrete, threatening objects that is impaired by the amygdala damage," Richie clarified.

Matthieu asked, "Would she feel no fear even when about to fall from a cliff?"

"No," Richie replied, "she would not feel fear, and it would be very dangerous to take her on a cliff."

Alan, picking up on a comment by an observer, Sogyal Rinpoche, said, "I was wondering whether there might be some real significance in the picture of the little baby, which is almost an archetypal representation of vulnerability."

"There might be," Richie agreed. "The little bit of commentary she provided when she drew this was that the first thing that came to her mind about fear was an infant who might get himself into danger through crawling."

Coming Back to Calm

We left it at that, and Richie moved on to how people differ in their emotional reactions. "There are such profound differences among people in how they respond to the same event. We believe that this is the key to understanding why some people are prone to destructive emotions and why other people may be much less vulnerable.

"When I talk about these differences among people, I am talking about differences in the brain—but that does not mean that those differences are genetic. There is a lot of reason to believe that many of these differences in the brain are a product of people's experience.

"One of the most important differences we have studied is what I call 'recovery function.' This refers to how long it takes for a person to come back to a quiet baseline condition of calm after being provoked by an emotion." This was another way of talking about what Paul Ekman the day before had put in terms of the "refractory period" and the time needed to release its grip on the mind.

"There are big differences among people that we can measure objectively, not just by what people say," Richie continued. "On the basis of brain function we can show that certain people have a very prolonged response and others come back to baseline very quickly.

"When a person is provoked by threatening pictures, people who come back to baseline quickly are those who have less activation in the amygdala and whose activation is shorter in duration. They are people who also show more activation in the left prefrontal cortex—the area important for positive emotion. These are also people who report that their everyday experience is filled with feelings of vigor, optimism, and enthusiasm.

"These differences have been found in infants as young as ten months of age. But these differences are not stable—so a child at, say, three years of age who had a very long reaction to a stressful, negative event will not necessarily show that same reaction when he is thirteen. There is much less stability of these traits in early childhood than there is in adulthood. This implies that there is a lot of opportunity for the environment to shape our brain during these early years of life.

"I want to mention three other characteristics that are very important in this cluster of traits," Richie continued. "If people who recover very quickly from a negative event are asked to voluntarily control their emotion, to suppress their anger or fear, they are better able to do so. We can demonstrate that experimentally very rigorously. They not only spontaneously show a shorter reaction time and come back to baseline more quickly, but are also better able to actively control their emotion if you ask them to.

"The person who is able to recover quickly also has a lower level of cortisol, which plays a key role in stress. Cortisol is a hormone released by the adrenal glands, which sit over the kidneys but are controlled by the brain. When a stressful event occurs in the environment, most people will release cortisol, but the people who recover quickly have lower levels of cortisol in general, at baseline. We know that when cortisol is present at high levels over a long period of time, it may kill cells in the hippocampus"—which has been documented in disorders such as posttraumatic stress disorder and severe depression.

"The last point is that the people who recover quickly also have better function in certain measures of immunity, which implies that they may show better physical health as well. To give one example, they have higher levels of natural killer cell activity, a primary defense that the immune system uses to fight off many kinds of foreign antigens that enter our body, from cancerous tumor cells to the common cold."

These findings about the range of differences in the ability to recover from a disturbing emotion have great implications for helping people learn to modulate emotional stresses. In general, the range of differences found within a biological system suggests a potential degree of plasticity—that is, a potential for change on that dimension. For instance, studies correlating what people eat with their cholesterol levels have made it clear that cholesterol levels can be improved by eating certain foods and avoiding others.

When it comes to handling disturbing emotions, the question becomes whether people can learn to improve—for instance, to recover their calmness more quickly. This question would find some practical answers by the end of the day.

Anger: The First of Three Poisons

The Dalai Lama had specifically requested that the neurological basis of the three destructive states known in Buddhism as the Three Poisons—anger, craving, and delusion—be a topic of our meeting. Richie, having covered the neurological background, now addressed the first "poison," anger.

"There are a number of different kinds of anger that have been described in the psychological literature. One kind is anger directed inward, which typically means anger that is not expressed overtly. Another kind of anger is directed outward, which can lead to rage. There is also anger that is associated with some kinds of sadness. Finally, a kind of anger can be transformed into a constructive impulse to remove an obstacle."

That list intrigued the Dalai Lama. Wondering about the logic of the categories Richie proposed, he asked, "How are the distinctions between these types of anger made? Is it only differences in behavior or expression? Or are these distinctions drawn on some other basis?"

"They are drawn on the basis of several kinds of evidence," Richie answered. "One is through analysis of answers to questionnaires that subjects are given. A second is on the basis of behavioral data, and a third is on the basis of physiology. I will describe some of the physiological findings next.

"When a person reports that he or she is angry but doesn't express it, research has found that the person shows the pattern of right-sided activation in the frontal lobe that is also associated with other kinds of negative emotions. The person also shows activation of the amygdala. In infants who are crying in frustration, anger frequently occurs in conjunction with sadness—this anger, too, has been associated with this pattern of right-sided activation of the frontal lobes.

"Then there is a kind of anger associated with what we call 'approach behavior,' where someone makes constructive attempts to remove an obstacle. There are several ways this kind of anger has been studied. If you show a toddler a really interesting toy while gently holding the arms of the child, restraining it so that it can't play with the toy, the toddler will show facial signs of anger in response to the situation. When you confront children with that kind of restraint, they show a pattern of *left* frontal activation. This has been interpreted as an attempt to remove the goal blockage and to actually attain the goal—to play with the interesting toy.

"In adults, the same kind of anger has been studied in people trying to solve a very difficult math problem. Though the tough math problem is very frustrating, there is an active attempt to solve the problem and meet the goal. Again, when this happens, we find left frontal activation. This is a type of anger that, in the West, we might call constructive: anger associated with an attempt to remove an obstacle."

If It's Constructive, Is It Really Anger?

This notion of constructive anger led us back to the first day's discussion about the differences between Western and Buddhist psychology in specifying what is destructive in an emotion—here, anger.

Alan spoke for the Buddhist view: "While one is engaged in trying to overcome the hurdle, such as the difficult math problem, something constructive is taking place—we are solving the problem. But is the anger helping us solve that problem? Even though it's conjoined with it, is there clear evidence that the frustration, the anger, the irritation, and the exasperation are actually helping you accomplish the goal?"

"This is a very critical question," Richie acknowledged. "Anger, as well as any other emotion, can be deconstructed into more elementary constituents. There may be a certain quality that is often present in anger but may be present in nonangry states as well, which is the constructive piece."

To that point, Paul Ekman suggested, "It's the persistence. Anger can provide the constructive motivation of persistence to solve the math problem rather than abandon it."

"So why is it called anger?" the Dalai Lama asked, a bit perplexed that such constructive persistence, even when a response to frustration, should be seen as anger. That thinking was incongruent with the Buddhist category of anger, which by definition entails a distortion of reality, a skew in perception that exaggerates the negative qualities of things.

"It's called anger," Richie replied, "because people report that they're frustrated, and frustration is typically part of the anger family."

That answer, which seemed a bit circular, did not seem to speak to the Dalai Lama's perplexity, so I asked Richie to clarify the actual cognitive challenge that triggered the frustration among the research subjects. Richie explained, "Imagine I ask you, Your Holiness, to take the number 4,786 and subtract 19 from it and to keep subtracting 19 from each remainder, and I told you that the speed of your responses was a measure of your intelligence. When people are in the heat of this, they get very frustrated because it is very difficult to do very quickly. Some people give up. And certain people are more likely to persist."

Alan came at the issue from a fresh angle. "There is a very difficult challenge in Buddhist meditation called *shinay,* or meditative quiescence.[7] There is a question of how to develop the tenacity to accomplish this. And it's by developing a delight and faith and enthusiasm. A person who tries to develop meditative quiescence out of rage, anger, irritation, or exasperation is not going to get very far."

But the Dalai Lama said, "I am slightly in disagreement with what Alan was saying. Even in the Buddhist context, the sense of disillusionment and aspiration for liberation that Alan spoke about yesterday—the spirit of emergence—depends upon the extent to which you have a feeling of intolerance or disgust toward being under the control of the afflictions. One can no longer bear the suffering of *samsara,* one is disillusioned, even disgusted with it—and that is wholesome and constructive."

Alan countered that in this case, "one is indeed disgusted with *samsara,* but that has to give way to faith and delight in spiritual practice. I still maintain that you can't progress far along the path to liberation with the emotional state of disgust alone."

The Dalai Lama got us back on track: "Just to clarify the point—in this kind of constructive anger, there is definite activity on the left side."

"Yes," said Richie, "and the quality that's most important is persistence in overcoming an obstacle."

The Sniper's Plea for Help: Pathological Anger

"Your Holiness, I'd like to now move on to the pathological kind of anger that can lead to rage and to violence, and what we know about it from the perspective of the brain. Someone prone to pathological rage may be unable to anticipate the negative consequences of the extreme expression of anger. This inability to anticipate those negative consequences appears to involve not just the frontal lobe but also the amygdala. There is a very recent study showing atrophy or severe shrinkage of the amygdala in people with a history of severe aggression.[8]

"The idea here is that the amygdala is needed for anticipating negative consequences, and people prone to pathological extremes of rage are unable to foresee the consequences their rage will have.

"Your Holiness, in the United States there was a fellow by the name of Charles Whitman who killed several people and himself, shooting from a tower on the campus of the University of Texas in Austin. He left behind a note begging society to examine his brain for possible clues to his pathological condition. When an autopsy was done on his brain they found a tumor pressing into his amygdala. Although this is just a case report, it again suggests that there may be something important in the connection of the amygdala to the pathological expression of violence."

Craving: The Second Poison

Shifting gears, Richie moved on to the neurochemistry of craving. "There is a chemical in the brain called dopamine, and virtually all forms of craving that have been studied involve abnormalities of this chemical system. Most of this research has been done on drug craving, but the abnormalities are also involved in pathological gambling, where people have a craving for playing games of chance, often going into great debt. The dopamine abnormality appears to be generic to craving of all kinds. Recent research indicates there are actually molecular changes in the dopamine system that arise over the course of craving and that powerfully alter the way this system works."[9]

Dopamine plays an important role in reward and in the pleasurable feelings that occur in response to reward. But Richie pointed out that addictions are driven not by this biology alone but also by habits that are learned. "Craving is also something that is very powerfully conditioned, so that stimuli or objects which were previously neutral can take on tremendous significance through learning. Let me give you an example. If a drug addict typically takes a drug in a particular room or with a particular set of paraphernalia, that setting or equipment alone can actually produce brain changes akin to the drug itself.

"One study showed cocaine addicts a videotape of the equipment they used to administer themselves cocaine—and found changes in the brain similar to those produced by the cocaine. The study found that one area, called the nucleus accumbens, is particularly activated by craving. It is an area very rich in dopamine and appears to be involved in all forms of craving and addictions.[10]

"We make a distinction between the circuitry in the brain associated with liking—enjoyment—and the circuitry associated with wanting. Often these two go together, so that we want things that we like. But in craving, the circuitry associated with wanting appears to be strengthened and the circuitry associated with liking appears to be weakened. Because our sense of liking or enjoyment declines and our wanting increases, we want more and more and we like less and less. We just keep wanting—but we need more to enjoy it as much. This is a major problem that underlies craving. There are many examples where the liking circuit has been dramatically disrupted in forms of addiction—for example, even with cigarettes and nicotine addiction."

Delusion: The Third Poison

As Richie moved on to delusion, his last topic for the morning, there was a dramatic clap of thunder nearby as a rainstorm rolled through.

"Now I would like to turn to delusion, how we understand it as neuroscientists, and the ways in which this may be similar to or different from the Buddhist understanding."

That prompted the Dalai Lama to ask, "In Buddhism we have a very clear sense of what we mean by delusion. What do you mean by 'delusion' in this context?"

Richie replied, "What I mean by delusion is afflictive emotions obscuring our ability to see the world clearly."

The Dalai Lama pressed for a more precise distinction. "In Buddhism, we can speak of delusive appearances as well as a deluded grasping or apprehension of reality. How things appear and how you grasp on to them may both be delusional. Are you referring to both?"

"More to the apprehension of reality," Richie clarified. "We think of delusion as the biasing by emotion of perception and cognition. Delusion involves the influence of the emotional circuits of the brain on the circuits of the brain responsible for perceiving things or apprehending the world, and also circuits that are involved in thought."

"So," the Dalai Lama clarified, "it's the bias that comes in your perception."

"Yes," Richie agreed. "It very much relates to Matthieu's comments yesterday about apprehending reality as it is. These are influences that obscure our capacity to perceive reality. They reflect how emotion disrupts both our perceptions of reality and our thinking. For example, people who are generally anxious and apprehensive focus their attention on threat-related cues. People with social phobia, for example, are fearful of many social situations, such as being with other people, being evaluated by other people, speaking in public—things of that sort. When they are shown a picture of a neutral face, one that shows no emotional expression, they show activation in their amygdala, which normally people only show in response to a fearful face."

Richie described the anatomical connections from the amygdala to parts of the system that processes vision. "The amygdala has projections all the way back to the primary area in the brain where visual information is first received. This provides a mechanism through which our negative emotions can influence our perception of visual information from the first moment."

The Dalai Lama commented, "There is a clear distinction in Buddhism between actual visual perception and the mental awareness of the visual perception. Are you suggesting that these connections back in the visual cortex are even influencing visual perception itself?"

"Correct."

"In Buddhist epistemological texts, one speaks of different conditions for delusions where even visual perception, for example, can be distorted. These are the conditions immediately preceding a mental state. More particularly, a mental cognitive state can actually influence the visual perception."

"So these data are very consistent with the Buddhist view," Richie said, going on to describe an experiment that made the same point. "Say you're shown two words—'knife' and 'pencil'—one above the other, and then immediately afterward a dot appears and you have to hit a button as soon as you see the dot. Sometimes the dot is in the location of the word 'pencil' and other times the dot is in the location of the word 'knife.' People who are anxious are much faster at responding when the dot appears in the location of the emotional word that represents a threat, like 'knife.' This is very clear and can be easily demonstrated."

Then Richie reinforced his point dramatically. He showed a slide on which there was a set of words, each printed in a different color—"apple" in purple and "house" in yellow. Some words were emotionally charged, like "bloody" and "torture." And all the words were written in Tibetan, not English, creating an appreciative stir among the Tibetans in the room.

This was a form of the Stroop Test, a classic psychological test of how emotions sway perception, in which people are asked to name the color in which a word is printed. Richie explained, "If you are anxious, you will be much slower in naming the color if it is an anxiety-evoking word, because you're disturbed and so your ability to access the name of the color is disrupted. This is another example of emotion influencing our perception: The speed at which you can say the word is affected by the emotion itself if you're anxious.

"Your Holiness, I'd like to end now with a quote that I've found inspiring. It's from *The Art of Happiness,* your book with Howard Cutler: 'The systematic training of the mind, the cultivation of happiness, the genuine inner transformation by deliberately selecting and focusing on positive mental states and challenging negative mental states, is possible because of the very structure and function of the brain. But the wiring of our brains is not static, not irrevocably fixed. Our brains are also adaptable.' "

Richie had quoted that same passage at the end of an article he wrote on neuroplasticity in the millennium issue of the *Psychological Bulletin.* It captures Richie's original vision of what psychology could be—what drew him to the field. Indeed, those words describe a beautiful marriage of his intellectual and personal interests. For Richie, the Dalai Lama himself represents the embodiment of desirable emotional qualities, such as equanimity and compassion, and the possibility that these are qualities we can all realize—the capacity for human transformation.

On that optimistic note, there was applause, and Richie put his palms together in a salute to the Dalai Lama, who took his hands between his own, touching his head to them in a gesture of appreciation.

9

Our Potential for Change

In the best-selling book *The Monk and the Philosopher,* Matthieu Ricard and his father, the French philosopher Jean-François Revel, engage in a wide-ranging dialogue on science, Buddhism, and the meaning of life. In the book, Matthieu argues that for two millennia or more Buddhist practitioners have been utilizing what amounts to an "inner science," a systematic method for transforming the inner world to produce a better human being—more selfless and compassionate, with greater calm and equanimity. One result of that program, he observes, is relief from the tyranny of destructive emotions.

Today, psychology has begun to embrace the same quest—not from a religious basis but from a scientific one. For psychology, the underlying quest is to influence the operation of the brain in ways that enhance emotional balance. When it comes to quelling destructive emotions, that quest seems all the more compelling.

In the morning Richard Davidson had pointed out that the brain interweaves emotion and intellect—raising the possibility that the positive potential of this connectivity might allow us to bring more intelligence to emotional life. More particularly, the dictum—unexplored in the morning's proceedings—that repeated experience modifies the brain raises the question of how we might best educate the emotions. These practical themes were to resonate through the afternoon's discussion—but not before we got off to a surprising beginning, dealing with questions about the most subtle levels of mental life.

After lunch, as an indication of his eagerness, the Dalai Lama again arrived early, as people were still gathering. He chatted with the few participants who had already arrived about the light hail that had fallen at lunchtime. As the AV crew quickly adjusted the microphones, Alan Wallace seized the moment to ask a question of his own before the session started.

Alan's question picked up on an earlier theme of the day, the links between mental activity and brain function. "Since we're not really formally assembled right now, I would like to ask His Holiness a question. Do you think that—at least at the level of gross mental functioning—there are likely to be neural correlates for each state of mind?"

The Dalai Lama replied, "There is no reason to believe that the very subtlest state—called 'innate mind,' the very essential nature of awareness itself, which is its luminous nature—would have neural correlates, because it is not physical, not contingent upon the brain. But for all other mental processes that manifest throughout the course of a human life, it is certainly possible."

With his mention of "innate mind" the Dalai Lama broached a topic that has been one of his strong personal interests in brain science. His Buddhist perspective included the notion of the continuity of mind on the subtle level. That is, while he agreed with neuroscience that gross mental events correlate with brain activity, he also felt that on a more subtle level of consciousness, brain and mind are two separate entities.

Indeed, he saw the automatic assumption in cognitive neuroscience that brain and mind are invariably two sides of the same activity as limiting the scope of scientific inquiry. That assumption, he felt, meant that science looked for its answers only within an arbitrarily limited framework. With so many new developments and discoveries in brain science, perhaps scientists might break out of this paradigm and expand the parameters brain science had set for itself.

For instance, one phenomenon he would like scientists to study is what Tibetans call "abiding in the state of clear light" after death. In this state, it is said, some advanced practitioners are able, at the time of death, to remain in a meditative state for several days after the breath stops, during which time their body shows no signs of decomposition. While this is, understandably, a rare occurrence, he had recently heard of an ordinary monk who, witnesses told him, had stayed in the clear light state for four days after his death.

At the other end of life, the Dalai Lama also wondered if science could yet tell the exact point when a developing fetus becomes conscious, or sentient. From the Buddhist perspective, that point would mark when this subtle consciousness awakened in the mind.

Subtle Influences

These considerations led the Dalai Lama to another line of questioning that might allow for the possibility of a subtle awareness that can drive the brain and body. "There is something here that I am very interested in: a very subtle cogitation, almost beneath the threshold of consciousness. When one is simply sitting quietly and pondering something, and out of this quiet thinking you start to get angry, without any external stimuli at all, where is the causal arrow going? Are there any compelling empirical grounds for asserting that the brain gave rise to that subtle cogitation leading to anger or other emotions? Or might this subtle threshold or quasi-conscious cogitation be having an impact upon the brain—which, of course, would then have a reciprocal influence, arousing other emotions?

"There is no question that the body's various states of balance or imbalance—good or bad health—influence mental states. That has been very well established. But I am interested in the extent to which the mind itself, and specific subtle thoughts, may have an influence upon the brain. In that case, it would not be a one-way correlation of brain to mental activity but a correlation of mental activity to the brain."

As they arrived, the participants had begun to focus on this conversation. Now Francisco Varela picked up the thread, drawing on cognitive neuroscience. "I think His Holiness touches on a very important point, which in modern science is called the idea of emergence (of course, in a different sense than the word is used in Buddhism). In mathematical terms, it might be said that the emergent state follows as a consequence of a global state. The mental condition has to have a downward influence on a small, local neural component. So not only does the brain give rise to mental states, but the mental state must also be able to modify the brain condition. This is necessarily true. However, it's not an idea that has been explored very much because it seems counterintuitive to Western assumptions. But it is logically implicit in what science is saying today."

Then the Dalai Lama took the topic in a surprising direction: "I am wondering about not only the philosophical but even the theological influences that still exert themselves upon modern brain science. Owen, you mentioned the Kantian context for modern science. But if you look at the theological foundation for Western science, which is passed down with unquestioned assumptions, there is no notion of a continuity of consciousness from lifetime to lifetime—it's assumed to be impossible from the outset.

"Since, from the Buddhist perspective, we consider all other mental processes to be derivative of the innate mind, the luminosity that is the fundamental nature of awareness, one could say that all mental processes that have been studied by neuroscience are emergent properties of this essential nature of awareness. I think there is quite a different perspective in modern neuroscience, where they are understood as emergent properties not of some essential luminosity of awareness but of the brain. That's a big difference."

Is the Mind the Brain's Puppet?

Alan pursued the implications. "As Francisco has pointed out, most of the literature assumes a bottom-up influence: The brain does this and the puppet mind follows exactly what the brain does. But Richie has been pointing out how experience and the environment modify the brain in very tangible, rather gross ways as well as at the molecular level. But I haven't heard how attitudes modify the brain.

"His Holiness raised the question of whether your thoughts themselves might have an impact on the brain when you're simply sitting quietly and cogitating. Doesn't the causality work both ways? Wouldn't it be helpful, with all the prestige and the authority that you have from a neuroscientific perspective, to start using other language?

"When you just say 'experience and environment,' frankly, as an individual, I feel disempowered. Speaking affectively, not rationally, it feels like I have to now find the right environment that will have a good effect on my brain. I have to look for the experiences to come to me. I still feel a pawn, which I also do when I hear about the brain doing all this stuff to me. But if psychology today started using different terminology, saying that your attitudes, thoughts, and values will also modify your brain, it would give us a cognitive basis for thinking that we can do something with psychological hygiene and emotional education—the idea His Holiness has here. You have to feel this effort is grounded in reality."

The Dalai Lama took up the point. "When you have such a total emphasis on environment, brain, and so forth, it seems that you have to look to somebody else in order to change. They have to do it for you rather than you doing it yourself. Even many religious practitioners feel that any good change in their lives will come from outside, for example, from God, without much effort from one's own side. I think that's the greatest mistake."

"I think there is a little misunderstanding," Richie Davidson responded. "Whenever you have certain thoughts or emotions that you generate yourself—for instance, if you're just sitting there and you generate an image of a visual scene—you are controlling your brain. You're changing the brain. We can demonstrate that in a laboratory precisely. We know that people voluntarily change their brain all the time.

"If you think about 'emergent property' in the way Francisco is using it, the thoughts or emotions you're referring to are emergent properties of the brain, which then in turn have influences on other brain systems. Internally generating feelings of lovingkindness or compassion, or images of a certain kind, invariably will involve changes in the brain. There is a very substantial literature in science now that has shown we can do that. When I move my hand, I'm changing my brain, according to our understanding in modern neuroscience. I think that perhaps we need to better convey that message."

"What is important about Richie's point," Francisco elaborated, "is that even in trivial things, like moving your arm, the illusion of will that everybody accepts is already a manifestation of that downward causation. The whole thing is always working like that in the brain—both up and down causation."

While no one picked up on Francisco's provocative phrase "the illusion of will," Owen Flanagan pointed out that philosophy has grappled with the same questions about mind and brain. "One major tradition in the West, sometimes called Cartesian dualism, is what one philosopher calls 'the myth of the ghost in the machine.' The idea was that there is a little, incorporeal soul that interacts with the brain, as Descartes thought, through the pineal gland. The consensus now among philosophers is to believe that the mind *is* the brain. This is not to say it's true, but this is what most of us working in this area believe.

"It's certainly true that there is upward and downward causation. Our higher-level thoughts can change our bodies, but the higher-level cogitations, despite being emergent properties, are themselves brain processes. The way His Holiness asked the question, I detected the possibility of a dualistic view, that at a certain point there is more than brain activity—there are thoughts, which are not themselves brain events, which are affecting brain events. However, the orthodox view in the West right now among philosophers, and I think most neuroscientists, would be that every mental event, no matter how exotic it is, even if it's a state of luminosity, will be some brain state or other."

When the Mind Drives the Brain

Undeterred and highly engaged, the Dalai Lama pursued his interest in those mental processes where the mind might drive brain activity. He noted, "When the eyes move, it is obvious why one's visual perception changes, but when you shift your attention within the visual field while holding the eyes steady, it seems like a purely mental event. It's not to say there wouldn't be neural correlates of this shift of attention, but it seems to be a clear case of what Francisco has called downward causation—the mind influencing physiology." He then asked how that shift in awareness was thought of in scientific terms.

Richie Davidson, whose work relates directly to this question, answered, "The phrase that has been used in cognitive neuroscience is 'spatial attention,' where you can keep your eyes focused but still be aware of information in the periphery."

"In this selective mechanism, what is actually being shifted?" the Dalai Lama asked. "It seems apparent that there are two distinct processes going on here. One is the simple visual perception itself, and the other one is something quite distinct, which is picking out and identifying, discerning, judging things in that field—but again, not directly correlated to where the visual gaze is directed. And so the question I am posing is, does this mental cognition have a correlation in another part of the brain distinct from the visual cortex?"

The Dalai Lama went on to propose some thought experiments, asking what would go on in the brain during passively viewing whatever is in the field of vision versus keeping the eyes open while concentrating attention on a sound.

"Your Holiness," Richie replied, "that is an excellent question—you have anticipated the current research program in the brain mechanisms that underlie attention." The ability to selectively attend to specific attributes of the visual field without moving the eyes, Richie said, involved parts of the frontal lobe and the parietal cortex. Attending to a sound, however, activated the frontal lobe and its connections to the auditory cortex. And in the instance where the eyes were open but attention passive, there would be a deactivation in the frontal lobe's control mechanisms that select attention, but continued activity in the sensory systems for vision.

As Richie answered the Dalai Lama's questions his hands were continuously in motion, with very clear, elegant, precise gestures illustrating each phrase—almost like a master conductor. He was far less restrained than when he had been presenting his prepared material.

In the morning Richie had brought along a prop, a plastic model of the human brain, which had sat on the table in front of him all day, unused. Now, however, Thupten Jinpa reached for the model to help clarify what had been said—but, giving up, passed it on to Francisco to take out the relevant structures to show everyone.

Meanwhile, the Dalai Lama continued his line of thinking: "Let's take two different situations in which the mental cognition may be more dormant, rather than reaching out and identifying. One is involuntary, where you are fatigued and the mind is vacant, spaced out. That part of the brain is presumably deactivated. But there is another possibility where your mind is very, very clear and you voluntarily choose not to have that mental identification and so forth activated. Would there not be some neural correlates for each of those two situations as well, voluntary and involuntary? Are those distinct, identifiable within the brain?"

At this point, Francisco took off the plastic wrapper on the brain model and put the assemblage in front of Richie—and it promptly fell into pieces, to much laughter from everyone.

"A fractured brain!" Richie exclaimed, then continued, "To answer Your Holiness's question, scientists have not studied that explicitly, but there are very specific predictions that we would make. Scientists talk about an increase in the signal-to-noise ratio in a state of alertness. The sensory, perceptual, and mental information in a state of alertness has a bigger signal in comparison with the background noise; it's going to show a high level of activation. But when we're tired, there will be a lot of background activity in other parts of the brain that will be irrelevant, and we would predict less activation in the visual area of the brain. So when we choose to be alert, we should see a more distinct pattern of activation associated with both sensory and mental events."

That prompted the Dalai Lama to seek a further clarification. "Aside from the case where one is simply exhausted, have you identified the neural correlates when you're very fresh and your senses are very alert, but you consciously choose not to mentally engage, judge, identify, and so forth with whatever is coming to the senses?"

Here the Dalai Lama seemed to be getting at a meditative state similar to what—during the experiments in Richie's lab at Madison—Lama Öser had called "open awareness," in which the person remains vividly aware of any mental activity but is not caught up in it. Awareness remains still and even. While the mental activity would seem to indicate a degree of neural activity, the Dalai Lama wondered whether any neural process that might correspond to this "inactive" state of awareness had been investigated.

"That hasn't really been studied," Richie replied. But within a year or so Richie would be investigating exactly that in Madison.

Impulsive Versus Reasoned Emotion

At that point, the Dalai Lama looked over at me and nodded to indicate that we should begin the formal session for the afternoon. I started by asking him, "Are there any questions you had that you still wanted to ask or any points you wanted to have clarified?"

After our sessions, the Dalai Lama told me he had been intrigued by the relationship between emotional states and the activity of the left and right frontal cortex and the amygdala, and impressed by the fact that there was now a much more sophisticated way of looking at the correlation between mental states and the brain. He sensed that there were potentially strong connections with Buddhist psychology, though precisely how brain science would map on this theory of mind was not immediately clear. He wondered, for instance, about what that might mean for the role of reason, or thinking in general, in wholesome or destructive emotions—since reason, too, was a function of the frontal lobes.

After a long pause, the Dalai Lama said, "We had a lot of scientific data on negative emotions like fear, anger, and so on. Everyone experiences these; they're very natural. I am interested in hearing from the neuroscientific view whether one can detect a qualitative difference that Buddhists would perceive between two types of emotions. On one hand, there are these impulsive emotions, such as anger. They may differ in degree with different individuals, but there is no suggestion that you can deliberately cultivate them or enhance their capacity.

"On the other hand, there are emotions such as compassion and the sense of disillusionment toward the unenlightened state that Buddhists speak about. These are emotional states we can actually enhance if we deliberately cultivate them through prolonged practice and familiarity. Take faith, for example. There is a pure blind faith that is spontaneous, but there are other types of faith that are grounded in admiration and appreciation of qualities—what the Buddhists would describe as faith grounded in understanding.

"Can you envision a neuroscientific study that would measure if there are any appreciable differences between these two types of emotion, impulsive and reasoned emotion?"

"Your Holiness," Richie responded, "yesterday you mentioned that certain types of positive emotions were much more likely to arise from reason, whereas certain negative emotions arise more spontaneously. In terms of neuroscience, that's an extremely intriguing observation. This morning I showed some evidence to indicate that certain types of positive emotions are associated with activation in the left frontal lobe of the brain. This is also an area where certain types of reasoning occur."

The Dalai Lama was showing keen interest as Richie continued, "And there is a strong suggestion that we can use our reasoning skills to increase the activation in this area, which also, in turn, can promote certain types of positive emotion. The stronger the activation in the left frontal area, in some studies that have already been done, the more there are certain positive emotions, such as vigor, zeal, and persistence."

I thought the Dalai Lama would also be interested in the role of the frontal lobes in the kinds of impulsive emotional acts he was contrasting with the reasoned emotions, and so asked Richie about relevant research.

"I didn't have time to talk about this earlier," Richie said, "but there is evidence that in certain types of spontaneous negative emotion—for example, when people commit violence or some other antisocial act impulsively, without thinking about it—there is underactivation in the frontal lobes. A paper just came out showing that there is actual atrophy, a smaller frontal lobe, in individuals who have a propensity for this kind of spontaneous antisocial behavior—behavior without thinking before the act.[1]

"Your Holiness, one thing that this does suggest is that there are certain kinds of thoughts we might cultivate to strengthen our positive emotions, and that those thoughts should be associated with changes in this area of the brain. That is something that we need to study."

Unchaining Thoughts: The Pigeon Warriors

Matthieu Ricard spoke up. "We have been speaking a lot about the possibility of change. How does that happen within the context of contemplative training? We know that emotions last for seconds, that moods last for, say, a day, and that temperament is something that is forged over the years. So if we want to change, obviously we need to first act on the emotions, and this will help to change our moods, which will eventually stabilize as a modified temperament. In other words, we must start by working with the instantaneous events that take place in our mind. As we say, if we take care of the minutes, the hours will take care of themselves.

"How do we proceed in terms of firsthand experience? The refractory period and all that will be a bit abstract for someone who wants to deal with his or her emotions right now. So one of the key points has to do with the way the chaining of thoughts occurs, the way one thought leads to another.

"My teacher told me a story about a former warrior chief in eastern Tibet who had forsaken all his martial and worldly activities and gone to a cave to meditate. He stayed there for a few years. One day a lot of pigeons alighted in front of his cave and he gave them some grain. But as he was watching, the host of pigeons reminded him of the legions of warriors he had had under his command, and that thought made him remember his expeditions—and he again grew angry thinking about his former enemies. These recollections soon invaded his mind, and he went down in the valley, found his former companions, and went to war again!

"That exemplifies how a small thought can grow into a full-fledged obsession, like a tiny white cloud that swells into a mighty dark cloud crisscrossed with lightning. How can you deal with that?

"When we speak of meditation, the word used in Tibetan really means 'familiarization.' We need to familiarize ourselves with a new way of dealing with the arising of thoughts. At the beginning when a thought of anger, desire, or jealousy arises, we are not prepared for it. So within seconds, that thought has given rise to a second and a third thought, and soon our mental landscape becomes invaded by thoughts that solidify our anger or jealousy—and then it's too late. Just as when a spark of fire has set a whole forest on fire, we are in trouble.

"The basic way to intervene has been called 'staring back' at a thought. When a thought arises, we need to watch it and look back at its source. We need to investigate the nature of that thought that seems so solid. As we stare at it, its apparent solidity will melt away and that thought will vanish without giving birth to a chain of thoughts. The point is not to try to block the arising of thoughts—this is not possible anyway—but not to let them invade our mind. We need to do this again and again because we are not used to dealing with thoughts in that way. We are like a sheet of paper that has been rolled for a long time. If we try to flatten it down on the table, it will roll again the moment we lift our hands. This is where training takes place.

"One may wonder what people do in retreats, sitting for eight hours a day. They do precisely that: They familiarize themselves with a new way of dealing with the arising of thoughts. When you start getting used to recognizing thoughts as they arise, it is like rapidly spotting someone you know in a crowd. When a powerful thought of strong attraction or anger arises that you know is bound to lead to a proliferation of thoughts, now you recognize it: 'Oh, that thought is coming.' That's a first step. That helps a lot to avoid being overwhelmed by this thought.

"When you have got used to that, the process of dealing with thoughts becomes much more natural. You don't have to struggle and apply specific antidotes to each negative thought, because you know how to let them vanish without leaving any trace. The thoughts untie themselves. The example given is that of a snake. If it happens that it has made a knot with its body, it can undo that knot effortlessly, without needing any outer help. Finally a time will come when thoughts come and go like a bird passing through the sky, without leaving a trace. The other example given is that of a thief coming into an empty house. There is nothing to lose for the owner and nothing to gain for the thief.

"This is an experience of freedom. You don't simply become apathetic, like a vegetable, but you have gained mastery over your thoughts. They can't lead you by the nose anymore. This can only happen through sustained training and genuine experience.

"This is also how you can gradually develop certain qualities that will become a second nature, a new temperament. Let's take an example about compassion. There was a great nineteenth-century hermit called Patrul Rinpoche. Once he told one of his disciples to go to a cave and meditate for six months, thinking of nothing else but compassion. In the beginning the feeling of compassion for all beings is bound to be contrived, artificial. Then, gradually, the mind becomes permeated with compassion; it remains in one's mind without requiring any effort.

"After six months had gone by, the meditator was sitting at the opening of his cave and saw a lone rider down in the valley, singing. The yogi had some kind of clear premonition, a strong feeling, that the man was going to die within a week. Then the contrast between the sight of that man joyfully singing and the sudden intuition the yogi had made him boundlessly sad about conditioned existence, what Buddhists call *samsara.* At that, a genuine, overwhelming compassion pervaded his mind and never left it again. It had become second nature, the true meaning of meditation. Seeing the man was the trigger, but what was essential was the prior familiarization. The incident would not have had the same effect if he had not spent six months soaking himself in compassion.

"We are talking about how to help society. If we aspire to contribute something to our society—to achieve a new vision of things—we need to begin with ourselves. We need to decide to transform ourselves, and that can come only through training, not through fleeting ideas. That's the contribution that can come from Buddhist practice."

Throughout Matthieu's speech, the Dalai Lama leaned forward intently. Then, taking his glasses off, with a completely sincere tone, he said, "Very good, wonderful."

Paul Ekman, too, had been listening with rapt concentration.

Enslaved by Emotion

The Venerable Amchok Rinpoche spoke very softly from his seat behind the Dalai Lama: "To what extent might destructive emotions also be strengthened by reasoning, in the same way that positive or constructive emotions might be strengthened?"

Richard Davidson responded, "I think that there is a class of destructive emotions that arise spontaneously, as His Holiness described. The emotion arises, to use Paul Ekman's term, with a long refractory period; once the emotion is triggered, it takes over. There is some evidence to suggest that those emotions are associated with unconstrained, or less constrained, activation of structures like the amygdala that are interconnected with the frontal cortex."

Such impulsive emotions are weakened by reasoning, rather than strengthened by it, Richie argued: "Very active reasoning will activate the frontal cortex and inhibit the amygdala. And so, according to this neuroscience understanding, the very act of reasoning should actually reduce this particular type of destructive emotion. That's not to say that there aren't some destructive emotions that may be strengthened by reason. There probably are. But the class of destructive emotions that arise very strongly, with spontaneity in the moment, would probably be counteracted by reasoning."

Paul Ekman was on the edge of his seat, waiting to jump in. "My question is about the term 'reasoning.' In the example I gave yesterday of my own experience in the grip of emotion, I had a lot of thoughts: 'Is she out with another man? Has she been hit by a car?' You could say they were unreasonable thoughts, but I don't think there was an absence of the use of cognitive abilities—which I presume means the frontal lobes."

Richie disagreed. "I think your thoughts in that case, Paul, were driven by the emotion, rather than the thoughts driving or regulating the emotion. Your thoughts were consequences of the emotion."

"I was enslaved by the emotion," said Paul.

"We're talking about using thought to regulate the emotion in a more intentional and voluntary way," Richie said. "Your thoughts in that case weren't intentional. They were arising spontaneously as a consequence of the emotion. It was only when you tried to override the emotion, when you had some distance from the event, that you began to cultivate more intentional thoughts that suppressed the anger."

"I think it's more complicated," Paul answered, "because intermixed with all of that was the deliberate awareness and effort that I should be careful not to act on these thoughts and feelings. That's another kind of thought. I'm worried about the level of precision we can gain when we can say that the good kind of reasoning, that is not enslaved, involves the frontal lobe. And that other kinds of conscious reasoning that are not voluntary, but directed by emotion, do not involve that part of the brain at all."

"Patients with frontal lobe damage," Richie pointed out, "cannot voluntarily direct their thoughts. That is the crucial difference."[2]

The Dalai Lama jumped in. "From the Buddhist point of view also there are different kinds of reasoning. Some are valid and others are not. For example, the reasoning involved with enhancing compassion is grounded in valid experience or some valid observations. But there are other forms of reasoning that can give rise to a greater degree of anger. You may think that someone has done something to you unfairly, which may not be the case, and then you start pondering on it. It's a kind of reasoning, but it doesn't really have a sound basis, and the extent to which it supports the emotion is also not very great.

"Am I right in thinking, Paul, that you are suggesting that it may be too simplistic to associate valid reasoning with the frontal lobe activity and other kinds of reasoning elsewhere?"

"Yes," said Paul.

"Yes," Richie echoed. "And that's not what I wish to imply. In the grip of unwholesome reasoning, one can plan to commit some unethical or violent action, thinking it through and working out all the details in one's mind in a very premeditated way. That also involves the frontal lobes in a very unwholesome way. So I don't mean to suggest that any activity in the frontal lobes is necessarily going to be wholesome. That's not the case at all."

While this hinted at a more direct reply to Amchok Rinpoche's original question about the deliberate ideological cultivation of destructive emotions such as hatred, we left the fuller implications unexplored. As the daily news affirms, there is an abundance of unwholesome application of the frontal lobes, as a variety of poisonous pedagogies teach the people of one group to hate those of another. But at this point our focus shifted to remedies.

Educating the Heart

I took us back to an earlier comment made by the Dalai Lama. "This gets back to His Holiness's point, that we need to have a very sophisticated understanding of the complexities of destructive emotions if we are going to be skillful in finding remedies for them—particularly when it comes to the question of how to educate people to overcome them. Matthieu laid out a model, from Buddhist training, of first making an effort to bring to mind a positive state, such as compassion, and then repeating it so that it becomes familiar, a habit, at which point it becomes stable. That seems to suggest a general model for how we might begin to change these processes and help people get more control over destructive emotions.

"That's something I know we're very interested in, Your Holiness," I added, hoping to get us focused on practical applications—ways to help people overcome their destructive emotions.

Mark Greenberg spoke up. "I wanted to make a point and then direct a question to Richie. This is telling us that we're not just interested in developing reasoning, but we're also interested in educating the heart. There are two fundamental processes here. Both need to be engendered. The question, then, is, do you think if we, as adults, were to promote lovingkindness through training, that this might also affect the recovery period from the negative emotions?"

"Or how strongly you felt them, or how often?" I added.

I knew that Richie would have answered the question in the affirmative, but Matthieu jumped in and took our thoughts in another direction. "In a study of children recovering from trauma following a catastrophe, they found that there was a significant difference in the recovery time of children in Bangladesh who were from Buddhist communities. Children who were raised with Buddhist values recovered significantly faster from the calamity and had much less trauma than children from other cultural backgrounds. It seems due to the way they are educated, with the idea of cultivating gentleness.

"In Tibetan society, for instance, it is extremely rare to see children deliberately trampling insects. I remember traveling in France with a group of Tibetan monks in a bus, and the driver killed a bee at one point. The Tibetans were really shocked. The study of children in Bangladesh found this compassionate attitude correlates with a better faculty for recovering from stress and trauma."

The Dalai Lama wanted to add something to Matthieu's story of the monk who meditated on compassion for six months. "From the Buddhist point of view, the success of his meditation on compassion depended on the purification of negativity and the enhancement of positive qualities, of virtues. The meditator was not simply repeating 'compassion' like a mantra every hour, every second—'compassion, compassion, compassion.' That is not the process of familiarization. The process rather involves directing every conscious thought toward the goal of cultivating compassion so that whatever activity the individual engages in, it is always from that orientation. There is a kind of single-pointed dedication. This is what gave rise to his experience."

Matthieu elaborated, "These practices are sometimes quite difficult. In the sutras, it explains how to do that in every single gesture. When getting up, one thinks, 'May I get up to deliver all sentient beings from suffering.' When tying one's belt, one thinks, 'May I cultivate the belt of mindfulness.' When coming down the steps, 'May I go down again to take beings from suffering.' When opening a door, 'May the door of liberation be opened for all sentient beings.' When closing it, 'May the door of suffering be closed for sentient beings.' In that way, every instant is filled with the thought of compassion. Compassion is bound to become part of your mind stream."

"I think Matthieu's description of the training makes a tremendous amount of sense from a neuroscience perspective," Richie Davidson said. "We can begin to think about how this kind of training, where every action is associated with the thought of cultivating compassion, actually changes the brain. There's every reason to believe that a training so profound and systematic can affect our brain in some way. We can begin to specify what brain regions and which connections may be strengthened to facilitate recovering quickly from a trauma of the sort Matthieu describes; there is research that is a model for how to understand the benefits of this type of training. But nothing like this has ever been approached scientifically, simply because the types of intervention we have dealt with in the West are at nursery-school level compared to what Matthieu is describing."

Forty Hours for Compassion

Throughout this discussion, Paul had been nodding in agreement. Now he asked, "What if the governor of California were to say to you, Richie, or to you, Your Holiness, 'I'll give you forty hours to train all the prison guards if you think as a result they'll be more humane, more compassionate'? To get forty hours would be an incredible achievement, but it is possible. I know of places where government officials have been willing to grant that much time. Of course, that time is short compared to the thousands of hours you're talking about. If we're to change anything about how people behave, is there anything that could actually be achieved in those forty hours?"

"I have a story about that," Matthieu replied. "It's about someone who was teaching meditation in a prison. It was not specifically Buddhist, just mind relaxation. He was dealing with hardened criminals, people who were already in for life and who continued to kill each other while in prison. One of them, a gang leader, began this training just because it was something new to try. He said at one point in that training—it happened in a very dramatic way—that it was as if a wall had suddenly collapsed. He realized that until then, he had been functioning only in terms of hate.

"Previously all his relations with others were about hate and domination, and that suddenly disappeared. That says a lot about plasticity, that trying certain new ideas doesn't necessarily need thousands of hours. The gang leader tried his best to go along with that new feeling, tried to share it with a few other people who were training with him. Sadly, after one year, he was himself killed in the prison, but for the last year of his life he functioned in a completely different way."

"Does that satisfy you?" I asked Paul.

"No," he said. "I'm still waiting to hear from Richie and from His Holiness."

The Dalai Lama gave him an answer: "There is a classic meditative procedure in Tibetan Buddhism for cultivating compassion, called 'exchange of self for others,' where you imagine putting yourself in the place of the victim. You switch positions."

"Do you think implementing this could have the same benefit for the guards?" Paul asked the Dalai Lama.

"Of course it will be a good learning experience," he replied.

Compassion Is Not Intrinsically Religious

Mark Greenberg suggested that Paul broaden the question beyond his concern with prisons. "What if we did lovingkindness training, or some kind of meditation training, with teachers as a way of making them care for their students more? Of course, there would be differences in their ability to accept such training. The big question then is, for those who would resist it or find it too awkward, could we find ways to do it that would be so secular they would find it acceptable? That's a major question for us in our work with teachers, because many teachers don't have much compassion for their students."

The Dalai Lama made an emphatic gesture, pointing with his finger as though hitting a nail on the head. "That's a key point. The cultivation of lovingkindness and compassion is not intrinsically a religious endeavor. It has really a much more general pertinence and general applicability. You don't have to be religious or buy into a religious doctrine to do it. This is why I think it is important to develop techniques that are secular and not simply religious in orientation."

"Is forty hours enough time for this kind of training?" Paul asked again.

"I think that forty hours would be enough," Matthieu assured him. "People rarely think about what others are really feeling. Doing this would be starting something that's bound to continue. If people spent that much time focusing on this way of perceiving things, it could make a huge difference."

I wanted to draw the Dalai Lama into focusing on what might be included in such a program. So I turned to him and said, "Richie suggested that if people, even prison guards, actually cultivated lovingkindness, it would change the way they experienced destructive emotions. They would recover more quickly, and they would be more prone to positive emotions. Then there's the question of secular applications of the many, many skillful means for cultivating positive ways of being found in Tibetan Buddhism. Leaving Buddhism aside, can you think of others that might be modified for the general population and that might have practical applications for helping people in this way?"

The Dalai Lama was particularly animated as he replied, "I have addressed the issue of secular and moral ethics at quite some length. The problem is, in terms of public awareness, the term 'ethics' seems almost a luxury. If we get around to it, that would be fine, but in the meantime, things like education and health are not considered luxuries; they are imperatives. For example, in science and medical research, there is an enormous amount of investigation being done on exactly what type of nutrition is needed for full brain development in children, what type of exercise they should be getting as they are growing, and so forth.

"Health is never considered to be a luxury. And likewise education is not considered in our society to be a luxury—it, too, is an imperative. Yet when we look at the education system itself, what children are getting is just information. They are learning how to read, and getting more and more information that will enable them to eventually get a job.

"But where is the education and research going into really developing the mind? People say, 'Oh that would be nice, but it does not have the imperative urgency connected to education or health.' So we need another term, not 'moral ethics,' not 'secular ethics,' but something like 'peaceful society' or 'social flourishing' or 'human flourishing'—something that does not have an ethical or anything like a religious connotation. Maybe instead of religious or ethical studies, it would fit better in social sciences or something like that, so it would be secularized.

"The aim is to ask what can we do from medical or scientific research to bring about greater social well-being: a flourishing of peace, harmony, a sense of well-being in individuals and the society as a whole. This should become an imperative just like health and education. Then under that umbrella we could raise questions about exactly how children should be educated, not just to learn mathematics and so forth but to be able to counteract destructive emotions and cultivate wholesome or positive emotions."

"Well, we have good news for you," I told him. "Tomorrow Mark Greenberg will describe exactly that program."

"Which we call social and emotional learning," Mark added.

The Dalai Lama responded with delight at this name, saying, "Oh, that's good, isn't it?" Then he added, "This should be of universal applicability. Just as, for example, if you get an education in Beijing, or anywhere in the world, you study mathematics. It's not considered Western or Chinese—it's universal. In a similar fashion, social and emotional learning should be considered everywhere to be just as imperative as standard science, mathematics, reading, and writing."

"Your Holiness," I told him, "it is actually becoming an international movement, not just in the United States but in other countries—Israel, Korea, the Netherlands, to name a few."

"This is a good reason why Jeanne Tsai and I are presenting together tomorrow," Mark added. "If we think about this as global or universal, we have to consider how culture interacts with it."

An Adult Education Program

Paul, quite energized today, was persistent in keeping us on a particular track. "Mark will provide us a good grounding for children, but the world is in a great deal of trouble right now because of adults. I hope we can spend some time designing a curriculum for adult education. If we had such a curriculum, I am quite confident we could get it tried, and we might even be able to get some support to show its efficacy. You couldn't assemble a better group than you have sitting in this room to come up with that curriculum."

Gesturing toward the Dalai Lama, I said, "Could we turn to one consultant right here?"

"Adults have already gotten a little crooked," the Dalai Lama replied. "They are like an old gnarled tree as opposed to a nice young sapling that is malleable. When you get to be an old geezer it's harder to fix," he said with a laugh. Then he continued, "Of course, this is not at all to discourage the challenge, because it does need to be done. We need to do it as well as we can, but it will be a greater challenge. But if ten people get some benefit, or even one, it's worth it—certainly no harm in trying."

"So," I asked him, "what would you suggest?"

"I don't know, I don't know," he replied thoughtfully. But he had begun to ponder the question.

Secularizing Buddhist Practice

Mark Greenberg was inspired by Paul's suggestion. "I want to go forward with what Paul's talking about," he said. "In the secular training we might do with adults, we have already talked about the idea of putting ourselves in the position of the other. I am wondering if there's a way of secularizing your discussion of the chaining of emotion," he said, turning to Matthieu, who had told the story of the warrior and the pigeons.

"That seems to me pretty secular," Matthieu replied. "There isn't an implied belief in any aspect of faith. There is a tradition that's been used and developed over thousands of years of contemplative experience, but you could explain it in a simpler way. In itself, it doesn't require a particular religious position or even a philosophy. It's just very pragmatic."

That brought to mind the work of Jon Kabat-Zinn at the University of Massachusetts Medical Center in Worcester.[3] Using an adaptation of mindfulness meditation, which trains people to carefully observe their moment-to-moment thoughts and feelings without reactivity, Kabat-Zinn had helped medical patients find peace of mind, which eased their physical pain, suffering, and symptoms. I said, "There are applications of mindfulness from Buddhism that are used in hospitals. Buddhism is never mentioned. It's just for patients' own good—and they get very enthusiastic about it in that situation.

"Likewise with empathy. In the treatment of criminals who have molested children, the first step is to have them reenact the crime from the child's point of view, because it's the lack of empathy that allowed them to do it in the first place. That's akin to the meditation practice of taking the position of the other person."

Matthieu commented of one of the lamas observing our meeting, "Sogyal Rinpoche has been involved in some very successful programs with dying people that implement the consequences of Buddhist practice without necessarily bringing in Buddhist ideas." In his popular work *The Tibetan Book of Living and Dying,* Sogyal Rinpoche introduced to the West a traditional Tibetan approach to helping a dying person and his or her loved ones with the spiritual and emotional dimensions of confronting death.[4]

"In Buddhist practice," Richie observed, "according to my limited understanding, a certain level of concentration is often cultivated before some other practices are introduced. Matthieu's example of a person learning to associate every action with thoughts of compassion and lovingkindness is an extraordinarily difficult thing for most people to do, because they are at kindergarten level in their concentration and attentional abilities. Your Holiness, what would you counsel about an adult curriculum for individuals who don't have a very well cultivated ability to concentrate?"

Matthieu remarked: "There is no point trying to do that kind of training for hours at the beginning. It is better to have short repeated sessions, like exercises. You could have a three-minute exercise going around your house and thinking that way. That gives you a taste for it. Or you could do it just ten minutes a day at the beginning."

How Our Emotions Create the Problem

The Dalai Lama now spoke up. "I would like to present something inspired by the traditional Buddhist concept of the Four Noble Truths, but brought into the secular arena. It's not simply a technique like that of thinking a particular thought each time you open a door and so forth. It is much more analytical and cogitative.

"It's looking first of all at the tremendous problems plaguing our society today. As you pointed out, Paul, there's a lot of suffering. But instead of looking for all the causes outside ourselves, economics and so forth, let's agree we all have destructive emotions and then ask ourselves what the nature of these destructive emotions is—really investigate them, analyze them, and look at their effects. What impact do our destructive emotions—hatred, prejudice, and so forth—have on the society as a whole? What role are they playing in the tremendous problems and sufferings that society is experiencing right now?

"Once one sees by careful analysis the relationship between the internal problems and the external problems we are experiencing here, that inspires one to raise further questions. How about plasticity—mental plasticity? Are these destructive emotions to which we are subject at all malleable? Can we diminish them? If we were to diminish them, what kind of impact would that have on society as a whole and on the myriad problems that society is experiencing?

"Once we raise that question, if you come up with a hypothesis that we are not completely hardwired, that our brains and minds are plastic, with a possibility for growth and transformation and for diminishing these destructive emotions, then we can ask how we might go about doing that. One possible strand of methods for destructive emotions might very well be what Matthieu has brought out here, but we would have a much broader context for understanding and investigation.

"That's exactly the kind of investigation and education that should be brought into the school system. Little children see all the problems out there, but where are they ever educated to relate their own emotions to the problems that are besetting society? Where is the education to help them attenuate their own negative emotions and cultivate positive emotions?

"There is so much research that has already been done in terms of physical health. Everybody in this room has heard the importance of exercise, nutrition, and so forth. But there is not just one technique for getting exercise. You can go to a gym, you can play sports—there are all kinds of things that emerge as a response to an understanding that is derived from investigation."

Alan commented, "Why would people very likely not take Matthieu's technique, for example, so seriously? They might pick it up, try it, say 'That doesn't work,' and move on to something else. Why? Because in most cases that practice is not embedded in a whole field of understanding that makes such a practice an imperative and not a luxury."

The Venerable Kusalacitto weighed in with a report on programs in his own country, Thailand. There for centuries education had been done in the temples, where as a matter of course positive qualities were cultivated. But in the last century secular and religious education had been separated, and many Thai monks were worried that children no longer received the character-building lessons. So about thirty years ago they started offering summer camps where children learned, for instance, how to meditate and how to think about living an ethical social life. In one game, each child would write down on a piece of paper things they wanted to give up, like anger, delusion, and envy, and put the paper in a bowl to leave behind symbolically instead of taking it home.

Seeing that their children returned after a month at camp more positive in their emotions, many parents said they wanted to experience the same thing. So the monks started a short-term adult camp, where they started on Friday evening and finished Sunday afternoon—about forty hours altogether. The adults learned the same things as the children, and many of them were very satisfied when they finished the course. The *bhante* finished, "Maybe this information could be useful when we're thinking about how to formulate the curriculum for a short course."

We then broke for tea. During the break, the enthusiasm among participants—especially Richie, Mark, and Paul—for adult education in the emotions was palpable. There were animated conversations about designing a program to implement these ideas and about demonstrating that it worked by evaluating it with behavioral and biological measures.

A Gym for Emotional Skills

After tea, I started our session again by acknowledging, "Something has been kindled here—a resolve among us, a serious interest in implementing the kind of program His Holiness has been talking about. Let's just continue."

Paul took up the topic by proposing that there were some excellent psychological techniques for increasing interpersonal skills and competencies such as empathy, and that additional ones should be drawn from Buddhist methods. "We should put in the best from both vantage points. I also think the training must be alive, interactive. It has to be experiential, not didactic."

The Dalai Lama nodded in agreement and listened intently as Paul went on. "I think that in the last few hours, I've gained some of Richie's optimism. I now believe that if we make a serious effort, we will succeed in making a change in people. Then we might be overwhelmed with the demand because there is a hunger. It is the same hunger that motivates the world's interest in you, Your Holiness. There is a hunger for being able to change our inner lives and how we deal with others.

"There are all kinds of crazy things that are offered, but nothing, I believe, that's well planned and combines the best of West and East. I wish we would spend a significant portion of our meeting getting a concrete, specific lesson plan. I keep saying it should be a lesson plan for adults, partly because I'm an adult, but partly because it is the adults in the positions of power who are making bad and often cruel decisions."

Richie added, "One of the things we were also talking about during the break, Your Holiness, is combining the development of this kind of curriculum with assessment of changes in behavior and the brain. We should actually be able to demonstrate that such a curriculum, if successful, could change the brain, as well as behavior, for the better. Evidence of that sort could be very powerful, in the same way that there is evidence for exercise helping the heart."

Paul piped up, "Emotional-skills gymnasiums offered all over the place!" As the laughter died down, he added, "Seriously! People would seek it out if they knew it was a possibility."

"In Tibet it's called a monastery," Alan deadpanned.

Paul continued, "You could involve the people who are buying *The Art of Happiness* and *Emotional Intelligence.* There are huge numbers of people who hunger for more than just reading. Reading is just the first step; now we have to provide something that they can do."

Owen had an idea. "To respond to His Holiness's challenge to us to come up with a term for this, I want to suggest the ancient Greek term *eudaimonia,* which Augustine also used. It doesn't have an intrinsically religious connotation. It's as old as the hills, but it is exactly what we're talking about: human flourishing. Which is what we all want and have always been wanting, though our education has not served us well in this."

"Is there a place called a eudaimonium?" I asked, joking. "Like the gymnasium?"

"Going back to Richie's point," Paul said, "when you first start playing tennis, you don't get many balls over the net. But as you learn, there are changes in your brain that are the basis of the skills that allow you to get the balls over the net. That is the model: We need to become emotional tennis players. We need to have more emotional skills. I don't know if this is the time to get specific about that curriculum . . ."

"Take a shot," I encouraged him.

"I have three things in mind," Paul ventured. "First, we have to teach people to be more sensitive to the subtle signs of emotions in others, in their faces, their voices, and posture. We have the techniques to do that now, and we know that it's very learnable. Many people aren't very good at it, but anybody can become quite good at it in a couple of hours.

"Second, we have to give people training in the internal sensations of emotion, so that they become more aware when emotions are beginning. The emotions physically feel different from each other, and you can educate people about bodily sensations. It's a little harder, but it's a kind of self-awareness. There are acting techniques that we can utilize to help people learn to pay attention to this."

"Mindfulness of bodily sensations does the same," I pointed out.

"The third," Paul continued, "is really borrowing from the late professor Norman Kagan, who developed a program called Interpersonal Process Recall.[5] You take two people—often a husband and wife, but any two people who are already engaged with each other, who care about each other. You videotape them while they try to settle a conflict. After they have settled this conflict and come to a single agreement—that's the goal—then each of them sits with an interlocutor, someone who goes over the videotape and asks them to unpack and talk about the feelings they were having that they didn't say: the responses to the other person, what was going on when they felt they were losing control. This is done with each person separately. Then they're brought back to have the conversation again.

"I'm not saying do it in exactly this way. But the nub of it is to give people practice in dealing with emotional conflict repeatedly, with coaches who can help them better understand the process and practice new ways of handling it. This program was widely used, actually, with prison guards in a couple of states."

Jeanne Tsai, who would present the next day, had been listening carefully. Now she spoke up. "A lot of the things we're proposing here are techniques that are used in Western psychotherapy now. For example, Norman Kagan's techniques have been used with couples who are having problems in their relationships. We can also borrow from cognitive behavioral therapies. Many people don't realize how their thoughts are linked to their emotions, resulting in particular behaviors. The key is to think about using these psychotherapy techniques with people who don't have psychological disorders, who perceive themselves as not having any problems, but who would benefit from these techniques as well."

"In Tibet it is a little different from modern Western self-perception," Alan pointed out. "From the Buddhist perspective, we're all 'sick.' That's why we suffer."

The Business Case for Emotional Education

"I find a problem with addressing this to adults, because it's very difficult to reach them," Matthieu said. "I don't mean that a generation should be sacrificed, but it's obvious that if we started with the school system, others could see its usefulness. Then we could have the equivalent of adult schools that derive or emerge from the children's programs. Otherwise, how do you reach adults except through the media?"

Mark said, "Matthieu raises an important question, and maybe, Dan, you can speak to it. What benefits might industry see in having more emotionally intelligent workers? One of the things we learn with children—it's true of myself, too—is that repeated practice is a necessity; people cannot learn from short instances alone. And the practice has to take place daily, or at least regularly, and there has to be some important encouragement to engage in it. Because it is very hard to change, weekend workshops may have limited use. Often that is the problem with one hour of psychotherapy a week.

"That's where we can learn a lot from the Buddhist use of repeated practice. Knowing that, how do we build a model that includes repeated practice? I started thinking about industry, for example, because people come to work every morning."

"As it turns out," I answered, "there is a very good business case for what His Holiness is suggesting. It's good for the bottom line."

"What's that?" the Dalai Lama asked about the unfamiliar phrase "bottom line."

"Profit," explained Alan.

"This may be a point of leverage," I continued, drawing on data from my books *Working with Emotional Intelligence* and *Primal Leadership,* in which I had analyzed extensive findings showing that productivity in workers and effectiveness in leaders were associated with emotional intelligence.[6] "For example, if you take salespeople, some might sell a million dollars' worth a year and some a hundred thousand. When you compare the stars with those who are average, what separates them? It turns out that it isn't technical skill or intelligence. It's how well they manage their own feelings—particularly the afflictive emotions—how motivated they are, how persistent they are, and how well they handle relationships. Just what you're suggesting, Paul—how sensitive they are to how other people are feeling, how smoothly they interact, and so on. That's what makes the difference—and that's the very domain we're talking about.

"You can see the same thing in leaders who are extremely successful. For example, a global company has presidents of different divisions, and some of those divisions are more profitable than expected, some less profitable. When you look at the leaders of the divisions, you find the same difference: How well they handle their own emotions and their relationships matters for business results. The ones who can't manage their anger and who blow up at people make those who work for them very anxious; they don't do as well in terms of the performance of their division."

"But," the Dalai Lama asked me, "wouldn't you agree that those who are more aggressive in their work seem to be more successful?"

"Aggressive in what sense?"

"Arrogant, assertive."

"It turns out not to be true."

"In the long run," the Dalai Lama replied, "I entirely agree. To be honest, sincere—that person may be more successful in the long run. But the other may do well just temporarily . . ."

To that point, I answered, "There are studies that show how a leader's emotional style affects the emotional climate of the people who work for him or her. If the emotional climate is positive, profits go up because people give their best effort. If people don't like the boss, if they feel bad when they're working, then it harms the company because people just do a good-enough job—not their best. The leaders whose styles are most positive are inspiring. They can articulate shared values for what they're doing that employees find meaningful or compelling, then keep reminding them of that mission. Those leaders create a positive climate and see a very positive outcome.

"Likewise, leaders who spend time making relationships harmonious among people, getting to know them, have a very positive effect. The same is true for leaders who take a person aside and ask, 'What do you want for your life, your career? How can I help you develop the way you want to?' Leaders who are collaborative, who make decisions by listening to what everybody thinks, are also very positive in their impact.

"But the leader who is coercive, who says, 'Do it because I say so,' has a bad effect on the climate. The arrogant leader can be effective in narrow situations, when there is a real emergency and it's important to follow orders. But if that's the only way you lead, it's very negative.

"So in industry, as you were suggesting, Mark, there's a strong rationale for introducing this kind of curriculum. How to help people change in this way in a business setting has also been studied, and it's very much like Matthieu's model. You can't do it in a seminar. You can't do it in just a weekend, because you have to help people change some basic habits—and that takes using on-the-job situations as continual learning opportunities. If a boss has a bad temper but wants to improve, he has to practice each day in every situation he can, over many months; then he changes."

New Problems, New Remedies

As the Dalai Lama later told me, he was quite satisfied that most of the group seemed to agree on the importance of developing a practical program. But he also felt cautious. He had too often seen groups feel good about plans that were never implemented. Then, too, he wondered if what this small group felt was so important would be seen as interesting, or even relevant, by the wider world.

So the Dalai Lama raised a strategic concern. He noted that people readily agreed on the urgent need to grapple with problems such as poverty and disease. But once a society became more prosperous and healthy, another level of problems emerged, one where the pall of destructive emotions was a cause. At that point, the answer lay in helping people with their mental states, he said, noting, "That way we can build a better world, a better family for every individual. But the appeal of this may be very limited. We've gathered a few individuals here from the universities from all sorts of backgrounds, but you're all here because you have some kind of interest in this.

"But I want to know whether your recognition of the need for a whole mission of change, and also the possibility of developing some kind of training, is a reflection of a wider recognition in the society, particularly in the university, among your colleagues. Or are we representative of a very small minority here? Otherwise it's like an echo in this one room."

"My own view," Richie responded, "is that it's broader than just this room. For example, the American Psychological Association, which is the largest organization of psychologists in the world, about forty-five thousand psychologists, has launched an initiative called Positive Psychology to focus on human flourishing. And they've used the word 'flourishing.' They say that we have spent too much time focusing on negative traits and we now need to turn our attention to positive traits. I think there is some recognition in the academic community that the time is ripe to turn our attention to these things."

The Dalai Lama nodded, satisfied.

Paul added, "I believe it's more than in the academic community. It's in the business community, it's in the medical community. It's not that there's a recognition that we can learn something from Buddhist practice—it's a recognition that we're not solving the problem. That's the recognition, and it is very widespread."

"Yes, that's it," the Dalai Lama said, emphatic.

A Consensus on What's Wrong

"I'd add a longer-term perspective," Mark Greenberg said. "The breakdown of religious practice for many people and the breakdown of neighborhoods in many cultures, not just in America, have caused a fragmentation that has led to many aspects of violence. I often have to respond to the media regarding violence. The first question is always 'What do we do about these violent children?' The next question always comes to the broader issue: 'What's wrong with our society?' Why are we operating without the right kind of social controls, as well as the right kind of inner development?"

"What do you mean by 'social control'?" I asked. With a totalitarian spin, that phrase could be ominous.

"The amount of violence in the media is an example of a lack of social control in America," Mark answered. "Lack of gun regulation, of course, is another one. We know that causes a much higher rate of violence in our society than in many other societies."

The Dalai Lama observed that if our discussion reflected a wider recognition within society and within many disciplines, "then wouldn't it be beneficial, instead of us trying to map out the curriculum or framework, to take it further by drawing in a wider number of people? And include them as colleagues in dialogue, and then try to flesh out the specifics? Then we could introduce a very clear, practical plan or proposal to send to some department of a certain government, and maybe even the United Nations as well."

Francisco Varela entered the discussion with a different perspective. "Your Holiness, you've heard the opinion of some of my friends here, who are all from the United States, and it may not be completely universal. The United States is a very peculiar culture. The situation in my country now, France, is not quite like that. France has centuries of placing enormous importance on education that is oriented to rational performance, in the truly Western style of reason over emotion. Children have a fantastic education but are extremely focused on intellectual performance. To start moving that white elephant, as it were, is going to take a long time, and there is no public awareness or recognition of the need for any form of learning in parallel to deal with one's emotions and relationships. This would be, for France, a pioneering idea.

"Although everybody acknowledges that social violence is a problem and there is currently a revision of the educational system going on because of that, it is a revision within the traditional parameters. There are little things here and there, but I want to be a little less optimistic about our current situation."

The Dalai Lama agreed that European countries such as France might be more resistant to trying such a novel educational approach. But he felt that America, being so diverse and so much younger a country, might be more open-minded, offering a laboratory for experimentation, and that if there was some success, European countries might eventually follow.

The key point, he felt, was to take action. He had seen too many other such discussions raise enthusiasm about good works, only to have people's resolve later dissipate. So he cautioned, "It is important for us to make sure that the conversations we have here don't remain simply as expressions of opinions or aspirations, but rather to try and implement them practically. Somebody has to change how things are implemented, so how do we reach there with, as we say, warm heart? The conversation itself is good karma, but it has to go beyond our accumulation of good karma to be implemented into society."

Paul, responding to His Holiness's point, proposed a meeting to plan the curriculum we had been discussing. And, in fact, he took action: That meeting was held in Boston the next year, with an expanded group, to plan the program and its scientific evaluation.

Help for Natural Scatterbrains

Getting back to the content of the program, Matthieu suggested, "One point we would certainly add to Paul's three points is a short session of introspection. After all, the best thing we can do is to look in the mirror of the mind. Even a few minutes of that gives us a new perspective."

"We could do that in small but repeated doses over a period of twenty or forty hours," Paul agreed.

"How many people do three minutes of introspection a day, quietly?" Matthieu asked.

Owen, who was emerging as our resident skeptic, interjected a note of caution. "Just to make sure that we don't try to reinvent wheels that are already out there, we would need to look into what is being done already, at least in the area of moral education in public schools in the United States. The late Harvard psychologist Lawrence Kohlberg did important work on this, and many schools I know have applied his techniques. For example, young children in these schools get to play 'moral musical chairs,' which involves taking other people's perspectives. These schools try to run themselves as communities. It's like Dan's model: The principal and the teachers command respect but they still sit down with the students to make sure that everything is going okay. I would be interested to find out how much of this is out there.

"One reason for pessimism even in the United States is Mark's point about the lack of social controls. When Americans hear about things like 'ethical training' or 'emotional intelligence training,' they think you are imposing some kind of value system. But they don't recognize that there already is a value system imposed. We know, for the same reasons that we can't get gun control passed, that certain kinds of curricular reforms, despite being obviously good things, can be met with huge resistance unless they have the right name. So I like some of the ideas that have come up here."

"On that same note," Alan Wallace said, "roughly a hundred years ago William James published a marvelous little book, extremely readable, called *Talks to Teachers,* drawing from his principles of psychology and applying them to education.[7] One of the central themes is what he calls 'sustained voluntary attention.' He points out that some people seem to be naturally scatterbrained, whereas other people tend to be more collected, more able to pay attention.

"He elaborated, in fascinating ways, on the role of sustained attention in morality, in education, and in a myriad of other very important facets of human life. He said that an education system that could help train students to develop their ability for sustained voluntary attention would be the education system par excellence. In Buddhism this is called mindfulness or introspection, as well as *shamata* training, meditative quiescence. You have to cultivate both.

"In conversations that I had with a senior professor of education at Stanford who had done a lot of fieldwork in junior high schools, he said that a huge portion of classroom time was spent just getting the students to pay attention. A relatively small portion was spent actually teaching them something. James raised the possibility of this training in sustained attention, but he said, 'I don't know how.'

"Buddhism has a tremendous strength here—but such a training program doesn't have to be Buddhist. You don't have to talk about karma or the Four Noble Truths, or limit the practice to breath awareness, which ten-year-old kids won't do. That could be another area for ingenuity and research—thinking about ways, again in short sessions, of developing the ability for sustaining attention. Maybe it could be done with the body, with various activities. I think we would be finally, a hundred years later, responding to the challenge William James presented to us, and for which there has been no response in the Western education system. That's one more element in the curriculum."

Our day was drawing to an end, and, to wrap up, I turned to the Dalai Lama. "You've given us a challenge which we seem to be quite enthusiastic about. I think something will actually come of this, Your Holiness. I have been requested to ask you, if we actually go through with this program and want to have the seminar where we draw in a wider public, would you come?"

"Since the suggestion was made by me, I would definitely go." Then he added, "Of course, I don't have to be there. But if there is any possibility of my contribution there, I'm always ready to come and participate."

"We will keep all of this in mind when we plan," I assured him. "This has been a very fruitful session."

And with that the Dalai Lama stood and wished all a good night. As he left the session, the Dalai Lama was pleased by the group's enthusiasm for a practical program on helping people counter their destructive emotions. He thought of a Tibetan expression, that "his words had been sent out in the wind"—he had made his own wishes clear, whatever was to happen.

As for Richie, he told me how surprised he was that the day's discussion ended in a plan for action—but the prospect was appealing. And though the Dalai Lama did not know about it, he would have been pleased that after dinner, a group of the participants met to continue this day's discussion—planting the seeds of what was to become a program for helping adults, called Cultivating Emotional Balance.

Day Four: Mastering Emotional Skills

March 23, 2000

10

The Influence of Culture

In the mid-1960s, the young Paul Ekman visited Margaret Mead, one of the great anthropologists of the last century, to talk about the research he was about to undertake. Paul was about to travel to New Guinea to do research on facial expressions with a remote tribe, a people whose cultural integrity had not yet been contaminated by extensive contacts with outsiders, let alone modern media. Ekman was to bring them photographs of Westerners expressing basic emotions—fear, disgust, anger, sadness, surprise, and happiness—to see if members of the New Guinea tribe would recognize them.

Mead believed that, like customs and values, facial expressions varied from culture to culture, and was cool about Ekman's project. Behind her coolness, she later revealed in her autobiography, was a social agenda. Like many social scientists of her day, she promoted the overweening power of culture as a retort to racists of her time—from colonialists to fascists—who seized on supposed innate differences between peoples as "proof" that they were biologically inferior. By emphasizing the malleability of human nature, Mead and others argued that differences were not biologically determined but were due to conditions that could be altered and improved.

But, as the Dalai Lama has argued in *Ethics for the New Millennium,* the shared human condition—beginning with our common biology—makes brothers and sisters of us all, despite cultural differences. Indeed, as he had reported to us, Ekman's research provided powerful evidence for that common humanity: the New Guinea tribe members were able to recognize the emotions being expressed by a group of men and women whose culture and society were utterly different from their own.

In showing that the universality of emotional expressions points to a common biological heritage of mankind, Ekman joined the scientific agenda promoted by Darwin—whose work he started to read in earnest. As Ekman wrote in his recent commentary to Darwin's *The Expression of Emotions in Man and Animals,* "Social experience influences attitudes about emotion, creates display and feeling rules, develops and tunes the particular occasions which will most rapidly call forth an emotion." In other words, culture shapes what emotions we display when. But, he adds, "The expression of our emotions, the particular configurations of muscular movements, appear to be fixed, enabling understanding across generations, across cultures, and within cultures between strangers as well as intimates."

A maxim in social science holds, "In certain ways every person is like all other people, in certain ways like some other people, and in other ways like no other person." While Paul Ekman's research on facial expression has largely focused on the first level (the universals) and somewhat on the third (individual differences), the study of culture focuses on that middle level, where people of similar culture show distinctive commonalities in the human repertoire. Jeanne Tsai brought this perspective to bear on our discussion, sharing research she and others had done on culture and emotions.

The influence of culture on emotion has been a lifelong interest for Jeanne; it was the central focus of her studies and research as an undergraduate, in graduate school, and—at the time of our meeting—as an assistant professor at the University of Minnesota (she since has joined the psychology department at Stanford University). She brought to her study an insider's sensitivity; her parents, both university professors, were immigrants from Taiwan.

Jeanne's parents came to the United States as students in the physical sciences. Jeanne's first language was Taiwanese—her kindergarten teacher told her parents not to speak Taiwanese to her so that she would not acquire an accent. (The irony was not lost on Jeanne that—because English was her parents' second language—the better advice would have been for them to speak only Taiwanese to her, so she would learn her English from native speakers!)

Jeanne grew up in Pittsburgh, where few other Asian American families lived. Then the family moved to California, where Jeanne later attended Stanford for her undergraduate studies and Berkeley for her graduate studies. It was only after she moved to California, with its much larger Asian American population, that Jeanne began to realize that many of the things she believed and the ways she and her parents acted were related to her Asian upbringing.

More particularly, Jeanne began to see the many ways in which she felt—and feels—very Taiwanese. Among these were a sense of humility and loyalty, and a sensitive attunement to and concern for how others feel. The self-effacement that stems from these attitudes, Jeanne realized, often gets misread by European Americans as low self-esteem or lack of confidence. Such realizations spurred Jeanne's interest in the impact of culture on psychology, a topic she was able to explore at Stanford, where she found she could meld her scientific and personal interests.

By the time she did her senior thesis on differences in relationships between young and old in Chinese Americans and European Americans, the field of cultural psychology—which had an early heyday in the 1960s, then faded—was reviving. At the same time, her classmates were caught up in the identity politics of the late 1980s, with questions of what it meant to be Asian American very much on the minds of Jeanne and her friends. That led Jeanne to question the extent to which culture influences who we are and how we feel, think, and behave—in other words, as a psychologist, to incorporate culture into the scientific dialogue about human behavior.

Jeanne chose to do her graduate work at Berkeley so she could study with Robert Levenson, an eminent researcher who was beginning to explore how emotions vary across cultures, genders, and ages. The research Jeanne began then, and has since continued, was to be her subject this morning.

The Day Begins

In the opening moments while people were seating themselves, I asked the Dalai Lama in an aside, "Are you feeling better?" Like the weather, which was clearing, his cold was "better today," he said, but a lingering cough still bothered him throughout the day.

Although the monk in attendance kept the room spotlessly clean, with a care that showed his reverence, he wouldn't touch the materials that the scientists left on the table. By this morning the green tablecloth was strewn with papers, cameras, and the brain model lying in pink pieces, in addition to the usual recording gear. It was like a snapshot of debris left behind by the high energy that had built in the group the previous day and continued through our evening discussion, where more plans had been laid for the program to cultivate emotional balance.

To start us off, I returned to the analogy of weaving a rug. "Yesterday we continued to weave our design, and a pattern is emerging very clearly. Richie talked about the neurological basis of the afflictive emotions—what's going on in the brain during the experience of the Three Poisons, and how you can intervene in that process for the better. It is clear that brain science can't really speak to some issues of deep interest from a Buddhist perspective, such as whether or not consciousness is solely in the brain. But it has much to say about what we all can do to benefit our emotional lives. Some key principles were described, one of which is that experience and learning shape the brain, so that we can design training that will allow people to better handle these destructive emotions."

Turning to the Dalai Lama, I added, "Our afternoon discussion, I thought, was quite animated. There was lots of energy around the idea of creating an action plan to give people practical methods to put into practice the principles of the secular ethics that you yourself have been describing. This is a very worthwhile agenda, and we should pursue this collectively—not just with ideas, but with action. After our break, Mark Greenberg will describe some programs for schoolchildren that are already showing promising results.

"But first we're going to step back from all this and look at a fundamental issue. If there is to be such a program, it should be for everyone. We need to pay attention not just to the ways that people are the same, which is what we've been looking at so far, but also to some important differences, particularly in relation to culture. What is the impact of culture on emotion? Does it fundamentally affect how we would approach this project? What issues should we keep in mind as we go ahead?

"We're very fortunate to have with us Jeanne Tsai, who is the daughter of Taiwanese parents who emigrated to America. She grew up in a Chinese-speaking bilingual home and has addressed the issue of culture as a psychologist with an understanding both from personal experience and from an objective scientific approach. Research is best guided when people have an intuitive understanding of the topic, as does Jeanne. She is going to address the issue of culture and emotion, which I think is a fundamental part of our discussion."

Throughout my introduction, Jeanne was beaming with contained anticipation. At first glance she seemed to have an almost deferential manner, but as Jeanne began to speak, she displayed a calm and powerful assurance and articulate clarity. And though she seemed to feel a bit nervous at first, as she spoke directly to the Dalai Lama her tension fell away.

The Dalai Lama had specifically requested a scientific participant representing an Asian culture, and he seemed even more attentive than usual this morning, despite his troublesome cough. He sat forward in his chair throughout most of Jeanne's presentation. As she talked, her gracefully contained gestures underscored her soft voice.

Differing Selves

Jeanne began by telling the Dalai Lama she was very honored to have the opportunity to talk with him about culture and emotion. She then plunged in: "In American psychology, there is a growing interest in how culture influences human behavior and in understanding how psychological principles apply to individuals of different cultural backgrounds, particularly non-Western backgrounds. This is because of the increasing cultural diversity of the United States, because of the increasing globalization of the world, and because there are more and more individuals like myself, who have been exposed to multiple cultures, entering the dialogue of psychology in the West.

"Today I would like to talk to you about how culture influences our emotions and what we feel. A few days ago Paul Ekman spoke about the aspects of emotion that are true for individuals of different cultures, but I'll point out how culture can result in differences in our emotions. These differences are particularly important when we consider how to promote constructive states and behavior and how to minimize destructive ones. We know from work in the United States, for example, that many treatments that seem to be effective for Americans of European descent are not as effective for Americans of Asian descent. For example, psychotherapy—going to someone for help with emotional problems—is something many members of Asian cultures don't like to do.[1]

"How does culture influence emotion? Cultures are similar and different in a number of ways. Social scientists have identified one way Western and non-Western cultures differ: in views of the self, which in turn influence emotion, or how we feel." Jeanne explained that the inner core of the self seems less swayed by culture, while an outer layer of the self appears heavily influenced by culture. That outer layer would be her subject today.

Though any broad cultural orientation, such as views of the self, runs along a continuum, Jeanne emphasized the extreme types to make her point. "One type of this outer layer is what psychologists Hazel Markus and Shinobu Kitayama call an 'independent' self—typical of individuals living in Western cultures—which views the self as separate from others, including parents, siblings, coworkers, friends. Such people view the self as being comprised of values, beliefs—internal attributes.[2]

"In contrast to this, there is an 'interdependent' self, much more typical of individuals living in Asian cultures. Such people see the self as connected with others, as very much part of a social context. The interdependent self is defined in terms of social relationships. Japanese, Chinese, Korean, and Taiwanese cultures are the particular cultural groups that have been studied most. Little, if any, work has been done on Tibetan culture."

The Dalai Lama, who now lives in India, asked, "What about Indians?"

"Some of the work has been on Indians.[3] Members of different Asian groups differ in the types of relationships they focus on. It seems that members of Chinese culture focus more on their family relationships, whereas members of Japanese culture seem to focus on both family members and coworkers. The number of their significant social relationships appears much greater.[4] I would expect that Tibetans have an even larger social circle." Jeanne was thinking (although again did not say) that, given the strong influence of Buddhism, Tibetans would focus on treating all individuals as important.

"I'm not so sure," the Dalai Lama said with a laugh. "For example, there are nomad families who are really quite isolated living out on the steppes."

Jeanne continued, "How do we know that these different views of the self really exist? Although there are examples from literature and the arts, as psychologists, we like to ask individuals about themselves. So we ask individuals of different cultures: 'Who are you?' Americans with independent selves would say, 'I'm outgoing, I'm friendly, I'm smart, I'm a good person,' whereas members of Asian cultures say, 'I'm a daughter or son, I work at this company, I play the piano.' They define themselves more in terms of social roles than internal attributes."[5]

Always quick to bring up facts that seem to disconfirm a theory, the Dalai Lama asked, "Then how would you account for the Western cultural tradition of assigning the family name as the surname? There is still quite a strong identification with the family there. Tibetans don't do that."

"That's true," Jeanne said, adding, "We haven't studied Tibetans yet." She was accustomed to such challenges. For her, the existence of counterexamples simply attested to the complexity of culture and to the fact that within any culture there are contradictions to the dominant cultural model.

In a tacit affirmation of just that point, Thupten Jinpa added, "Tibetans are already talking about the need to use family names because otherwise there is confusion. There are so many Tenzins around that if you call the name in a crowd, six people will answer"—which got an appreciative laugh.

Have It Your Way, or Others Before Self?

Jeanne got us back on track: "These different cultural views of the self influence an individual's goals in life. One life goal of someone with an independent self is to separate, to distinguish self from others. Such people do this primarily by expressing their internal beliefs, saying how they feel, and emphasizing the importance of themselves, particularly in relation to other people. In the United States we see these messages all the time. We're told to 'express ourselves'; that's a famous song by Madonna. We're told by advertisements to 'have it your way'; that's the most important way. And a very famous proverb says that 'the squeaky wheel gets the grease'; only by making a loud noise and making your opinions known do you get attention.

"But these goals are different from those of someone with an interdependent self, which are to connect with others and maintain relationships. We do this by moderating our internal beliefs and by minimizing the importance of ourselves in comparison to other people. Interdependent messages include the Japanese proverb 'The nail that stands out gets pounded down.' Here at the Tibetan Children's Village I saw a photograph of a celebration at the school, where it says, 'Others before self,' which is also an interdependent message.

"These differing views of the self influence different aspects of emotion. I'm going to talk about three. First, they alter what constitutes a desirable emotion. I'm going to give you two examples of this. The first is based on the idea that Westerners value self-enhancement whereas Asians value self-effacement. So in the West, we like to say very positive things about ourselves."

Here the Dalai Lama broke in again, unconvinced about the distinctions being drawn so sharply between Easterners and Westerners, which went against the grain of his own belief that people are more similar than different. "Is this based on statistical evidence?" he asked. "Can you make generalizations?"

"Yes," Jeanne assured him. "In general."

Still skeptical, he again cited a contrary example: "There may be exceptions, of course—for example, the famous saying from Mao Zedong that the winds from the East will overrun the winds of the West." This was said with a wry smile.

"There are exceptions," Jeanne granted. In the interests of making an argument, Jeanne had found, cultural psychologists are forced to talk about differences in their more extreme forms—while, of course, recognizing the considerable variation that exists within cultures. She had found initial resistance to be a common reaction among people hearing about cultural psychology for the first time, particularly those who feel that focusing on cultural differences may divide rather than unify people. Still, Jeanne—like myself—was a little surprised by the Dalai Lama's seeming resistance to the notion of cultural differences; we had expected he would be very intrigued by cultural influences on emotion.

Feeling Good About Yourself

Jeanne continued, "Asians value self-effacement; because we want to promote relationships with others, we're more critical of ourselves. This is perhaps best illustrated by the concept we call self-esteem—how we regard ourselves. We measure it by giving people questionnaires that include such statements as 'On the whole I am satisfied with myself; I feel that I have a number of good qualities; I take a positive attitude toward myself.' People with high self-esteem agree strongly with these statements, and people with low self-esteem don't.

"In American culture we think it very, very important to have high self-esteem. In California, millions of dollars were given to the school system to improve student self-esteem. We think that high self-esteem is good and low self-esteem is bad; low self-esteem, for example, is related to depression and feelings of anxiety. What's interesting is that when one measures self-esteem in very large groups of Americans and members of Asian cultures, there are differences in normal levels of self-esteem."[6]

Self-esteem had been an area of heated focus at an earlier meeting between the Dalai Lama and a group of psychologists that I had moderated in 1989. Back then he had been shocked to hear, for the first time, that a common problem among some Westerners was that they did not think well of themselves—that is, they had low self-esteem. What surprised him most was the idea that people could have so little compassion for themselves—that their kindness so easily extended to others but ignored themselves. But the very idea that low self-esteem should be a problem reflects the flip side of American views of the self: the overly high regard most people hold for themselves, and so the anxiety felt when one does not measure up to some inflated self-image.

That would have been, for Jeanne, a perfect illustration of the point she was trying to make: that because American culture values high self-regard, Americans think that anyone who doesn't have such high regard has a problem. In many other cultures, however, to have such a high regard for oneself would be perceived as equally problematic.

Now Jeanne showed a slide ranking several groups of college students on their levels of self-esteem, from lowest levels to highest, as follows:

1. "Never been abroad" Japanese
2. "Been abroad" Japanese
3. Recent Asian immigrants
4. Long-term Asian immigrants
5. Second-generation Asian Canadians

6. Third-generation Asian Canadians
7. European Canadians

European Canadians were the group with the relatively highest self-esteem.

"The more exposure a group has to American culture, the more their self-esteem increases," Jeanne noted. "For Americans, the normal average is higher than what's average and normal for Japanese."[7]

"Are there specific studies that show whether being wealthy gives you greater or lower self-esteem?" the Dalai Lama asked. "My speculation would be that people of more affluence might have greater self-esteem and people who are more impoverished might have lower self-esteem, on average. I was wondering whether that would turn out to be true when studied."

"It's possible," she replied, thinking of the many complex factors at play that make it hard to examine directly the relationship between socioeconomic status and self-esteem.

Then, summing up, Jeanne said, "The idea here is that Asians, because they have a lower average self-esteem, would appear to be psychologically less healthy in mainstream American culture. But they're not—it's just that their normal view is to not enhance themselves as much as Anglo-Americans."

What's Desirable: Conflict and Romantic Love

Jeanne's second example of cultural differences in desirable emotional states had to do, ironically, with interpersonal conflict. The data compared European American and Chinese American couples who were dating, and it came from research Jeanne had done with Robert Levenson at Berkeley.[8] "Because of their views of the self, Westerners value being different from others, whereas Asians value being similar to others," Jeanne reminded us. "Westerners value conflict or disagreement more than Asians because it's an opportunity to express their internal state, and therefore conflict feels better for Westerners than it does for Asians. It feels bad for both groups, but it feels a little better for Westerners."

Jeanne's data also showed that there was a continuum, based largely on how acculturated the Chinese Americans were. The more "Chinese" the Chinese Americans were, the less positive emotion they showed during their conflict conversations.[9]

"There is a genuine love?" the Dalai Lama asked about the couples.

"Yes," Jeanne said. "They say they love each other, and they have been dating each other for at least one year—which is a long time for college couples." At that, the Venerable Amchok Rinpoche could hardly contain his laughter.

Jeanne asked the Dalai Lama, "Can you guess what the strongest area of disagreement was for these couples? It's the same for both European Americans and Chinese Americans."

He thought a long time before answering, "A question of marriage?" He explained his thinking, that "without proper marriage, they would choose freedom, break up. That's a very Western attitude. The Asian couples might be very different—the problem might be getting their parents' permission, or at least agreement."

I asked Jeanne if these Asian American couples would need their parents' permission to marry, and she said, "Yes, some of them might," though she didn't think these couples were at that point.

"The parents' approval matters a lot with Asians," the Dalai Lama commented, "regardless of whether there is a real imposition from the parents' side. Even in the Western context, if the relationship between the father and daughter is very good, the good daughter will take into account the good father's feelings."

He laughed gleefully at this last remark, looking straight at Paul. On the previous day, Paul and his daughter Eve had had a private conversation with the Dalai Lama, and Eve had asked for his views on how to avoid destructive emotions in romantic love. He had given some surprising advice: to envision the negative aspects of the person you're involved with, to bring them off the pedestal of idealization to make the other more human. That way, he said, your expectations from the other person will be more realistic, and you'll be less likely to feel let down by what they do. He also advised that love needs to go beyond simple attraction to include mutual respect and friendship.

That advice seemed pertinent to Jeanne's findings. Picking up the thread of her comments, Jeanne said, "What's interesting, Your Holiness, is that the strongest area of disagreement for both the European American and the Chinese American couples was the same. They were all worried about jealousy. It all had to do with one partner spending too much time with another person."

The Dalai Lama brought his reasoned logic to the realm of passion. "If human beings are truly rational and if they are able to utilize their faculty of intelligence well, then in a modern secular society where there is a lot of sexual freedom, there should be less premise for jealousy because there is a lot of freedom."

"Yes," Jeanne replied, "but we're not rational beings all the time."

Alan observed, "Isn't the implication that college romances aren't very rational?" getting a laugh from the Dalai Lama.

"All romances," Paul quipped.

That prompted a more serious question from me for the Dalai Lama about the Buddhist view on the subject: "Jealousy is clearly an afflictive emotion, right? Is romantic love?"

After a good deal of discussion in Tibetan, Alan explained that it's difficult to translate the exact meaning of "romantic love" into that language. Romantic love had been unpacked for the Dalai Lama to mean "that in many cases it's not simply attachment in the afflictive sense but a more complex mixture of attachment, caring, and affection." That explanation had come from Thupten Jinpa, who, though once a monk, is now married and the father of two.

Indeed, as Alan observed, at these meetings with scientists the two ex-monks—he and Jinpa—sometimes offered in back channel their own views on such issues as a balance to those of the lifelong monk, the Dalai Lama. The Dalai Lama had at first assumed that "romantic love" was the same as sexual desire and, from the Buddhist perspective, came under the category of a mental affliction. But Alan raised an objection, pointing to the issue of afflicted compassion as a parallel; as he pointed out, they were dealing with hybrids where one element may be seen as afflicted, while the other is not. To which Jinpa added that the nonafflicted aspects of romantic love included feelings of closeness, empathy, companionship, and other aspects of a warm and enduring love.

The Dalai Lama concluded, "Romantic love is complex, for it includes not only sexual desire but a human element as well. For instance, people don't feel romantic love for an inanimate object, though they do feel attachment. So romantic love usually includes both sexual attraction and such human elements as lovingkindness and compassion. That being the case, it is not true that romantic love is simply a mental affliction, because it's multifaceted, with some elements being afflictive and others wholesome.

"Even so, from the Buddhist point of view, although it may not be one of the afflictive emotions, it is an afflicted state because the basis of that love is strong attachment. And this attachment colors the love that you feel, the sense of intimacy and closeness toward the object of attachment. The question is whether there could be appropriate forms of that attachment, and even from the Buddhist point of view, you can say yes. Even attachment can be very useful because the associated lovingkindness and compassion are beneficial."

Jeanne then summed up the reactions of the romantic couples while they talked about some area of conflict in their relationship. She assessed negative reactions, such as anger, belligerence, and fighting, as well as positive ones, such as affection, happiness, and validation of the other person. "We found that there were no culture differences in the amount of negative emotional responses, but there were differences in the amount of positive ones. The European Americans experienced more positive emotion during conflict than did the Chinese Americans, supporting the notion that in Western cultures, conflict is more desirable than in Asian cultures."[10]

Easygoing Asian Infants

"Another way in which cultural views of the self influence emotions is in the physiological component—how our bodies respond. As independent selves, European Americans place a greater value on high arousal states because it's important to be in a pleasant state. So they show higher physiological arousal during emotion, and then tend to be slower to return to a low arousal state during the recovery period.

"In contrast, interdependent selves place a greater value on lower arousal states. Independent selves are focused on themselves and want to feel positive—but our own high arousal may make other people feel bad. So interdependent selves want to show lower arousal during emotion, and they may be faster to return to a lower arousal state so that other people won't feel bad. In other words, for interdependent selves, one's own emotional state should have minimal impact on other people's emotional states."

Then Jeanne turned to corroborating data from Jerome Kagan, a developmental psychologist at Harvard, who compared the physiological reactions of four-month-old infants from Beijing with European American infants of the same age.[11] "They showed these infants a number of sensory stimuli, moving objects, and then looked at their behavior. They found that the European American infants cried more, vocalized more, and fretted more—they looked more worried."

The Dalai Lama was intrigued, leaning in and gesturing forcefully as he discussed the data with the translators. He sought an explanation. "This is very interesting. Are there any significant differences in the experiences they have had for the first four months?"

"That's the question," Jeanne said. "That's what we don't know."

"This is crucial," the Dalai Lama said. If there was a difference in their experience, that might rule out a genetic explanation. Differences observed even so close to birth could be due to environmental influences in utero working through the mother's emotional reactions, or in how babies are handled and responded to from birth onward.

"Right," Jeanne said, picking up on the implication. "We don't know if these differences are genetic."

"Is there an understanding from the developmental psychological perspective," the Dalai Lama asked, "at what stage the child has a cognitive recognition of the mother?"

Jeanne deferred to Mark Greenberg, a developmental psychologist. "It depends on the sensory modality," Mark explained. "In the first days of life babies can differentiate their mother's breast pad from another mother's by smell."

"Immediately?" the Dalai Lama asked. "So there's a spontaneous feeling of dependency."

"In the auditory channel, they can recognize the mother's voice from birth," Mark said. "Visually it takes a while longer because the visual system is not complete."

The Dalai Lama's passion for experiment came to the fore: "I have a speculation here directed to you, Mark. If you gave the newborn baby its own mother's breast one day and the very next day gave it another woman's breast to drink from, would there be any resistance, any difference in the baby's response?"

"Yes," Mark told him.

Richard Davidson added another research finding. "If you play a voice over a loudspeaker on the mother's abdomen when she is pregnant in the third trimester, the fetus responds physiologically differently to the mother's voice than to the voice of a strange mother—even before birth."

Still, Jeanne observed, "it is unclear whether these differences are genetic or due to differences in the early environments."

"And what if the children are from Taiwan?" the Dalai Lama asked.

Jeanne replied with a smile, "I'd like to do that study."

The Dalai Lama pursued the issue of environmental influences. "It may also make a difference whether the child was brought up in an orphanage or day care right from the beginning."

"Yes," Jeanne agreed.

"If the parents are at work, the infants may be in day care," the Dalai Lama said, still pondering Kagan's data from Beijing. "In a Communist system that often happens."

"Yes, that's right."

"So we can't say it's the Chinese or Asian influence."

Jeanne agreed again, adding, "We haven't been able to deconstruct the reasons why there might be these cultural differences. But one possible reason is views of the self." The Dalai Lama's questions made Jeanne wish that cultural psychology as a science was further along. All of the things that he mentioned—practices of child rearing, the varying quality of parenting across cultures—could well be sources of the cultural differences Kagan and others have found. At this point there was just too little data to identify the cultural factors.

The Dalai Lama raised another point: "Since Communist China is such a unique Asian society, where there is deliberate social engineering—if you want to use that word—it may not be a representative example of all Asian communities."

"That's true," Jeanne agreed. "But other Asian groups who aren't influenced by Communism show similar differences in comparison to Westerners or European American culture."

Jeanne went on to present just such data, comparing Chinese American infants—children born in the United States to Chinese parents—and European American infants.[12] The same pattern emerged: "The basic finding is that the Chinese American infants were better able to calm themselves after being agitated than were the European American infants."

Again the Dalai Lama had a question about methodology: "I am wondering about the differences or commonality of conduct of the family environment in which these children are raised."

"Unfortunately," said Jeanne, "the authors of the study grouped the infants only by their cultural heritage and didn't look at other specific factors that might influence these differences."

Jeanne was finding the Dalai Lama's questions astute in pointing out what was not known in cultural psychology, as well as in suggesting possible mechanisms by which culture may be exerting an influence. She summarized that, for whatever reasons, "Asian infants are less aroused and better able to calm themselves than Western infants. Some evidence suggests this difference is retained in adults—for instance, in the couples study, the Chinese American couples showed less heart rate activity during conflict than the European Americans."

Jeanne then cited supporting data from a study of the startle reflex, just like the one that Paul Ekman and Robert Levenson had done with Lama Öser. In this study, Chinese Americans recovered more quickly—their heart rate calmed sooner—after hearing a loud, startling noise than Mexican Americans.[13] In general, the larger the startle reflex, the greater a person's typical emotional reaction. These data, Jeanne said, suggest there may be something about cultural environment that influences how we respond physiologically to emotion, but too little is known about this as yet.

Focus: On Oneself or on the Other?

Yet another cultural difference is that during emotional events, Asians tend to focus on others and Westerners on themselves. "Of course, there are differences among Asians and among Westerners," Jeanne cautioned, "but the general idea is that Westerners will think about themselves during a social interaction, whereas somebody who has an interdependent self will think of the other person during that interaction. When we ask people about when they experienced the most intense emotions, we find that Asians talk about events that have to do with others more than themselves. With Westerners it's just the opposite: Their most intense emotions come up concerning events that happened to themselves."

The emotional case in point was shame, an emotion particularly salient in Asian cultures, where shame is often spoken of in terms of being negatively valued by others, or "losing face." Jeanne presented data from one of her own studies comparing the Hmong, a Southeast Asian group from Laos, and European Americans. She read aloud a European American male's description of a shame experience: "I accepted a job to be an assistant manager and I thought I'd be good at it. About five months later it dawned on me that I was really bad at it and I was really ashamed about how bad of a manager I was. I was embarrassed and ashamed at my poor performance."

"In contrast, a Hmong American female wrote about feeling shame this way: 'I'm an 'X', which is a Hmong name. We had a pastor, he is an 'X' too. He got caught having an affair with one of his churchgoers. They're not close to us by blood, but just the fact that they carry our name brings shame to the name. They were having a three-year-long affair and that made me feel really ashamed.' It was somebody else's actions that made her feel shame. They didn't even know each other—but they belonged to the same clan (the primary social unit in Hmong society), and so shared the same name."[14]

Another example came from a study of college students who were asked to read hypothetical scenarios in which they had to imagine that they did something wrong or that their brother did something wrong. "The Chinese felt much more shame and guilt when their brother was responsible for an action than did Americans," Jeanne said.[15]

Then she summarized, "Compared to Westerners, Asians experience more shame and guilt, as well as pride, when others are responsible, because their views of the self are based more on others. So cultural views of the self appear to influence how we experience emotions—what's a desirable emotion, whether we put our attention on ourselves or on others. Culture seems to get into our bodies, influencing our physiology.

"I think that these cultural differences have implications for how we develop programs like the ones we spoke of yesterday. For example, if we come up with a program for the development of emotional competence, it's likely that Americans will think everybody else needs the program but they themselves don't need the program—whereas it may be different in Asian cultures."

To that, the Dalai Lama riposted wryly, "I don't know how uniquely

American that is, because even Tibetans, when they hear teachings of the Buddha being given, on the whole would think, 'Well, that is for others,' as if to say, 'They need it, not me.' "

That led Jeanne to wonder if the same would be even more true among Americans when it came, say, to cultivating compassion. Jeanne cited studies showing that Americans, more than members of other cultures, think they're above average, better than most people. "Unfortunately, that attitude is very American. We need to design programs that are seen as appropriate so they're acceptable to members of different cultures. I think that by acknowledging cultural differences and incorporating them into our programs, we can really begin to achieve universal training toward compassion."

As Jeanne concluded, the Dalai Lama took her hands and bowed to her.

Recognizing Similarities

Though the Dalai Lama was keenly interested in Jeanne's presentation as she spoke, he felt a basic skepticism about the importance of cultural differences relative to mankind's common heritage and the universality of the human predicament. During a later discussion he raised an intriguing issue: "I am slightly puzzled as to why you keep insisting that there is this fundamental difference between Easterners and Westerners in terms of emotional management. What we are talking about may be a factor of spirituality. The differences may not really lie in different cultures as such, or ethnicity, but rather in differences in the legacy of religious traditions.

"For example, in the Judeo-Christian tradition, where the primary focus is on a Divinity and the whole spiritual orientation is toward achieving transcendent union, there is less emphasis on correcting the internal emotional life or creating equilibrium within oneself. Genuine faith toward God the creator, and acting from genuine love for God, leads to genuine love for other human beings. Then such things as killing, stealing, or raping are against your belief in God. That's a very powerful message about becoming a good human being.

"But the ultimate aspiration of a practicing Buddhist is the attainment of nirvana. The emphasis is within oneself, so then these negative emotions and the resulting actions become important; now we have to know what's going on within the mind. In Buddhism, then, the aim is different. From the cultural perspective, you see, Buddhists have a fundamentally different orientation toward emotion. From that point of view, even subtle degrees of grasping the reality of self and the world becomes obstructive and negative.

"So maybe the difference really comes from the fundamental orientation: toward the transcendent or toward internal development. But, putting religious belief aside, we are not talking about these subtle differences here. Now we are talking about secular ethics. And when it comes to that, I don't believe there are any fundamental differences between Westerners and Easterners. This is my fundamental belief."

Then, becoming more animated, he added, "Sometimes I believe scholars overemphasize differences within their field. They don't take a holistic view—seeing how it's unified. They focus on small differences. Even within myself, just one person, there are so many differences: the morning Dalai Lama, afternoon Dalai Lama, evening Dalai Lama. A lot of differences—in state of mind, even empty or full stomach."

We were back to the central issues raised in that long-ago conversation between Paul Ekman and Margaret Mead: the social agenda implied by cultural studies. Jeanne agreed with the Dalai Lama's point that both cultural similarities and differences exist and that within individuals there is considerable variability in their behavior. Indeed, at a certain level, individuals are fundamentally the same. However, she felt that the magnitude of cultural differences remained open to scientific inquiry and was what she and others were trying to determine. She also agreed that one's decision to focus on cultural similarities or differences did depend somewhat on one's social agenda. Her interest in cultural differences was largely in reaction to their being completely ignored in most American scientific contexts, creating a need to bring them to the attention of Western psychology in the first place. Jeanne was acutely aware that when Western psychology spoke of "universals" in emotions, they too often really meant "mainstream white Anglo-American." Similarly, she realized that the Dalai Lama, whose goal was to unite people of different cultural traditions, wanted to focus primarily on the ways in which they were similar, or the universal nature of human experience.

Now Jeanne took up the Dalai Lama's point. "First, definitely the dominant religious traditions in Asian and Western cultures differ, and they may explain the cultural differences in emotions that I've described today. What's interesting is that in the studies that I showed you this morning, the Chinese Americans weren't Buddhist. They were Christian, too, and still there were those differences.

"But," she added, "I agree with Your Holiness that there are lots of individual differences within each cultural group, and really, what these cultural views of the self represent are different overall ways of being that individuals are reacting to. Of course there are Westerners who are very interested in Buddhism and who are probably more interdependent. But still, each individual within a cultural context has to react to the dominant messages in some way.

"In the United States, for example, there is a message that you as an individual are special and you should promote how special you are. It doesn't mean that every single American in this room feels that way, but it does mean that they are responding to some larger cultural message. I think that is really where the cultural differences lie."

The Individual Versus the Collective

I knew from my travels that many Western cultures were not nearly as individualistic as American culture; some were more collectivist, as in Asia. "In Scandinavian cultures," I mentioned as a case in point, "the ethic is very much like in Asian cultures, that you shouldn't stand out." Jeanne's data had, in fact, shown that European Americans of Scandinavian heritage are less emotionally expressive than those whose ancestors are from the central and southern parts of Europe, especially during happiness.[16]

Jeanne acknowledged that others had done much research comparing differences in individualism and collectivism across different Western cultures.[17] "But," she added, "studies still need to be done to see whether a collectivistic Western culture is more individualistic than Asian culture."

"It is something of an anomaly," the Dalai Lama observed. "We have the classic Western religion of Christianity in which there is one creator, and in Judaism of course, and Islam too for that matter. In all three Mediterranean religions, these so-called Western religions, there is the unified belief in an external creator who created the whole of creation, including every creature. We are all alike in the sense that we are creatures of the one creator, which gives us a common root and which means, of course, that we're all brothers and sisters, the same family with one father. If you follow the theology, that would imply a sense of nonindividuality, of uniformity and homogenization.

"A classically Asian or Eastern religion like Buddhism has no such notion of an external creator creating everything. Rather, the circumstances of each sentient being are brought about by one's own individual karma, which casts us into this world. Even the world we're experiencing arises from our karma. One of the four laws of karma is, if you do not create the cause, you will not experience the result. If you have created the cause, you will definitely experience the result. All of this is individual, so the experiences you have are tied into your individuality. The world you're existing in, you created as an individual. There is no external source that is common to everyone.

"That would imply a very strong element of individualism in Buddhism, whereas it seems the tables are turned. So then I wonder, if there are no theological grounds, there must be some other factor accounting for this interdependent self in Asia and the strong individualism in the West. What other factors might there be?"

Jeanne conjectured, "It could be that economic factors and family unit have an influence. I think it's a multitude of factors that influence the self. What you're speaking to is the complexity. It's not so simple. It's not the case that all Western cultures are this way and all Asian cultures are that way. For example, within an individual culture we have more and more bicultural individuals, like myself, who are influenced by more than one culture. In some contexts I'm very independent and in other contexts I'm very interdependent. It's very complicated how these manifest themselves within an individual."

Alan added, "When we look at religion—for example, Christianity—it's very important to see its historical development. In the Protestant Reformation there was a very strong emphasis on the individual relating to God without the intermediary of a priest, and less emphasis on the community. In the Enlightenment period, again, there was strong emphasis on individual reason. I think this strong emphasis on the individual is a rather recent event. I suspect that in medieval Christianity—prior to the Protestant Reformation—you would find something much more similar to this Asian modality."

"Which brings up the point," Jeanne concluded, "that cultures change all the time."

That point, the Dalai Lama felt, was key. As the Dalai Lama later told me, he still had qualms and methodological questions about generalizing when it came to cultural differences, if only because cultures evolve. He had seen in his own culture that simply communicating with other cultures outside brings change. It might be useful to know about differences such as the degree to which given emotions are expressed by a group—but even so, everyone feels the same emotions underneath. As a figure on the world stage, the Dalai Lama preferred to focus on commonalities and then nod to differences as needed. His core belief, that people are essentially the same at the fundamental level, meant that he did not look at whether someone is Chinese or Indian or American, but rather sought to find solutions for the human dilemmas faced by everyone.

At the tea break there was a much more personal exchange between Jeanne and the Dalai Lama. She had felt it important to let him know that she empathized with the Tibetans in their struggle with Communist China. He told her that he felt no animosity toward the Chinese, and of the great respect he had for Chinese culture. She took the opportunity to tell him that while honoring their Chinese heritage, many Americans of Chinese descent also sympathized with the Tibetan struggle. When he told her how moving this was for him, Jeanne's eyes filled with tears—and so did his.

11

Schooling for the Good Heart

As I was writing my 1995 book *Emotional Intelligence,* I searched for ways to make the case that children could benefit greatly from an emotional education in schools. In those days, however, that was a radical idea for education, and there were few schools that were actually doing what I was arguing for. Fewer still were the emotional literacy programs that had any data to support their effectiveness.

One of the rare exceptions was an emotional education curriculum codeveloped by Mark Greenberg, who would be our next presenter. The PATHS (Promoting Alternative Thinking Strategies) curriculum helped deaf children learn how to use language to better understand and manage their emotions—to become aware of and recognize their feelings and those of others, and to regulate them.[1] Those skills also happen to be the main elements of emotional intelligence, and in my book I cited Mark's program as a model for teaching emotional literacy—called now by educators, as Mark had mentioned, "social and emotional learning."

After the tea break, we shifted our focus to social and emotional learning. I pointed out that many schools have already put into action for children the kind of program for adults we had been formulating the previous day. I told the Dalai Lama that Mark, a pioneer in creating one such widely used program, would tell us about them. I added that his program—in something rare for education—had undergone rigorous evaluation to show its actual effectiveness, building the scientific case for expanding education to teach children to be intelligent about emotion.

Mark, I pointed out, frames his work as more than education—it's also primary prevention, a strategy for lowering the risks young people face in life. At Pennsylvania State University he holds the Edna Peterson Bennett Chair in Prevention Research and directs the Prevention Research Center for the Promotion of Human Development. And he oversees part of two large federal grants, one (funded at close to $60 million over thirteen years) a collaborative project with four other universities to test a curriculum to lower children's risk for violence, crime, and dropping out of school.

"The idea behind his work," I continued, "is that if we teach children these things now, we can prevent problems later, particularly the problems that come from afflictive emotions—violence, suicide, drug abuse, and so on."

Mark Greenberg grew up in the baby boom generation. He was raised in Harrisburg, Pennsylvania, and educated at Johns Hopkins University. It was there that he had his first psychology course, with Mary Ainsworth, a leading developmental psychologist, and was smitten by the field. Ainsworth was a colleague of the British psychologist John Bowlby; both were world experts on how parents' early bond with children forms the basis of the capacity for loving attachment throughout life. Mark became fascinated by how personality develops as a function of personal relationships in the early years.

Going on to graduate work at the University of Virginia for training in developmental and clinical psychology, Mark began his work with deaf children by chance. One day he was sent to give an IQ test to a five-year-old hearing-impaired child, who, Mark realized, became frightened when his mother left the room. Intrigued, Mark started to do research on parent-child attachment in the hearing-impaired. That led to an interest in behavior problems among deaf children and how they might be prevented—which, in turn, led Mark and his colleague, Carol Kusché, to develop the PATHS curriculum, designed to prevent those problems.

The PATHS program was evaluated rigorously. It proved to work so well that the principals of the schools where it had been tried among deaf students asked whether the other students could take it, too. Today it is in broad use in over a hundred American school districts as well as several other countries, including the Netherlands, Australia, and England.

With PATHS, Mark became a pioneer in a new specialty in psychology: the field of primary prevention, which seeks to protect children from later problems through teaching them key skills for living. The growing movement in social and emotional learning seeks to include basic lessons in life skills in every school's program. Mark is codirector of research for the Collaborative for Academic, Social, and Emotional Learning, based at the University of Illinois at Chicago under the directorship of Roger Weissberg.[2]

Mark was eager to share this expertise with the Dalai Lama, and to link it to the development of capacities of the prefrontal lobes that underlie social and emotional development. But there was another strand of Mark's life for which this encounter held particular meaning, for since his college days Mark had also been a student of meditation. Mark saw Eastern psychologies such as Buddhism as offering the West a missing expertise.

The methods of psychotherapy and psychology aim to help people develop a healthy ego—emotional maturity, a sense of self-efficacy, and the like. But the goals of Western psychology basically stop there. As transpersonal theorists such as Daniel Brown and Ken Wilber have argued, Eastern psychology, while recognizing that you have to build a healthy ego before you can let go of it, also focuses on the next step: the development of the self past the ego. We had touched on some of this difference earlier in our discussions, in terms of Buddhist and Western methods for dealing with destructive emotions.

Most salient for Mark, the Dalai Lama himself represented a model of how to balance spiritual concerns with social action. And Mark was fascinated by the importance the Dalai Lama gave to learning how to handle destructive emotions—the focus of Mark's own work. Finally, Mark felt, from both the scientific and the spiritual perspectives, that the challenge comes down to the balance of mind and heart—and how best to help children find that balance.

Educating the Heart

For his presentation, Mark wore a maroon Tibetan vest. He had joked the night before that all the presenters were looking more and more Tibetan every day and would be in robes by the end of the week. Though he speaks softly, Mark's natural rate of speech is quite rapid, and, like Owen, he had to make a conscious effort again and again to slow himself down.

Mark began by thanking the Dalai Lama and the Mind and Life Institute for bringing their attention to the problem of destructive emotions, and said he felt it was both a blessing and a joy to share his thoughts. He also introduced his wife, Christa, as a professional partner in his work. Many of the things he would say, he pointed out, were the result of his work with her and other colleagues over the last twenty years.

"I thought that I'd start with a quote from Your Holiness: 'Even though a society does not emphasize this, the most important use of knowledge and education is to help understand the importance of engaging in more wholesome actions and bringing about discipline within our minds. The proper utilization of our intelligence and knowledge is to effect changes from within that develop a good heart.'

"My talk will focus on the Western psychological knowledge of some of the factors that can educate the heart—that can make a good heart. I found His Holiness's analogy to the immune system fascinating and very useful. Our secular goal should be to support a healthy emotional immune system. Thus when destructive emotions arise—and they will—we can apply our intelligence, our educated heart, to more effectively deal with emotions in the moment. I want to emphasize that it's emotions in the moment that are the issue, because we can learn many useful things to do when we're in the heat of an emotion.

"In child development research we call this immunity 'protective factors.' Today I want to talk about both protective factors and risk factors that influence children's emotional well-being. I will discuss infancy for a few minutes and then spend most of the talk, as Dan said, on the practical issues in teaching social and emotional skills to children in schools.

"It was very interesting yesterday to hear His Holiness say that in a Buddhist text, the model often used for compassion and empathy is a mother-infant relationship. It was also interesting to hear you say today in your comments on romantic love that attachment can be necessary and supportive at certain stages in development. Given the essential nature of the parent-infant relationship, I would like to make three points about infancy. First, research indicates that when parents recognize their infants' negative emotions—their anger and sadness—and help them to cope with those emotions, children over time develop better physiological regulation of their emotions and show more positive behavior.

"On the other hand, when parents ignore or punish infants for showing these emotions, or get angry at them—I see many parents who get angry at their infants and toddlers for getting angry—over time, children, knowing that certain emotions can't be shared, shut them down. This makes a child overstressed, both physiologically and psychologically, because the emotion is still there, and it puts an obstacle in the way of developing a basic trust between the child and adults. Mary Ainsworth's observations of infants and their mothers identified such patterns. By one year of age, some infants will avoid contact with the mother rather than go to her when they are upset and distressed. They have an approach/avoidance conflict about having emotional and physical contact. We know that infants who have those problems are not learning a healthy way to manage their emotions.

"The second point is that one of the most important of many factors that place infants at risk is maternal depression. Mothers who have high rates of sad feelings, who are lethargic and depressed, have children who later show higher rates of aggression, anxiety, and depression. Richie Davidson, in previous research, has shown that adults who are depressed have lower activation in the left frontal lobe. The work of Geraldine Dawson indicates this same pattern in mothers who are depressed.[3]

"In addition, Dawson has now shown that, by one year of age, infants whose mothers are depressed show the same pattern: less activation of their left frontal lobes. So even in infancy, children who have depressed mothers show less positive emotion and an unusual brain activation pattern. A critical issue here is that relationships in infancy set the course for later social-emotional development. The amount of positive emotions, like joy, in the relationship in infancy is critical to setting the correct brain pathways. We know that each developmental period matters for emotional development, and we must start at the beginning."

In short, making babies happy grows the circuitry that will help them have positive feelings like joy throughout their lives. The Dalai Lama later told me he was pleased to hear about this finding. He often mentioned this biological longing for affection as a key point in his own humanitarian view of ethics. His own view was that there is a biological need for such caring, akin to the body's need for food. And here was more scientific ammunition.

Mark's third point focused on how broader social and emotional deprivation affects the infant's brain. "We know that deprivation can affect levels of the neurotransmitter dopamine and, as a result, can affect brain development and brain plasticity. So it should be of great concern that there is a growing number of children around the world who are residing in orphanages where they are deprived of care and a close emotional relationship between the children and the caregivers. We're going to see a large increase in the number of orphans, especially in Asian and African countries, over the next decade due to AIDS. For example, in South Africa twenty-eight percent of women who are pregnant are HIV-positive, so it's estimated there'll be a million orphans in South Africa alone in the next decade. Addressing this problem is of critical concern."

At that somber thought, the Dalai Lama—whose emotions typically are writ openly on his face—showed an intense sadness, almost as if he were about to burst into tears. Recovering after a moment, he shook his head and closed his eyes for a moment, as though offering a brief prayer.

The Prefrontal Window for Emotional Competence

"Now I'd like to move to the preschool years," Mark continued. "This is a period in which there is a great deal of learning and the brain is being shaped. There are very important social skills that begin to develop between the ages of three and seven. These skills are very similar to the ones His Holiness has often talked about. They include the ability to have self-control, to stop and calm down when one is upset, and the ability to sustain attention, which Alan talked about yesterday.

"Children also show great growth in their emotional awareness during this period. In the early phases of language development, they have very few words for emotions. However, in the preschool years, there is a dramatic growth in the child's ability to talk about emotions and to recognize emotions. And last, children can begin to plan and think ahead for the first time. For example, we can ask a four- or five-year-old questions about what the child would do when teased by another child. At that age children can begin to use their new cognitive skills to think ahead and create alternative ideas or plans.

"These developmental skills combine information from our emotions and our thinking skills. They are now recognized as processes that all have important correlates in the frontal lobe, so this is very much in line with what Richie was talking about yesterday. For instance, a persistently aggressive style of play in children at the age of five or six is not likely to fade away—such children are likely to continue to be aggressive. At least half of children who show early aggression are going to persist in that aggression through adolescence. And as they persist, they will become worse and turn more toward cruelty and violence."[4]

Mark's writings make clear that children who strike out impulsively are displaying a failure to integrate their emotions and their reasoning. Impulsive aggression stems in part from a failure to plan ahead, combined with poor controls on emotional impulse. Both planning and impulse control are functions of the prefrontal lobes.

Significantly, frontal lobe damage in young children—whether from an accident or from disease—appears to have a very low recovery rate. That is particularly troubling, because the prefrontal lobes are the critical areas for the integration of reasoning and emotion. Unlike, say, the language centers of the temporal lobes, the prefrontal lobes show much less recovery from damage.[5] If a young child has damage to the temporal lobes, other areas will take over language capabilities and the child can develop reasonably normal language skills. But if the damage is to the prefrontal areas, such substitution typically fails to occur, and the child grows up impaired socially and emotionally.

These neurological data underscore the significance of the prefrontal area for the development of healthy emotions in children. The frontal lobes, as Richie said, have evolved and grown dramatically in humans compared even to other primates. Because this area is the newest part of the brain in evolution, it seems to have little redundancy with other areas.

Even so, the prefrontal area itself is quite plastic, shaping its circuitry as the result of the experiences and learning we undergo, particularly during the surprisingly long period during which this area continues to grow anatomically. The brain is the last organ of the body to become anatomically mature; the progressive mental and social milestones of a child's development reflect its continued growth. The prefrontal areas are the last part of the human brain to become fully mature, continuing to show anatomical growth into the mid-twenties—making life's early years a key window of opportunity to help young people master the most helpful lessons for life. That was the implication of what Mark said next.

"On the other hand, children who have good planning skills and are aware of their emotions by the time they enter school, at the age of five or six, are at much lower risk for later having problems of aggression and anxiety disorders. We know that by the time children enter school there are very clear pathways going into the future, though the patterns are not completely stable.

"This is partly related to the concept of selective perception, which we've talked about already. Children who are aggressive or who have a chip on their shoulder are very vigilant—they're looking around to see who's going to hurt them next, because they've been hurt before. They're very reactive; they jump quickly. A classic situation in school is lining up. Children have to line up many times during the day, to go to lunch and come back from recess, and so many things happen in the lining-up process.

"It's these little, everyday events that are so telling. A child may be bumped in line by another child, and instead of first looking at the situation to see what's happening, an aggressive child will often quickly react with aggression, and then a fight will begin. It's those quick emotional reactions that we're interested in here. Children who have had a history of aggression are primed, in a way; they're ready to see damage being done to them even when it's not true or when it's accidental.[6]

"As Matthieu mentioned yesterday, schools may be the only enduring institution that can provide the universal education to build emotional health. During the past twenty years or so, I and other colleagues in America and elsewhere have begun to scientifically test whether we can intervene effectively in the schools to build emotional health. I'm very happy to say that we now have scientific evidence that, using the PATHS curriculum two to five times a week, we can be successful in improving children's well-being.[7] When taught with high fidelity, PATHS can build children's social and emotional skills as well as improve some of their thinking skills. We shouldn't think about social and emotional skills separately from these thinking skills. In the

Buddhist model, intelligence includes both. In America, we've often separated these. We think about children's social development and their cognitive development separately, but we know that there is great interconnection."

Getting Practical: You Can't Think Until You're Calm

"For the remainder of my talk," Mark said, "I'm going to become practical. I would like to use our own work with PATHS for the past nineteen years as an example of how to work in the secular and quite conservative structure of the educational system—a very difficult structure to change. We've worked in the public schools in America, although our work has also been used in England, the Netherlands, Canada, Belgium, Australia, Wales—a variety of places around the world. Not France yet, though it's been translated into French," he added, getting some laughs at what had become our running joke.

"I want to begin by saying that I think our work is still primitive. I'm not suggesting that it should be seen as a complete model, but really as just a place to begin. Further, I should note that our work has greatly profited from the work of many other prevention researchers, most especially Maurice Elias, Roger Weissberg, and Myrna Shure.

"We know that effective curricula have at least these five characteristics. First, they focus on helping children calm down. This relates to how we can decrease the recovery period from emotional arousal that Paul discussed on Tuesday, be it for anger, jealousy, or excitement. Second, they increase awareness of emotional states in others. The third characteristic may be more Western: the outward discussion of feelings as a way of solving interpersonal difficulties. Fourth is a very important skill: planning and thinking ahead so that one can avoid difficult situations. And last is considering how our behavior affects others; this is part of what empathy and interpersonal concern are about.

"To illustrate this I'll give you some of the guidelines, what we think of as ideas to live by, that we teach the teachers and children. Then I'll talk about specific procedures that we use to develop each of these skills.

"We have a rule structure that we're creating for children and teachers; you might call it an ideology about how emotion works. There are four main ideas we want to teach children. The first is that feelings are important signals. They can arise from inside our body or they can come from outside, as a signal from someone else, and they provide very important information. This information could be about oneself—something that one needs or desires—or it could be about the needs of others.

"We teach children that this information shouldn't be ignored; it should be investigated. Becoming aware of emotions requires understanding how we know what we feel about the situation, how we can put those feelings into words, and how we can recognize those feelings in others. I think that corresponds in some ways to the idea of bringing intelligence—and the Buddhist notion of flourishing—into the picture: to be able to use our reason not to suppress emotions but to consider them and then make decisions about them.

"That is one guideline, that emotions are important signals. We don't merely tell this to children—we provide them with tools to practice, as I will describe later. This is important because many children are afraid of their feelings—often they cannot separate their feelings from their behavior. In fact, many adults have a hard time doing this. It is complicated and occupies much time in most forms of adult psychotherapy. So it's very important that we help children understand that their feelings are different from their behaviors.

"We talk about this in a very simple way. We place signs in the classroom that say, 'All feelings are okay. Behaviors can be okay or not okay.' It's important for children to realize that everyone sometimes feels jealousy, greed, disappointment—the entire spectrum of feelings. But feelings are distinct from behavior, and thus we say that behaviors may be okay or not okay.

"How might this be taught in a lesson? Let's take a lesson on jealousy as an example—a very important emotion for children. We'll have children show on their faces how a jealous person might look. During a lesson we would discuss jealousy and would show them pictures of the different ways a person feeling jealous might look. We might tell a story about a time when a child felt jealous and how the child resolved it. We may have the children take turns talking about a time when they were jealous, or draw a picture, or write in their journal about jealousy. We'll talk about behavior—what you can do when you feel jealous. The feeling of jealousy may be very difficult to control when it arises, but we can make decisions about how to behave.

"The second guideline is to separate feelings from the behaviors. The question is, what kinds of behaviors are okay or not okay? That takes a lot of time for many children to discern. Often when they have certain emotions, let's say anger, and they've been punished for something, they fuse together the emotions they felt and the behavior that they were punished for. They also believe that even feeling certain emotions is already being bad. It's very important to help children see that feelings are just a part of us. They arise and we need to look at them. There's nothing wrong with feelings—they are natural.

"The third guideline we tell children is that you can't think until you're calm. This is a sort of a mantra, if you will, in our classrooms. It relates to

Matthieu's idea that emotions condition the mind to see in a certain way, as well as to Paul's experience of the phone call with his wife. We tell children they must calm down first so that they can see clearly what's happening, and then see what to do about it. What action should be taken about the emotion? We say this over and over again. And we teach specific ways to calm down when they have these feelings."

The Dalai Lama wanted to know, "When you tell the children first of all that they should calm down so they can assess the emotion and see what to do about it, isn't that already telling them to modify their emotions?"

"Well," Mark replied, "it's telling them to handle the arousal. We don't want them to get rid of the emotion. We want them to calm down so they can say to themselves, 'I'm angry. Now what can I do about this? Why am I angry?' We tell them to modify the arousal of that emotion—not that the emotion shouldn't be dealt with, but that first we have to calm down and use our intelligence."

Paul Ekman clarified that this involves decreasing the intensity of the emotion.

The point was that in this program, any emotion was okay—but the actions it led to might not be. This contrasted markedly with the Buddhist view that certain emotions themselves are not okay. The Dalai Lama took a long moment to think about this before signaling Mark to continue.

"The fourth guideline that we use is the golden rule," Mark went on. "We think this is a very important, age-old piece of wisdom. We say to children, 'Treat others the way you want to be treated.' The idea here, of course, is to invoke taking the perspective of others.

"These are four fundamental guidelines that we try to put across to children on a repeated basis, over and over again—not only to the children, but also to the teachers, the principal, and other staff working with the children."

The Dalai Lama came back to what he had been getting at in his earlier questioning. He asked if there wasn't a bit of contradiction "when you tell the children on one hand that all emotions themselves are okay, if not the behavior, but as soon as a child shows an emotion such as anger, you say, 'Calm down.' Wouldn't it be more congruent to say, 'I see that you're very angry. I get angry, too, but it would be better not to be so angry'? Help the child to diminish the anger."

Mark answered, "That is exactly what I think we do. I'm not sure there is a contradiction. When I talk about practical ways to do this, I think you'll see that's exactly what we're doing."

Doing Turtle

Getting to the practicalities, Mark told a PATHS story—accompanied by pictures—for children three to seven years old. "This is a story about a little turtle. This little turtle liked to play by himself and he liked to play with his friends. He liked to watch TV and play games outside, but he didn't really like to go to school very much."

At first the Dalai Lama did a double take, seemingly a bit startled to realize this was a story for children, not a true account. Catching himself, he tapped his head, and, clearly charmed by the tale, nodded and smiled at each part.

"He didn't like sitting in a classroom and listening to the teacher for long periods of time," Mark narrated. "It was very hard for him. Often the little turtle would get angry at his friends. His friends might take his pencil or push him, or bother him in some way, and when that happened, the little turtle would get very, very angry. He would often hit back or he would say mean things to the other child. After a while, other children didn't want to play with the little turtle."

At this point, Mark said, the pictures would show the turtle alone on the playground by himself. "And the little turtle felt upset," the story went on. "He felt angry and he felt confused, and he felt sad because he couldn't control himself and didn't know how to solve his problem. Then one day he met a very wise old turtle who was three hundred years old and lived at the edge of the town. He said to the wise old turtle, 'What can I do? School is a problem for me. I can't behave myself. I try but I always fail.' The wise old turtle said to him, 'You already have the solution to the problem inside yourself. It's your shell. When you feel very upset or very angry and you can't control yourself, you can go inside your shell.' "

Mark, who often works with deaf children, demonstrated the sign for this, wrapping one hand over the other fist and retracting the thumb that sticks out like a turtle's head.

" 'When you're inside your shell you can calm down. When I go inside my shell,' the wise old turtle said, 'I do three things. I tell myself to stop; I take one long deep breath, or more if I need to; and then I tell myself what the problem is.' The wise old turtle and the little turtle practiced this idea. And the little turtle said he wanted to try this when he got back to his class.

"The next day he's doing his work when another child begins to bother him. He starts to feel the anger welling up inside; his hands are hot and his heartbeat is going up. He remembers what the wise old turtle said, and he folds his arms and legs into his shell, where it is peaceful and no one can bother him, and he thinks about what he should do. He takes a deep breath, and when he comes out of his shell he sees his teacher smiling.

"He tries this over and over again. Sometimes it fails and sometimes it succeeds, but little by little he learns how to control himself by using his shell. He makes friends and he likes school more because now he is a turtle that knows how to manage himself.

"After we tell the turtle story we have the children act it out. One day a child might be the wise old turtle, the next day the little turtle, the next day the teacher. They act it out from different points of view.

"There are a few important points in the story, as I'm sure Your Holiness sees. First of all, the turtle learns to become aware of his feelings before he acts out destructive behaviors. The second is very important: The turtle learns to take responsibility for himself. The fact that he can control himself can lead to a feeling of satisfaction. It's a part of growing up and becoming mature.

"We use this story to teach a skill," Mark continued. "We teach these young children to 'do turtle.' We teach this in different ways, depending upon the context, but we always teach it in a way that uses the body. For most children we teach them to do this," and Mark crossed his hands over his chest, taking a deep breath.

"I'd like everyone to do this for a minute. Take a deep breath. It's very calming—and not only that, you can't hit anybody when your hands are like this," Mark said jokingly.

The Dalai Lama retorted with a wry smile: "But you can throw nasty glances!"

At that point Mark had everyone in the room "do turtle," saying, "We teach children, starting out at the very beginning, by rewarding them with an ink stamp of a turtle for doing this when they're upset and calming themselves down. This gives the teacher a visible sign that the children are calming down. But even more important, the Russian psychologists Vygostky and Luria talked about how motor planning is very important to learning. We believe that children learn from the outside first through physical actions, and then it becomes more conceptual in the mind. We want them to associate an action with this idea of calming down. And in addition, it is very hard to do something physically aggressive in this state.

"Our work began in 1981 with deaf children using sign language. Because deaf children often have very deprived language, we would have them do turtle by doing this," Mark said, again making the sign for a turtle in his shell. "But over time, we thought crossing arms was better, because it incorporates the deep breath, which calms them.

"To calm down is often difficult; in some way it's almost as if they're holding themselves back. It needs great support from adults. When a teacher encounters a child who looks very upset and angry, the child often can't calm down alone. We suggest the teacher take the child's hand and say, 'I see you're very upset. Let's calm down together. I'll do it with you. Let's take a deep breath together,' and then 'Now, are you feeling calmer?' It's just like a mother and a baby where the mother 'scaffolds,' or structures, the interaction. In the same way, teachers need to do this many times for children to internalize this essential skill.

"Another thing we're teaching children simultaneously with doing the turtle is what we call self-talk, or talking to oneself as a way of controlling behavior. Sometimes it is called verbal self-control. The idea is to talk to oneself and to use language as a substitute for the acting-out behavior or the emotional overdisplay."

Here Mark made a crucial point: that self-regulation abilities are the prerequisite for acting responsibly. Moral teachings alone, without the underlying skills to follow them, are not enough. "We think that unless children can learn how to calm down when they're truly upset, nothing else that we'll teach them about moral development or about feelings will make much difference. It's the primary, critical issue. It's very difficult; it takes repeated practice. As an adult, I'm still working on it.

"We only use the turtle technique with younger children. It is too immature for older children; they would be embarrassed by it, and they have less need for it. But younger children, in this three-to-seven-year-old period, have much more emotional instability and difficulty with behavioral control than older children."

Showing What You Feel

Then Mark showed a slide of cartoon images of human faces, each standing for a different emotion: a smiley face for happiness, a grumpy face for anger, and so on. "A second goal is to teach children about feelings. Starting developmentally with their simple feelings, over the elementary years we progress to more complex feelings. First of all, we color-code them. We talk about yellow feelings, or comfortable feelings. We never discuss them as good or bad; all feelings are okay. We use the word 'comfortable,' which is a word that children understand very easily at young ages. Then we talk about blue feelings as feelings that are uncomfortable. We talk about the feelings as being comfortable or uncomfortable because of how they make the children feel inside (although this does get complicated at times). For example, with 'scared' or 'afraid,' we usually teach the opposite at the same time, in this case 'safe.'

"Lessons are multimodal—the teacher will show pictures of people's faces and bodies, maybe talk about a time when she felt those emotions when she was a young child, tell a story, and have the children talk about when they have experienced these feelings. In addition, at the end of the lesson, she hands out a 'feeling face' on a small card to each child, and each child puts it on a ring and keeps these faces on his or her desk. Similarly, the teacher has a set of faces on her desk, and, if we're able to penetrate a school completely, the principal has a set too.

"The child begins with a few 'feeling face' cards on his or her ring, and slowly the ring becomes full of more and more faces. These faces are used throughout the day to express and develop awareness of their inner states of being. Just as we taught the children to do turtle—because it is a behavior that they can use anytime during the day, especially in the heat of the moment—in a similar way we use these 'feeling faces' during real situations. For example, at certain times—maybe at the very beginning of the day, or after children come in from lunch and are very excited—the teacher will say, 'I'd like everybody to look through their faces and show the one they're feeling.'

"Over a number of grades, we teach a variety of feelings, starting with basic ones like happy, sad, scared, and safe, and then moving to somewhat more complex ones like disappointed or proud; then to even more complex ones like embarrassment and humiliation. By the time the children are eleven years of age, we are discussing quite complex experiences such as feeling rejected and feeling forgiveness.

"By the way, we also teach 'private'—which is a white card—in the first few lessons so that children realize that they don't have to show what they're feeling. They can feel very comfortable or very uncomfortable, but they don't need to show it. In fact, we learned this from a deaf child. In the early years we decided we would hand out some empty faces with no emotion on them and see what the children did. One child wrote on an empty face 'nobody's business.' He didn't want to tell anybody how he felt on that day.

"Our early experiences with PATHS led to two conclusions. One is that we underestimate children's abilities, and the other is that they can teach us quite a bit about which emotions we should introduce. Another example of this was a deaf child who was about nine years of age. He said to his teacher one day, 'I need a new face. I have a feeling I want to have a face for...' She said, 'What is it?' And he said, in sign language, 'Mean/happy.' She said, 'What is mean/happy?' He said, 'It's when I trip someone and they fall down and I laugh.' We spent a year in our laboratory deciding what feeling that was and decided upon the word 'malicious.' That's a very powerful word.

"There is a way in which teaching children about feelings not only helps them to recognize what's going on inside themselves or what's going on inside another person, but also shows them how talking about feelings can actually often solve problems. Let me give you an example with 'malicious.'

Teasing is a very difficult problem for children, and many children just can't respond effectively to being teased. Adults will often tell them to ignore the teaser, who will go away. In some cases that is true, but it is very hard to ignore teasing. Children often think they're ignoring the teaser, but they're giving enough cues to keep the other child going, because a child teases to get a reaction.

"So when we teach children the word 'malicious,' we teach them that they can say to a person who teases them, 'You're just being malicious.' They are now commenting on the feeling of the other rather than reacting to the behavior. It's a way of metacontrolling the situation. I was visiting a classroom one day and saw a child being teased by another. The child being teased said to the teaser, 'Are you feeling malicious? Did you have a problem earlier today?' It is a very different kind of reaction than reacting by feeling hurt. The child stopped teasing."

Laying Down Pathways in the Brain

"Teasing is a good example of a very complicated phenomenon. First of all, when children are being teased, sometimes they feel very hurt and humiliated, sometimes they just feel confused, and sometimes they feel it actually makes them a part of the group. It's very complicated, but generally when we talk with children in the classroom, they say that all teasing is bad and negative. As they get older, we see a different form of this kind of behavior, which is gossip. By the time they're ten years old, children are in cliques and they gossip and tell stories about each other, which is again very, very painful. It's extremely hard for children to manage their emotions when children are telling false stories about them. So we spend a lot of time at the older ages talking about gossip."

"What seems to be emerging here in dealing with the problem of teasing among children," the Dalai Lama commented, "is the suggestion that because they haven't developed fully their faculty of intelligence, they don't understand the context. But my own personal feeling is that you don't really need a high level of cognitive faculty to understand teasing. Often teasing is really play—a game that we can see in animals too. Dogs often bite each other playfully. They seem to understand that this is not malicious."

Mark responded, "This is where it is very important to be able to calm down when one is being teased and see clearly whether someone is just trying to have fun or is really trying to hurt. Children who are either aggressive or easily hurt react to teasing right away, almost automatically. We don't know how this works in the brain; it may be that there are certain circuits that are primed to be especially sensitive to this.

"Teachers are faced, just like parents, with problems that are sometimes insoluble. Two children run in from the playground and one says, 'He took my ball.' 'No, no, he took my ball, I had it first.' 'I had it first.' The problem is that the teacher never saw the first event. Or there is an event that happened two days before that initiated the problem. You rarely know who started the problem; you can suspect but you don't know. What happens often is that because the teacher doesn't want to deal with this, he or she will say, 'Okay, both of you go sit down. You both have a time-out.' Both are punished.

"We advise teachers that when the children run in with all of this emotion, the first thing that often happens is that they begin to get emotionally upset themselves. We suggest that teachers might say, 'You're looking very upset, and now I'm starting to feel it too. We all need to calm down.' One way of doing this is for the children to go find their feeling faces and find out what emotion they're feeling. This is the idea, theoretically, of activating the left frontal lobe"—the area that Richie said helps inhibit disturbing emotions.

"It's using that language center in the reasoning part of the brain to now begin to understand and, in that way, manage the emotion. Sometimes it works and sometimes it doesn't, of course," Mark finished.

"This is very true," the Dalai Lama agreed. "From the Buddhist perspective, what is being done here is to skillfully divert the focus away from the strong emotion so that the mind can first be brought to a neutral state."

Nodding, Mark added, "And we believe that developmentally, at this period from three to eight or nine, when children are learning to label emotions, we can lay down these pathways in the brain. We don't know much about the pathways between the amygdala and the frontal lobe, or the hippocampus and the frontal lobe, and there are lots of structures in the brain in between those with pathways that we don't understand very well. But we think that laying these abilities down as habits at this critical stage in life is very important. If the same skills have to be taught later, it requires relearning. And relearning is always harder than first learning."

Here again, Mark enunciated a basic rationale for educating the emotions in children: Helping them acquire effective emotional skills while the crucial circuitry first develops its pathways is far easier than having to try to change how those pathways operate once they are adults. The ounce of prevention, as always, is worth a pound of cure—or years of psychotherapy, drug counseling, or prison, for that matter.

Zones of Peace in the Classroom

"In addition," Mark said, "we have a broader context in which we teach children problem solving and conflict resolution skills. In doing this, again, we use practical pictures and stories. For example, we use the Control Signals Poster—it's a traffic light, which children understand right away."

Mark displayed a poster of a stoplight, with each light standing for a step in the basics of self-control:

Red light: Take a long, deep breath. Say the problem and how you feel.

Yellow light: What could I do? Would it work?

Green light: Try your best idea. How did it work?

This poster—developed by Roger Weissberg and his colleagues at Yale University—was one I had seen on the walls of every classroom in the New Haven public schools when I went there in the early 1990s to write about a pioneering program in emotional literacy. Over the years the New Haven program—like PATHS, a national model—has spread widely, as educators from around the world have come to New Haven to learn how to create their own programs in "social development," as it is called there.

Mark explained the stoplight: "The idea is that when you feel an important emotion, it's a signal giving you information, and the first thing you need to do is stop and calm down. Of course, that's exactly what the wise old turtle taught the little turtle, the steps in the red light—take a long, deep breath, and talk through the problem and how you're feeling about it to yourself or to someone else.

"Then we begin to teach children the yellow light. The idea is to generate different solutions to problems, and we have them practice lots of different ways of solving problems through role playing. It's very important to create the right context. We want the teacher to create an atmosphere of the classroom as a family—a family away from home. This family should be a safe place, and therefore the solutions we develop should be ones that don't harm others. You don't have to become best friends with everyone, but you have to get along with people. Part of getting along is to understand that during the day you live in a classroom where we don't want to harm others.

"As a result of our philosophy, we don't spend a lot of time permitting children to generate aggressive, negative solutions—it's not productive. Instead we say, 'If your goal is to at least get along and do no harm, what could you do now if someone was teasing you? What could you do now if someone was talking behind your back? What could you do now if someone pushed you in line and you were feeling really angry at that person?' Then we have them try their ideas and at the end ask themselves how it worked.

"We put these Control Signals Posters everywhere. We put them in the classroom, on the playground doors, in the lunchroom, in the principal's office. In some schools, in the playground we put red cones—like traffic cones—in different places on the playground, and the children learn that when they're upset, they can go over and stand by the red cone and no one will bother them.

"In the back of the classroom sometimes we have what is called a 'peace table' or a 'peace chair.' In the past schools often called these 'time-out chairs.' They were put there to calm children down, but it was still perceived as a punishment by the child. So we put a red circle on the chair and said they could sit in it when they have a lot of emotion, to calm down and think about what they can do."

"So there's a zone of peace in every classroom?" I asked, thinking of the Dalai Lama's use of that phrase when he proposed making Tibet such a zone, free of all weapons.

"Well, we haven't done this in all classrooms," Mark replied, "but we have tried it and it works quite well. In many American schools we have a program focused on conflict resolution in which older children are taught how to intervene in the conflicts of younger children. Eleven-year-olds in the school are taught how to walk around the playground and intervene when they see younger children having a problem. In our PATHS schools, we have them wear a T-shirt that has the Control Signals Poster on it. That makes it very concrete. We put the symbols of the skills everywhere, so when the older child intervenes, they'll say, 'Let's go to the red light first because we have a problem. We'll calm down.' And then 'Let's go to the yellow light. First you talk and the other listens, and then the other talks and you listen.'

"We've done careful experimental studies of the PATHS curriculum, and we know from randomized controlled trials that the children who received this curriculum become better able to talk about their feelings and to understand other children's feelings."[8]

His scientific instincts piqued, the Dalai Lama asked about the methods used to conclude that the program worked. "In one school there would be some classes that wouldn't get this training and some classes that would get it?"

"No," Mark explained, "we usually have one school that gets it and one school that doesn't. Otherwise there would be contamination because if they have it, the staff naturally want to spread it throughout the school environment." But the comparison schools are in comparable neighborhoods, and the choice of which schools get the program is randomized, Mark assured us.

Then he went on to explain some of the ways they assessed what children had learned. "We ask them questions like 'How can you tell when you're angry or sad?' They become better at responding to these questions—better able to recognize and talk about their feelings—than children who don't have this training. They almost immediately show a reduction in their own self-report of symptoms of depression and feeling sadness. In fact, those are relatively easy symptoms to change. When children learn the power of talking about their feelings and sharing them, it is often a very important antidote to depression. Over time we also see reductions in children's aggressive behavior. These reductions are not dramatic, but they're significant, and we've repeatedly shown them across a number of studies.

"We could think about this like heart disease. We know there are certain factors related to heart disease such as diet, genetic factors, exercise. And we know that if we reduce these risk factors in the population, it will slowly reduce the amount of heart disease. In the same way, our work reduces the risk factors of not being able to calm down, not being able to take the other's point of view, not being able to think through a problem. So we're slowly reducing the amount of aggressive behavior and acting out of destructive emotions."

Wanted: Wise Elders

Mark then emphasized the power for children of seeing adults demonstrate these emotional skills. "In the school, it is critically important that teachers learn to model these skills and make them their own. For many teachers this is very difficult to do. It is quite demanding, and there are individual differences in how good teachers are at this. But if we give them regular weekly support by having one of our staff work with them, their modeling can have a profound influence on how children use emotional abilities.

"Even when I'm doubtful that I can get teachers to model calming down, talking to themselves, and modeling for children how to use their intelligence, many times it turns out they *can* do it. This fits with Aristotle's notion, which Owen mentioned, that virtues are harmonized by exposure to wise elders. This modeling by adults is critical. We find that when teachers don't model what they teach, the children don't use it.

"Of course, we don't want to leave parents out. John Gottman and other researchers have provided good evidence that many parents also do what we call emotional coaching.[9] When a child is angry or sad, they don't turn away from the child. They don't punish the child. They help the child to understand that their feeling will not overwhelm them, that it's okay and can be worked with, that it's a natural phenomenon. And those children show the same positive capabilities: better behavior and a better ability to manage their physiological arousal.

"The first thing I talked about this morning was how the parents of infants helped them to manage their emotions. In the same way, but at a different developmental level, parents and teachers of ten-year-olds are still helping. Paul may say that a parent of a twenty-year-old is still helping, because wise elders are important at every age. We're all looking for teachers.

"But we shouldn't think that childhood is the end of the zone for intervention. We don't know about adulthood, but we believe there is still plasticity in adolescence and beyond. Other programs that teach social and emotional learning to adolescents have been shown to reduce drug and cigarette use, and aggressive behaviors. We know that even in the adolescent period, these kinds of programs, examined carefully in experimental trials, have been shown to be effective.

"Although adults are important in children's lives, the heat of the moment is almost always in peer relationships. We know that the very best predictor in childhood of adult mental health is what other children say about a child during their school years.[10] Children see things about other children that adults often miss.

"Because of this, I think it's very important that this kind of work be universal, that it not be done just in the context of psychotherapy, with an adult teaching one child. Really, a parent can't do this all alone, either, because children's peer social context is very important. We have to create contexts in schools in which they see these skills as valued in their peer relationships, not just by adults but by other children. And children need to realize from an early age that this is really what growing up is about. In America this is quite a problem given the radical changes in the last twenty years in the amount of time adults spend with children."

The Dalai Lama turned to Jinpa and quietly told him how happy he was to hear Mark's report. All along he'd been saying there was a real need to bring something like this into education, and now something concrete and practical was being done. The Dalai Lama later told me, too, how pleased he was to learn of this systematic attempt to help children handle their destructive emotions. He was impressed both by the specifics and by the fact that these methods were actually being applied as part of children's education.

Modeling Compassion

Mark went on, "One of the things that we've spent less time on, possibly because of our Western view of the world and our focus on preventing psychopathology, is developing positive emotions. But we've begun to work on that over the last seven or eight years by telling children true stories about important people in the world. Some are children just like themselves who have done important things to help the world, and some are adults, like His Holiness.

"I thought I might give you an example of how we can use a story to weave PATHS into language arts and the reading curriculum, so we integrate these lessons across the school day. There's a story about a famous baseball player in America, Jim Abbott, who only has one arm. We're interested in teaching the idea of persisting through obstacles, and of course he had an enormous obstacle. He tells the story that when he was a child, everyone said he could never be a baseball player because he has one arm. We tell the story of his life and how he became successful, and then we ask the children about a goal they think they can't reach. We have them write it down and think of steps to reach that goal.

"Another example is Aung San Suu Kyi from Burma (now called Myanmar)," Mark said, getting a nod of recognition from the Dalai Lama, who knows her as another Nobel Peace laureate; he traveled to the Burmese border to be part of a Nobel laureates' demonstration to support her. "We use her life as an example to teach social responsibility, that sometimes you must give your life for something that is important. We tell the story of her being under house arrest for many years, and what the democracy movement is in Myanmar and why people feel so strongly about some things that they must persist in doing something about them, even if it means great sacrifice.

"After discussing her biography, we have the children do a short project to improve their school or their neighborhood. The idea is to transfer the understanding of certain emotions and goals that Aung San Suu Kyi had. Then they can see those same goals in themselves and that there are goals they should have for their community in the same way.

"Another example we've used is an Asian American woman named Maya Lin. She designed the Vietnam Veterans Memorial in Washington and the Civil Rights Memorial in Montgomery, Alabama. We use her life story to illustrate how one can use art to commemorate important things. We use a children's book about a father who takes his son to the Vietnam Veterans Memorial to see his grandfather's name—*The Wall,* by Eve Bunting. It's very powerful because it also brings in themes of death and war.

"We talk then about how walls can commemorate or memorialize important events in history. Then the class plans and conducts a project to commemorate something in their community. We don't know what it will be. It could be something that happened in the school during the year, or something historical in the neighborhood, but the idea is to move toward the ideal of social responsibility—and maybe the beginning of compassion.

"I speak humbly about these examples, because we are just beginning to learn how to work with positive emotions. We've been much more focused on managing destructive emotions. I'm very interested in your thoughts about different ways to develop compassion. I know that there is a many-thousand-year history in Buddhism of developing compassion in young monks, and I think we can learn a lot from some of those techniques, along with our own Western techniques.

"Maybe I should pose that as a question to His Holiness. Do any ideas come to mind for ways we can help develop compassion in young adolescents' minds?"

At that, the Dalai Lama asked in Tibetan what others present thought, at which point Matthieu commented, "There is a very small thing which I notice in some Tibetan families that I thought was wonderful. A child will make presents for everybody else on his own birthday and is happy to do so. These small things are not big principles, but they say something."

Mark agreed. "We know that for children, it's not the big ideas but the small things that happen every day that are so important."

A Repertoire of Compassion

Then the Dalai Lama shared his thoughts. "I believe that managing negative emotion is very important, but by itself it is not really going to solve the problems. Clearly in your program you recognize this point, the need for developing and cultivating the positive emotions. Although these positive emotions may not be directly applicable as an antidote in the heat of the moment, they will help prepare the child, or whoever it is, to deal with the negative emotions much more skillfully. As to what specific technique could be developed to do this, I don't really have any particular ideas—except that perpetual exposure of children to an atmosphere of genuine love and compassion, both within the family by the parents and also by teachers in the schools who have a genuine concern and care for the well-being of the children, will have a significant impact in itself. It is very difficult to try to teach the value and importance of compassion and love to children through words. Actions speak louder than words."

Mark had gone into the day knowing that the Dalai Lama virtually never talks as though he knows much about subjects such as child development, but Mark was struck by his suggestions. Agreeing, he said, "That's why we use examples and stories. I'll tell you another story we use with third-graders. This is a true story. It is a story about a thirteen-year-old boy who lived in the wealthy suburbs outside of Philadelphia. His name is Trevor Ferrell. One night he was watching the news on television and he saw homeless people on the streets in the downtown area of Philadelphia. He went to his father and said, 'We have some blankets in the garage. I want to take those blankets downtown and give them to people. They're sleeping on the grates where the steam comes out.'

"His father thought it was a strange idea, but he took him down there, and it was very rewarding to Trevor and his father. The next day Trevor started putting signs up in the grocery store and other places: 'Does anybody have blankets they don't use? Is there any food people don't need?' Within a week he had a garage full of food, and now in Philadelphia there are a number of warehouses that are called Trevor's Place that feed the homeless."

The Dalai Lama had been smiling and nodding rapidly in approval throughout Mark's tale.

"We tell this story and use it with the Control Signals Poster. We talk about how when Trevor felt that there was something really wrong, he needed to calm down and think, 'What can I do.' The idea is that it's not just adults like His Holiness who can be models, but there's something that children themselves can do. That's how we try to communicate, through story, but we're looking for new ideas."

Alan Wallace made a suggestion about cultivating the positive range of emotion. "You started out with the theme that all these emotions are natural and okay, and my first response was that they're not really all okay. My second response was that it may be good advice just to recognize them, and not judge them before you recognize them. But one could also say that, just as in Communism all people are equal but some were more equal than others, all feelings are okay but some are more okay than others. William James has a principle that I think is really brilliant, and I use it just about every day of my life: What we attend to becomes our reality, and what we don't attend to fades out of our reality. A fair number of the 'feeling faces' on the cards were negative. The children, especially when they get to the ages of ten, eleven, twelve, and on, could start developing a wider repertoire of cards of compassion, patience, friendliness.

"There is a central theme of the classic text *Bodhicaryavatara* or *A Guide to the Bodhisattva Way of Life*. When feelings arise, observe how they affect you. When a child expresses generosity, how does that feel? Watch not only how the other person experiences your generosity but how you feel when you're expressing generosity. They can start developing more and more sensitivity and awareness of the virtues without having to tell them, 'You should do this.' His Holiness has so often said that these virtues are natural. If they attend to them and start using cards for them, then they'll say, 'Wow!' "

"It's a wonderful idea," Mark said. "In the West, I think we're focused more on the destructive emotions partly because we work in the school context, where violence is driving all of the funding for these programs. But even at the early ages we haven't spent enough time on the positive. A simple example: As I was listening the last two days I started writing all the names of new lessons we should be creating. We don't have one on awe or wonderment. I've learned a great deal already about where I need to go next with the work, and I'm grateful to you."

The Dalai Lama, who had been particularly touched by Mark's presentation, raised his joined hands to his forehead in a gesture to honor Mark.

12

Encouraging Compassion

Why has Western science ignored compassion?

That had been the pivotal question in a telling interchange at the fifth Mind and Life meeting, on altruism and human nature. The question had been raised by Anne Harrington, a historian of science at Harvard University.[1] As she put it, "Historically, the more deeply our sciences have probed reality, the less relevant concepts like compassion become. Behind altruism is strategizing for genetic fitness," which is how evolutionary theory explains away such selflessness.

In contrast, she had noted, "when one employs Buddhist methods of exploring reality, one apparently arrives at a very different reality," one in which "compassion is basic, serves as a dominant framework for the dramas of life, and in which beings are all connected and not in struggle."

The Dalai Lama had replied that science was a relatively young discipline, and its current mainstream understanding of human nature as basically aggressive, selfish, and heartless seemed an arbitrary viewpoint at a particular stage in the evolving understanding of human nature.

Perhaps that negative spin was due to psychology following the lead of medicine, which focuses on disease rather than on health, observed Richard Davidson, who had organized the meeting. The bias in psychology toward studying negative emotions, he speculated, may reflect that bias.

To that point, Ervin Staub, a social psychologist at the University of Massachusetts, had replied that in the last thirty years some psychologists had begun research on altruism and empathy, though they had not yet linked those with the idea of compassion. And he thought the time was ripe for the field to pay attention to compassion as well as to positive emotions in general.

That very focus on compassion and the positive proved to be true of our afternoon session. As the afternoon began, I told the Dalai Lama I'd like to pursue a key point we had just discussed over our lunch at Chonor House: that the school programs Mark had described focused mostly on curbing disturbing emotions but not on cultivating the positive ones, which are antidotes to the destructive emotions. "We wonder," I said to him, "since Buddhism itself is a rich storehouse of methods for cultivating these positive emotions, if there aren't some techniques that could be adapted in the secular context for instruction in a program like this."

As he often does when asked directly for a solution, the Dalai Lama at first demurred, wanting to reflect a bit. "As Matthieu said in his presentation, in Buddhist understanding there are eighty-four thousand different kinds of afflictions of mind, and in response there are eighty-four thousand different kinds of antidotes. I would like to begin with that statement and then we'll see what you have to say, and maybe I'll have something to add."

I saw that Alan was eager to speak, and turned to him. He began by referring back to the classic *Guide to the Bodhisattva Way of Life*, by the sage Shantideva, that he had mentioned in the morning session. "There is a whole chapter devoted to cultivating patience or tolerance as an antidote to the problem of anger and hatred. Another approach goes back to the teachings on the Four Immeasurables—compassion, equanimity, empathetic joy, and lovingkindness." Here Alan was referring to a classic set of Buddhist meditation practices designed to cultivate these states.

"There lovingkindness is also diametrically opposed to hatred," Alan continued. "If hatred is an attitude or an emotion that can't stand another person's well-being—'I don't like it that you're happy because you're my enemy'—lovingkindness is just the opposite. It's wishing for the happiness and the sources of happiness for the other.

"And so the more you cultivate lovingkindness, the less you have to deal with anger and hatred. It's like having a strong immune system: You can go into an area with the plague, and you won't have to worry about antidotes because you're immune to it. Similarly with the other Four Immeasurables: Compassion is diametrically opposed to cruelty. Cruelty is delight in someone else's suffering, and even yearning to inflict suffering. Compassion is just the opposite—'May you be free of the suffering and the source of your suffering,'" Alan said, repeating a phrase used in the meditation practice itself. Such phrases are repeated mentally, along with generating the feeling of the compassionate wish, until both the thought and feeling become deeply ingrained and genuinely felt (even if they may not be at the beginning).

Then Alan came to a uniquely Buddhist concept, *mudita,* which refers to being joyous at the well-being or joy of another person. As is often the case with Buddhist concepts pertaining to emotion, there is no single equivalent word in English, suggesting that this is a concept poorly articulated in our culture.[2]

"The more you cultivate empathetic joy," Alan elaborated, "the more you will naturally be counteracting its opposite, which is jealousy—'I can't stand that you're happy; I can't stand that you're famous or wealthy.' In empathetic joy you delight in the good fortune of others, so you undermine jealousy before it even has a chance to arise.

"Finally, there is equanimity, which is diametrically opposed to attachment and aversion. The more you cultivate equanimity, once again, it's like having an immune system that enables you to carry a peace zone with you wherever you go."

Matthieu added, "There are also two complementary ways of generating positive emotions. One begins with reason, and the other begins with generating some basic emotions and then working on them.

"The first one is exchanging places with others. There is a series of gradual exercises on how first to equate yourself with others, then to exchange yourself with others, then to consider others as more important than yourself, and sometimes just to take others' point of view in seeing your own ego as selfish and arrogant. You start being upset at that ego from the others' point of view, just as you might ordinarily be toward someone else you saw as selfish." He added that an entire chapter in the Shantideva text that Alan had referred to deals with gradually more subtle ways of making this exchange.

"The other way is to generate a basic feeling of intense lovingkindness—for instance, by considering someone you love very much, the classic example being the very kind mother. And then you imagine that mother in a terrible situation. There is a lot of imagination used, because we're dealing with emotion. Say you imagine her as a doe being chased by a hunter. She jumps over a cliff and breaks her bones. The hunter comes and is about to give the final blow, and then she looks at you and says, 'Can you help me, son?' and you feel powerless. Or you imagine someone who is very dear to you having no food for months and asking you for a morsel. You do all this to generate a very powerful emotion of lovingkindness for someone you really love."

Once the feeling of lovingkindness becomes strong, then the meditator extends the feelings toward other people, and finally toward all living beings, as Matthieu explained. "Then you try to extend that to other beings by realizing that, in fact, there is no reason why you should not extend those feelings to all sentient beings. You can combine both complementary methods into something that you feel naturally and you can expand rationally."

"I have a more modest version of what you're suggesting," said Paul Ekman. "It's a technique that I have used when preparing myself for a situation that I know will be difficult. I have certain visual images that I use again and again because they're very rich ones for generating positive emotion. I focus my mind on those visual images and begin to experience the positive emotion, and then enter into that difficult situation in a positive state. That's one technique that I think is related to what you're saying, but much smaller.

"The other technique is based on my own research and also relates to something that Mark said. I make the muscle movements of a smile to generate a positive emotional state," just as his research had shown that intentionally evoking a smile actually stimulates the appropriate changes in the brain.

"I also use a slight variation on the turtle movement," Paul continued. "When I worked in a Stone Age culture in New Guinea, I found again and again that when people were ill at ease, they held themselves like this," he said, crossing his arms and placing his hands on his shoulders.

"I have pictures of hundreds of people standing there like this. I use this posture because I'm holding myself, warming myself, and it helps me. I don't know whether, when gripped by the emotion, I could get a grip on myself. I haven't yet tried that. So far, these methods are preparatory, when I can anticipate a difficult encounter."

Compassion: The Great Tranquilizer

Now the Dalai Lama had much to say. "Generally speaking, before engaging in a Buddhist practice you attend to what the purpose and benefits are. This is a very practical procedure. If you skip that stage and you are just told to cultivate compassion, most likely if you did it at all you would cultivate something contrived that wouldn't have much juice to it.

"For example, a classic procedure in Buddhism for cultivating compassion is to develop a way of viewing others as if each sentient being is your own mother. To verify by means of cogent reasoning that every sentient being has, in fact, actually been your mother in some life in the infinite past is a difficult task. But that's not the primary reason for viewing all sentient beings as your mother. Why do it? Because viewing an individual as your mother brings forth a sense of fondness, cherishing, gentleness, affection, and gratitude. When you recognize why you should do it, then even if you're not absolutely sure that every single sentient being has actually been your mother, seeing the purpose and anticipating the benefit, you can make the attempt.

"Similarly, if one has a very strong predilection for attachment—really, craving—one of the classic early antidotes involves a very strong use of imagination. You imagine the world to be covered with bones and skeletons. Of course, it's very disenchanting, a very unpleasing way to view reality. Why on earth would one do that? I'd much rather imagine the whole world covered with flowers. But you see that doing this will help calm your mind, which is presently afflicted with craving. This could be a useful temporary device to counteract what is disturbing you. You keep on coming back to this question of what is really disrupting your well-being. If you recognize that it's your own mental afflictions that are the problem, then you can see for yourself why you might want to pursue this antidote and do so with perseverance.

"Coming back to the issue of compassion, you can often get the impression that the cultivation of compassion and lovingkindness is something that we do for others, an offering we make to the world. But that's really a very superficial way to see it. I feel from my own experience that when I practice compassion there is an immediate direct benefit to myself, not for others. By practicing compassion, I get one hundred percent benefit, while the benefit to others may be fifty percent. So the main motivation for the practice of compassion is self-interest." The Dalai Lama noted that in Buddhist scriptures, a bodhisattva, who reaches a high level of spiritual attainment through practices focused on compassion, has great happiness and well-being because of cherishing others more than oneself and developing extraordinary degrees of compassion and lovingkindness.

"From my own small experience, I find that as soon as some kind of sense of caring or concern increases in my heart, this brings me more inner strength. The result: I feel less fear, more happiness. There are some problems here and there? Okay, no matter. If there is shocking news, sad news, I may be uncomfortable for a few seconds, but then I recover very swiftly and there is peace again"—confirming an observation Paul Ekman had already been struck by in observing the Dalai Lama's emotional reactions.

"I think the practice of compassion is like a medication that restores serenity when one is very agitated," the Dalai Lama concluded. "The great tranquilizer is compassion."

Throughout this discourse on compassion, the Dalai Lama was exceptionally animated, almost buoyant, using very forceful gestures—it was clearly a topic of conviction for him.

Matthieu put the discussion in a broader social context. "If you read the Declaration of Human Rights, there are fifty-eight or so articles. But in our dealings with others, it seems that one basic article that could define human rights is to recognize that others want to be happy just as much as we do. As much as we don't want to suffer, neither do others. Therefore, they have exactly the same rights because their wish is the same as ours. That summarizes the whole Declaration of Human Rights."

How Compassion Changes the Brain

Our discussion returned to themes from Richie Davidson's presentation on neuroscience the day before, with Francisco Varela making a link to compassion. "I've found a very interesting connection with the practice of cultivating compassion by exchanging oneself with others, where at the beginning we use our imagination to generate an emotion that is slightly contrived, but then we get used to it and we carry it through. There is more and more evidence that perception and imagination are very closely linked mental functions. Of course you can make a distinction, but there is a tremendous amount of overlap of the mental image and the perception of a real situation.

"Therefore, you can learn and modify with the imagination in a physiological sense. This is the idea of neuroplasticity. From the neuroscience point of view, this is not surprising; it should work. One good example: Techniques have been developed recently by sports coaches who will train skiers, for example, in the summer by having them lie down in bed and imagine skiing on the slopes. The fact is, when they actually put their skis on, they're much better. It works the same way with this compassion training."

I highlighted the implication: "If these practices are actually effective, wouldn't it suggest that there must be an underlying neural change? The practice, from a neurological point of view, involves repeating the habit enough that it changes the circuitry in the brain so that the goal we seek to achieve—for example, equanimity and compassion—becomes actual reality at the level of the brain." Knowing his research was relevant, I turned to Richie and asked, "Would that be the case?"

"Yes," Richie said. "Matthieu's comments the other day were very clear about this. When we first begin a practice of this sort, we generate a transient state of compassion or other positive emotions, which can come and go. But when it's practiced more consistently, it becomes more of a mood or a temperament. As a temperament, there is some evidence to indicate that a part of our brain has changed in a relatively permanent way."

Francisco cited the finding that trained musicians enlarge relevant parts of the brain. In other words, hours and hours on the violin change the amount of cells involved in musical performance, and enhance their conductivity.[3] That prompted Richie to tell the Dalai Lama about a study that had only recently been published in *Nature,* a very prestigious journal, on London taxicab drivers.[4] "The areas of the brain that enable the drivers to navigate turned out to be strengthened after the first six months of driving through the London streets."

The Dalai Lama remembered something in classic Buddhist texts that describes the progressive stages of mastery in meditation practice and that seemed relevant to the neurological explanations just given. It begins with a surface intellectual understanding of the words and their meaning—for instance, "compassion." With prolonged reflection, that understanding becomes clear and certain—the person has confident intellectual mastery of the concept and can successfully implement it in meditation practice. At first the evoking of compassion may take deliberate effort and feel simulated. But as practice matures, the actual feeling of compassion comes naturally and spontaneously, arising easily. Finally, it takes no effort. "These stages are called the understanding, or wisdom, derived from hearing, thinking, and meditation," he concluded.

Francisco responded to the Dalai Lama: "The interesting thing about the neurobiological evidence is that the sense of familiarity and effortlessness comes from the fact that our bodies have changed. The brain has rearranged itself, and we are a different being because of those changes. The familiarity has resulted in lasting changes in the brain."

Jinpa added, "A metaphor that is used in the Buddhist textual tradition is oil soaking the cloth. You can't really separate the two."

Cultivating a Culture of Gentleness

"Mark said something that I think is very important," I pointed out. "He said that first learning is easiest. Later learning takes more effort, as you say, because it's relearning. Can we help children learn these things in the first place so that the brain follows those pathways? Mark, maybe you can comment a little on how these lessons at the right age interplay with the development of the brain areas that Richie was talking about—the prefrontal areas, the amygdala, the hippocampus—that is, the areas involved in regulation of emotion. These are the areas that, as you said, are the most responsive to learning and experience."

Mark answered, "There is a great deal of development in the frontal lobe during early and middle childhood. We don't understand it all yet, by any means, but it happens just when these issues of self-control and being able to use language to talk to yourself begin to develop in the brain. It's then that these brain mechanisms are beginning to come online.

"I'll give you an example. I received an email last night from a teacher. We have now begun to do our work with children who are three and a half and four years old, so we're modifying our methods to find out how they will work at this younger age. The teacher, who works with children in poverty in a Head Start program, had taught the children the turtle story over the last few weeks. Last week she visited the homes of three parents. In each case the parents told her that the children spontaneously did this at home, as if it was natural. One mother said that she had begun to get upset, and her daughter, who is three and a half, told her that she should do turtle!

"What you're saying, Dan, is right, I think. This relates to what Matthieu said about a culture of gentleness. He gave the example of not killing a fly. If you killed a fly around Tibetan children, it would upset them. There is a cultivation of gentleness that, frankly, we don't see very much in America."

"I think we just saw a demonstration of exactly this gentleness," I said, "when His Holiness found a little gnat." Only minutes before, I had been struck by a spontaneous enactment of this sort of compassion in action. As the Dalai Lama had been speaking, he noticed a tiny insect crawling on the arm of his chair. He paused, bent down to peer at it, and gently flicked it away with a folded tissue to protect it—then he checked to see it was safe where it had fallen, and he saw that it was still on his chair. While Thupten Jinpa was translating his remarks, the Dalai Lama used his tissue to pick up the bug. He passed it to the young monk beside him, who took it out to the garden and set it free.

The Dalai Lama explained, with his characteristic laugh, "I was afraid I might inadvertently put my hand down on it and accumulate that type of karma where you don't really intend it, but you still get a little bit of karma. The gnat seemed afflicted with a broken leg and wasn't in good shape, so we removed it from harm's way. It's probably just because I'm in a good mood now! If I were in a bad mood..." He made a mischievous gesture as though he had squashed the bug, bringing peals of laughter.

"I think it was Owen," I commented, "who said that when people are in a good mood they're more altruistic. You've just proven that"—a remark that brought a laugh from the Dalai Lama.

"Once the mood becomes a temperament you're always in a good mood," Richie added.

"So the question is," I asked, "how can we raise children to be always in the kind of mood where they would do what His Holiness did?"

Mark gave an example. "I sometimes tell teachers a story about two brothers, one who was never satisfied and one who always seemed satisfied. On Christmas morning they got their presents, and the children were up in their room playing with them. The child who was never satisfied had a new computer and games and a little robot, but when his father asked if he was happy, he said, 'No. Now all the other children will be jealous of me, and then the batteries will die and I'll have to buy new batteries,' and on and on.

"Now, the other little boy had gotten a load of horse manure for Christmas. When his father went to his room, he found him happily playing in it. His father said, 'Why are you so happy?' He replied, 'There must be a horse in here somewhere!' And so we try to tell teachers that we want children to have that more optimistic attitude. It is very interesting how such buoyancy is a very important characteristic in the Buddhist model."

Counteracting Cruelty

Paul Ekman shifted our focus to how the brain learns negative behavior. "The first time one acts in a seriously cruel fashion may be the most difficult. But if you continue to act in a cruel fashion, you are in all likelihood changing your brain in such a way that cruelty now becomes your temperament. And cruelty becomes your way without thought or reservation. We see a lot of that.

"When you are faced with someone who has already established cruelty as their way rather than compassion, and they are about to act cruelly toward you or toward another, what can we do? How can we respond to lead that person away from the cruelty?"

"It depends on the context," the Dalai Lama pointed out. "In any specific situation there is a question whether you really have the ability to do anything or not. If you think there is a possibility, then the first option to consider is peaceful means, theoretically speaking. You would use reason or try other gentle measures to persuade the person not to engage in the cruel act.

"Clearly, I'm putting on the Buddhist hat again. There are four modes of enlightened activity that are laid out sequentially for a bodhisattva. The first option is pacifying, where you try to calm the situation with words, with reason, with comfort, or what have you. If that doesn't work, the second option is a slightly stronger mode: causing expansion or increase by giving the person something. You give them a gift. You give them something that will calm the waters. It could even be giving knowledge, or it could be giving something tangible to rectify the situation, to solve the problem.

"Where that's not possible, then you go on to the third option, which is domination or power. You use your greater power to subdue the person, the country, or whatever it may be. There are some situations where even that won't work, and then the final option is ferocity or wrath—even violence is a possibility. Among the forty-six secondary precepts of a bodhisattva, one of those is a vow to engage in a forceful response in a situation that calls for altruistically motivated force. So with wrathful compassion there can be violence. Theoretically speaking, violence can be permissible if it's done out of compassion.

"But in practice it's very difficult and is done only when, with a harmful person, there is no other way to change their cruel attitude. Because once we commit violence, the situation is very unpredictable, and violence generates more violence—many unexpected things can happen. It's much safer just to wait and see. Then, under those circumstances, maybe try some prayers, or curse—if nothing can be done, then maybe just shouting some words!" he added with a laugh.

"These are the modes for a bodhisattva who is still on the path and has to go by trial and error, not knowing exactly what is appropriate in a situation. Whereas one of the qualities of a Buddha is knowing immediately and unerringly exactly what is appropriate. A Buddha doesn't have to use trial and error." He noted, however, that we are not on that exalted level, but rather somewhere "back on the bodhisattva path."

"Your Holiness, is it harder to be cruel to someone who emanates lovingkindness?" Paul wanted to know.

"Generally speaking, yes," the Dalai Lama replied. "I very often quote a statement from *A Guide to the Bodhisattva Way of Life* to the effect that generosity is much easier to cultivate than tolerance or forbearance. The reason is that all of us have chances to show generosity. You can go anywhere and people are always very happy to accept your gifts, your generosity. However, tolerance and forbearance can only be cultivated when we meet with adversity, with an enemy, with cruelty, and so they are more rare.

"The author, Shantideva, encourages himself and his reader: When you see a situation of adversity or cruelty, you should really respond with *fiero,* the delight of meeting a challenge, because now you have an opportunity to cultivate patience. These opportunities are not so easy to come by. Especially if you do not inflict harm on others, they are less likely to inflict harm on you. The further along you are on the path, the less people will be antagonistic to you."

The Venerable Kusalacitto added a cautionary story from the Pali sutras. "One day the Buddha happened to meet with a horse trainer, and the Buddha asked him, 'What are your methods to train a horse to run very fast?' The trainer said, 'I divide horses into three types. The first is very quick at learning. When I just show the riding crop, they will run fast—that's the very best kind. The second kind of horse I have to whip again and again, otherwise it will not run. But the third kind is very difficult. Even if I whip again and again, it will lie down and not stand up and run.'

"The Buddha asked him, 'What do you do with those horses?' The horse trainer said, 'I don't even bother with them.' The Buddha said that training human beings was the same. Only some of the people could be trained; some were untrainable. He would lead them as far as their previous karma would allow, but he could not help them beyond that."

Richie Davidson cited data suggesting that there might be at least some hope for helping seemingly impossible cases, such as criminal psychopaths. "In the United States some scientists have studied a group of psychopaths who are incarcerated for cruel acts. One characteristic of psychopaths is that when they are confronted by rewards and good things that they want, they focus their attention so much on those things—on the object of desire—that they're insufficiently attentive to the possible negative consequences of what they might do to get what they want.

"It's been found, though, that if they are trained to pause, to develop patience, they begin to pay more attention to the cues of the possible negative consequences, and they actually show improvement. With criminals who are in jail, this improvement can happen over a fairly short period of time. It suggests there may be certain techniques that we haven't yet tried systematically but which are worth trying, even in populations that are very hardened and difficult to train."

Empathy and Loving Composure: Antidotes to Cruelty

Matthieu went back to Paul's query about how best to relate to a cruel person. "You need two hands to clap. If someone is not at all in the mood for conflict, it is much more difficult to get in a fight with that person. It is difficult to judge just by texts and biographies, but we find many stories of meditators and hermits in Tibet who encountered bandits and even sometimes wild animals. When the bandits suddenly come into the presence of someone who is very serene, with loving composure, their attitude and initial intention completely subside, just like pouring cold water on boiling water. There are plenty of stories like that, and some of them are bound to be true."

Jeanne Tsai turned the question back to Paul: "From your work, is there any evidence to suggest that certain facial expressions or body postures are disarming to people who are behaving in aggressive ways?"

After reflecting for some moments, Paul concluded there was no direct evidence for this. "It appears that people who act cruelly aren't moved by signs of suffering or fear—they depersonalize. Part of the issue is how to reassert that they are dealing with a fellow human being. People whose job is to be cruel report that they don't respond to the other person's pain. The surprising thing about such people is that, supposedly, they are nice to their families. It's hard to believe, but that's what they report. So there is also a negative side to this plasticity of the brain: One can learn to no longer regard people as people."

This reminded me of data about people who have been torturers. I said,

"Research on people who worked for dictatorial regimes in Latin America and Greece shows that the process by which they became torturers is a very methodical indoctrination. It begins by first seeing the people who are victims as evil, not as people. The very first step is to deaden yourself to the other person as a person"—to depersonalize, as Paul had said. "Then they are very slowly made to do something that at first is very unpleasant, and then made to repeat it and repeat it until they become inured to it. There must be some unfortunate brain changes that go along with this."

Matthieu took up the theme. "Of course you all know the stories of child warriors in Africa who are forced to kill someone to break the barrier of their sensitivity to killing. I also heard stories of ordinary people who were forced to work in concentration camps. Many of them said that although the first week they were in tears all the time, after a few weeks they became insensitive."

I added my own tale, one showing how the absence of empathy opens the way to cruelty. "A man in California is in prison for killing his grandparents, his own mother, and five female students at the University of California. My brother-in-law was interviewing him for a research project and asked him, 'How could you do it? Didn't you feel any pity for your victims?' This murderer said very matter-of-factly, 'Oh, no, if I had felt any of their suffering I couldn't have done it.' He didn't feel a thing for them, and that was the key to his cruelty."

How to Cultivate Empathy

I concluded, "I think that the teaching of empathy very early in life is extremely important in this general curriculum we're talking about, if only as an inoculation against human cruelty later in life."

The Dalai Lama took up the question of how to cultivate empathy. His answer offered an insight into one reason he so often extended our discussion to include the implications for animals—and why he was so solicitous of that small bug on his chair.

"One way you can develop empathy," he explained, "is to start with small sentient beings like ants and insects. Really attend to them and recognize that they too wish to find happiness, experience pleasure, and be free of pain. Start there, with insects, and really empathize with them, and then go on to reptiles and so forth. Other human beings and yourself will all follow.

"On the other hand, if you murder little insects and dismiss any possibility of their wanting pleasure and avoiding pain, then when you come to animals that are more and more like us, it's easy to dismiss them. Even if a dog is wounded and it yelps, you don't experience the pain. Since you've already gotten into the mode of disregarding the pleasure and pain of an insect, now it's easier to disregard a bird, a dog, and even another person who cries out. With the attitude 'I don't feel it,' you dismiss that pain. You would never feel the empathy until it actually hits your own skin.

"If you have greater sensitivity to the pain and suffering of animals," the Dalai Lama continued, "then all the more you will have a greater sensitivity and empathy toward other human beings. It is a uniquely Buddhist phrase to refer to other sentient beings as 'mother sentient beings.' The point is, how you perceive sentient beings makes a difference."

Mark noted, "This confronts us with many problems in the West. For example, in the town where I live, school is closed on the first day of hunting season so that everyone can go sport hunting. When I think about trying some of these ideas with children, I would come up against real philosophical opposition from almost forty percent of men in the rural area I live in."

"And then there's fishing," the Dalai Lama added.

"I am wondering how to deal with the clash of values," Mark emphasized.

"It's conceivable," the Dalai Lama suggested, "there could be a worldwide ban on sport hunting at some point, but it's almost impossible to conceive of a similar ban in relation to fish or poultry on a global scale."

The Puzzle of How to Live a Good Life

Owen had a different kind of reaction—one that took us back to my beginning question about how to cultivate positive emotions. "I'm more convinced than I was even before I spoke with His Holiness on the first day that we are consistently talking about ethics. The emotions are a little piece of the puzzle of how to be a good person, how to live a good life, how to create compassionate, gentle, nonviolent people. Mark's work is vitally important. We have been talking about plasticity and how we can even teach old people like ourselves to change, but we've all acknowledged that it's harder. We have an expression in English that you can't teach an old dog new tricks. It's not quite true, probably, but I think the kinds of interventions that Mark uses with young people are very, very important.

"I just made a list of some of the main virtues and wholesome states of mind: fairness or justice, love or charity, patience, compassion, generosity, gratitude, tolerance, courage, honesty, self-knowledge. Or principles such as treating each person as if he is worth no more than any other person and acknowledging that oneself is worth no more than any other. The kinds of things that Mark was talking about this morning are ways to get young people to be able to live lives like that. In some sense, what we're really doing here is moral philosophy and trying to foster secular ethics. There is no way around that."

The Dalai Lama nodded in agreement. Even so, as he later told me, he felt a bit wary about talking in terms of morality, feeling that when beneficial practices or techniques are described in terms of moral development, it lessens their appeal to many people. Some people, of course, are drawn to such development, but only a select few. He sensed that often the attitude is, "Yes, it would be wonderful to be a moral person, but I don't really need to bother." Making an extra effort to be moral is not so universally appealing as, say, being a healthy person.

Better, then, to couch it in terms of a point of necessity—no one says they don't need good health or happiness. He saw that many people had taken up yoga not for its spiritual benefits but for better health. Likewise, the more effective way to present a program for cultivating positive emotions would be in terms of good health or happiness.

Presenting scientific evidence or analysis of how positive emotions can be cultivated and of what is destructive in emotional life, he felt, is the best way to approach the public—not talking about any specific set of ethics or morals or any religion. Even within our own dialogue, he worried that our emphasis on the Buddhist perspective might be a bit excessive, so that the applicability might seem restricted. His goal was to reach all humanity—we have these destructive emotions because we are human, and so we all need a better awareness of them.

Happiness, Virtue, and Positive Illusions

At this point Owen shifted the focus once again, to a finding related to Jeanne Tsai's talk, particularly the data on the inflated sense of self-esteem that typifies individualistic cultures. Owen said that he wanted to cite data that "might make you worry about the individualistic Western view of the self. Philosophers have historically discussed the relationship between virtue and happiness, and I pointed out on the first day that there was general agreement that a virtuous person is a happy person—that true happiness only comes with virtue.

"Adding mental health to the picture is a pretty new thing. Consider the criteria developed by psychologists or psychiatrists to determine what constitutes a mentally healthy person. The list varies, but interestingly enough, on no list that I looked at when I did my research does goodness ever appear.

One characteristic that does get on everyone's list is accurately understanding oneself and the world. So in other words, a mentally healthy person, according to Western definitions, is someone who is not deluded, who sees things accurately.

"But it turns out when North Americans have been studied, the people who score very high on criteria of happiness and caring for other people are pretty seriously self-deluded. Let me explain what I mean by self-deluded. These are called 'positive illusions' sometimes, but it's a question whether they're truly positive. Most Americans think they and their loved ones are much better-looking than everyone else. They think that they and their loved ones are smarter. When people give a musical performance or a speech, they judge their own performance much more highly than other people."

The Dalai Lama, who had been chuckling quietly through this, quipped, "Maybe the Europeans won't agree on that."

To which Richie made the by-now-inevitable retort, "Except in France."

And Francisco riposted, "Well, many Europeans do have that point of view about the United States."

Owen returned to a more serious note, but again with data that brought laughter: "I understand. But I'll just tell you about two more findings, from studies of American professors. Suppose that Richie, my friend Paul here, Francisco, and I write a paper together. It's published, and we go out and toast each other and we all agree that we each did twenty-five percent of the work. Six months pass. Someone asks Richie what percentage of the work he did on that paper. He says thirty-three percent. They ask Paul, and he says thirty-three percent. Francisco and I also did thirty-three percent. So suddenly there is a hundred twenty-six percent of work. The more time that passes, the more self-serving our perception becomes. Twenty years later we all remember that we did seventy-five percent of the work!"

Owen continued, "But there is another set of mistakes made by Americans who fall into this group of being generally happy and well-adjusted. Suppose a person is told that the probability of an American woman getting breast cancer is one in nine. If you ask one of these happy women what she thinks the probability of her getting breast cancer is, she will say, 'Very low in my case.' It's the same with car accidents and all kinds of diseases. Even when you tell people what the normal rates are, they radically underestimate the probability that this will happen to them. The reason this is important is that the people who are found to make the most realistic self-appraisals, at least among North Americans, are mildly depressed!"

Owen concluded, "As Jeanne said this morning, talking about how the self is configured by culture, American culture does very much emphasize high self-esteem. But in gaining high self-esteem we don't see things correctly. When Jeanne and I first met last December she pointed me to some recently published research on Japanese people. In Japan, they don't make these same overly optimistic errors, but it remains to be seen whether they're happier or more virtuous."

The Dalai Lama picked up on Owen's point about self-esteem. "From a Buddhist perspective, we do not take self-esteem as such to be a virtue or an absolute good. If one has an exaggerated sense of self-esteem, one faces falling into arrogance, which is a mental affliction. Then one is encouraged to engage in an antidote that would deflate the mind a bit. On the other hand, if you so deflate it that you wind up with very low self-esteem, then you should do discursive meditations on the preciousness and value of human life and your own Buddha nature, the luminous nature of your awareness. Meditating on such things raises your sense of self-esteem.

"The issue is really not simply self-esteem as an absolute good, but finding a realistic and balanced degree of self-esteem. If you have inflated self-esteem, it leads to a much greater level of expectation, which then leads to greater vulnerability to disappointment and disillusionment. It's a chain."

Richie made an important distinction: "In the research that Owen was describing, it is true that the more positive emotion people report, the more they show these kinds of illusions, but the correlation is not perfect. There is a small percentage of people who show high levels of positive emotion but don't show these illusions. Those might be interesting people for us to study. They may show only moderate self-esteem—not inflated—and more accurate perception."

Matthieu went back to Tibetan spiritual practice, where, he said, "it is really important to cultivate humility. If you ask a great scholar what he knows, he will say, 'I know nothing.' Sometimes this creates a very interesting situation. I remember once two very great scholars from Tibet came to a monastery in Nepal, to Khyentse Rinpoche, one of the great teachers of the last century. One of them was asked to give some teachings, and he said, 'I don't know anything.' Then he added about his friend, 'And he also doesn't know anything.' He took for granted the other's humility!"

With that, we broke for tea. During the tea break, Mark talked to the Dalai Lama about giving training in the methods of social and emotional learning for teachers in the Tibetan schools. The Dalai Lama invited Mark or one of his colleagues to come to Dharamsala to share the methods with Tibetan teachers during their yearly training meetings.

What's Wholesome Where?

After the tea break, the mood shifted. While our earlier interactions had been more formally directed toward the Dalai Lama, in the closing hour of the day there was more spontaneous, direct interaction among the participants.

I started with a point that had been raised during the tea break. "How do you skillfully combine what Jeanne said this morning with what Mark said? How do you bring these lessons into schools or to people in a way that respects and uses well the cultural differences? Mark was saying that the children in these programs are taught that all emotions are okay. From a Buddhist point of view, however, all emotions are not okay. This is just one example of the differences, as Jeanne pointed out, between the way emotions are valued from culture to culture. How do you take such differences into account?"

"We don't know," Mark replied. "Our North American and European conception that talking about feelings is a good idea may be very effective in our culture, but not necessarily in others. We should recognize that these curricula in some way are an artificial replacement for a lack of harmony.

"I believe that everything I talked about this morning is fundamentally universal—the idea of self-control, becoming aware of internal states of mind, planning ahead, using one's intelligence. I think the differences are very small details. For example, each day in PATHS a different child is picked to be the teacher's helper. That child stands in the front of the room and helps the teacher with the lesson. The child might hold up the pictures or act in the role-plays.

"At the end of the lesson, the child gets compliments. First the teacher might say, 'You did a very good job today as a helper,' or 'You're a warm and friendly person,' or 'I like your shoes.' Then the child chooses two children in the classroom that he wants to compliment. Then lastly the child gives himself a compliment, in front of the whole group. The compliments are written down and sent home to the parent in a letter, and the parent is asked to add one more compliment.

"This is a very American idea, and I don't think it would translate well to Asian cultures. It's fluffing up the feathers, if you will, of the child in a way that builds some self-importance. We've done this in the Netherlands, England, and America, and parents are quite enthusiastic. They put the letter up on the wall at home. They say, 'Finally I hear really positive things about my child. It makes him feel good, and it makes us all feel good.' But the same idea might be contrary or awkward in some cultures."

Jeanne Tsai responded to Mark's point by telling a story about herself. "When I was graduating from high school we had a ceremony in which the principal called down each student one at a time. There was a spotlight on each student as the principal listed his or her accomplishments. All of my European American friends would beam as they walked down to the stage, smiling at the audience as the principal said that this student excelled at math or will go to such-and-such college.

"When it was my turn, I looked down at my feet when the principal was listing my accomplishments. That felt appropriate. I was being humble, which is how my parents taught me to be. Then I realized that my European American friends thought I was looking down because I was sad instead of proud. When I realized that, I looked up and started smiling, but my friends told me later that they didn't understand my behavior. That's an example of a cultural difference."

The Dalai Lama rubbed his head and laughed quietly.

But Mark put the question of cultural difference in perspective, saying, "Again, these are small issues, not fundamental ones—but as we move a model across cultures we need to be sensitive to them."

As an educator in America, Mark had been sensitized to issues of cultural diversity. Yet when, for instance, he went to other cultures, like the Netherlands or the United Kingdom, he often found that at first people there objected to his school programs as "too American," saying the programs would not work in their own culture. Mark would encourage them to modify the programs to fit better into their cultures, yet when he would return months later, he typically found they were doing them just as he had presented them, saying they seemed to work just fine. This pleasant surprise made Mark feel that the Dalai Lama's focus on the underlying commonality of human experience did not just make good ethical sense but was practical as well.

Praise, Kindness, and Effective Learning

In a quiet aside during the dialogue, someone in our group had made a suggestion to Mark for the PATHS program that he now brought up: to recognize and give compliments for altruistic acts—things the children have done to help others—rather than to give compliments on how they look and so on. "That was a very interesting idea," he said. "When I go back we'll try to focus those compliments in some classrooms."

The Dalai Lama suggested, "Praising children is one of the most effective ways to actually correct certain behaviors. For example, if you praise a child first before pointing out mistakes, saying, 'You're so smart, you'll be able to correct this,' this is a very skillful way of giving confidence to the child."

This moment was the biggest surprise of the day for Mark, who had expected the Dalai Lama to object to the idea of compliments as puffing up children's self-importance or inflating their ego—or at least making them too focused on themselves. But as Mark now realized, the Dalai Lama saw the need for children to develop a healthy sense of confidence and the feeling that their efforts are appreciated.

The Dalai Lama continued with his point on positive reinforcement. "When a trainer works with circus animals, whether lions or tigers—also killer whales—they don't do it just by beating them. They're always giving positive reinforcement, giving fish to the whale. Human beings are physically not too strong, but our minds are very strong, so the proper way to change people is through genuine kindness. Praise makes the child happy and enthusiastic. Having said that, I don't have the experience of even having spent one full day with a child! If I spent just one full class period with them, I'd probably box their ears!" At that, he broke into a laugh, miming this.

"Well," I advised, "remember the turtle."

He laughed again, started to cross his arms like the turtle, and said, "There is an expression that rhymes in Tibetan: 'If you are angry, bite your knuckles.' "

Richie added, "There are actually good scientific data, Your Holiness, showing that many different kinds of material are much more effectively learned with positive reinforcement than with punishment. Rewarding good performance leads to better retention than punishment."

Paul concurred. "Another study along that line about thirty years ago showed that if the teacher smiles when she gives the lesson plan, the students remember more of what she has said than if she doesn't smile. This is what you've been describing, teaching through kindness in a kind context. I think that's another universal."

I brought in another research finding: "Afflictive emotions actually interfere with the ability to take in and understand information. To the extent that children are upset, they can't learn well. In a way, bringing these programs into schools is helping educators fulfill their main mission. Studies of programs like Mark's found that after a year or two of these programs, the children's academic achievement improves."

That finding resonated with the Dalai Lama, as he later told me. For him, the deepest meaning of acquiring knowledge is to reduce the gap between distortions in our perception and reality. Embedded in this philosophical outlook is the idea that it is ignorance and our inability to perceive reality as it is that get in the way of fulfilling our aspirations. Through the process of acquiring knowledge we can get closer to reality and in that way resolve our problems. But as we had discussed over several days now, many of the destructive emotions get in the way of our perception of reality. In that sense, the Dalai Lama felt it important to build into the idea of education itself the notion that clearing the mind is an essential for learning.

Changing the Agenda

Paul brought us back to Mark's discussion about the deficits that might occur if the relationship between the parent and the child is impaired. "How do your techniques work with emotionally handicapped children who come from a very bad upbringing—say, depressed parents, or a parent who doesn't like physical contact?"

Mark replied, "Think about it as a public health problem. Some children come with a lot of history of damage and difficulty, and some come with very supportive parents. For normal children these programs just continue to build immunity, if you will. They help them think through problems more clearly, and they help them to get better at talking about their emotions. They don't decrease behavior problems because those children don't have those problems.

"We have the most impact on children who have emotional problems in the middle range, not serious ones." For example, Mark said that depressed children are helped the most by the social and emotional learning programs, but that children whose behavior is extremely out of control or who have very serious mental health problems need much more. And the program did not help much those children diagnosed with attention deficit disorder—in some cases because they have organic damage, as was also the case for children with fetal alcohol syndrome. He summed up, "These children have a very difficult time learning from experience. So there are clearly limits on what a public health model can do."

Mark then switched to a related public policy issue, the education of teachers. "Teachers go through four years of college education, but they are not required to enroll in a course that concerns what we've discussed here today—not in any university in the world. They learn about educational curriculum and they learn about the history of education. They learn their subject matter, like mathematics or science. They may learn how to reinforce and punish children—but they don't learn about emotional development. They don't learn how to make children more mindful in any sense of the word, or how to create harmony. If there is one single point on which we can make a great impact, it's by beginning to teach this to teachers before they go into the classroom."

"In a sense," said the Dalai Lama, "this is easier to implement as well because you are really getting at the source."

"Yes," said Mark, "it is easy to implement—but very difficult to get schools of education to see this as a central topic. I know of no university in America that requires a course on children's social and emotional development before teachers go into the classroom. This is a major public policy problem."

I offered a different perspective: "In America and other parts of the developed world, there is a growing sense that something is not working, particularly in how children are growing up. This becomes a motivator for change in schools. I was asked a month ago to go to Colorado, to speak to the state principals association—by a teacher in a town called Littleton."

I then told the Dalai Lama about the tragic incident at Columbine High School in Littleton, in which two students killed a teacher and twelve classmates before shooting themselves. "Unfortunately, such incidents are becoming more common. It's driving educators to be more open to change. Many of these programs in social and emotional learning come in as violence prevention programs. But, as you point out, if we're going to educate children in this, we need an atmosphere of lovingkindness—so we need this kind of program for teachers themselves."

"Being in academia," Alan commented, "I encounter that kind of resistance to change in the academics themselves. The challenge is that we ourselves—I was about to say 'they'—should actually strive to be better people, to bring greater altruism and so forth to the classroom, that we teachers should change. There is a lot of resistance not to the idea that society should change, that somebody else should change, but that we teachers should change. There is an inertia there and a fear: 'It would be too hard . . . I don't think I could do it . . . I can write books but would I be good at this? Maybe not.'

"Both from Christianity and Judaism as well as from science," Alan added, "we have very little hope that we can really change ourselves from inside. We think change comes more from outside. In Judeo-Christianity it comes from God's blessing or grace. In science it comes from taking drugs or from some type of gene therapy."

Richie was more optimistic. "I think this is a case where modeling is a very powerful form of learning. Mark was talking about modeling in his program. Think of the value of having in each school just one teacher who displays lovingkindness and compassion."

At this, I had the thought that while there are such devoted teachers to be found in schools, they are not held up as models. What's needed is both the expertise to develop such attitudes in teachers who don't bring it with them into the profession, and institutional support for it.

Richie went on to suggest that holding up such teachers as models, and encouraging others to be similarly compassionate, "would create a vision of hope in education. We have to take small initial steps, but through modeling that change can occur."

"That's a positive note," I said, "on which to end our session today."

At the end of the day, the Dalai Lama told me he was pleased with what he had heard about emotional education—it fit well with his own analysis of the deep meaning of "education" itself: that learning about the mind and emotions should be part of any concept of education.

Day Five:
Reasons for Optimism

March 24, 2000

13

The Scientific Study of Consciousness

The fifth day of our meeting was intended to remind us that our focus on destructive emotions was part of a larger agenda: exploring how Buddhist and modern scientific perspectives could together enrich our understanding of the mind. For the Dalai Lama, brain science offers Buddhist psychology information on the hardware that might fit its software, theories of mind. As he told me, learning the neurobiological basis of mental states was one of the ways Buddhist thinkers might gain the most from engaging with science. And brain science might offer a stronger corroboration—or challenge—for Buddhist theories of mind.

Buddhist epistemology makes the distinction between what is not found and what is found not to be the case. The neuroscience findings, the Dalai Lama felt, had so far presented no contradictions for Buddhist thought. And, in the spirit of investigating the mind, the Dalai Lama's interest visibly quickened when such findings were offered up, as was the case on this day.

On this last day of our meeting, as everyone stood for the Dalai Lama to be seated, he went around the circle of presenters, clasping the hands of each in turn. There was a heightened coziness in the room as we settled in. A gentle, soothing rain had fallen during the night; the weather had cleared, the air was crisp.

Today we would return from the realm of practical applications to our larger scientific agenda. Francisco Varela would be our first presenter, and Richie Davidson our second. Because the Dalai Lama knew Francisco so well, I simply said with a smile, "As you know, Francisco Varela holds research posts at many prestigious institutions in France—but because my French is so bad, I will spare you all the embarrassment of my mispronouncing those names, and simply introduce Francisco."

A Radical Theory

Of all the scientists who traveled to Dharamsala for this dialogue, Francisco Varela's life journey may well have been the greatest—certainly in distance, if not in time. Francisco was born in Tulcahuano in the south of Chile, where his father, an engineer, was in charge of the work at the port. Francisco's vacations were spent in Monte Grande, a remote village of just fifty or so people high in the Chilean Andes, where his grandfather lived, and where life was much as it had been in the nineteenth century: no roads, no television, no radio. He considered Monte Grande his spiritual home.

A voracious reader with a knack for science, Francisco was largely bored with school and an average student until college, where his performance in biology under his mentor, Humberto Maturana, earned him a scholarship to Harvard for his Ph.D. The year was 1968, the peak of the wave of radically rethinking social institutions that was then sweeping the world.

As a graduate student, Francisco was fascinated by the deep philosophical question of neuroscience: How does the mind emerge from the brain? In the spirit of the time, he was deeply critical of the then-dominant paradigm, one that modeled the human brain on the information processing system of a computer. But, as befits a scientist, he started with the basics, focusing his research on the eye of the honeybee, a complex visual system totally different from the eye of a vertebrate, let alone that of humans. His advisor, Thorsten Wiesel, was later to win a Nobel prize for research on the visual system.

In 1970 Francisco passed up a job offer at Harvard to take a post at the University of Chile—a move motivated in part by the election of Allende, whom Francisco, left-leaning himself, avidly supported. It was a time of hope and openness in Chile, with an egalitarian socialism promising a new social and economic order.

The optimism of the moment was reflected in an open-mindedness in the atmosphere of the university as well. With his old mentor (now colleague) Humberto Maturana, Francisco undertook research at the frontier of biology. Francisco and Maturana developed a radical theory of "autopoiesis" (that is, self-production), which explains how a living system emerges and maintains a continuing identity even as all its components are in continual flux.[1] A cell, as he put it, "bootstraps itself out of a soup of chemistry and physics"; as a self-organizing network of biochemical reactions, it produces molecules that then create a boundary that constrains the network itself.[2] The cell, in other words, is self-created.

Rather than reducing life to its molecules, auotopoiesis sees the organism as more than the sum of its parts. Properties of the whole emerge from the dynamics of its parts but cannot be explained simply as the totality of its elements. The theory applies at all levels of life, from a single cell to the immune system, the mind, and even communities, as Varela and Maturana later proposed in their 1987 book *The Tree of Knowledge*.[3] In the early 1970s, the theory of autopoiesis was considered heretical, although it now influences thinkers in fields ranging from philosophy of mind and cognitive science to complexity theory.

But then came the dark days of 1973, after the military coup led by Pinochet, when the university was under police control and Francisco was faced with the threat of having his lab closed down if he did not denounce friends connected with Allende. Francisco's work with Maturana came to a halt. Worse, the police were rounding up many of Francisco's friends and associates. He himself had been active in leftist politics, and he sensed that it was only a matter of time before the police came looking for him too. Francisco fled with his first wife and three children to Costa Rica, the farthest point they could afford to reach that was still accepting Chilean political refugees. Arriving with just $100 to spare, he got a job teaching biology at the university there.

A Mind-Stopping Encounter

The next break came a few months later, when he was offered a job at the University of Colorado in Denver. Arriving there in 1974, Francisco soon ran into Jeremy Hayward, a Cambridge-educated physicist he had known at Harvard who now had given up his scientific career to study with Chogyam Trungpa, a Tibetan lama. Trungpa was an anomaly at the time, a highly revered lama who had fled Tibet at the same time as the Dalai Lama, in 1959, and gone on to get an Oxford education. He became one of the early prominent teachers of Tibetan Buddhism in the West at a time when it was still astonishing to meet a Tibetan lama in America.

At the time, Francisco felt as though his life had been wiped as clean as a blank slate. The horror of the violent coup d'état in Chile, the sudden destruction of a world of sense and meaning, left him feeling adrift. There were no satisfying answers to explain the human cruelty he had witnessed. All the years of philosophy and rationality, of Marxism and science, couldn't help him; his sense of a meaningful universe was suspended. So when Hayward said, "Come and meet Trungpa," Francisco decided, "What the hell—why not?" And he went.

A rationalist with no interest in Eastern philosophy or religion, Francisco nevertheless found himself intrigued by Trungpa's presence—his sharpness, his humor, his quirkiness. At one point as they talked, Francisco told Trungpa about his confusion and his sense of not knowing what to do. Trungpa gave Franscisco a full, penetrating look and asked, "Why do you want to do something? How about doing nothing?"

At that, Francisco felt his mind stop. Doing nothing was a radical proposal for someone used to constant mental activity, to continual analysis. But as life had shown, sometimes all that doing just led to more confusion. Now *whammo*—suddenly there was an alternative, peace of mind, and it just might make sense. "But how do you do that?" Francisco asked. "I'll teach you," Trungpa replied—and on the spot showed him how to meditate.

Meditation became a kind of love affair for Francisco, a passion. Soon he was going off to a center in the Rockies for monthlong retreats. Meditation fed a hunger that he had long felt. He realized that beneath his know-it-all, rationalist, scientist self, the very ground of his existence was alien to him. In meditation he found a feeling of just abiding in the ground of his being without having to articulate it or express it in any way. There was a simple joy, a pleasure, in just being that felt natural and good—even fascinating.

Reluctantly at first, Francisco started to read the classics of Buddhism and the commentaries, which allowed him to discover the beauty of Buddhist theory, not just as a practice but as a philosophy, even a science of mind. As he got a firmer grasp on the Buddhist view, he started to reflect on its relationship to the view he got from science.

Trungpa had recently founded the Naropa Institute, a university focusing on Buddhist themes, in Boulder. With Jeremy Hayward, Francisco and others designed a summer program on science and Buddhism. Contrasting Perspectives in Cognitive Science pulled together a diverse, high-level group of twenty-five specialists in Buddhist and scientific perspectives on the mind. But this initial encounter between Buddhism and science proved a disaster. Rather than a dialogue, the foray became a confrontation, with neither side hearing what the other was saying. There were heated arguments, dreadful misunderstandings. There was no hint of the spaciousness dialogue requires, let alone the friendliness essential to it.

Paradoxically, that disaster was to prove useful in designing the later Mind and Life dialogues. Mainly it was a cautionary lesson for Francisco that just getting top scientists together with Buddhists was not enough—they had to be scientists open to the dialogue (as was true for the Buddhist side, for that matter).

Then came a meeting with the one Buddhist who was perfect for such dialogue: the Dalai Lama. In 1983 Francisco was invited to a meeting in Austria on spirituality and science where the Dalai Lama was among the speakers. At a meal early in the conference, Francisco was seated next to the Dalai Lama. "Are you a brain scientist?" the Dalai Lama asked him—and immediately launched into a series of questions about the brain. Their discussions continued informally on the side during the rest of the meeting, leaving both with a hunger to continue their talks.

Though Francisco had returned to teach in Chile in 1980, in 1984 he worked in Germany at the Max Planck Institute, moving on to Paris a year later, where he joined the Center for Research on Applied Epistemology, a think tank at the Ecole Polytechnique. By 1988 he had been appointed director of research at the Centre National de la Recherche Scientifique. During the years he was taking on his new responsibilities in Paris, Francisco was unable to follow through on meeting with the Dalai Lama.

Then in the spring of 1985, while speaking with his good friend Joan Halifax, Francisco learned that a meeting on Buddhism and science was already being planned by a group led by Adam Engle, who had also heard about the Dalai Lama's interest in meeting with scientists. Francisco immediately picked up the phone and called Adam, who told him that the meeting they were planning with the Dalai Lama would focus on the intersections between Buddhism and physics. Francisco argued convincingly that the meeting would be more fruitful if it focused on Buddhism and the cognitive sciences, and asked if he could join the team to organize such a meeting.[4] The two joined forces in planning what has since become the series of Mind and Life meetings, with Francisco as the founding scientist, Adam as the administrator.

This meeting would be Francisco's fourth, and from his base in Paris he was now recognized worldwide as a leader at the interface between neuroscience, psychoneuroimmunology, phenomenology, and cognitive science. In addition to his academic posts, he had contributed over two hundred articles to scientific journals, mostly on the biological mechanisms of cognition and consciousness, and had written or edited fifteen books, many translated into several languages. As a scientist, Francisco was hard to categorize. He had moved smoothly from neuroscience to immunology, from cognitive science to philosophy of mind to theoretical biology. His erudition was vast, combining precision in research with a creative fertility in theory.[5]

Sadly, though, Francisco had long been fighting a battle with hepatitis C; just months before, after a tense wait for a donor, he had received a lifesaving liver transplant. Until the last moment, we had not been sure he would be able to come to Dharamsala. With him was his wife, Amy Cohen, an American-born psychoanalyst who had hoped to come to the Mind and Life meeting in 1991 but was then pregnant with their son Gabriel and so stayed home. During our meeting Francisco was taking a cocktail of medicines, and, with Amy, carefully monitoring his health. Now, on the final day of the eighth Mind and Life meeting, Francisco began what would be his last scientific presentation to the Dalai Lama.

A Gift of Life

"Your Holiness," Francisco said, "like my colleagues before, I'll offer just a little thought before we begin. It seems to me wondrous that I am here with you once more. It is a truly amazing thing that we have been able to keep up over the years. This time, even more so, it seems like a gift of life that I can be back here to have this opportunity to talk to you." As Francisco added, "Your support and kindness through difficult times was very, very essential for me," he looked for a moment as though he was on the verge of tears.

In a sense, the Dalai Lama may well have been responsible for Francisco being alive at that point. Francisco had been diagnosed with liver cancer due to hepatitis C in the spring of 1997. After surgery, he was told he would have to get on the list for a liver transplant. But Francisco questioned how far he should go in trying to preserve his life and was seriously considering not putting himself on the list—thereby guaranteeing a quicker death.

As he was pondering this decision, Francisco received a fax out of the blue from the Dalai Lama, who said he had heard about the illness and hoped Francisco would do everything possible to continue his life. Francisco took this as a sign as well as much-needed emotional support. With that encouragement, he decided to put his name on the list for a liver transplant, which he received in the year before our meeting. The surgery, always risky, resulted in Francisco spending an exhausting three months in intensive care while his body seemed to be rejecting the new liver. By the time he came to Dharamsala, though, Francisco seemed surprisingly chipper.

The most seasoned of the presenters, Francisco had been in the hot seat many times before. But there was a difference today, as he later confided to me—as he opened his talk, he felt a bit overwhelmed. This was a moment that very well might not have happened had circumstances taken a different turn.

As he took the presenter's chair, Francisco felt an upwelling of gratitude to the Dalai Lama for having been so supportive during the rocky months. When the Dalai Lama had greeted Francisco at the morning tea break on day one—the first they had seen each other since the surgery—the Dalai Lama simply held Francisco's head and hand in a long, prayerful silence. Sitting next to him now, Francisco was overwhelmed by a sense of the Dalai Lama's personal warmth and caring, and felt an intimate closeness. Indeed, it seemed more like a reunion than a scientific proceeding—like talking to an old friend.

That somber mood quickly took a lighter turn as Francisco started up his laptop to do a PowerPoint presentation—the first of the meeting, and apparently the first the Dalai Lama had seen. When the initial LCD display came on the screen, the Dalai Lama exclaimed, "Very impressive!" Then came the first graphic: an animation of the title sweeping across the screen. At that there was spontaneous applause, and His Holiness uttered the Tibetan equivalent of "Wow!"

"I knew you would like that, Your Holiness," Francisco said with a laugh, and continued, "We want to introduce the idea of expanding this project, to see how we can move further in collaborative research growing out of the Mind and Life Institute. First I and then Richie will touch on things that are actually being done along these lines. This is an opportunity to discuss this basic question: How can the neuroscientific study of consciousness and the meditation tradition actually collaborate?"

Breaking the Taboo of Subjectivity

"I know that you have always manifested a great interest in the relationship between consciousness and brain, and to me also this is a fascinating area, as well as for a lot of our colleagues here. Science has evolved greatly in this regard: Ten or fifteen years ago, 'consciousness' was a dirty word; today there are conferences on the topic, and many people trying to work on it.[6]

"I think there are two important reasons why this is so, Your Holiness. One is that there are new, noninvasive methods to work with humans, and the second is the renewed openness in the scientific study of consciousness. These two factors combine, making it possible for us to work further in this collaborative effort."

As Francisco saw it, a turning point had come at a conference held in Tucson in 1994, where a young philosopher from California, David Chalmers, gave a paper about what he called "the hard problem of consciousness." Chalmers argued that it was impossible to study consciousness without asking people what they are experiencing—a rather commonsense proposal that was, for neuroscientists who had been relying on high-tech machinery to probe the brain, rather radical.

Francisco by then had been grappling with the hard problem of consciousness for decades. The behaviorists, remember, had vanquished such testimonials about people's experiences from scientific study in the middle of the last century, charging that such data were hopelessly biased. Francisco had been busily refuting this stance in a flurry of publications. His book *The Embodied Mind*—published in 1991 but begun ten years before—argued that Buddhist training in mindfulness meditation offered a method to help people become "first-person" collaborators—reporting on their own experience—in the study of consciousness.[7] In 1996 Francisco proposed that this approach, which he called neurophenomenology, offered a way to answer the hard problem of consciousness—a method explored in detail in his 1999 anthology *The View from Within*.[8] And in 2002 his last book, *On Becoming Aware: The Pragmatics of Experiencing* demonstrated the scientific usefulness of the approach.[9]

Francisco continued, "This renewed interest in the study of consciousness is not obvious from outside this funny thing we call scientific culture, but it is becoming more and more clear that there is tremendous value in bringing back data from the first-person method. This means that you take into account your subjective experience. Some people might call this lived experience, or phenomenology, or the personal level. We're using 'phenomenology,' 'experience,' and 'first-person' synonymously. Although the terminology varies—whatever you want to call it—what has been shunned in the past by science, the subjective, is becoming more and more important.

"There is now a whole variety of first-person methods that are more or less sophisticated. Part of the discussion going on today concerns which methods to use under which circumstances. The tradition of meditation is a fundamental one, but there are others, and we would like to examine them in a wider context."

Getting the Other Half of the Story

To illustrate his point about the need for first-person data in neuroscience, Francisco raised the question of what happens in the brain when you have a mental image. "Suppose that I show you this piece of paper," he said, holding up a blank sheet, "and then I tell you to close your eyes and imagine it. The question is whether that image is of the same nature as the image that you see. It was thought that you could find the answer by looking to see whether or not the visual cortex was active. The answer that came from the laboratory is interesting, because it is neither true nor false. In some kinds of visual imagery the visual cortex is indeed very active, as if you were seeing the image. But for other kinds of visual images, it is not.

"For example, you might tell a person, 'Close your eyes and imagine that you're drawing a map from here down the path to our hotel, Chonor House, and then on to Dharamsala.' In such tasks the visual cortex is not very active during imagination, while, of course, it would be active if you drew the map you had imagined. There are also individual differences in brain function: For the same task, about half of the population has the visual cortex active, and the other half does not. This is evidence in answer to your question this morning, of whether brain patterns are the same for all people. In fact, it seems that personal style in visualizing could result in very different patterns of activation."

This finding, in Francisco's view, argued for the need for first-person data in neuroscience. No matter how robust the neuroscientific method for studying the mind, key interpretations of data can be missed without getting reports from the person being measured. If, for example, the studies on imagery used brain-imaging techniques alone, the results would have been utterly confusing—about half the time the visual cortex lit up in people and half the time it did not, depending on the experimental paradigm used.

If the imaging data were simply analyzed in terms of the group averages, the scientific result of all those studies would be to end up empty-handed. What's missed, Francisco pointed out, is the differing effects on the visual cortex of the different visualization strategies people use. The only way to truly understand what's going on is to ask people for a precise report of what they are doing mentally while their brain activity is being measured. Without the first-person data in such studies, then, neuroscience is half blind.

An Inner Expertise

"Another key point," Francisco continued, "is that this work, which is still very young and developing, makes it obvious that you just cannot have people do first-person observation without measuring the degree of training they have. Being able to walk into a garden and see the plants doesn't make one into a botanist; that requires training.

"This idea—that people vary in their abilities as observers of their own experience—may seem completely obvious to you, Your Holiness, but you will be surprised how nonevident, almost revolutionary, it is among researchers in the West. Everybody knows that you have to train to be a sportsman, or a musician, or a mathematician. But when it comes to observing one's experience, it is as if there is nothing to learn—it's just there. You cannot underestimate the degree to which there is a culture of blindness about this."

So Francisco proposed a corrective to this problem: using objective methods—what he called second- and third-person methods—to corroborate first-person reports. The "first person" is the one having the experience; the "second person" is a highly trained interviewer; the "third person" refers to the objective measurements science applies. "The basic idea is to combine the first-person method, which requires training, with the empirical third-person approach, which is neuroscience as we know it. Take an EEG study, where we can detect the kinds of electrical activity going on in the brain. You have two sides of the story: the signal that comes from the machine as the third-person approach, and the first person who can give his own account and say, for example, that he was experiencing surprise. The idea, then, is that by combining these two sources of data, we can get much closer to understanding not only the experience but its biological and organic basis.

"So, in summary, the starting point is a rediscovery of the importance of the first-person view, and the working hypothesis is that the first-person description can work reciprocally with the empirical approach. A necessary basis, of course, is the cultivation of a sustained discipline of observation—which is a new idea for the West."

This idea intrigued His Holiness, who saw that meditation practitioners might be just the kind of people needed.

A False Start

"Backtracking for a second, Your Holiness, do you remember that in 1992 a few scientists, including Richie, came here to do some studies with yogis and monks?"

Francisco was referring to an earlier foray into collaborative research that arose from the third Mind and Life meeting, when the Dalai Lama invited him to study the brain activity of advanced meditators, yogis who lived in small huts in the mountains above Dharamsala. Francisco was joined by Richie Davidson, Davidson's colleague Cliff Saron, and another researcher, Greg Simpson, with Alan Wallace as translator.

Every day for a few weeks, the research team—armed with a letter of introduction from the Dalai Lama—would lug its EEG instruments and related machines high into the mountains to meet with one or another yogi. And each day they met skepticism and obstacles. Among them was the reluctance of most yogis to allow their brains to be measured at all. As one more or less cannily put it: "What those machines measure may have nothing to do with what happens during my meditation. So it may look like nothing is happening, which could lead to doubt in the minds of Buddhist practitioners." And so he—and the others—declined.

For Francisco that failure produced some productive lessons. One was that it was naive to ask a yogi who has been meditating for twenty years and who has no interest whatever in science, to participate in a scientific experiment. Instead, you need to work either with Westernized Tibetans or highly experienced Western practitioners, where the collaboration becomes possible. The second lesson was that testing under such rugged conditions meant that research was limited to measurements possible in the field, which were superficial compared to the rigor and precision of those available in a research center. Better to bring the yogi to the lab than the lab to the yogi.

"It was an extremely interesting experience," Francisco continued, "but we realized that in order to really study the abilities that were our concern, we needed the technology to look into their brain state. The psychological measurements we used then, such as reaction time, just weren't enough. So what we're using now is a more elaborate, electrical technique. Why electrical? Because the moment of experience is very fast. Techniques such as metabolic studies of blood flow are very, very useful, but they're slow. It takes minutes to get a picture of how a little more blood comes to here or there in the brain.

"But a moment of experience is like that," he said, snapping his fingers. "What we need to study is a thousand times faster, on the order of milliseconds, not seconds. So the technique had to be based on electrical or, eventually, magnetic measurements. We focus on a very, very simple mental condition and use the surface measurements of electric changes by an electroencephalogram. Or magnetic fields, with a very sophisticated machine, essentially a kind of quantum device, that could not be brought here to Dharamsala. You don't just measure—there's a lot of data analysis. That's where the progress has been, in new techniques for extracting quite a bit of information from a simple measurement."

The Brain's Melody

Francisco then mapped out two complementary goals he saw in the research agenda for the Mind and Life Institute. His own work would focus on the dynamics of mental activity within a moment's time, while Richie Davidson explored lasting changes in the brain over a much longer time span: months or even years.

"For example, when anger arises, there is a refractory period where you just have time to catch the anger arising and try to suppress the action that will follow. It follows that you need to understand very precisely the dynamics of the emergence of that state. You need to understand in great detail a moment of experience. How does a moment of consciousness, a moment of cognitive activity, a perception, or an emotion actually arise? If we understood it better, then we could clarify how to apply that understanding to work with it. But very little is known about the minute details of how it arises."

At this, the Dalai Lama perked up; he had a keen personal interest in just this question. Though the ensuing presentation seemed quite esoteric to many in the room, from the Dalai Lama's perspective it was to be one of the richest parts of the entire week.

"When we perform a cognitive act—for example, we have a visual perception—the perception is not the simple fact of an image in the retina. There are many, many sites in the brain that become active. The big problem, Your Holiness, is how these many, many active parts become coherent to form a unity. When I see you, the rest of my experience—my posture, my emotional tone—is all a unit. It is not dispersed, with perception here and movement there.

"How does that happen? Imagine that each one of the sites in the brain is like a musical note. It has a tone. Why a tone? Empirically, there is an oscillation. The neurons in the brain oscillate all over the place. Each goes *whoomph*"—his arms rising as in an expansive gesture—"and then *ffhhh*"—falling in deflation. "The *whoomph* is when different places in the brain oscillate, and these become harmonized. When you have a wave here and another there, from different parts of the brain, several become synchronized, so they oscillate together.

"When the brain sets into a pattern—to have a perception, or to make a movement—the phase of these oscillations becomes harmonized, what we call phase-locked. The waves oscillate together in synchrony."

"Am I right in understanding your metaphor," the Dalai Lama asked, "that each of these oscillations is like a different tone and when they are combined together you create music?"

"You create music, exactly," Francisco agreed. "Many patterns of oscillations in the brain spontaneously select each other to create the melody, that is, the moment of experience. That's the *whoomph.* But the music is created with no orchestra conductor. This is fundamental."

Francisco mimed a conductor, waving his arms in the air. "You don't have a little man in there saying, 'Now you, and you, and you.' It doesn't work that way. So again, to understand the large-scale integration of the whole brain, the basic mechanism is the transitory formation of synchronous groups of neurons that are distributed widely. This was a beautiful discovery that gives us an account of how a moment of experience can arise."[10]

Families in the Brain

Here the Dalai Lama donned his familiar debater's hat as the scientific interlocutor: "Does this process vary from individual to individual? Would it be faster in some cases? Is it stable? Does it depend on age?"

"Those are very good questions, Your Holiness," Francisco replied. "It's probably very constant. There seems to be a universal law of how the brain works—we see the same thing even in animals. However, the specific patterns that arise certainly change from individual to individual depending on their learning and their unique history. Quite frankly, the answer to that is still unclear.

"If you put electrodes on different parts of the brain, you can measure oscillating signals. Then you put another electrode on another part of the brain, and what you see is another oscillation—a *whoomph.* And they enter into synchrony: They start and stop together. That's the basic mechanism."

The Dalai Lama asked, "Within one specific brain location, will there be a difference in what can be detected, depending on how far apart you put the two electrodes?"

"Absolutely," Francisco said. "We use a cap of electrodes that covers the brain. We are interested here in locations that are really far apart because we're interested in the large-scale integration. The small scale is a different story—where the neurons are so tightly together they are almost inevitably synchronous because they are interconnected. They are like a family because they are so close together. But the question is, can a family here in Dharamsala have synchronicity with a family in Delhi? That's the analogy. That's a different story because it requires they have a mechanism to get synchronized."

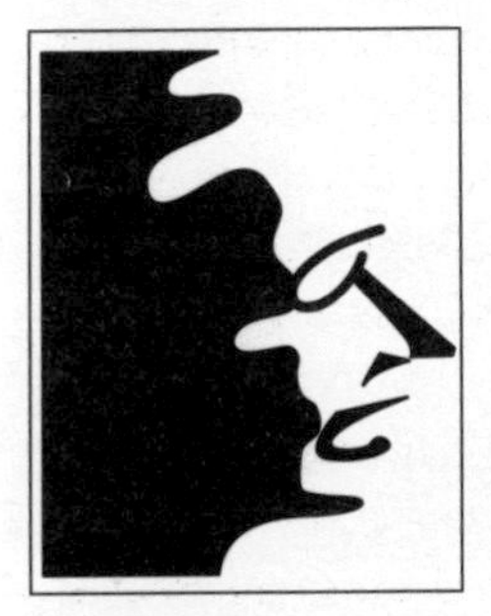

Perception condition

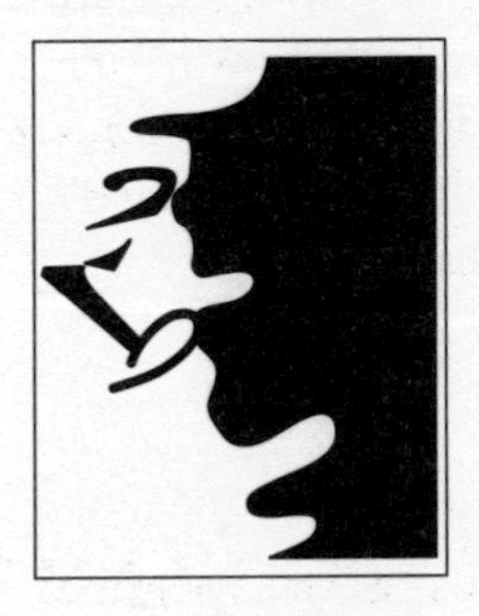

No-perception condition

Then Francisco showed a slide of an extremely high-contrast black-and-white image that on first glance seemed just a set of blotches, but with more scrutiny suddenly revealed itself to be the face of a woman.

"Do you see it now?" he asked. "Once you see it you cannot stop seeing it, right? These are called moony faces, like the man in the moon—in other words, high-contrast faces. They're not easy to see, but most people can immediately detect them with a little attention.

"These faces are easily recognized when they are presented right side up." Then, showing the same image upside-down, he asked, "But now, do you see a face there? Very few people ever do. The upside-down stimuli are much more difficult to read. For the purpose of the study, we call the first image the perception condition—people eventually see the face—and the more difficult one the nonperception condition, because people usually don't recognize it at all."

The Anatomy of a Moment in the Mind

At that, Francisco displayed a chart showing the sequence and timing in his experiment deconstructing a moment in the mind.[11] While volunteer subjects in Francisco's Paris lab had their EEG measured, they were simply asked to press a button the instant they could recognize an image. The sequence occurs with extraordinary rapidity, so fast that it must be tracked in milliseconds—thousandths of a second.

As the chart showed, during the first 180 milliseconds, when the black-and-white pattern is presented, the person's mind begins to stir into action. The act of recognition takes place from 180 to 360 milliseconds after the initial presentation—that is, by about the end of the first third of a second. The person's brain goes back to resting from that act of recognition during the next sixth of a second. The movement—the person pushing the button—occurs during the following sixth of a second. The whole sequence ends before three-quarters of a second has elapsed.

"When it starts, there's about a tenth of a second where nothing happens. I like to think of it as everybody's trying to get started, going *rrr-rrr-rrr,*" he said, making the noise of an engine revving up. "Everyone is trying to make allies to form the synchronous groups," he pointed out, referring to the first head on his chart, where there were barely any connecting lines—and the image had not yet been recognized.

On the second head, there were suddenly many cross connections, indicated by black lines, as alliances were made by brain cells in disparate areas. "Then the groups begin to form; there is a pattern that emerges. This is truly a case of emergence, because nobody told them to be synchronous—say, between this electrode and that electrode. They self-synchronize with each other. That corresponds, we know from all kinds of other evidence, to about one-third of a second after the stimulus—to the moment the person actually recognizes a face.

"From that moment of recognition on, you can see lots of green lines, which mean the opposite of synchronous. Everything in the brain is going out of synchrony. Everybody is oscillating on their own. The whole *whoomph* is now going *poof,*" he says, waving his hands wildly around his head. "In other words, the brain says, 'Erase that oscillation pattern.' "

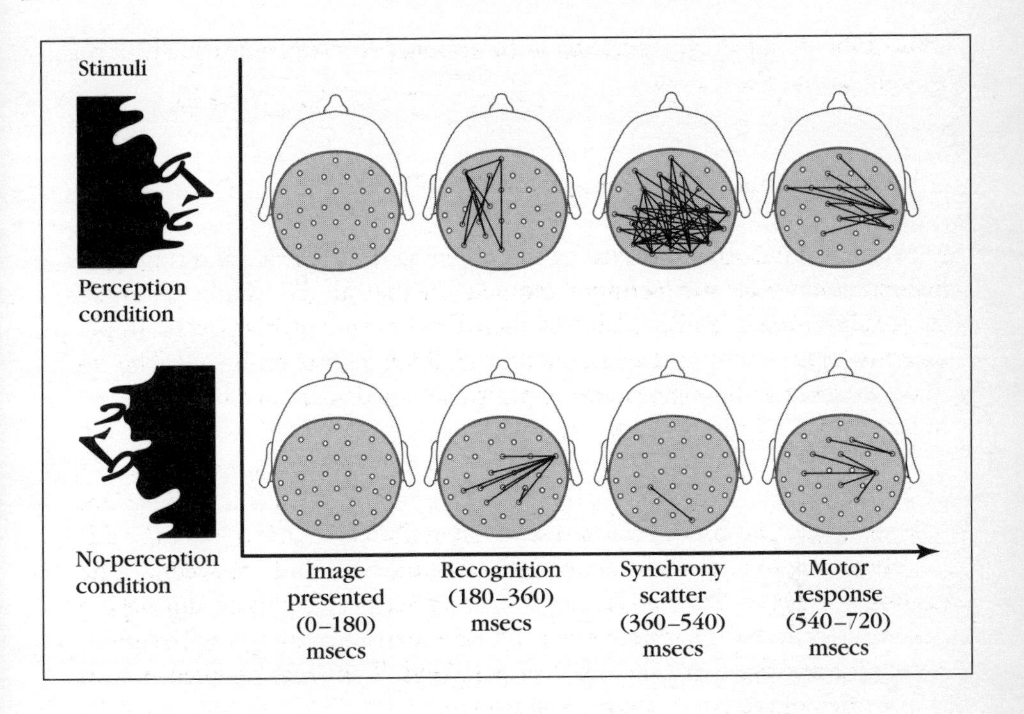

Tracking Subtle Movements of the Mind

The Dalai Lama had been listening with particular attentiveness, gently rocking back and forth in his chair. Now he asked, "Could you conceive a study where instead of showing a visual stimulus, you have an auditory stimulus—a sound? Then could you see these processes—in the second stage this synchrony, and in the third this dissynchrony? And then compare that dynamic to the visual stimulus, to see if there's the same pattern in the third stage?"

"We have done that experiment," Francisco replied, "and you will see the same patterns. We have done experiments with audition, with memory, with conflict of attention between visual and auditory. The answer is always the same: You have one particular pattern at the moment of the arising of the perception, and then you have a moment of recognition, and then you have a new pattern being formed at the moment of the action, which is pushing the button.

"Another set of synchrony arises in a new group of neurons as the person remembers that he has to push a button. The recognition arises, and then *poof*, the dissynchrony. Then the person remembers to push the button, and that needs a new pattern or synchrony in a new pattern of neurons."

"It's almost as if once a synchrony is formed, the role of those neurons is finished," the Dalai Lama observed.

"That's right—they are transient. And that's what I like. It's like the transience of mental factors." Francisco was referring to the basic elements that compose each moment of awareness in the Buddhist Abhidharma model of mind. "They come and they go, and they correlate to transient patterns in the neurons. That was clearly a big discovery for me. The brain actively undoes itself; it creates a gap where the transition from one moment to the next is actually marked. There is recognition and then action, but they are punctuated. It's like saying 'perception, comma, action,' rather than a continuous flow. This is systematic; we have seen it in all kinds of different conditions."

Timing the Mind

Francisco's results accord with those of other researchers who have been timing the fine movements of the mind. Benjamin Libet, a neurosurgeon at the University of California Medical School at San Francisco, found, for example, that electrical activity in the motor cortex begins about one-quarter of a second before a person is aware of his or her intent to move a finger. And there is another full quarter second between the awareness of the intention to move the finger and the beginning of the movement itself. Like Francisco's work, Libet's unpacks otherwise invisible, fine-grained components that in our experience seem a single, solid event: the recognition of a face, the movement of a finger.

The Dalai Lama pursued such an unpacking of a moment's mental activity in his next question: "The measuring device you use seems highly sensitive, to milliseconds. So is there still a gap between the initial exposure and the recognition if you show a photograph of a face that is so familiar that the person would instantly recognize it without having to actually think about it or recall from memory?"

"We have actually done that, and the answer is that the gap shortens but it is still there," Francisco replied.

At this point there was a heated discussion in Tibetan on the issue of whether there is an initial phase of nonconceptual awareness before memory and other aspects of cognition create Francisco's *whoomph*. The Dalai Lama, pleased at this opportunity to explore a topic of high personal interest to him—the distinction between conceptual and nonconceptual processes in the mind—continued, "Would you agree that this would indicate that the first moment is nonconceptual, purely a visual perception that apprehends the form in question, and the second is conceptual, which recognizes, 'Oh, this is that'? This seems to corroborate Buddhist psychology."

"Which leads you to decide to push the button," Francisco said. "It's only when I say 'Oh, I recognize that' that it leads to the moment of decision, where you then push the button. So it is a conceptual moment. The first one is just the pattern being perceived, without the conceptual process."

The Dalai Lama pushed on, intrigued by the implications he saw: "Would you agree that this corroborates a point in Buddhist psychology, that the first moment is a purely visual perception that is nonconceptual and the second moment, no matter what its duration might be, is when the conceptual mind apprehends, 'This is that'? For example, as I look at Alan Wallace here, I immediately recognize his face without having to figure it out. Grossly speaking, it seems like it's instantaneous, but in fact—"

"In fact it's at least two hundred milliseconds," Francisco interjected.

"This is exactly the Buddhist point of view," the Dalai Lama continued. "Even though, grossly speaking, it seems to be instantaneous, in reality it's not instantaneous. First there's an impression, and then the labeling—the conceptual recognition—and it's a sequence."

"Absolutely," Francisco agreed. "Typically, under normal conditions you cannot compress a mental moment to less than a hundred and fifty milliseconds. Even when it's something that's virtually immediate."

This is, in fact, a key point in Buddhist epistemology. The first moment of, say, a visual cognition is pure perception—a raw percept without a label—but shortly thereafter comes a mental cognition, the murmur of a thought, drawing on memory and enabling one to recognize and label the visually perceived object for what it is. Realizing that the first moment of cognition is nonconceptual and that those thereafter are conceptual offers a gateway, an opportunity for inner liberation, in the Buddhist model. This insight into the nature of our ongoing construction of reality represents a necessary step (though not in itself a sufficient one) toward freeing the mind from the inertia of mental habit.

As we entered this territory in our discussion, we left behind most people in the room, including many of the scientists. But the Dalai Lama was keenly interested to hear what science had found about what happens during the arising in the mind of a moment of experience, and to see how these findings fit with Buddhist models as described in the texts he was familiar with. This was a rare opportunity to hear a detailed scientific description of the process, and he found striking parallels between the scientific and Buddhist views, the two versions largely supporting each other.

Modern Evidence on an Ancient Debate

"In Buddhist epistemology," the Dalai Lama explained, "there has been a lot of debate on the nature of perception and how it engages with the object. There is one school that maintains that the visual experience perceives the object in a naked way, without mediation by a mental representation. The eye organ comes into immediate contact with the object. This has been critiqued by other epistemologists who argue that there is something called *namba,* which roughly translates as 'aspect.' This is also akin to a mental representation, or in this case a visual image created in part by the mind—and this is what actually organizes random sensory data into a coherent image at the sensory level. And then the sensory experience arises. It is not a simple sort of representation, a mirroring image.

"According to Tibetan philosophical understanding, there are four major Indian Buddhist schools of thought on this. The first school, Vaibhashika, is the one that accepts the idea of perception being a simple case of mirrored representation. All the remaining three schools argue that it's a more active process, with a role being played from the subjective side that organizes through this *namba.*" He added that all the schools agreed that there were fundamentally two distinct modes of cognition, one nonconceptual and one conceptual; the disagreement centered on whether even the sensory perceptions are necessarily distorted.[12]

The debate dates back more than a thousand years. In brief, the issue is whether we visually perceive objects in themselves (without mediation by an "internal" image) or whether we visually perceive objects in the outer world by way of "internal" mental representations. The latter view is held by the more philosophically sophisticated schools of Indo-Tibetan Buddhist philosophy.[13]

The Dalai Lama was pleased that science had started to find methods to dissect the different stages within a single experience and so could offer fertile cross connections from these findings to fine points of Buddhist thought. There had been an animated discussion in Tibetan of whether it made sense to posit that the initial moment of a sensory experience is shaped by thought or a mental image, as Jinpa argued. But here Jinpa was a lone voice, and the Dalai Lama did not buy his argument.

Francisco put science's stake in the ground: "Neuroscience says that internal active organization occurs not only in the perceptual sphere, but it happens in the larger context of the rest of other mental conditions such as memory, expectation, posture and movement, and intention. Seeing, for instance, takes into account what we perceive through the senses, but shapes it depending on these other conditions."

The positions in Buddhist philosophy resonated for Francisco with similar debates in science: "For example, to say that an emotion colors a perception is one interpretation that I myself am not very satisfied with because it suggests there is a perception and then an emotion is layered on top. There is another point of view, in which emotion—that is, the tendency toward motion—is like a predisposition with which the organism goes to meet the world. It is not that you have the perception and then you paint it with emotion; it is that the very act of encountering the world, the perception, is already intrinsically emotionally shaped. There could not be a perception without an emotional component. I would distinguish as a distortion a very deluded perception when that emotion becomes, for example, so very prolonged that it is dysfunctional or pathological. But even normally there is no such thing as perception without emotion."

A Subtle Interest

Richie Davidson offered an example. "Your Holiness, with certain kinds of visual objects that are more complex—for example, a neutral face that is not expressing an emotion—the very initial reaction across ten people will not necessarily be the same because of the emotional temperament of each person. Within the first two hundred milliseconds there is a difference in their reaction to the face between a person who is anxious and a person who has a calm temperament," Richie explained. This immediate difference in patterns of neural activity has been detected in the fusiform face area, a part of the brain that registers faces, and occurs in response to neutral faces that are liked versus disliked.

It struck the Dalai Lama that this difference could still be due to a conceptual process. He clarified, "My real interest here is very subtle. Even within that first two hundred milliseconds where you're already seeing differences from one individual to the next, is there a point, maybe in the first hundred milliseconds, that is just the visual perception—the mere appearance—and then the conceptual cognition clicks in the second hundred milliseconds? Is there any evidence for that? My hypothesis is that the first hundred milliseconds would be the same for all ten people and the variations for temperament would come once the conceptual apparatus is involved."

Richie started to say, "The evidence would suggest—" but was cut off by Thupten Jinpa, who, in the spirit of the debater, was raising a challenge: "I would make a counterargument that the preceding mental state will already influence the initial moment of visual perception."

The Dalai Lama took the challenge in stride. "Yes, in principle, the first moment of visual perception will be influenced by a preceding mental state—but only in the sense that the clarity of the experience is drawing its basis from the previous moment; it won't modify the sheer appearance of it. In the second moment, when you get into judgment—the good or bad feeling you have about it—that's a new event. But I still suspect that there is a very brief moment—a tenth of a second, perhaps—where your temperament, health, age, and so forth are not likely to influence the sheer visual perception itself."

Francisco answered, "I don't think that we can determine that to that level of detail, Your Holiness, but there seems to be quite a bit of evidence that when I see an image, the way it comes in and is treated and shaped also continues what was there before. In what the brain does to shape it, expectations and memories and associations will affect it—but they do not determine it. I think I would agree more with Jinpa that something would be carried on from the previous moment. I don't think there is any evidence that you can have a pure visual appearance. It always will be in the context of what just happened or other events of the past in working memory. I don't think we can really determine a fine, fine moment when there will be just perception."

"How could you check that out neuroscientifically?" Alan wondered.

"Well, that is a good point. We might be able to if we could refine this kind of analysis," Francisco answered. "This particular analysis is bad for answering that, because we can only resolve down now to about seventy milliseconds."

A Brilliant Suggestion

Richie wanted to point out that the data here are clear and support the Dalai Lama's hypothesis. The very early components of the brain measure used to measure these extremely quick bits of mental activity reveal that for the first seventy to one hundred milliseconds people react in a highly similar way. The differences among individuals in brain activity begin to emerge after about a hundred milliseconds—Richie was struck that the research record was exactly as the Dalai Lama suggested.

"There is a method," Richie said, "using the same kind of electrical measurements where we can actually detect activity in the brain stem before it gets to the highest part of the brain, the cortex. The brain stem is very unlikely to show differences across people. You're more likely to see commonality there. That might be the moment that you're describing, which really is similar and does not reflect like or dislike, or expectations. It's just the pure sensory information coming in."

The Dalai Lama murmured, "That's it, that's it," indicating that this was precisely the focus of his interest.

Alan continued the line of inquiry: "According to Buddhist epistemology as I understand it, that moment is so brief that the ordinary person cannot ascertain it."

"Right—it's within the first thirty-five to forty milliseconds," Richie said.

"If it's impossible to corroborate on first-person testimony, then it's hard to imagine how you could get at it just through neuroscience," Alan pointed out.

"Why not?" Francisco asked. "If we can make more-refined methods to distinguish the dynamics of the arising of a perception, it is not impossible. But with today's indirect techniques for measuring the brain stem, that is very tough, so more precise methods would have to be developed. We're getting a little better already—resolving at the level of dozens of milliseconds, which is already something. But the more subtle levels are lost. This is part of the collaboration—if there is such a thing as a first-person ascertaining of that. There could be, in principle."

The Dalai Lama offered a specific theory to test experimentally: "My hypothesis is that for sensory perception in general, that first moment is nonconceptual; you're simply getting the impression. In the second moment, some kind of identification clicks in. You would expect that to hold across the board. But I suspect that when you close your eyes and get a purely mental image, you would not have that sequence of a simple image followed by added identification. Probably the identification would come in simultaneously."

"Actually," said Richie, "there you don't get the brain stem involvement, so that's exactly right! That's a brilliant suggestion! With pure imagery, mental imagery, the brain stem component—which is within the first forty milliseconds—does not arise. It all happens just in the cortex, so it fits perfectly with what you say. But when actually looking at an image, the sensory processing activates the brain stem."

"I was wondering," the Dalai Lama added, "whether one could see a difference between a situation where you have just visual perception and another where you go through a thought process at the same time as being aware of what you are seeing—for example, liking or disliking. Another case would be having the visual perception and then closing your eyes so you are no longer looking but going through the related thought process. Would you envision a difference in the brain activity of these instances?"

Richie answered, "In one case the visual stimulus is present and in the other case it's absent. In one case you will have brain stem activity and in the other case you will not. There is an issue as to whether we could be aware of the activity in the brain stem. According to modern neuroscience, the only way to become aware of activity in the brain stem is for that activity to reach the cortex, and so there is a paradox"—that is, we can't know it, since we depend on that information reaching the cortex to experience it.

Richie added a telling afterthought: "Maybe there is a process by which very accomplished yogis can become aware of activity in the brain stem before it reaches the cortex, but we do not know anything about that in the West."

Within the year Richie would be testing just such accomplished yogis in his laboratory at Madison.

First-Person Science

Francisco—pressed by time—returned us to our initial theme, the importance of first-person accounts. "Just to conclude, Your Holiness, I want to begin to combine what we just saw—the face-recognition experiments—with first-person accounts as a tool for analysis. We have now begun to do the same kind of experiments, but instead of just presenting slides and asking the person to push the button, after each presentation now we ask the person to give an account of his or her experience and state of mind preceding the stimulation: 'I was distracted . . . I was thinking about my girlfriend . . . I was really prepared.' You get a very rough, minimal—but nevertheless phenomenological—first-person account.[14]

"These are intelligent but not highly trained subjects; nevertheless, you find that you immediately discover different kinds of preparedness." One group had what he called "stable readiness"—they were just relaxed and waiting. Readiness with some degree of expectation typified the second group. A third group was slightly distracted. And finally, there were those people who were totally unprepared—doing something else, such as daydreaming.

"If we take the data for these four categories, we can see how they differ under these different conditions of mind," Francisco said. There was a great deal of oscillation and activity in those who had the stable readiness, both with and without expectation. By comparison, those in the unprepared state showed patterns that were much less coherent and synchronous; these people were daydreaming or distracted, not ready.

"There ought to be brain activity because they're distracted," the Dalai Lama observed. In other words, the thoughts that distract us are themselves brain activity.

"That's exactly right," Francisco agreed.

"So there would be two cases of unpreparedness," the Dalai Lama went on. "One is where the mind is active but distracted, and the other is a simple lack of concentration, where the person doesn't really care. You're just falling into laxity, to use a Buddhist term, just getting dull." Here the Dalai Lama was drawing on a classic typology in Buddhist practice, described in detail in the literature on meditative quiescence: excitation, in which the mind is agitated or distracted, and laxity, in which the attention "implodes" and has lost its sharp edge of vividness.

Francisco replied, "The point here is simply to see the difference when you are asked to do a task. Here you have a whole group of cases where the person is just distracted, and the patterns are so different that they don't combine into something stable. Whereas when you do the task very precisely, they always combine into a stable pattern."

Francisco went on to another point: "This was done with subjects who were not highly trained. What we're going to do now is to take trained meditators who can go into much finer detail in describing a moment of experience. For example, we want to work with people from the monasteries in Dordogne in the south of France; we hope to have well-trained Buddhist practitioners come to the lab and do this kind of experiment. It is obvious that if we can find differences even with ordinary people, then with more expert people we should be able to really go into much finer detail. This is where there is a true possibility of collaboration, not just in principle but in a very concrete sense."

Going Back to Things Themselves

I wanted to continue the discussion about the scientific attempt to understand what happens in the moment of perception or experience, and the very fine-grained Buddhist analysis of just that. This seemed a point where Buddhist insights might become a guiding source of theoretical hypotheses for science. So I asked about the value that might be added by having such expert observers: "If we're going to use a first-person methodology, what can people really notice—both ordinary people and highly trained people?"

Francisco replied by pointing out that the first-, second-, and third-person methods—that is, the person having the experience, a skilled interviewer, and objective methods—"are really just different ways to validate this kind of data. There are different styles of validation, all part of what can become intersubjective knowledge—knowledge that is valid in common and not just my private idea. For example, a meditator who is sitting has, in some sense, an immediate experience. He might remain silent with no expression of his experience at all, in which case this cannot become part of the data that we can use. There has to be at least an expression, a report; if he doesn't express himself, others cannot share this knowledge.

"If there is a second person involved, there are two extremes possible. One is a really expert second person, for example a skillful teacher who could really lead a meditator on the path by asking the right questions—'Did you notice this?' There are also other techniques in the West, such as methods of interviewing where one guides a person in reliving a certain experience in memory with complete recall. There is another interview technique, not so directive, that extracts knowledge that otherwise wouldn't be easy to obtain.

"All of these have drawbacks, strengths, and weaknesses. There is also a more trivial form of the second-person method where you just ask a person to complete a questionnaire. That is, in fact, the way the first-person techniques existed for a long time in psychology and in cognitive science. Though well established in cognitive science, it remains a very limited method because the second person is not an expert in the sense of being able to coach the first-person report. Then, of course, there is the third person, the methods for objective measurements.

"Let me present what I call different 'lineages' for the first person. Of course the Buddhist tradition is a very important lineage, which covers both the first person as such—self-reports—as well as an expert second person. The relationship between a teacher and his student becomes extremely sophisticated; it is not just a trivial 'Fill out this questionnaire.'

"There is also in the West a truly unique tradition of phenomenology. In this, the first-person account is considered to be the basis of how to think about mind and the world. In phenomenology there have been several methods developed that correspond to both second and first person. For example, William James could be seen as belonging to this tradition, and particularly Edmund Husserl in Germany, who created this whole style of work. This is quite different from other philosophical schools in the West, particularly the empiricist tradition, or American philosophy of mind."

The Dalai Lama wanted to know, "Is there a very simple definition of phenomenology? Is it just description?"

Francisco answered, "My colleagues across the table there will correct me, but basically Husserl's point of view was that one cannot think about oneself and the world without doing what he called 'going back to things themselves'—in other words, to just the way things appear. Not to have any a priori assumptions about what the world should be—there should be God, there should be matter, there should be this or there should be that—but to simply look, simply have the way the world presents itself be the basis. This is what he called the phenomenological reduction.

"So it's a very meditative approach. When you want to analyze something, the first thing you do is to suspend all of your ideas about it, all your preconceptions, all of your habitual patterns and just see what you see and start from there as the basis. That was Husserl's great contribution, and in fact he built a whole philosophy on that basis, a century-old tradition that has continued."

"Am I right in thinking," the Dalai Lama asked, "that the basic standpoint is to forget about, or to bracket, whatever metaphysical or religious views that might exist, and simply start from your experience? Wouldn't that require a kind of arrogance deep down, thinking that I have the ability to know everything?"

"Not to know everything," Francisco replied, "but to know the basis. There is a certain arrogance in the same way that it might be seen as arrogance for a meditator to say, 'I'm going to look in my mind and see it as it is.' "

"The point is," the Dalai Lama asked, "in the final analysis, doesn't the knowledge have to be verified by one's experience? Similarly, no matter how sophisticated and complex a philosophical system is, at the end of the day validation has to come by relating to one's experience."

"That was exactly Husserl's point, that the basis is validation through experience," Francisco answered.

"This is a very basic Buddhist standpoint," the Dalai Lama observed. "There is a similar spirit in a Buddhist scripture where the Buddha is asked a number of questions and ultimately says to relate it to your experience."

Francisco observed that Husserl's school has "very elaborate descriptions about time and about space. They have great discoveries, but the method—how to communicate to a young student how to phenomenologize about this or that—remains rather vague and obscure. It is not a tradition where the method has been really elaborated. That's where I think Buddhism can make a great contribution to this philosophical tradition independent of its use in science."

Beyond Naivete: Yogis as Expert Phenomenologists

Working with Richie, Francisco said, he had come up with a way of fitting all of these different first-person lineages and methods together that made clearer the possibilities of this approach. The first person is one dimension, distinguishing the beginner from the master in degrees of expertise. The second person is another, distinguishing between a naive second person and an expert coach.

The third dimension to explore, he proposed, was time. "You can either report the immediate situation, or else you can go back in time and remember, for example, what you experienced two days ago, or a month ago. There are a number of new techniques in cognitive science and experimental psychology for either immediate self-report or recollected self-report, and there are problems with both of them. What we are trying to do is to define different cases, and not to think that the first person method is just one thing. For example, in the classical studies on hypnosis, you need an expert coach to induce the hypnosis, and a person under hypnosis, who is probably a beginner reporter and is making an immediate report.

"In the classical verbal report in most experimental psychology, you deal with beginners and immediate or intermediate time, and the second-person level is quite naive."

"That's just why having a highly adept meditation practitioner come into the lab would be a very valuable contribution," I pointed out.

Francisco agreed, saying that would make possible exploring the entire range of experience. But, he added, "in fact, science, so far, has explored only the little corner where naive subjects report to naive second persons."

Richie chimed in, "In the field of emotion research, this is a very, very important point. Most emotion research that has relied on people's reports of their experience will ask people, on a very simple questionnaire, 'How satisfied are you with your life? Very satisfied, extremely satisfied, moderately satisfied, or unsatisfied.' You just have to circle a number.

"That," he continued, "actually is the basis for a very large scientific literature on what is called subjective well-being, but it is based upon such a cursory and undisciplined introspective examination of people's experience that it is no wonder it has been found to have many problems. So the idea of bringing into the laboratory observers who have gone through some systematic training to provide a richer description about their internal experience will be extremely important as we progress in this area. Particularly so when we begin to make finer distinctions among different attributes of the same emotion."

That idea had been proposed for years by Francisco, most notably in his book *The Embodied Mind,* but in more recent writings as well; Alan Wallace, likewise, had made a similar proposal in his own writing.[15] Owen, too, had been making converging arguments in philosophy of mind—indeed, this part of the meeting was a small epiphany for him, seeing how the rich taxonomy of mental states in Buddhism and the highly experienced observers of mind could further the agenda in brain science.

But when it came to practitioners who might have the extremely fine powers of discrimination that could be useful, say, in Francisco's research, where could they be found? The Dalai Lama felt that there might be some highly trained in practices such as Mahamudra and Dzogchen—advanced meditation techniques—who might have the capacity to be aware of such moments of experience (especially those who had refined what Matthieu had talked about on the first day as the "clarity" aspect of awareness). Even so, he questioned whether they would be able to articulate this experience, which would depend at least in part on how well informed they were about the technical terms for such states of mind.

The Dalai Lama pointed out that monks—and even, to some degree, children at the Tibetan schools set up in refugee communities in India—study rudiments of Buddhist psychology. Some monks, of course, study systems of Buddhist psychology and epistemology in depth. But the Dalai Lama thought that if these topics were taught "not just in isolation without practical application, but together with modern cognitive neuroscience, then there would be a lot more interest." The monks would learn to relate their experiences with contemplative practice back to both theoretical frameworks—an idea Francisco found fascinating.

A New Kind of Collaborator

One of these studies' main take-home messages for science is in how to connect experience—the phenomenology of a mental state—with its brain activity. As Richie said, "Using highly seasoned practitioners as scientific partners would enable us to have more faith in the relations that we see between what people report of their experience and particular changes in the brain, making those connections with more precision. That will be an important research strategy for us in the future."

Such skilled practitioners represent a new class of collaborators for brain science, individuals who can generate and report on their internal states with unparalleled accuracy. That sharp inner awareness had been an elusive holy grail for a group of American psychologists at the beginning of the twentieth century. Called "introspectionists," these psychologists hoped to study the mind through the inner observations of their subjects. In one method, for instance, volunteers (even then, typically college students) would write down as quickly as they could their stream of thought verbatim, supposedly tracking the fluid meanderings of their mental states.

But because such methods yielded virtually nothing of use—if only because those subjects had no particular expertise in or discipline for the task—the movement sputtered out, a scientific blind alley. (One unexpected benefit of introspectionism was for literature rather than psychology: The writer Gertrude Stein, while a student of the psychologist William James at Radcliffe, learned the method of free-associative writing that was to become her trademark in literature.)

Now, nearly a century later, the aim—if not the means—of the introspectionists could be attempted anew. Tools such as the fMRI and computerized EEGs offer an unprecedented precision in observing the brain at work. And skilled meditators offer a promising pool of collaborators who can work as peers with scientists. Just such a collaboration was envisioned more than a decade ago by Francisco, who argued that the biological signature of a state and the inner experience of its contours need to be studied together to get a complete picture.

In a rather surprising way, the Dalai Lama also sees great promise in this collaborative approach to the scientific study of human consciousness. Indeed, he later told me one reason he has been insisting on introducing scientific education into the curriculum in monasteries is not simply to inform monks about scientific theories, but to focus on a select group, from which might emerge some monks whose scientific education can be taken to the highest levels.

His hope, he explained, "is that one day in the future we may be able to produce a scientist who is also a Buddhist practitioner." His vision of monks who would develop high-quality scientific expertise along with traditional depth as practitioners means that, sometime in the future, it would be these monks who would be doing the scientific research—on themselves.

But, taking the long view of someone who thinks not just in years but in centuries, the Dalai Lama recognized this will take a goodly time. With an impish smile he added, "It is conceivable that the good results of this collaboration are not something we will see in our lifetimes."

A Collaboration Emerges

At this point I announced the morning tea break. But the momentum of the discussion between the Dalai Lama and Francisco was so strong, they just kept talking into the break.

"There are two very different ways of being unprepared," said the Dalai Lama, pressing a previous point. "One is to use *shinay* (that is, calming meditation) terminology—where you're falling into laxity, where the mind is inactive, just kind of empty. The other way of being unprepared is very different, with excitation, agitation, distraction. In the latter, your mind is caught up in thinking about the past or anticipating the future; you're single-pointedly focused, but on something else. I would expect to see different types of brain activity for these, though both fall under the rubric of unprepared. You would need to divide those two."

"This is a very good suggestion," Francisco agreed. "We need to have people with that expertise. Most people only think that they are either distracted or expectant, but with a more highly trained person you can ask them to focus on what kind of distraction they had."

At this point the tea break ended, and their discussion broke off—though the collaboration was to go on. For Francisco, the measure of success for his presentation was how engaged the Dalai Lama was. By that standard, he was very pleased, even if he didn't fully finish all the talking points he hoped to cover.

Francisco, though elated by the Dalai Lama's questions and proposals, was also a bit frustrated by not being able to pursue in more detail the ideas that emerged about using expert meditators as collaborators in research—one of his central passions as a scientist. But that further exploration would come just a few months later in his lab in Paris. There, with Lama Öser as his collaborator, Francisco would put into practice some of the critical experiments on the neurological impact of meditation that had been pointed to today in Dharamsala. And those experiments, it would turn out, would become part of Francisco's legacy, among his last acts on the stage of science.

14

The Protean Brain

For the Dalai Lama, the primacy of fact over theory in the search for truth represents a particularly appealing aspect of modern science. Any theory, any law, any dogmatic statement in science can be overturned tomorrow if the right piece of fresh data reveals it to be wrong. Research provides a self-corrective mechanism, a way for science to pilot itself in pursuing truth.

Richard Davidson's topic for our last morning offered a prime case in point. For decades brain science held as a given that the central nervous system did not generate new neurons. Every student of neuroscience was taught this truth; it was seen as hard fact, not theory. But this unshakable dogma was shaken—indeed, shattered—in the late 1990s, largely through research in molecular biology at the cellular level.[1] What had only recently been viewed as definitely established has now been shown to be utterly false.

That finding—that the brain and nervous system generate new cells as learning or repeated experiences dictate—has put the theme of plasticity at the front and center of neuroscience.[2] Richie believes that neural plasticity—the brain's ability to reshape as experience molds it—will reshape psychology itself in coming years. His own research has been leading the way in infiltrating psychology with new insights from neuroscience.

As Richie replaced Francisco in the presenter's seat, I suggested how he would add to our morning's dialogue: Francisco had focused on what happens within a moment of experience, and Richie would now turn to the lasting effects of training the mind and how that affects the brain.

"Your Holiness," Richie began, "I would like to return to our theme of destructive emotions and talk about some antidotes to such emotions and how we can think about those antidotes in neuroscientific terms—specifically, how the use of certain meditation practices in changing brain function and other bodily activity over a long term may have lasting effects. We're addressing here the idea of really changing temperament by altering the brain in ways that endure.

"One of the ways to think about antidotes to destructive emotion is by facilitating the activation of regions of the frontal lobe that suppress or modulate the activity of the amygdala. The amygdala has been shown to be very important for certain kinds of negative emotions, and we know that specific regions of the frontal lobes reduce this activity of the amygdala. Through this mechanism we can change the brain so that a person will show less negative and more positive emotional reactivity."

"Are you suggesting," the Dalai Lama asked, "there might be a possibility of developing drugs that could help reduce the negative emotions, to change emotions by creating change in the brain?"

"It's a good question," Richie replied. "The problem with drugs is that when you give a person a pill, it affects chemicals throughout the brain." In other words, because medications work by impacting chemical systems that have far-flung purposes throughout the brain—and the rest of the body—they inevitably produce unwanted side effects. Medicine, of course, accepts these as the price of a remedy.

"Or might it be an electrical intervention, or some other kind of medical intervention?" the Dalai Lama asked again. "Is that a possibility you're pursuing?"

"I'm actually going to pursue the use of meditation as a way to change the brain," Richie answered.

But first he addressed the question of new interventions, describing one that stimulates the brain with a special high-powered magnet that when brought close to the brain induces a current in the brain itself. Several research groups had found that using this device to stimulate the left frontal lobe in depressed patients reduced their symptoms.[3] But there were some limitations to the method, including its most serious drawback—that it caused severe headaches for an hour or two after each of the sessions. And to work, it required two or three sessions a week for two months.

"Is there any degradation of intelligence, the ability to reason, or any other mental faculties?" the Dalai Lama asked.

"At this point we don't know," Richie replied. "Longer-term studies have not been done. My preference is to use other methods that are more internal"—that is, under control of the person, like meditation.

"Yes—and they're safer," the Dalai Lama agreed.

Shifting Temperament

Richie went on, "We have talked over the course of the week, Your Holiness, about how when a negative event happens, some people are disposed by temperament to react strongly, immediately. It's an automatic response; Paul Ekman used the phrase 'refractory period' for when the emotion is very difficult to stop once it's initiated. A person is not receptive to new information while in the grip of emotion.

"One possibility is that the cultivation of certain skills may facilitate the disruption of the automatic negative emotion. That would give a person an opportunity to pause and shorten the refractory period—and to become more conscious of that initial moment of the arising of the emotion so that it can be cut off before the negative effects occur.

"In the cognitive restructuring we have talked about, Your Holiness has provided some very valuable information for us as Western scientists. For instance, I found it extremely intriguing when Your Holiness mentioned that

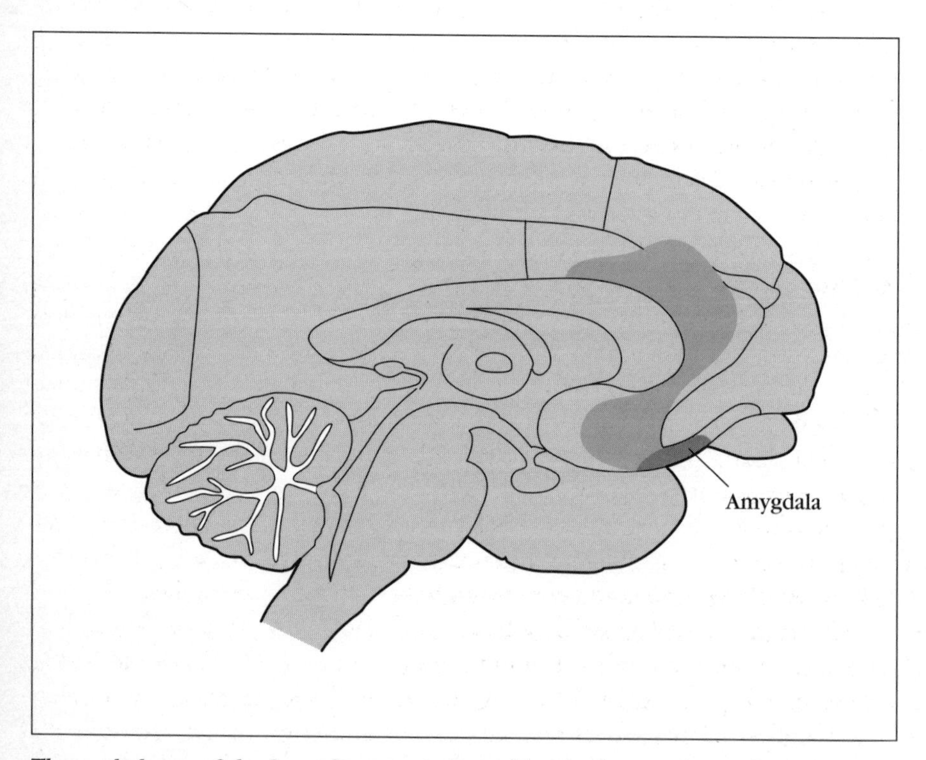

The medial area of the frontal cortex, indicated by shading, is the prefrontal area most heavily connected with the amygdala.

positive emotions were more likely to arise as a consequence of deliberate thought, whereas negative emotions often arise more spontaneously.

"There is an approach in the West called cognitive therapy, which involves teaching people to think differently about the upsetting events in their lives. Instead of automatically cultivating a habit of negative emotional reactions, they reason about what upsets them—and they're able to have a more positive response. Finally, there is the cultivation of positive affect itself, which we believe can be a direct antidote to the experience of certain kinds of negative emotions.

"I would like to turn our attention now to the brain mechanisms that allow these kinds of antidotes to work, and how practices like meditation might affect these brain mechanisms."

Putting up his first slide, Richie went on, "This diagram shows the key areas in the frontal lobe. The medial portion, deep down in the lobe, is the area most heavily interconnected with the amygdala."

"Is the amygdala the area that is very closely related to the negative qualities of experiences such as depression?" the Dalai Lama wondered.

"Yes," Richie told him. "The amygdala is more active in people who are depressed. It is more active in people who have posttraumatic stress disorder. It is more active in people who are anxious. The medial area of the frontal cortex plays an inhibitory role: When this area becomes more active, the amygdala shows a decrease in activation. People differ in their temperament in the extent to which these areas of the prefrontal cortex are active and the amygdala is correspondingly underactive."

This difference in temperament due to prefrontal activation sheds new light on some puzzling data. One study of people's sense of well-being found negligible differences in satisfaction with life between paraplegics, ordinary people, and lottery winners. The data on paraplegics was especially startling. While losing use of one's limbs is of course devastating, a surprising number of people start to feel positive moods only a few weeks after the accident that disabled them. Within a year most are back to feeling about as upbeat (or downbeat) about life as they had been before the accident. Likewise, most people who lose a loved one are back to their normal mood range a year or so later. And there is virtually no difference in daily moods between people who are extremely wealthy and people who have very modest incomes.

In short, there is amazingly little connection between one's life circumstances and our predominant moods. On the other hand, studies of identical twins reared apart show that they have very similar levels of positive or negative moods—if one twin is typically upbeat and enthusiastic, the other will be; if one is morose and melancholy, so will be the other. Such findings have led to the proposition that each of us has a happiness set point, a biologically determined ratio of good-to-bad moods. And because the set point is biological, life's upsets or triumphs may budge it for a while, but it will tend to settle back to our customary level.[4]

That suggests, too, that there is little we can do to change it; after all, biology is destiny, is it not?

Not so. At least, that is the implication of Richie's findings—he found a way to shift that set point for the better.

A new slide displayed a brain image showing small bright spots—indicating heightened activity—during positive emotions. Richie commented, "In this particular study we searched through the entire brain to see what area is most strongly associated with a person's reports of positive emotion in their everyday life, like zeal, vigor, enthusiasm, and buoyancy. It's in the left frontal cortex.

"This is the same area most strongly associated with decrease in amygdala activation. So the question then is, how can we strengthen this area that inhibits the amygdala so that we can increase a person's positive emotions and decrease the destructive emotions? Inspired, Your Holiness, by many of your teachings, we have explored whether meditation will have effects in the long term on this area of the brain and whether that may also help to decrease negative emotions and increase positive emotions."

Alan wondered, "Would compassion in which there is empathy for the other person's suffering—perhaps even to the point of weeping with compassion—show up in the left frontal area?"

"We don't know—and this is part of the collaborative work that we would like to pursue," Richie answered. "We do know that people who score high on measures of positive emotion also report engaging in more altruistic action. But that's on the basis of their reports; we don't know if their actions actually correspond."

In fact, compassion was one of the conditions tested in Richie's later research in Madison.

The Case of the Happy Geshe

"I would like to now turn our attention to two experiments that we have done, Your Holiness. One is a case history with just one person, but it is very revealing and intriguing. The second is a more formal experiment that we have recently completed with Jon Kabat-Zinn, who presented to Your Holiness at a previous Mind and Life meeting.[5] Jon Kabat-Zinn has been developing methods to use mindfulness meditation in a large variety of populations, including medical patients, employees in the workplace, prisoners, and inner-city populations in various places in the United States.

"In a project that Francisco, I, and a number of others were involved with, we had the opportunity to study one monk who came to our laboratory in Madison. We were able to place electrodes on the monk's head and measure the brain electrical activity to see whether, just in his everyday, baseline state, the activity in this region associated with strong positive emotion and a decrease in the amygdala activation was, in fact, particularly active."

When Davidson showed a slide of the monk being hooked up to the EEG in the laboratory, the Dalai Lama recognized him and said with delight, "That *geshe* is currently the abbot of one of the major monasteries in India!"

"Something very interesting and exciting emerged from this," Davidson continued. "We recorded the brain activity of the *geshe* and were able to compare his brain activity to the other individuals who participated in experiments in my laboratory over the last couple of years. We had a hundred and seventy-five individuals whom we tested previously, using the identical measures."

As Davidson showed the slide comparing the *geshe*'s ratio of right-to-left activation, he revealed the finding: "The *geshe* had the most extreme positive value out of the entire hundred and seventy-five that we had ever tested at that point."

"Even in his everyday life, he is a very, very good person," the Dalai Lama remarked. "He has a very good sense of humor and is quite laid-back. And he's an excellent scholar."

The Dalai Lama knew the *geshe* as a monk-practitioner and a scholar but not as a yogi, in the sense Tibetans usually use the word—someone who spends long periods of time meditating alone on retreats. The annals of Tibetan Buddhism are filled with the accomplishment of great yogis in the past, and the Dalai Lama knew that there are today many dedicated yogis spending years and years in retreat. He had once asked his Office of Religious Affairs to inquire about highly accomplished meditation practitioners who might cooperate with researchers. The inquiry included not just Tibetans, but Indian yogis, as well as practitioners in the Theravada, *vipashyana,* and other Buddhist meditation traditions.

However, the Dalai Lama felt it was important that scientists realize that being a yogi, whether Tibetan Buddhist or from other traditions, did not in itself guarantee a person had found freedom from negative emotions. That depended, he noted, to a large extent on the practices involved; the ancient Vedas of India are replete with stories of extremely angry or jealous yogis.

By contrast, the *geshe,* an ordinary practitioner living a monk's life, was spiritually advanced, in the Dalai Lama's view. As a dedicated Buddhist scholar, even this "laid-back" monk would constantly check his own mind to be sure his life was his practice—and that was the likely reason he showed such strong effects in Davidson's research.

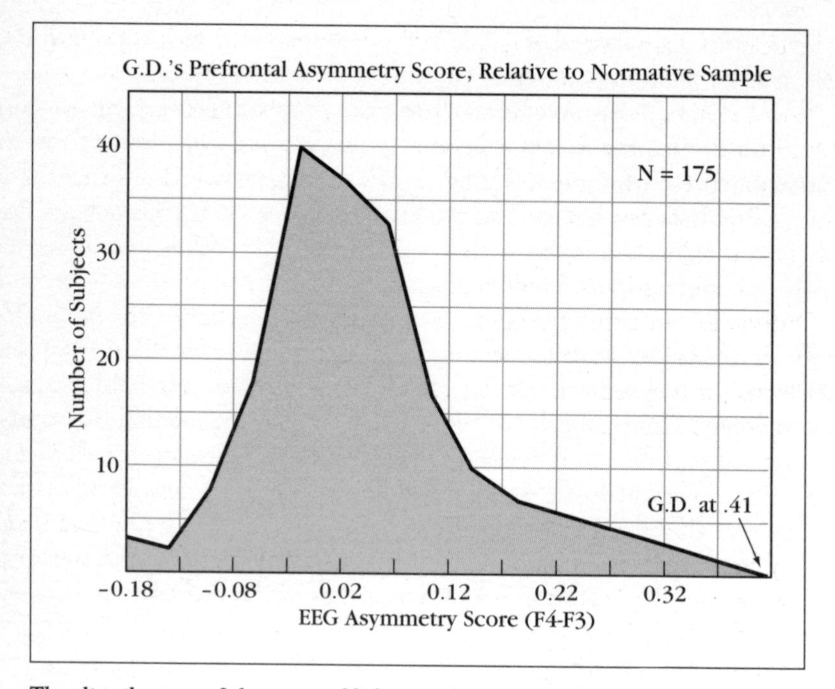

The distribution of the ratio of left-to-right prefrontal activity in 175 test subjects. Negative emotions activate the right prefrontal area, positive the left; the ratio of the two predicts the range of moods a person is likely to feel day to day. The *geshe* ("G.D.") had a value higher—that is, more positive—than any of the 175 other people tested.

The Happy Outlier

The joyful *geshe* is an outlier, in statistical terms, as his ratio of left-to-right activity was at a point way beyond the rest of the bell curve for positive emotion. Exactly what might account for the *geshe's* extremely positive value was an open question. As an ordinary Tibetan Buddhist monk, he would have routinely done many meditative practices that might have contributed to shaping his brain response. Indeed, Richie mentioned that the *geshe* had done daily practices, such as one aimed at cultivating compassion, for more than thirty years.

For me, the *geshe's* data was an epiphany of sorts, as in my mind there was little question that such sustained practice in itself was the cause. Since my first trip to India in the early 1970s as a graduate student studying meditation systems, I had been intrigued by a palpable quality of being—a lightness—that distinguished many of the people I met who had practiced meditation for years, whether as part of a daily monk's routine, as with the *geshe,* or as a yogi doing more prolonged and intensive retreats.

Now I realized what may have drawn me so. This shift in the brain—the leftward tilt in their emotional set point—was apparently one of the fruits of spiritual practice. Two thousand years ago the writers of the Abhidharma, the classic of Buddhist psychology, had proposed that progress in spiritual practice could be tracked by a ratio: how often and how strongly wholesome versus destructive emotions grip us. Modern brain science seemed to be bearing this out.

Ordinarily, our emotions come to us as our life conditions change, shifting for better or worse. But meditation practitioners gradually develop an inner locus for their emotional states, an equanimity less vulnerable to life's ups and downs. Gradually, the Abhidharma proposes, the meditator's moods are governed more by an inner reality rather than by outer events. *Sukha* is the Sanskrit term for this sense of repleteness, of an inner contentment and calm joy that abides regardless of external circumstances. *Sukha* differs from ordinary happiness or pleasure, which typically depends on what happens to us. In this respect, *sukha* seems to reflect that leftward prefrontal tilt—in essence, a highly positive set point.

From the Abhidharma perspective, "all worldlings are deranged," as the Buddha provocatively put it, in that they are vulnerable to the distortions and skews in perception caused by destructive emotions. The ultimate state of well-being, by contrast, is one in which not a single such destructive emotion stirs—and in which positive states such as compassion, lovingkindness, and equanimity dominate the mind.

When I first studied the Abhidharma model of mental health while still a graduate student in clinical psychology at Harvard, that notion appealed greatly. It offered a positive psychology, a model of human development that pointed beyond limits of the prevailing theories of the West. But while it appealed as an admirable ideal, it seemed an unlikely reality. Now, with the data point from the *geshe* documenting an extremely positive prefrontal tilt, that range of human development seemed a real possibility.

To be sure, many people I've known have a positive, optimistic tone that bespeaks the leftward tilt. In fact, Richie himself is one of the most perpetually upbeat people I've known. When I once asked where he fits on the left-to-right ratio for happiness, he said, "I'm definitely to the left—just not three standard deviations," like the *geshe.*

That leaves some important questions in explaining the extremely positive readings from the *geshe.* Was it just some unique oddity of the *geshe,* a genetic accident, say—or did his brain measures reflect progress along a continuum of positivity that any of us could aspire to?

The next part of Richie's presentation explored just that point.

Biotech Meets an Ancient Technique

While the results with the *geshe* were very intriguing, Richie pointed out, the data were from just one person—and a very unusual person at that. Could similar changes in brain activity be observed in ordinary people? To answer that question, he and his colleagues decided to examine people who worked for a biotechnology corporation.[6]

Because of the intense competitive pressure in the biotech industry to get new products developed and to market, said Davidson, "the employees in these corporations often have to work under very severe deadlines. Even in the best environments, they report tremendous amounts of stress. So we felt that we could do an experiment and also be of benefit to people at the same time."

Richie asked Jon Kabat-Zinn, of the University of Massachusetts, to collaborate with him. As he explained, "In the West, Jon has had perhaps the most experience in using mindfulness meditation practices that have been secularized, and teaching them to a wide variety of the population. Jon was very enthusiastic about collaborating with us; he agreed to fly out from Massachusetts to Madison, Wisconsin, every week for ten consecutive weeks to conduct the training himself.

"The participants were identified in July when we asked people at this company who were interested in learning meditation to sign up. Before the meditation groups began, all the participants came to the university and had their brains measured by EEG. We also assessed some other biological systems. After the assessment was completed, which was in September, participants were then randomly assigned to either the meditation group or to a group that we call a 'wait list control group,' where they were simply told that we couldn't accommodate all of them. They would join a later group for the same training."

The Dalai Lama wanted a clarification: "Is it because there was not enough space or was it deliberate?"

"It was deliberate," Davidson explained, "so that we had a group against which to compare—people who came from the same corporation, reported the same stress, and had the same interest in meditation. Everything about the two groups was the same. At the time we did our initial assessments, we ourselves did not know which person was going to go to the meditation group and which person was going to go to the wait list control group.

"Then the meditation group took the standard training that Jon Kabat-Zinn offers. It consists of one two-to-three-hour class each week for eight weeks plus a one-day retreat.[7] We got permission from the chairman of the corporation to allow the employees to take time off to go to the class."

The Dalai Lama smiled broadly on hearing this—apparently a company policy he could endorse.

"We set up a very nice room in the company as a meditation room. After the sixth week, there was a one-day full retreat in silence. In addition, each participant was asked to practice for forty-five minutes per day. At the end of each day, each of the participants filled out a little questionnaire reporting honestly how much they actually practiced. Those were not given to Jon Kabat-Zinn until the training was finished; they were held for later analysis. The training ended in mid-November; we purposely arranged for the training to go through the fall because at the very end of the training every person in both the meditation group and in the wait list control group was to be vaccinated with an influenza vaccine."

The flu shots given were the same as those offered by doctors to their patients every flu season. "What was the significance of that?" the Dalai Lama asked.

Davidson elaborated, "By taking blood samples at different points after the vaccine, we can get a quantitative measure of the functioning of the recipients' immune system. In that way we were able to determine whether meditation had any effect on the immune system.

"There is an interesting anecdote, which has not been reported, which relates to this. When the United States went to the Gulf for the Desert Storm War, before the soldiers went they all received the hepatitis A vaccine. It turned out that a large percentage of the soldiers did not show seroconversion in response to the vaccine. That is, they got the vaccine but it didn't work. The assumption was that because they were so stressed about going to the Gulf War, it interfered with their immune system and so they didn't show the normal immune response to the vaccine. There was also a recent study published that found that the family members who are caregivers of patients with severe Alzheimer's disease show a very poor response when they're given influenza vaccine.[8] So we know that stress can have a big impact on these immune measures."

Davidson also knew from his own research that high activity in the left prefrontal area predicted that a person's immune system would respond better to the vaccine, converting it into more antibodies against the flu. But in this study he wanted to go the next step, to assess the effect of mindfulness training.

"The logic in this experiment was to see whether meditation, as an antidote to stress, can have a beneficial effect on the immune system. This had never before been asked in this context. At the end of the study the participants got the vaccine. They were also brought back to the laboratory and we put the EEG cap back on and assessed their brain activity. We did the same thing again four months later. The participants in the wait list control group went through the identical assessments; the only difference was they had not yet had the meditation training. They only began their training after all the assessments ended.

"I would like to share with you four findings and one observation that came from this study. The first finding was, as you would expect, that the participants in the meditation group reported that their anxiety level went down. Their negative emotions went down and their positive emotions went up compared to the participants in the control group. We very much expected that to happen and other studies have shown that, so it was not a surprise. But we were particularly interested in whether the brain activity changed in the way that we had predicted.

"When all the participants were first tested from July to September, before we assigned them to their respective groups, there was no statistical difference in EEG measures of activation in the left frontal part of the brain associated with positive emotion. But at the third assessment, four months after the meditation training ended, the meditation group showed a significant increase in left-sided activation from before they began."

The stronger the leftward tilt in prefrontal activity, the more positive emotions in their daily life people reported after the meditation training. But, Davidson added, the control group actually went in the other direction. "They were getting worse. One interpretation is that we promised the control group that they were going to get the meditation and then had them go through very elaborate testing, and they were getting very angry at us (with reason). But we did give them the meditation at the end.

"Here is the finding that we are actually the most excited about because it's so unusual. It has never been demonstrated before. We found that the meditation group showed a stronger immune response to the influenza vaccine compared to the control group—enhanced immunity. This is the reverse of the effects of stress on the vaccine response, and it shows that meditation can markedly increase the effectiveness of the vaccine. Other research has shown that this actually correlates with the decreased likelihood of getting influenza if you were exposed to the virus."

In earlier research, Richie had found that people who show the distinctive leftward prefrontal tilt in brain activity associated with the positive emotional qualities also have a more robust activity on some parameters of immune function. These earlier findings led Richie to the conjecture that the more positive a person's disposition, the bigger and better their immune system's ability to mount an antibody response to a flu vaccine. The mindfulness group displayed a larger response to the flu vaccine, and—most interesting—the larger the leftward tilt in a person's brain activity, the greater the beneficial response to the flu vaccine.

The Dalai Lama was particularly interested in Richie's report of the immune measures. He felt that they corroborated his own view that emotions such as anger or stress are harmful to human life. On the other hand, peace of mind and a compassionate attitude offer a countervailing, positive force. And these were scientific findings: Without speaking of religion, God, or nirvana, there was a sound basis to say that the one set of emotions are harmful, the other beneficial. It was, as he had said before in these meetings, more ammunition for his secular ethics.

A Bit of a Puzzle

Richie concluded that though he was excited about these findings, he felt cautious, too, viewing them as very preliminary because they were based on a small number of people.[9] He said he hoped to repeat the study using MRI measures rather than the EEG measures in the first round; MRI would allow probing deep within the brain so that they could look directly at the amygdala. Since the EEG data reflected left frontal activity, he could only infer that the amygdala shows decreased activation with mindfulness; the MRI could confirm that.

Then Richie turned to a piece of the data that was puzzling him. "At the end of each day, as I mentioned, we gave people a little questionnaire to tell us how much they practiced. We believe people were giving us honest reports, because some said they never practiced outside the class. We examined the extent to which both the immune changes and the changes in brain activity were correlated with the amount that people reported they actually practiced. We found that there was no correlation. Zero."

The Dalai Lama made a light comment: "So maybe they were better off—they didn't do a lot of hard work."

Richie went on, "Your Holiness, one possibility we considered is that people who were in the meditation group were practicing spontaneously, during the day, just in their everyday life. When a stress was about to occur, they would begin to come back to their breath or begin to notice the sensations arising in their body, as they were taught in the meditation class."

The Dalai Lama supported Richie's theory: "If mindfulness was being taught, this is something that could become manifest even in your daily activities."

There is yet another explanation for Davidson's data. Essentially, he found that for these beginners in meditation, just going to the eight classes—which included thirty or forty-five minutes of meditation—plus eight hours of meditation during the daylong retreat was enough to produce the range of benefits in mood and in brain and immune function. The meditation in each weekly class plus that in the retreat meant everyone had a minimum of fourteen hours of practice. The puzzle was that the additional daily meditation time put in by some of those in the classes did not seem to boost those benefits. In other words, there was not a linear dose-response relationship, where, for instance, the more medicine a patient takes, the better the recovery.

Yet Richie's results are quite parallel to what has been found in studies of exercise and heart disease among sedentary people. For those who have never exercised, the greatest initial health benefit comes when they first go from being sedentary—getting zero exercise—to doing two or three hours of exercise per week; it's a tipping point. There is relatively less added gain from an additional three hours per week of exercise. So another possibility is that fourteen hours of meditation, the minimum amount for those in Kabat-Zinn's classes, was the tipping point for the benefits found in Davidson's research.

Whatever the explanation, Richie concluded, "To summarize, we are very encouraged by this, Your Holiness, and we are energized with vigor and zeal"—a sly reference to the earlier discussion of the wholesome emotions in Buddhist psychology. "And we hope in the future to continue this kind of collaboration where we take some of the important insights from Buddhism and begin to examine the longer-term effects as they transform the brain and the body to make us happier, and maybe even healthier."

"Wonderful!" the Dalai Lama exclaimed.

The Quest to Understand States of Mind

By now, the meeting's final hour, the table in front of the presenters lay littered with the detritus of the week's work: books and notebooks, the disassembled plastic model of the brain, Palm Pilots and cameras, AV equipment, water bottles . . .

I started our final discussion by asking the Dalai Lama, "In terms of what has been presented to you, is there some kind of research that you would think particularly useful?"

After a long pause, the Dalai Lama began by tying Richie's earlier presentation on the neurology of destructive emotions to the data he had just presented. "When Richie was making his presentation and examined what kind of antidotes could be applied to deal with negative emotions, I felt that 'antidote' was already an evaluative, judgmental term. It may be possible to frame what we are interested in in such a way that we simply examine what mental states oppose or counter others, similar to the terminology used to describe the relationship between the left prefrontal cortex and the amygdala.

"Let's take one example, of a deflated or listless emotional state. You can't just say uniformly that a deflated state of emotion is a negative one or a destructive one, because it all depends on the particular circumstances. If one is feeling very haughty, with an inflated sense of self-esteem, then at that time it would be good to deflate one's mental state. On the other hand, if at times one feels very low self-esteem or maybe falls into depression, at that time a deflated state would be not helpful. So you can't say uniformly that it's one or the other; rather, you would have to see in context where it is useful.

"Likewise, you could look at different types of emotional states and try to evaluate them by context as well as in terms of what state is diametrically opposed to them. Comparing this to matter, it would be like identifying an acid or a base. Neither is positive or negative, but they are incompatible and will neutralize each other."

Now the Dalai Lama turned to a very different topic. "Another interesting point is that when one is dreaming, normally one's sensory faculties have gone dormant, so you don't hear or see. On the other hand, if a person is dreaming and you shout at them, then they do hear you. They wake up. This would seem to imply that the grosser level of sensory awareness is dormant but there must be some subtle level of awareness that enables you to be aroused when somebody shouts at you. That would be an interesting area to study."

Then he wondered, "When you're experiencing dream imagery, exactly what part of the brain is being activated, and how does this relate to the earlier discussion of which part of the brain is activated in straight perceptual awareness as opposed to mental conceptual cognition?"

Richie replied, "The areas in the brain that are responsible for visual perception are also the areas that are activated during dreaming. In addition, Alan Hobson and his colleagues at Harvard Medical School have carefully studied the emotional content of dreams, and it turns out that in ordinary people, about two-thirds of dreams have anxiety as their predominant emotional content. Very recent studies have indicated that during dreaming the amygdala, which has been associated with certain types of negative emotions, is particularly active and the frontal lobe is particularly underactive. So in these natural states there is a dynamic balance between these two areas—as amygdala activity goes up, the prefrontal activity goes down." In other words, the rampant amygdala, unrestrained by the prefrontal area, plays a role in spawning the emotional reality of the subconscious as revealed in our dream life.

The Dalai Lama asked, "If while dreaming one is experiencing lovingkindness or compassion, or even cultivating them, would this correspond to an activation in the frontal cortex?"

"That's very interesting," Richie responded. "We have recently published a study where we found that people who have a lot of positive emotion in their waking life also show this pattern of left frontal activity during dreaming. They show this pattern of more positive emotion during dreaming—and they are the one-third that don't show the anxiety dreams."[10]

"So," commented the Dalai Lama, "having a wholesome mind not only has benefit in the daytime but also while you're sleeping."

He was referring to classic Buddhist lore on the benefits of virtue, which holds that a wholesome state of mind just before falling asleep will carry over into one's dreams. Buddhist texts also name good dreams as one benefit of cultivating positive emotions like lovingkindness and compassion.

"That's absolutely right," Richie agreed. "There is a very strong correlation between the waking and the dreaming emotions."

Owen offered a clarification. "It would be wrong to leave the impression that one-third of people have positive dreams. The point is, about two-thirds of dreams across the board are negative. Some people tend toward more positive ones, but you rarely find a person that is consistently positive. Another interesting feature about dream affect is that the emotions in dreams tend to go downhill. You start with a neutral dream; they usually get worse and almost never get better. I remember I had a dream once that involved a potentially very nice episode with Marilyn Monroe." (At this, the Dalai Lama asked his translators, "Who's she?") Owen continued, "I woke up from it and wanted to go back to sleep and have it go a certain way. It didn't happen."

Matthieu provided the opposing view. "From accounts of past teachers and hermits, it seems that there are plenty of examples of practioners who develop the faculty to be aware that they are dreaming and who can transform voluntarily the nature of their dreams: a dream that starts quite dramatically with evidence of negative influence and then all of a sudden, this cycle is dispelled and the dream flourishes in a very positive way." Indeed, just such a positive influence is one of the goals of the practice of dream yoga, or lucid dreaming.[11]

Anger Without Delusion

Alan Wallace, in his alternate role as philosophical coordinator, refocused the discussion by coming back to the major theme of our meeting, destructive emotions, and drawing a stark contrast between the Buddhist and the scientific positions. "We started off by seeing quite an important and fundamental difference between the Buddhist perspective and the notion from the scientific perspective that all of our emotions have a role. For science, all emotions are okay—we don't really want to get rid of anger or any of the so-called destructive emotions, but only to find the appropriate measure and circumstance for them. In Buddhism there is a very clear difference: We want to completely eradicate all mental afflictions from the root so they never come back. The idea is that, in principle, they are never really appropriate and even a small amount is still a small amount of a disease or a poison."

He went on to note the differences between Western and Buddhist views of normality; for the West, normality is the goal, while in Buddhism it is but the starting place.

"In the Western perspective, being normal is fine. From a Buddhist perspective, being normal means that now you're ready to practice Dharma; now you're able to recognize that we are here in an ocean of suffering because our minds are dysfunctional, because normal people are heavily subject to mental afflictions.

"So it seems like a big difference until you look closer. Drawing from Paul Ekman's report especially, a couple of factors stand out. First, when anger arises it biases our perception and cognition, and there is a refractory period during the anger when you don't even have access to your own intelligence. Similarly in Buddhism, anger is by definition an afflictive mental state that derives from delusion and always distorts one's cognition of reality. If there is something like anger that does not arise out of delusion and does not distort one's view of reality, then we would not call it anger.

"This raises a very interesting research point that Richie and I have talked about—whether it is possible for an emotion to arise that looks a lot like anger but has little or no refractory period and little or no bias of perception and cognition."

Speaking about a higher level of spiritual attainment, Alan said, "You may feel some strong energy when you see injustice, but it would be less and less a mental affliction. So here's the real question: If anger can be constructive, wouldn't it be more and more constructive if it were less and less delusional?"

The Dalai Lama noted another important distinction: "Desire and dislike by themselves are not mental afflictions. To feel that one dislikes Brussels sprouts is not a mental affliction unless it is conflated with attachment. Likewise, with anger, the sheer fact that there arises a rather rough or tough mind—like the English expression 'tough love,' a forceful mental state or emotion—does not necessarily imply that the mental affliction of anger, which by definition is delusional, has arisen."

A Constructive Anger

Paul had been trying to get the floor for some time. "There are two different issues you raise, both complex and interesting ones. The first is whether in a constructive episode of anger, or any other emotion, one is really biased during this refractory period. I would like to propose two things. If it is constructive anger, the refractory period is short, and we are more able to respond to changes in the circumstances that caused it. Second, 'biased' is the wrong word. We should think of it as *focused*. It's a narrowing, but also a focusing in the moment. One's attention is focused around the event that has brought forth the anger and around one's response to it.

"When the refractory period is longer, it not only focuses but biases. That is, I believe, when you bring into it things that aren't in the situation. Take my example of the phone call with my wife, who will not be at all pleased about my talking so much about her in her absence. The fact that I brought my relationship with my mother (an angry relationship in which I was never able to show my anger to her) into that situation meant that I was not responding just to my wife. I was responding in a biased fashion, and the refractory period was correspondingly longer.

"The wonderful thing about emotions is that they focus you, they get you started. And then you're free to respond to what happens next. That's why they are adaptive. When they're maladaptive, you have a long refractory period and you respond to things that aren't there. I do believe there are things that can help. If you're burdened by external concerns that you keep bringing into the situation, you can learn what they are. You want to be free of those so you can respond to the moment, without bias."

Richie spoke up. "I want to pick up on two issues related to the idea of bias. As you saw in the pictures of the brain I showed on Wednesday, the amygdala and the hippocampus are adjacent to one another. The amygdala is importantly involved in negative emotion, the hippocampus in aspects of memory. It is not an accident that our brains were constructed in such a way that these two structures are right next to each other, with very extensive interconnections.

"When we see an object that elicits some emotion, it is almost invariably the case that it also triggers associated memories. When Paul began to think about his relationship with his mother, the amygdala and the hippocampus were talking to each other. And so, in most cases, it is true that there is an influence or coloring—we don't have to use the word 'bias'—that the emotions provide to our perceptions and that comes from these other parts of the brain."

With a tone of satisfaction, Paul noted, "I've had the experience again and again this week I have in reading Darwin: Every time I think of something, Darwin has already thought of it. I'm finding many of my own thoughts confirmed and sharpened here. That's really part of the great delight for me at this meeting."

A Compassionate Wrath

"I think Alan is raising an incredibly important challenge to our Western scientific study of emotion," Richie said, taking up the discussion. "I don't think science has really grappled at all with the idea that there may be more wholesome elements of negative emotion that can be preserved. Using anger as an example, there may be a kind of compassionate wrath, a forceful compassion that retains some of the qualities of anger but doesn't have the biasing or delusional component."

The Dalai Lama nodded in agreement as Richie added, "In the study of cognition, scientists have begun to deconstruct certain cognitive processes. We no longer think of attention, memory, or learning as a single unitary construct. For each of those, there are many different forms and many different subtypes. Similarly with emotions like anger and its multitude of forms: Certain forms may be stripped of the qualities that have the biasing or delusional component. That has not been studied, but one of the consequences of this meeting, for me, is a challenge to now begin to see if we can identify how that kind of process may actually work in the brain."

Matthieu offered an analogy. "It's the same as when we look at a wall from afar. It looks very smooth in the distance, but if you look from very near, the pits and bumps become obvious. Likewise, one finds distinctions in attachment on closer inspection. Obviously, attachment—or desire, or obsession—is one of the most destructive, obscuring mental factors. But within attachment you can also find components of tenderness and altruism, just as you can make distinctions within anger.

"Also, when we say that anger is altogether to be discarded, I think we should make a distinction between anger as an arising emotion and what comes in the chaining of thoughts that follows. That is very important because it's precisely what makes the difference between someone who is trained and someone who is not trained. What we want to get rid of altogether is the ordinary expression of anger that will be perceived as animosity in most cases, except when we have to act in a very energetic way to stop someone from jumping over a cliff. Usually what we call anger is an expression of animosity toward someone.

"We say that in the first stage of training of a meditator, anger will arise in the same way, but it's what happens just after that that makes a difference—whether we are enslaved by the anger or can let it go in the second or third moment without consequences. Of course, ultimately, in the state of Buddhahood, the anger has no more reason to arise. That is the third step. And we mentioned briefly that the moment anger arises in itself, in its own nature, it's not always fundamentally, intrinsically negative. We mentioned the aspect of clarity. In the same way, if we are able not to be carried away by desire but rather to look at its nature, it is also an aspect of bliss. Likewise, in confusion there is an aspect of freedom from concepts. None of these have the intrinsic property of being either positive or negative. It's all a question of whether we're enslaved by emotion."

Paul responded, "If there was no memory of anger, we wouldn't ever learn anything about anger experiences, but some of the things that we learn and apply don't fit, and that's where this longer refractory period occurs. But we have also learned ways of acting when we are angry. I believe that what nature gives us is not necessarily the impulse to attack the person, but to deal with the obstacle. But in the course of growing up and observing others, our experience may be just the opposite. We may learn that when angry we don't deal with the obstacle, but instead we deal in a hurtful fashion with the person who is causing the obstacle." He demonstrated by taking Owen by the shoulders and shaking him.

"That's a learned element of anger that becomes automatic, and which you have to unlearn. There are processes we can use to become conscious and to unlearn those automatic responses or memories and perceptions. They can be both good and bad for us, but the Darwinian view I have been trying to maintain is that it's not built into the emotion. It gets acquired in the course of unfortunate experiences. Is everybody like that? Some of us start out with temperaments that make it easier for us to learn things that are going to be harmful, and so we have more of a struggle to deal with that. But still, I am much more optimistic now than I was last week that even temperament should be viewed not as fixed but as changeable."

At this point our clock had run out. So I began a final summing up. "I think that this event has been very fruitful, certainly from the scientific side, Your Holiness, and I definitely hope for you too."

At that, the Dalai Lama put his hands together in a salute of appreciation.

"This is really an offering to you," I continued, "as well as a very rich experience for us. I know it changes everyone who participates, and we'll all go back doing what we do in a different way and in a better way for having been able to discuss these things with you. So I profoundly thank you, Your Holiness."

And the Dalai Lama responded, "I would like to say thank you to all. The task that we are engaged in is something that is truthful and also noble." He added that over the thirteen years of Mind and Life meetings, there had been the kind of learning and development that comes from a sincere quest.

Then he continued on a note of caution. "One thing that we have to be aware of is that when things go really well and when we confront success, sometimes there is a danger that one's motivation and objectives may get sidelined. Therefore I feel it's very important to remain steadfast with a strong principle and committed to that original ideal that we all had. If we pursue our task with that approach, then of course we will have greater success in the future.

"The presentations that all the scientists and participants made showed the rigor and detail of your work, which is very impressive. And also, I felt that when each of you was making your presentations, not only were you giving the information, but also there was a genuine human feeling that was coming through. That I very much appreciate—the whole atmosphere created is really something special. That's most important. Whether we can capture that atmosphere as we go on with our lives, I don't know. At least we've enjoyed it here. Thank you very much."

And so ended the rich weaving of our intellectual tapestry, this intricate, sometimes exhilarating dialogue. Its impact on the life and work of many of those who participated would prove equally rich.

Afterword: The Journey Continues

Our journey to Dharamsala had the flavor of a pilgrimage—not just a trip that fades away until an album of snapshots is the only reminder, but rather one that leaves those who take it transformed in some way. There was no doubt for all of us who participated that our meeting with the Dalai Lama had been a high of sorts—but it also left some persisting traces in our lives and work. And, like any group of pilgrims, each of us brought home uniquely individual lessons.

Our journey back started with what was supposed to be a four-hour drive to the airport in Jammu, from where we would fly on to New Delhi. It was largely downhill, and we anticipated a much shorter ride than on our way up. But every car, truck, and motorized ricksha seemed to pass our lumbering bus, which, fitful at best on the narrow and twisting mountain roads, took a seemingly interminable eight or nine hours to get us there.

As we reached the Jammu airport, the lofty intellectual discourse on destructive emotions ran up against a more sobering reality: The city was under martial law, soldiers everywhere. A few days before, terrorists had murdered more than thirty Sikhs in a district just outside Srinagar, the nearby capital of the seething province of Kashmir. The whiff of terrorism—the mobilization of destructive emotions in the service of psychological warfare—lingered in the air. At the airport, we were surprised when Indian soldiers hand-searched each of our bags, confiscating sharp objects, even batteries. (We had no idea this was an augury of air travel security that would become routine in our own cities in the not too distant future.)

Still, our group remained as though wrapped in a protective bubble. Our feelings were pretty much summed up by Paul Ekman, who reflected that his experience meant he would have to revise some of his own scientific writings on the smile. He had written in the past that people can't maintain a genuine "Duchenne" smile—the one that signifies true enjoyment and puts crinkles around the eyes—for a long period of time. But he'd noticed a slight Duchenne smile on his own face for extended stretches during the week, and was keenly aware of the sense of continual pleasure that goes with it.

In fact, although he generally hates meetings and avoids them (or leaves early) if he can, Paul had found himself rapt throughout. The five days had seemed like one, he said. His attention had been so keen that his experience of time changed—typically a sign of being in flow, the state of energized absorption. He spoke for us all.

Each of us was touched personally, to be sure. But the more tangible impact of our meeting was manifest in a variety of projects that emerged in the weeks and months afterward, each of which reflected new thinking and refocusing of people's work.

Philosophy Reconsidered

One of the first signs of this impact came just two weeks after our meeting, when Owen Flanagan gave the John Findley Lecture at Boston University, and the topic he chose was "Destructive Emotions." Although he had acted as the in-house skeptic for much of our week, in his lecture (and in a later article with the same title published in the journal *Consciousness and Emotion*) Owen introduced into Western philosophical discourse the Tibetan Buddhist stance on destructive emotions that the Dalai Lama and others had offered in Dharamsala.

For instance, he contrasted the common Western assumption that our biological programming for emotions was a given—that we could do little to modify even harmful emotional reactions—with the Tibetan Buddhist claim that destructive emotions could be greatly reduced. "Some Tibetan Buddhists," as he put it, "think it possible and advisable to overcome, even eliminate" emotions such as anger or hostility, which Western philosophers see as natural and immutable.

He questioned the notion that destructive emotions necessarily serve some vital, adaptive function in evolution. He noted that every wisdom tradition urges us to assert some control over them, from the Bible, Confucius, and the Koran to Buddhist texts—as well as moral philosophers from Aristotle, Mill, and Kant onward. Owen echoed Richard Davidson's argument that despite some skepticism among neuroscientists about plasticity, the evidence "abounds that we are plastic" and so potentially able to exert the emotional self-control religious traditions have encouraged.

Owen added as a final thought that he liked Tibetan Buddhism for the message it gave us all as we "engaged in the project of finding methods for 'overcoming the genotype.' We are animals, to be sure, but unusual ones, capable of breaking out of, adjusting, and modifying what Mother Nature has tried to make us be."

Owen went on to elaborate these themes in the book he had been writing while he visited Dharamsala, *The Problem of the Soul*, in which he grapples with how to reconcile humanistic and scientific truths, and thus find meaning when advances in cognitive neuroscience drastically challenge our image of ourselves as humans capable of free will or possessing something akin to a soul. He proposes that because it has built so carefully on a phenomenological approach to reality, "Buddhism, almost alone among the great ethical and metaphysical traditions, holds to a picture of persons that is uniquely suited to the way science says we ought to see ourselves and our place in the world."

- Owen Flanagan, "Destructive Emotions," *Consciousness and Emotions*, 1: 2 (2000), 259–81.
- Owen Flanagan, *The Problem of the Soul: Two Visions of Mind and How to Reconcile Them* (New York: Basic Books, 2002).

A Challenge for Psychology

Where two systems of thought intersect, there is greatest potential for cross-fertilization. That certainly had been the case with Buddhist and Western systems of psychology during our meeting, and the fruitfulness of our exchange between intellectual paradigms inspired another article—this one aimed not at philosophers but at psychologists.

For this article—designed to demonstrate the utility of such dialogue for generating research hypotheses in psychology—Alan Wallace and Matthieu Ricard wrote from the Buddhist perspective, and Paul Ekman and Richard Davidson from that of Western psychology. The article, "Buddhist and Western Perspectives on Well-Being," emphasizes challenges from the Buddhist model to basic assumptions in psychology about the nature of well-being.

For instance, Buddhism posits the possibility of *sukha*, "a deep sense of serenity and fulfillment that arises from an exceptionally healthy mind"—a concept with no parallel word in English, nor a direct equivalent in psychology (though some psychologists have recently begun arguing for a more "positive psychology," which might embrace such concepts). Moreover, Buddhism posits that the capacity for experiencing *sukha* can be developed in those who try, and offers a set of methods for attaining this state. That training starts with positive shifts in fleeting emotions that lead to more lasting changes in moods, and eventually to a shift in temperament.

This notion challenges modern psychology with a model of optimal human functioning that surpasses its own. The article proposes that psychologists study expert Buddhist practitioners to assess any connected changes in brain function, biological activity, emotional experiences, cognitive abilities, or social interactions. That program, of course, has begun, as reported at the Madison meeting in Chapter 1.

The article's integration of ideas from Buddhist and Western psychology parallels changes our Dharamsala meeting brought about in the book Paul Ekman had been writing, *Gripped by Emotion.* For Paul, the conversation with the Dalai Lama crystallized ideas that were parallel to his own thinking or confirmed his own hunches. Among the ideas he had come up with on his own that were echoed in Buddhist thinking, for instance, were the different strategies for dealing with destructive emotions, depending on whether it is before, during, or after they occur. By the time he finished the final draft, Paul had woven many of these ideas throughout the book.

- Richard Davidson, Paul Ekman, Alan Wallace, and Matthieu Ricard, "Buddhist and Western Perspectives on Well-Being," manuscript submitted for publication.
- Paul Ekman, *Gripped by Emotion* (New York: Times Books/Henry Holt, 2003).

Investigating the Mind

The cross-fertilization between Buddhist thought and the mind sciences has taken yet another form, one that expands the conversation to include a wider circle of scientists. The day our Dharamsala meeting ended, the Dalai Lama agreed to come to Harvard University to take part in a Mind and Life meeting where researchers in the biobehavioral sciences will explore with Buddhist scholars how their differing perspectives can enrich the scientific study of the mind. The guiding question for the meeting will be: "Can modern science make use of Buddhism's 2,500 years of investigating the mind?"

This eleventh Mind and Life meeting—called "Investigating the Mind"—has been organized by Richard Davidson, working with Anne Harrington, a director of Harvard's Mind/Brain/Behavior Initiative (which will cosponsor the event), who had participated in Mind and Life V, on altruism and compassion. They have mapped out a two-day meeting, with sessions devoted to three subjects: attention and cognitive control of mental activity, emotion, and mental imagery. Now scheduled for September 13–14, 2003, "Investigating the Mind" will be the first Mind and Life event partially open to the general public, although the sessions are aimed primarily at researchers in the fields of psychology, cognitive science, neuroscience, and medicine—and most especially at graduate students who are seeking topics for their dissertation research.

Western researchers on attention have had scant interest in Eastern methods for attentional training, even though understanding the mechanisms for enhancing attention is a shared focus of scientific efforts. In Buddhism, though, training that increases the mind's ability to sustain attention is seen as the gateway to expanding the capacity for control over our inner life, and the bedrock of spiritual practice. The session on attention seeks to make up for this missed opportunity by exploring the implications for modern researchers of the Buddhist understanding of attention.

Emotions represent a parallel opportunity for science. Western psychology has largely assumed that emotions are inevitably able to swamp reasoning and the ability to exert control over the mind; Buddhist training offers practice in strategies for managing emotions. One focus of the session on emotions will be examining scientific assumptions about the limited extent to which emotions can be voluntarily controlled. Other topics include exploring the power of compassion, an emotion largely ignored in Western science.

Finally, in the session on imagery scientists will hear about Buddhist methods for systematically generating and controlling mental images—a system unparalleled in Western science, and one that could enhance the ability to study the images that populate the world within.

In addition to the Dalai Lama, those speaking for the Buddhist tradition include Alan Wallace, Thupten Jinpa, and Matthieu Ricard, as well as Georges Dreyfus, a professor of religion at Williams College who attained the *geshe* degree while a Tibetan Buddhist monk, and Ajahn Amaro, a Briton who is abbot of a Thai Buddhist monastery in California.

From the science side, "Investigating the Mind" has attracted an A-list of a dozen or so eminent researchers. For the session on attention, the main scientific presenter will be Jonathan Cohen, a psychiatrist who directs the Center for the Study of Brain, Mind, and Behavior at Princeton University. The session on mental imagery will have as the main presenter Stephen Kosslyn, chair of the psychology department at Harvard University and a psychologist in the department of neurology at Massachusetts General Hospital. And the old hands Richard Davidson and Paul Ekman will be among the participants for the session on emotion. During the final session Jerome Kagan, the eminent developmental psychologist at Harvard University, will reflect on the significance of the dialogue.

In the Mind and Life tradition of bringing a philosopher's view to the conversation, Evan Thompson, a philosopher at York University in Toronto, will join Kagan in offering reflections. Thompson, who has long participated in the dialogue between Buddhist thought and Western science and philosophy, was a close associate of Francisco Varela, and a coauthor with Varela of *The Embodied Mind: Cognitive Science and Human Experience,* which explored the contribution of Buddhist thought to scientific study of the mind.

Some of the participants have already shown an active interest in expanding their own research, notably Stephen Kosslyn at Harvard University, whose research focuses on visual imagery. Kosslyn was intrigued enough by premeeting dialogues with Matthieu Ricard about the heightened imaging abilities cultivated through meditative visualization that he has begun studies of advanced practitioners such as Lama Öser.

- Mind and Life XI, "Investigating the Mind: Exchanges Between Buddhism and the Biobehavioral Sciences on How the Mind Works." Boston, MA., September 13–14, 2003. For more information on this meeting, please visit its website: www.InvestigatingTheMind.org.

Inspirations for Teachers

To philosophy and the scientific study of the mind, add education as a field that stood to benefit from our Mind and Life meeting. As he left Dharamsala, Mark Greenberg said that the Dalai Lama had inspired him to think of ways to help children more with their positive emotions—a genuine shift of emphasis. Programs such as PATHS, he realized, had been successful in helping children manage the negative, reactive aspects of their emotions—calming down, self-control, managing anger. But he now saw that a separate, and equally valuable, goal would be to help children cultivate a "positive mind": attitudes such as optimism, tolerance, and caring for others. Doing so, he felt, might well help with the first goal, handling the troubling emotions.

He envisioned writing lesson plans to encourage emotions such as compassion for children as young as six, and to do research on the effects of lessons about caring, forgiveness, and social responsibility on twelve- and thirteen-year-olds. A more specific suggestion from our meeting—that younger children be encouraged to compliment each other for being helpful—has now been implemented in some of his school programs. And, Mark reports, the reactions have been good: Teachers say this simple practice has had a positive effect on classroom climate.

Another inspiration for Mark came during the conversation about training teachers. He was intrigued by the thought of having teachers spend perhaps five minutes in small groups each morning before the school day to become more aware of their intention for the day. They might reflect on why they are teaching, on what they hope for, on the children they would teach that day, on the children's need to be loved and cared for, on how they could help the children manage themselves better when they misbehave, and on ways to help the children become more empathic and caring. Mark wanted to study what the effects on the teachers—and their students—might be simply from getting centered and positively focused in this way at the start of the day.

Mark had also been inspired by Richard Davidson's reports on brain changes in meditators. It made Mark wonder about the neurological effects in children's brains of his programs in social and emotional learning, and he resolved to find neuroscientists to work with. That research collaboration has been designed and, at this writing, a grant proposal for it has been submitted to the federal government.

Perhaps the most personally meaningful moment for Mark had come at the tea break after his presentation on emotional learning programs, when the Dalai Lama invited him to come back to Dharamsala to share his expertise with Tibetan teachers. He asked Mark to share his ideas at yearly teacher training sessions that gather faculty from the Tibetan Children's Village in Dharamsala and other schools in the Tibetan refugee settlements around India. Despite some early difficulties finding dates that would work, Mark has now scheduled that trip back to Dharamsala.

- For information on PATHS, see www.colorado.edu/cspv/blueprints/model/ten_paths.htm.

The Madison Project

For Richard Davidson, those five days in Dharamsala had a major impact on his research agenda. Over the previous years he had developed a strong interest in neuroplasticity, the capacity of people to transform their own emotions, behavior, and brain function. The meeting strengthened his resolve to pursue that scientific agenda, expanding it to include how meditation might cultivate positive emotions. While in the past his work had focused on reducing negative emotions, he was now tremendously interested in research on how to help people develop a greater capacity for compassion or joy.

Richie had been struck that many important positive qualities—including compassion and lovingkindness—are not currently found in the present Western psychological lexicon of emotion. He now felt they should be put at center stage because of their critical importance for psychological science, not to mention their value to individuals and to society. Now a new generation of scientific tools—particularly brain imaging—could assess the lasting impact of centuries-old methods on cultivating these emotions, and so put the study of positive emotions on psychology's scientific agenda.

Toward that end, Richie has been inviting to his Madison lab highly experienced meditation practitioners such as Lama Öser, who typically have done several years of intensive retreat, to be collaborators in brain imaging studies. In Dharamsala the Dalai Lama had agreed to visit Richie's lab in Madison the following spring (as we saw in Chapter 1), which gave him an impetus and deadline for starting the research. That research has already started to show promising results. He now expects this research program to last for several years, as highly advanced practitioners are tracked down and invited to the lab and as their data are analyzed. He plans to gather enough data to publish his findings in a top-tier scientific journal—studies of six or so meditators might do it, given the extreme precision of MRI data.

In a sense, this professional focus brings Richie's career full circle. During his graduate-school years at Harvard he had a strong scientific interest in meditation—his doctoral dissertation had been on attention in meditation. However, he later turned away from meditation research, partly because it was mostly based on self-report measures and (by today's standards) skimpy physiological data measuring transient effects. He knew that these momentary changes were not the goal of practice—what was most interesting was the transformation of everyday life. Now, with his brain-imaging abilities, he has the scientific tools to study those persisting changes.

- For more information, see http://keckbrainimaging.org and http://psyphz.psych.wisc.edu

Cultivating Emotional Balance

Of all the participants, perhaps the one on whom the proceedings had the most profound impact was Paul Ekman. During that long, bumpy, and dusty bus ride from Dharamsala to the airport at Jammu, Paul reflected on what this week might mean to him on his return to life as a research scientist.

Before coming he had heard, with his usual skepticism, stories about how the meetings changed the scientists who attended. Now it had happened to him.

Most strikingly, he felt in touch again with what had brought him into psychology in the first place. "I've spent more than forty years in the psychology of emotion—and my original motivation was doing what I could to help reduce human suffering and cruelty." As he put it, "I've returned to my own roots and motivations—and that allows me to take what I've learned in forty years and use it for my original goals."

So, he added, the week had given him "a renewed sense of what I can do with this next, last epoch of my own life." Although he had been winding down his obligations, for the first time in nearly a decade he felt like taking on a new one: the mind-training program for adults envisioned during our meetings, now called Cultivating Emotional Balance.

At Madison, Paul summarized his progress to date for the Dalai Lama. "In Dharamsala I heard you ask for research that would show the benefits of a secular version of meditation. A number of us took up your request, and the approach that we've developed combines meditative practices with psychological techniques from the West. Our design includes a control group and uses both psychological and biological measures before, just after, and a year later, so we can see what the helpful effects might be."

Paul was stunned and moved when, in response to hearing about the plans for the program—and the need to raise funds—the Dalai Lama pledged $50,000 from his book royalties toward the money needed, a concrete sign of the importance he places on this scientific agenda.

Cultivating Emotional Balance has at its core the secularized mindfulness training that Richie and Jon Kabat-Zinn had done research on, as reported in the Dharamsala meeting (see Chapter 14). But in addition to learning mindfulness, participants would also benefit from additional methods from Western psychology, such as those for positive conflict resolution taken from research on marital interactions, or instructions from Paul's research in recognizing subtle facial expressions of emotion. The overall program could enhance every aspect of emotional intelligence: awareness of, and the ability to handle well, one's own and others' emotions.

Many of those who were part of our conversations at Dharamsala have also had a hand in planning the Cultivating Emotional Balance program: Alan Wallace and Matthieu Ricard as well as Jon Kabat-Zinn have been active in designing the mindfulness training. Mark Greenberg, who had been among those at our meetings who most enthusiastically embraced the notion of an emotional education program for adults, has signed on as a scientific coordinator, helping to design the assessment of its effectiveness. And Jeanne Tsai will draw on her expertise in the study of emotion by designing and conducting measures of interpersonal awareness that will be used to assess the program's effectiveness. At this writing, the pilot phase has been designed.

- For updates on progress, see: www.MindandLife.org

The Exceptional Persons Project

A related project had its roots in a surprisingly powerful private exchange Paul Ekman had with the Dalai Lama during a tea break on Wednesday. As his daughter Eve asked the Dalai Lama a personal question about relationships, His Holiness alternately held, and affectionately rubbed, each of their hands. That small encounter, Paul later recounted, was what "some people would call a mystical, transforming experience. I was inexplicably suffused with physical warmth during those five to ten minutes—a wonderful kind of warmth throughout my body and face. It was palpable. I felt a kind of goodness I'd never felt before in my life, all the time I sat there."

This was a unique moment for Paul, a feeling of being embraced with generosity, concern, and compassion. And that moment came on top of the Dalai Lama having said during the discussion what a good father Paul was. Somehow that combination touched the very roots of Paul's motivation in life.

A year or so later, Paul related that experience—and changes he had felt since—to a particularly traumatic incident in his life. "My father was a violent man. When I was eighteen I told him I had decided to study psychology, not medicine, like he had—he was a pediatrician. And he said he would give me no support. I asked him if he wanted me to feel toward him as he did toward his own father, who had also refused support for his education. He knocked me to the floor, and when I got up I told him that was the last time he was going to hit me, for I was bigger and I would hit him back. I left home, not to see him again for a decade."

Since that time, Paul added, "About once a week for the last fifty years I've had an anger attack that I regretted." But things changed on the day in Dharamsala when Paul had that private encounter with His Holiness. "After that, I didn't even have an angry impulse for the next four months, and no full episode of erupting in anger for the whole last year. I'm someone who has struggled his whole life with flare-ups of anger, but even now, almost a year later, they're very rare. I believe that physical contact with that kind of goodness can have a transformative effect."

In psychology perhaps most of all the sciences, autobiography informs theory—the life experience of the psychologist offers one source of raw material for theorizing. And, ever the scientist, Paul tells me he wants to investigate the transformative quality of interactions with extraordinary beings such as the Dalai Lama. That resolve led him to the Extraordinary Persons Project, which he had described at Madison—and in which Lama Öser had been his first experimental subject (as described in Chapter 1).

Because such extraordinary research subjects are few and far between, they are being shared, studied in different ways at different labs. At Madison, Richard Davidson uses brain-imaging methods to study the long-term neurological effects of meditation practice, while at the University of California, Paul employs methods such as assessing accuracy at reading emotions from facial expression to gauge the impact on empathy and other emotional skills.

- For updates on progress, see: www.paulekman.com

A Two-Way Exchange

The Venerable Ajahn Maha Somchai Kusalacitto (to give his full title) added an intriguing perspective on these research projects, a reminder that the dialogue between Buddhism and the mind sciences is a two-way exchange. In a conversation with a visitor from America several months after the Dharamsala meeting, he said how important it was to study accomplished meditation masters with scientific methods, and so measure the effects spiritual attainments have on the brain.

One reason he favored such research had to do with the increasing problems he saw in Thailand—the social costs of disturbing emotions as manifest in, for instance, increased rates of child abuse. Scientific studies documenting the benefits of Buddhist practice, he felt, would have an influence in Asian countries, where he feared there was beginning to be a real lack of understanding of the value of Buddhist teachings and practice. As he put it, "The influence from the West will be important in stimulating interest and acceptance of the values of Buddhism. If we Thais do something ourselves, we will tend to ignore it—but we get excited about something that comes from the West."

A Curtain Falls

As for Francisco Varela, the sad news came a few days before the Madison meeting. We heard that a virulent recurrence of cancer had been found in his transplanted liver, and that despite an aggressive round of chemotherapy, it had spread. The doctors had given up; there was nothing more medicine could do for him. He was at home with his family and would not be coming to Madison. Instead Adam Engle, who had cofounded Mind and Life with Francisco, arranged for a live two-way video hook-up via the Internet. Francisco would be a virtual presence, watching the meeting in Madison on a computer monitor in his bedroom in Paris.

After that meeting we all wrote our heartfelt thoughts to Francisco on a card, to be delivered to him in Paris the next day by his research associate Anton Lutz, who had stood in for Francisco in Madison.

Francisco died, at home, just a few days later. Watching the Madison presentation to the Dalai Lama from afar dropped the final curtain on his life in science.

Notes

Chapter 1: The Lama in the Lab

1. The six states studied, in transliteration from the Tibetan, are: visualization, *kyerim yidam lha yi mig pa;* one-pointed concentration, *tse chik ting ngey dzin;* vast compassion, *migmey nyingjey;* devotion, *lama la mögu;* fearlessness, *gang la yang jig pa med pey mig pa;* open state, *rigpa'i chok shag.*
2. Sharon Salzberg, *Lovingkindness* (Boston: Shambhala, 1995).
3. Startle lore includes a cross-cultural oddity: At least five languages around the world have a word for people who are hyperstartlers, that is, individuals with an extreme reaction to being shocked by a surprise. Such people, from childhood on, have a hair-trigger startle reflex, and their startle response is exaggerated to the point of slapstick—at least that's how it seems to onlookers. In all five cultures hyperstartlers are favorite targets for teasing; for the fun of it, people delight in sneaking up and surprising them. See Ronald C. Simons, *Boo! Culture, Experience, and the Startle Reflex* (New York: Oxford University Press, 1996).
4. Still, neuroscientists do not know with certainty what accounts for this change—whether the change is in the synaptic weight as added connections bulk out neurons, or whether an uptick in the number of neurons may also be playing a role. T. Elbert, C. Pantev, C. Wienbruch, B. Rockstroh, and E. Taub, "Increased Cortical Representation of the Fingers of the Left Hand in String Players," *Science* 270, 5234 (1995): 305–7.
5. K. A. Ericsson, R. T. Krampe, and C. Tesch-Römer, "The Role of Deliberate Practice in the Acquisition of Expert Performance," *Psychological Review* 100 (1993): 363–406.
6. For instance, Paul Whalen, a neuroscientist and colleague of Davidson's at the

University of Wisconsin, has found that it is the amygdala, and related circuitry, that recognizes microexpressions. Whalen's research shows that the amygdala recognizes some expressions even when they are flashed very quickly and followed by what is called a masking stimulus (such as a neutral face) that blocks a person's ability to consciously see the emotional face. Typically, the emotional face is presented for about thirty-three thousandths of a second in these experiments. The results with Öser and the other advanced meditator on the test for reading microexpressions suggest that the appropriate brain measures might show changes in this amygdala-based circuitry as an effect of sustained pratice (though precisely which practice is not yet clear).

7. P. S. Eriksson, E. Perfilieva, T. Bjork-Eriksson, A. M. Alborn, C. Nordborg, D. A. Peterson, and F. H. Gage, "Neurogenesis in the Adult Human Hippocampus," *Nature Medicine* 4, 11 (1998): 1313–7.
8. Francisco Varela, "Neurophenomenology: A Methodological Remedy to the Hard Problem," *Journal of Consciousness Studies* 3 (1996): 330–50.
9. In this series of experiments, Öser's EEG was put through a sophisticated computer analysis to monitor the moment at which functional connections among different regions of the brain begin and end. Varela had devised a measure that showed whether groups of neurons started firing at a specific rhythm and then recruited neuron groups in other parts of the brain to their same rhythm—the basic dynamic that marks the involvement of a critical mass of activity throughout the brain needed to support a thought. This approach hinges on being able to isolate from the chaotic mass of ongoing mental activity a single, crisp perception. For that, Varela took advantage of the "Aha!" moment of recognition that comes when someone suddenly recognizes a shape from what initially seems a meaningless mass.
10. Perhaps the most dramatic effect was seen during the open state, when Öser's mental stance was one of neither preventing nor pursuing thoughts or perceptions, but "letting go" of everything as it arose in his mind without being attached to anything. The inner stance of the open state seemed to be reflected at the level of the brain, with little neural synchrony across the brain. By contrast, while Öser was in a state of focused attention, many other brain areas were recruited into synchrony at the moment of recognition.
11. Antoine Lutz, J.-P. Lachaux, J. Martinerie, and F. J. Varela, "Guiding the Study of Brain Dynamics by Using First-Person Data: Synchrony Patterns Correlate with Ongoing Conscious States During a Simple Visual Task," *Proceedings of the National Academy of Sciences of the United States of America* 99 (2002): 1586–91.
12. For instance, a much-touted study of meditation used SPECT, which makes an image of the rate at which areas of the brain take up a given type of molecule, in this case one that labels blood flow. A single period of meditation was compared with a resting period among subjects who varied considerably in their mediation experience. The data were valuable in highlighting general areas of the brain activated during meditation, such as regions of the prefrontal cortex. But the methods for analyzing the imaging data were relatively crude, and the study's usefulness was further limited by the fact that only a single meditation period was compared with a single

resting period, making it impossible to tell if the patterns found were repeatable, reliable correlates of meditation. Beyond these problems, the researchers went far beyond their data, making dubious claims about the role of the patterns of brain activity they observed in producing an "altered sense of space" in meditation that might produce a feeling of transcendence of one's ordinary boundaries. A. Newberg et al., "The measurement of Cerebral Blood Flow During the Complex Cognitive Task of Meditation: A Preliminary SPECT Study," *Psychiatry Research* 106, 2 (2001): 113–22.

13. The notion of altered traits of consciousness was proposed in an article Davidson and I coauthored while we were at Harvard together in the early 1970s—he still a graduate student and I, at the time, a visiting faculty member there. See Richard J. Davidson and Daniel J. Goleman, "The Role of Attention in Meditation and Hypnosis: A Psychobiological Perspective on Transformations of Consciousness," *The International Journal of Clinical and Experimental Hypnosis* 25, 4 (1977): 291–308.

Chapter 2: A Natural Scientist

1. The traditional cosmology was contained within the vast compendium of Buddhist theory known as Abhidharma.

Chapter 3: The Western Perspective

1. Alan Wallace's undergraduate thesis was eventually published in two volumes: *Choosing Reality: A Buddhist View of Physics and the Mind* (Ithaca, N.Y.: Snow Lion, 1989) and *Transcendent Wisdom* (Ithaca, N.Y.: Snow Lion, 1988), which includes a translation of Shantideva's work, together with the Dalai Lama's commentary.
2. A version of Alan Wallace's dissertation was later published under the title *The Bridge of Quiescence: Experiencing Tibetan Buddhist Meditation* (Chicago: Open Court, 1998).
3. See Daniel Goleman, ed., *Healing Emotions: Conversations with the Dalai Lama on Mindfulness, Emotions, and Health* (Boston: Shambhala, 1996). The same topic, low self-esteem, came up in an earlier dialogue; see Daniel Goleman, ed., *Worlds in Harmony: Dialogues on Compassionate Action* (Berkeley: Parallax, 1992).

Chapter 4: A Buddhist Psychology

1. Matthieu Ricard, *Journey to Enlightenment: The Life and World of Khyentse Rinpoche, Spiritual Teacher from Tibet* (New York: Aperture, 1996). Over his years as a monk, Matthieu Ricard first was guided in his practice by Kangyur's eldest son, Tulku Pema Wangyal, who later established retreat centers in the Dordogne Valley of France.
2. This ultrasubtle level is described in Tibetan texts as "the fundamental continuum of the luminous consciousness that is beyond the notion of subject and object."

Chapter 5: The Anatomy of Mental Afflictions

1. A mental image that is produced as a result of prolonged mental focus is considered to be a kind of a form; in Buddhist epistemology, the concept of form is not necessarily confined to material things. There are three kinds of form. One is the material, tangible object that we can see, with its visual qualities: shape, color, and so on. But the word "form" in this context does not just apply to visual forms but is a very broad usage, referring to the objects of all five senses, including, for example, "forms" of sound. The second kind is forms that are said to be visible but not obstructive or tangible, such as a reflection in a mirror. The third kind of form is purely an object of mental cognition.
2. These are five types of form belonging to the category of "forms for the mental consciousness": (1) forms arising from aggregation—the objects of the senses, (2) space forms, in the sense of the physical field in which perceptions take place, (3) forms arising from promises (this is particularly technical—it refers to forms arising, for example, when one takes monastic precepts), (4) imaginary forms, and (5) forms arising as the result of meditation. See Jeffrey Hopkins's *Meditation on Emptiness* (Boston: Wisdom, 1996), 232–35.
3. The mental images that arise from visualization during meditation are not afflicted.
4. The term in question is *drotok,* which refers not only to reification but to any time we superimpose upon reality qualities or entities that are not in fact present. The view of nihilism or denial applies whenever we deny anything whatsoever that is present.
5. Stephen Jay Gould, *The Panda's Thumb* (New York: W. W. Norton, 1980).
6. Thupten Jinpa's dissertation is being published by Curzon under the title *Tsongkhapa's Philosophy of Emptiness: Self, Reality and Reason in Tibetan Thought.*
7. Oliver Leaman, ed., *Encyclopedia of Asian Philosophy* (New York: Routledge, 2001).
8. Historically there was never a word in Buddhist philosophy directly equivalent to "emotion." As Georges Dreyfus (like Thupten Jinpa, a translator for the Dalai Lama—but into French—who also has the *geshe* degree, and who now teaches philosophy at Williams College) notes, confronted by Westerners using the term "emotion," some Tibetan teachers have recently coined a new word *(tshor myong)* for it. The term, which means literally "experience of feeling," has yet to take on common usage in Tibetan, and bears little meaning in the Buddhist context. See Georges Dreyfus, "Is Compassion an Emotion? A Cross-Cultural Exploration of Mental Typologies," in Richard J. Davidson and Anne Harrington, eds., *Visions of Compassion: Western Scientists and Tibetan Buddhists Examine Human Nature* (New York: Oxford University Press, 2002).
9. Dharmakirti's *Commentary on Valid Perception* (from Tibetan sources).
10. On virtuous anger, one Buddhist text, Shantideva's *Guide to the Bodhisattva Way of Life,* encourages practitioners to develop resentment toward their own mental afflictions and self-centeredness—a pragmatic use of the energy of anger in the service of spiritual goals—what might be called a virtuous anger. Similarly, Shantideva encourages practitioners to develop a sense of valor and self-confidence in their ability to achieve enlightenment, rather than having an afflictive pride—that is, an arrogant sense of one's supposed superiority. Vajrayana teachings also include transmut-

ing attachment into bliss, anger into clarity, delusion into nonconceptual wisdom—all via a process akin to a mental alchemy. See Lama Thubten Yeshe, *Introduction to Tantra: A Vision of Totality* (Boston: Wisdom, 1987).

11. Richard Lazarus, *Emotion and Adaptation* (New York: Oxford University Press, 1991).
12. Within the Indo-Tibetan tradition there are different nuances between the two main versions of the Abhidharma, as well as some between the Pali version and that in Sanskrit. Most of the differences among the various versions are minor. Within the Pali literature, for instance, there are two different versions of the list of mental factors, one listing fifty-two, the other just forty-eight. The two main versions of Abhidharma—the source for the lists of mental affliction—in the Tibetan tradition are the Abhidharma Samuccaya and the Abhidharmakosha; the Pali version is called Abhidhamma.

Chapter 6: The Universality of Emotion

1. Paul Ekman, *Gripped by Emotion* (New York: Times Books/Henry Holt, in press).
2. P. Ekman, W. Friesen, and M. O'Sullivan, "Smiles When Lying," *Journal of Personality and Social Psychology* 54 (1988): 414–20, as well as P. Ekman, R. J. Davidson, and W. Friesen, "Emotional Expression and Brain Physiology II: The Duchenne Smile," *Journal of Personality and Social Psychology* 58 (1990): 342–53. In an unpublished finding, John Gottman at the University of Washington compared happily married couples and unhappily married couples when they see each other for the first time at the end of the day. The happily married couples showed the smile with the muscle around the eye. Unhappily married couples show the smile just with the lips.
3. P. Ekman, M. O'Sullivan, and M. G. Frank, "A Few Can Catch a Liar," *Psychological Science* 10 (1999): 263–66.
4. R. J. Davidson, P. Ekman, S. Senulius, and W. Friesen, "Emotional Expression and Brain Physiology I: Approach/Withdrawal and Cerebral Asymmetry," *Journal of Personality and Social Psychology* 58 (1990): 330–41.
5. See Peter Salovey and John D. Mayer, "Emotional Intelligence," *Imagination, Cognition and Personality* 9, 3 (1990): 185–211, as well as Daniel Goleman, *Emotional Intelligence* (New York: Bantam Books, 1995).
6. The most generic Tibetan terms for thought also embrace emotions: *tokpa* and *namtok.*
7. See, for example, Daniel Goleman, "Buddhist Psychology," in Calvin Hall and Gardner Lindzey, *Theories of Personality* (New York: Wiley, 1978).
8. For a discussion of the significance of the mother-child relationship, especially pertaining to the meditative cultivation of compassion in Buddhism, see Tsongkhapa, *The Principal Teachings of Buddhism,* trans. Geshe Lobsang Tharchin (Howell, N.J.: Classics of Middle Asia, 1988), 95–107.
9. The Dalai Lama mentioned two examples: contemplating *shunya,* or emptiness, and the analysis of the interdependence of all things.

Chapter 7: Cultivating Emotional Balance

1. The Dalai Lama noted that the concept of *dhyana*—the levels of absorption in the development of concentrative meditation—and the subtleties of various contemplative states of mind are common to many other Indian traditions as well as Buddhism. The distinctions between levels are described in terms of the level of bliss, rapture, joy, or equanimity that characterizes each. Perhaps in other traditions where there is much more emphasis placed on such meditations and understanding the levels of concentration, as well as meditations reflecting upon the destructive nature of what we call the afflictions of the desire realm, there may be terms roughly equivalent to "emotion."
2. See, for example, R. J. Davidson and W. Irwin, "The Functional Neuroanatomy of Emotion and Affective Style," *Trends in Cognitive Science* 3 (1999): 11–21.
3. There are several versions of the list of mental factors among the various schools and branches of Buddhism. Another Tibetan source lists eighty mental factors; the main text followed in the Thai and Burmese tradition describes fifty-two mental factors but also mentions that actually there are a countless number. In short, the lists seem to represent a useful convention rather than an exhaustive account. Along with each wholesome or unwholesome state, five other neutral mental factors always arise: feeling, recognition, volition (etymologically, "that which moves the mind"), attention, and contact (the sheer naked detection, or contact, of the mind with a given object).
4. Alan explained what was meant here by reification: "If you simply apprehend a flower, then you simply know there's a flower. The reification is grasping on to the flower as something existing exactly in accordance to the manner in which it appears. The flower appears as if it exists from its own side, by its own nature, objectively, independently—that's how it appears. In the first instant there is simply a valid apprehension of the flower. But the grasping on to the flower as if it exists just as it appears—that is a false cognition, a misapprehension."

Chapter 8: The Neuroscience of Emotion

1. See Richard J. Davidson and Daniel J. Goleman, "The Role of Attention in Meditation and Hypnosis: A Psychobiological Perspective on Transformations of Consciousness," *International Journal of Clinical and Experimental Hypnosis* 25, 4 (1977): 291–308. At the same time Davidson coauthored an article showing that an attentional ability—being able to ignore distractions while focusing attention—was associated with distinctive EEG patterns, and that there was a continuum of this ability; R. J. Davidson, G. E. Schwartz, and L. P. Rothman, "Attentional Style and the Self-Regulation of Mode-Specific Attention: An EEG Study," *Journal of Abnormal Psychology* 85 (1976): 611–21. If there is a continuum, that in turn opens the possibility that people can be trained to improve. A third paper (R. J. Davidson, D. J. Goleman, and G. E. Schwartz, "Attention and Affective Concomitants of Meditation: A Cross-Sectional Study," *Journal of Abnormal Psychology* 85 [1976]: 235–38) showed that the more meditation experience a person had, the better that

individual was at this attentional task, suggesting that meditation training improved attention. But it was decades later that Davidson was able to do the brain research showing that, indeed, our early hunches had been correct.

2. Richard J. Davidson and Anne Harrington, eds., *Visions of Compassion: Western Scientists and Tibetan Buddhists Examine Human Nature* (New York: Oxford University Press, 2001).
3. B. Czeh, T. Michaelis, T. Watanabe, J. Frahm, G. de Biurrun, M. van Kampen, A. Bartolomucci, and E. Fuchs, "Stress-Induced Changes in Cerebral Metabolites, Hippocampal Volume, and Cell Proliferation Are Prevented by Antidepressant Treatment with Tianeptine," *Proceedings of the National Academy of Sciences of the United States of America* 98, 22 (2001): 12796–801.
4. Neurons grow throughout life span: P. S. Eriksson, E. Perfilieva, T. Bjork-Eriksson, A. M. Alborn, C. Nordborg, D. A. Peterson, and F. H. Gage, "Neurogenesis in the Adult Human Hippocampus," *Nature Medicine* 4, 11 (1998): 1313–7.
5. J. Davidson, D. C. Jackson, N. H. Kalin, "Emotion, Plasticity, Context and Regulation: Perspectives from Affective Neuroscience, *Psychological Bulletin* 126, 6, (2000): 890–906.
6. Daniel Dennett, *Brainstorms: Philosophical Essays on Mind and Psychology,* (Cambridge: MIT Press, 1981).
7. Meditative quiescence is also known by the Sanskrit term *shamatha.*
8. R. J. Davidson, K. M. Putnam, and C. L. Larson, "Dysfunction in the Neural Circuitry of Emotion Regulation—A Possible Prelude to Violence," *Science* 289 (2000): 591–94.
9. E. J. Nestler and G. K. Aghajanian, "Molecular and Cellular Basis of Addiction," *Science* 278, 5335 (1997): 58–63.
10. Areas activated by craving: H. C. Breier and B. R. Rosen, "Functional Magnetic Resonance Imaging of Brain Reward Circuitry in the Human," *Annals of the New York Academy of Sciences* 29, 877 (1999): 523–47.

Chapter 9: Our Potential for Change

1. A. Raine, T. Lencz, S. Bihrle, L. LaCasse, and P. Colletti, "Reduced Prefrontal Gray Matter Volume and Reduced Autonomic Activity in Antisocial Personality Disorder," *Archives of General Psychiatry* 57, 2 (2000): 119–27, discussion 128–29.
2. E. K. Miller and J. D. Cohen, "An Integrative Theory of Prefrontal Cortex Function," *Annual Review of Neuroscience* 24 (2001): 167–202.
3. Jon Kabat-Zinn, *Wherever You Go, There You Are: Mindfulness Meditation in Everyday Life* (New York: Hyperion, 1994).
4. Sogyal Rinpoche, *The Tibetan Book of Living and Dying,* ed. Patrick Gaffney and Andrew Harvey (San Francisco: Harper San Francisco, 1992).
5. Norman Kagan, "Influencing Human Interaction—Eighteen Years with Interpersonal Process Recall," in A. K. Hess, ed., *Psychotherapy Supervision: Theory, Research and Practice* (New York: John Wiley and Sons, 1991).
6. Daniel Goleman, *Working with Emotional Intelligence* (New York: Bantam Books,

1998); Daniel Goleman, Richard Boyatzis, and Annie McKee, *Primal Leadership* (Boston: Harvard Business School Press, 2002).
7. William James, *Talks to Teachers on Psychology and to Students on Some of Life's Ideals* (Cambridge, Mass.: Harvard University Press, 1983).

Chapter 10: The Influence of Culture

1. S. Sue, "Asian American Mental Health: What We Know and What We Don't Know," in W. Lonner et al., eds., *Merging Past, Present, and Future in Cross-Cultural Psychology: Selected Papers from the Fourteenth International Congress of the International Association for Cross-Cultural Psychology* (Lisse and Exton: Swets and Zeitlinger, 1999), 82–89.
2. H. R. Markus and S. Kitayama, "Culture and the Self: Implications for Cognition, Emotion, and Motivation," *Psychological Review* 98 (1991): 224–53.
3. See, for example, J. G. Miller and D. M. Bersoff, "Culture and Moral Judgment: How Are Conflicts Between Justice and Interpersonal Responsibilities Resolved?" *Journal of Personality and Social Psychology* 62 (1992): 541–54.
4. R. Hsu, "The Self in Cross-Cultural Perspective," in A. J. Marsella, C. DeVos, and F. L. K. Hsu, eds., *Culture and Self: Asian and Western Perspectives* (New York: Tavistock Publications, 1985), 24–55.
5. S. Cousins, "Culture and Self-Perception in Japan and the United States," *Journal of Personality and Social Psychology* 56 (1989): 124–31.
6. S. Heine, D. Lehman, H. Markus, and S. Kitayama, "Is There a Universal Need for Positive Self-Regard?" *Psychological Review* 106 (1999): 766–94.
7. Ibid.
8. J. L. Tsai and R. W. Levenson, "Cultural Influences on Emotional Responding: Chinese American and European American Dating Couples During Interpersonal Conflict," *Journal of Cross-Cultural Psychology* 28 (1997): 600–25.
9. J. L. Tsai, R. W. Levenson, and K. McCoy, "Bicultural Emotions: Chinese American and European American Couples During Conflict," manuscript under review.
10. Ibid.
11. J. Kagan, D. Arcus, N. Snidman, Y. F. Want, J. Hendler, and S. Greene, "Reactivity in Infants: A Cross-National Comparison," *Developmental Psychology* 30, 3 (1994): 342–45; J. Kagan, R. Kearsley, and P. Zelazo, *Infancy: Its Place in Human Development* (Cambridge, Mass.: Harvard University Press, 1978).
12. D. G. Freedman, *Human Infancy: An Evolutionary Perspective* (Hillsdale, N.J.: Lawrence Erlbaum, 1974).
13. J. A. Soto, R. W. Levenson, and R. Ebling, "Emotional Expression and Experience in Chinese Americans and Mexican Americans: A 'Startling' Comparison," manuscript under review.
14. J. L. Tsai and T. Scaramuzzo, "Descriptions of Past Emotional Episodes: A Comparison of Hmong and European American College Students," manuscript in preparation.
15. D. Stipek, "Differences Between Americans and Chinese in the Circumstances

Evoking Pride, Shame, and Guilt," *Journal of Cross-Cultural Psychology* 29, 5 (1998): 616–29.
16. J. L. Tsai and Y. Chentsova-Dutton, "Variation Among European Americans? You Betcha," manuscript under review.
17. S. Harkness, C. Super, and N. van Tijen, "Individualism and the 'Western Mind' Reconsidered: American and Dutch Parents' Ethnotheories of the Child," in S. Harkness, C. Raeff, and C. Super, eds., *Variability in the Social Construction of the Child* (San Francisco: Jossey-Bass, 2000).

Chapter 11: Schooling for the Good Heart

1. M. T. Greenberg and C. A. Kusché, *Promoting Social and Emotional Development in Deaf Children: The PATHS Project* (Seattle: University of Washington Press, 1993); C. A. Kusché and M. T. Greenberg, *The PATHS Curriculum* (Seattle: Developmental Research and Programs, 1994).
2. The Collaborative for Academic, Social, and Emotional Learning includes those doing basic research in the emotions and child development, teacher training, and preventive interventions; it also includes policy makers. Their unifying focus is providing scientific information on social and emotional learning to schools and the public, and promoting the use of effective science-based curricula. One of the services offered is a website, www.casel.org, which lists over two hundred school programs that follow the principles that work best—not only helping children master the essential emotional and social skills they need, but also boosting academic performance.
3. G. Dawson, K. Frey, H. Panagiotides, E. Yamada, D. Hessl, and J. Osterling, "Infants of Depressed Mothers Exhibit Atypical Frontal Electrical Brain Activity During Interactions with Mother and with a Familiar, Nondepressed Adult," *Child Development* 70 (1999): 1058–66.
4. Conduct Problems Prevention Research Group, "A Developmental and Clinical Model for the Prevention of Conduct Disorders: The FAST Track Program," *Development and Psychopathology* 4 (1992): 509–27.
5. S. W. Anderson, A. Bechara, H. Damasio, D. Tranel, and A. R. Damasio, "Impairment of Social and Moral Behavior Related to Early Damage in Human Prefrontal Cortex," *Nature Neuroscience* 2 (1999): 1032–7.
6. K. A. Dodge, "A Social Information Processing Model of Social Competence in Children," in M. Perlmutter, ed., *Cognitive Perspectives on Children's Social and Behavioral Development*, The Minnesota Symposia on Child Psychology, vol. 18 (Hillsdale, N.J.: Lawrence Erlbaum, 1986).
7. M. T. Greenberg and C. A. Kusché, *Promoting Alternative Thinking Strategies: PATHS*, Blueprint for Violence Prevention, Book 10 (Boulder: Institute of Behavioral Sciences, University of Colorado, 1998).
8. M. T. Greenberg, C. A. Kusché, E. T. Cook, and J. P. Quamma, "Promoting Emotional Competence in School-Aged Children: The Effects of the PATHS Curriculum," *Development and Psychopathology* 7 (1995): 117–36.

9. J. M. Gottman, L. F. Katz, and C. Hooven, *Meta-Emotion: How Families Communicate Emotionally* (Hillsdale, N.J.: Lawrence Erlbaum, 1997).
10. J. Coie, R. Terry, K. Lenox, J. Lochman, and C. Hyman, "Childhood Peer Rejection and Aggression as Stable Predictors of Patterns of Adolescent Disorder," *Development and Psychopathology* 10 (1998): 587–98.

Chapter 12: Encouraging Compassion

1. See Richard J. Davidson and Anne Harrington, eds., *Visions of Compassion: Western Scientists and Tibetan Buddhists Examine Human Nature* (New York: Oxford University Press, 2001). The interchange is reported on pages 82–84.
2. Although there is no single word in English that itself translates *mudita,* "delight in the happiness of others," a word that stands in stark contrast exists in German: *Schadenfreude,* "delight in the suffering of someone else."
3. T. Elbert, C. Pantev, C. Wienbruch, B. Rockstroh, and E. Taub, "Increased Cortical Representation of the Fingers of the Left Hand in String Players," *Science* 270, 5234 (1995): 305–7.
4. E. A. Maguire et al., "Navigation-related Structural Change in the Hippocampi of Taxi Drivers," *Proceedings of the National Academy of Science of the United States of America* 97, 9 (2000): 4414–16.

Chapter 13: The Scientific Study of Consciousness

1. See Humberto Maturana and Francisco Varela, *Autopoiesis and Cognition: The Realization of the Living* (Dordrecht and Boston: Reidel, 1980).
2. See the interview with Francisco Varela in John Brockman, *The Third Culture* (New York: Simon and Schuster, 1995).
3. Humberto Maturana and Francisco Varela, *The Tree of Knowledge: The Biological Roots of Human Understanding* (Boston: New Science Library, 1987).
4. In the fall of 1984, the Dalai Lama had been approached by Adam Engle and Michael Sautman in California, and had agreed to participate in a meeting on Buddhism and science. The four organizers of that first meeting—Adam Engle, Michael Sautman, Francisco Varela, and Joan Halifax—met later at the Ojai Foundation in California and agreed to work together, forming the kernel of what has become the Mind and Life Institute.
5. Among his books: Francisco Varela, *Principles of Biological Autonomy* (Amsterdam: North Holland, 1979); with Humberto Maturana, *Autopoiesis and Cognition: The Realization of the Living* (Dordrecht and Boston: Reidel, 1980); and with Evan Thompson and Eleanor Rosch, *The Embodied Mind: Cognitive Science and Human Experience* (Cambridge, Mass.: MIT Press, 1992).
6. Science's new openness to the study of consciousness is attested to, for example, by the founding of the *Journal of Consciousness Studies* in 1994 and the annual series of Tucson conferences, Toward a Science of Consciousness, at many of which Francisco Varela presented.
7. Varela, Thompson, and Rosch, *The Embodied Mind.* The arguments for the first-

person method in cognitive neuroscience are continued in two edited books, Francisco J. Varela and Jonathan Shear, eds., *The View from Within: First-Person Approaches in the Study of Consciousness* (London: Imprint Academic, 1999), and Jean Petitot, Francisco J. Varela, Bernard Pachoud, and Jean-Michel Roy, eds., *Naturalizing Phenomenology* (Stanford: Stanford University Press, 2000).

8. Francisco Varela, "Neurophenomenology: A Methodological Remedy for the Hard Problem," *Journal of Consciousness Studies* 3 (1996): 330–50; Varela and Shear, eds., *The View from Within.*
9. N. Depraz, F. Varela, and P. Vermersch, *On Becoming Aware: The Pragmatics of Experiencing* (Amsterdam: John Benjamins Press, 2002).
10. F. Varela, J.-P. Lachaux, E. Rodriguez, and J. Martinerie, "The Brainweb: Phase Synchronization and Large-Scale Integration," *Nature Reviews: Neuroscience* 2 (2001): 229–39.
11. E. Rodriguez, N. George, J.-P. Lachaux, J. Martinerie, B. Renault, and F. J. Varela, "Perception's Shadow: Long-Distance Synchronization of Human Brain Activity," *Nature* 397 (1999): 430–33.
12. There is agreement among three of the schools that, on the whole, there are instances of sensory perception that are undistorted. But the Prasangika Madhyamaka school maintains that all sensory perceptions are by nature deceptive, too, for they perceive their objects as existing according to their own inherent nature, whereas in reality they do not exist in that way.
13. These more sophisticated schools of thought include the Sautrantika, Yogachara, and Madhyamaka, the major views held by Tibetan Buddhist philosophers today.
14. A. Lutz, J.-P. Lachaux, J. Martinerie, and F. J. Varela, "Guiding the Study of Brain Dynamics by Using First-Person Data: Synchrony Patterns Correlate with Ongoing Conscious States During a Simple Visual Task," *Proceedings of the National Academy of Sciences of the United States of America* 99 (2002): 1586–91.
15. Varela, Thompson, and Rosch, *The Embodied Mind.* B. Alan Wallace makes parallel proposals in his book *The Taboo of Subjectivity: Toward a New Science of Consciousness* (New York: Oxford University Press, 2000), particularly the section "Observing the Mind."

Chapter 14: The Protean Brain

1. P. S. Eriksson, E. Perfilieva, T. Bjork-Eriksson, A. M. Alborn, C. Nordborg, D. A. Peterson, and F. H. Gage, "Neurogenesis in the Adult Human Hippocampus," *Nature Medicine* 4, 11 (1998): 1313–7.
2. See, for example, H. van Praag, G. Kempermann, and F. H. Gage, "Running Increases Cell Proliferation and Neurogenesis in the Adult Mouse Dentate Gyrus," *Nature Neuroscience* 2, 3 (1999): 266–70.
3. M. S. George, Z. Nahas, M. Molloy, A. M. Speer, N. C. Oliver, X. B. Li, G. W. Arana, S. C. Risch, and J. C. Ballenger, "A Controlled Trial of Daily Left Prefrontal Cortex TMS for Treating Depression," *Biological Psychiatry* 48, 10 (2000): 962–70.
4. See S. Frederick and G. Loewenstein, "Hedonic Adaptation," in D. Kahneman,

E. Diener, and N. Schwarz, eds., *Well-being: The Foundations of Hedonic Psychology* (New York: Russell Sage, 1999); P. Brickman, D. Coates, and R. Janoff-Bullman, "Lottery Winners and Accident Victims: Is Happiness Relative?" *Journal of Personality and Social Psychology* 36 (1978): 917–27.

5. Jon Kabat-Zinn presented at the third Mind and Life conference; see Daniel Goleman, ed., *Healing Emotions: Conversations with the Dalai Lama on Mindfulness, Emotions, and Health* (Boston: Shambhala, 1996).
6. R. J. Davidson et al., "Alterations in Brain and Immune Function Produced by Mindfulness Meditation," *Psychosomatic Medicine*, in press.
7. The course includes a calming meditation on the breath, as well as a meditative scan of sensations throughout the body. For more details of the training, see Jon Kabat-Zinn, *Full Catastrophe Living* (New York: Dell, 1990).
8. J. Kiecolt-Glaser et al., "Chronic Stress Alters the Immune Response to Influenza Virus Vaccine in Older Adults," *Proceedings of the National Academy of Science of the United States of America* 93, 7 (1996): 3043–7.
9. The meditation group had twenty-three participants and the control group had sixteen, suggesting the need to replicate the study with a larger group.
10. R. M. Benca, W. H. Obermeyer, C. L. Larson, B. Yun, I. Dolski, S. M. Weber, and R. J. Davidson, "EEG Alpha Power and Alpha Asymmetry in Sleep and Wakefulness," *Psychophysiology* 36 (1999): 430–36.
11. See, for example, the translated text and commentary on dream yoga in Gyatrul Rinpoche, *Ancient Wisdom: Nyingma Teachings of Dream Yoga, Meditation and Transformation*, trans. B. Alan Wallace and Sangye Khandro (Ithaca, N.Y.: Snow Lion, 1993). This was also a major topic in the Mind and Life meeting reported in Francisco Varela, ed., *Sleeping, Dreaming, and Dying* (Ithaca, N.Y.: Wisdom, 1997).

About the Participants

Tenzin Gyatso, His Holiness the Fourteenth Dalai Lama, is the leader of Tibetan Buddhism, the head of the Tibetan government in exile, and a spiritual leader revered worldwide. He was born to a peasant family on July 6, 1935, in a small village called Taktser in northeastern Tibet. He was recognized at the age of two, in accordance with Tibetan tradition, as the reincarnation of his predecessor, the Thirteenth Dalai Lama. The Dalai Lamas are manifestations of the Buddha of Compassion, who chooses to reincarnate for the purpose of serving human beings. Winner of the Nobel prize for peace in 1989, he is universally respected as a spokesman for the compassionate and peaceful resolution of human conflict. He has traveled extensively, speaking on subjects including universal responsibility, love, compassion, and kindness. Less well known is his intense personal interest in the sciences; he has said that if he were not a monk, he would have liked to be an engineer. As a youth in Lhasa, it was he who was called on to fix broken machinery in the Potala Palace, be it a clock or a car. He has a vigorous interest in learning about the newest developments in science and brings to bear both a voice for the humanistic implications of the findings and a high degree of intuitive methodological sophistication.

Richard J. Davidson is the director of the Laboratory for Affective Neuroscience and the W. M. Keck Laboratory for Functional Brain Imaging and Behavior at the University of Wisconsin at Madison. He was educated at New York University and Harvard University, where he received his B.A. and

Ph.D., respectively, in psychology. Over the course of his research career he has focused on the relationship between the brain and emotion. He is currently the William James Professor and Vilas Research Professor of Psychology and Psychiatry at the University of Wisconsin. He is coauthor or editor of nine books, the most recent being *Anxiety, Depression and Emotion* (Oxford University Press, 2000) and *Visions of Compassion: Western Scientists and Tibetan Buddhists Examine Human Nature* (Oxford University Press, 2002). Professor Davidson has also written more than 150 chapters and journal articles. He is the recipient of numerous awards for his work, including the Research Scientist Award from the National Institute of Mental Health and the Distinguished Scientific Contribution Award from the American Psychological Association. He is a member of the Board of Scientific Counselors of the National Institute of Mental Health. In 1992, as a follow-up from previous Mind and Life meetings, he was a member of a scientific team doing neuroscientific investigations of exceptional mental abilities in advanced Tibetan monks.

Paul Ekman is professor of psychology and director of the Human Interaction Laboratory at the University of California Medical School in San Francisco. He was educated at the University of Chicago, New York University, and Adelphi University, from which he received his Ph.D. His research has focused on emotional expressions (and their relationship to physiological changes) and deception, and he is the leading authority on facial signs of emotion. His cross-cultural studies of emotional expression led him to work in a Stone Age culture in Papua New Guinea in 1967–68, in Japan, and in a number of other cultures. Among his honors are receiving (seven times) a Research Scientist Award from the National Institute of Mental Health and an honorary doctorate in humane letters from the University of Chicago. He has published more than a hundred scholarly articles and edited or authored fourteen books, including coediting (with Richard Davidson) *The Nature of Emotion* (Oxford University Press, 1997). His most recent book is an annotated edition of Charles Darwin's 1872 book, *The Expression of Emotion in Man and Animals*, where he points to the relevance for contemporary research of Darwin's insights on the evolution of emotion.

Owen Flanagan is James B. Duke Professor of Philosophy and departmental chair, professor of psychology (experimental) and professor of neurobiology at Duke University. In 1999–2000, Dr. Flanagan held the Romanell Phi Beta Kappa Professorship, awarded by the national Phi Beta Kappa office to an American philosopher for distinguished contributions to philosophy and to the public understanding of philosophy. Dr. Flanagan works primarily on the mind-body problem, moral psychology, and the conflict between the scientific and the humanistic image of persons. He is the author of *The Science of the Mind* (MIT Press, 1991); *Varieties of Moral Personality* (Harvard University Press, 1991); *Consciousness Reconsidered* (MIT Press, 1992); *Self-Expressions: Mind, Morals, and the Meaning of Life* (Oxford University Press, 1996); and *Dreaming Souls: Sleep, Dreams, and the Evolution of the Conscious Mind* (Oxford University Press, 2000). He has also published numerous articles, including several recent articles on the nature of the virtues, the moral emotions, Confucianism, and the scientific status of psychoanalysis.

Daniel Goleman is cochair of the Consortium for Research on Emotional Intelligence in the Graduate School of Applied and Professional Psychology at Rutgers University. He received his B.A. from Amherst College and his M.A. and Ph.D. in clinical psychology and developmental studies from Harvard University, where he was later a member of the faculty. He cofounded the Collaborative for Academic, Social and Emotional Learning at the University of Illinois, Chicago, a research group that evaluates and disseminates school-based programs for affective self-mastery. He has focused on the interface between psychobiology and behavior, with a special interest in emotions and health. He was twice nominated for the Pulitzer Prize for his work as a journalist covering the brain and behavioral sciences at the *New York Times*. He has written or edited twelve books, including the international best-seller *Emotional Intelligence* (Bantam, 1995) and *Healing Emotions* (Shambhala, 1997), the proceedings of Mind and Life III.

Mark Greenberg holds the Bennett Chair of Prevention Research in the Department of Human Development and Family Studies at Pennsylvania State University, where he also is director of the Prevention Research Center for the Promotion of Human Development. He received his B.A. from Johns Hopkins University and his M.A. and Ph.D. in developmental and pediatric psychology from the University of Virginia. His research focus has included neuroplasticity in the emotional development of children, the study of parent-child attachment, and educational strategies that can lower risks of behavioral problems and promote social and emotional competence. Professor Greenberg has been a consultant to the U.S. Centers for Disease Control Task Force on Violence Prevention and is cochair of the research committee of CASEL (Collaborative for Academic, Social and Emotional Learning). He has published more than a hundred scholarly articles on child development, including a chapter on the neurological basis of emotional development in *Emotional Development and Emotional Intelligence* (Basic Books, 1997).

Geshe Thupten Jinpa was born in Tibet in 1958. Trained as a monk in south India, he received the *geshe lharam* degree (equivalent to a doctorate in divinity) from Shartse College of Ganden monastic university, where he also taught Buddhist philosophy for five years. He also holds a B.A. (honors) in Western philosophy and a Ph.D. in religious studies, both from Cambridge University. Since 1985 he has been a principal English translator to His Holiness the Dalai Lama and has translated and edited several books by the Dalai Lama, including *The Good Heart: The Dalai Lama Explores the Heart of Christianity* (Rider, 1996) and *Ethics for the New Millennium* (Riverhead, 1999). His most recent works are (with Ja's Elsner) *Songs of Spiritual Experience* (Shambhala, 2000), *Tsongkhapa's Philosophy of Emptiness* (forthcoming from Curzon Press), and the entries on Tibetan philosophy in the *Encyclopedia of Asian Philosophy* (Routledge, 2001). From 1996 to 1999 he was the Margaret Smith Research Fellow in Eastern Religion at Girton College, Cambridge University. He is currently the president of the Institute of Tibetan Classics, which is dedicated to translating key Tibetan classics into contemporary languages. He lives in Montreal, Canada, with his wife and two young children.

The Venerable Ajahn Maha Somchai Kusalacitto was born into a farming family in the far north of Thailand and was ordained as a monk at age twenty. After receiving a B.A. in Buddhist studies in Thailand and a Ph.D. in Indian philosophy at the University of Madras, he was appointed dean at Mahachulalongkornrajavidyalaya University in Bangkok, where he now holds the post of deputy rector for foreign affairs and lectures on Buddhist topics and comparative religion. He continues to publish scholarly works on Buddhism and serves as assistant abbot at the Chandaram Buddhist monastery, while also broadcasting on Thai radio and television and writing for newspapers and magazines on Buddhist topics. He is cofounder of an international society for Buddhists engaged in social issues, of a group advocating an alternative educational system in Thailand, and of an association of Thai monks dedicated to preserving the forest monastic tradition.

Matthieu Ricard is a Buddhist monk at Shechen Monastery in Kathmandu and a French interpreter since 1989 for His Holiness the Dalai Lama. Born in France in 1946, he received a Ph.D. in cellular genetics at the Institut Pasteur under Nobel laureate François Jacob. As a hobby, he wrote *Animal Migrations* (Hill and Wang, 1969). He first traveled to the Himalayas in 1967 and has lived there since 1972, becoming a Buddhist monk in 1979. For fifteen years he studied with Dilgo Khyentse Rinpoche, one of the most eminent Tibetan teachers of our times. With his father, the French thinker

Jean-François Revel, he is the author of *The Monk and the Philosopher* (Schocken, 1999) and of *The Quantum and the Lotus* with the astrophysicist Trinh Xuan Thuan (Crown, 2001). As a photographer, he has published several albums, including *The Spirit of Tibet* (Aperture, 2000) and (with Olivier and Danielle Föllmi) *Buddhist Himalayas* (Abrams, 2002).

Jeanne L. Tsai is on the faculty in the Department of Psychology at Stanford University. She received her B.A. from Stanford and her M.A. and Ph.D. in clinical psychology from the University of California at Berkeley. Her research has focused on the interplay between culture and emotion, exploring the impact of socialization on emotional experience, expression, and physiology. She has brought a diverse range of methods to bear in, for example, comparing differences in the physiology and experience of emotion between Chinese people and various other ethnic groups in America. Her articles have appeared in numerous scholarly journals and books, including *The Encyclopedia of Human Emotions* (Gale, 1999) and *The Comprehensive Handbook of Psychopathology* (Plenum, 1993).

Francisco J. Varela received his Ph.D. in biology from Harvard in 1970. His interests centered on the biological mechanisms of cognition and consciousness, and he contributed over two hundred articles to scientific journals on these matters. He also wrote or edited fifteen books, many of them translated into several languages, including *The Embodied Mind* (MIT Press, 1992) and more recently *Naturalizing Phenomenology: Contemporary Issues in Phenomenology and Cognitive Science* (Stanford University Press, 1999) and *The View from Within: First-Person Methods in the Study of Consciousness* (Imprint Academic, 1999). The recipient of several awards for his research, he was Fondation de France Professor of Cognitive Science and Epistemology at the Ecole Polytechnique, director of research at the Centre National de la Recherche Scientifique in Paris, and head of the Neurodynamics Unit at LENA (Laboratory of Cognitive Neurosciences and Brain Imaging) at the Salpetrière Hospital, Paris. He is the founding scientist of the Mind and Life series and has published several articles and books on the dialogue between science and religion, including *Gentle Bridges* (Shambhala, 1991) and *Sleeping, Dreaming, and Dying* (Wisdom, 1997), covering the first and fourth of the Mind and Life dialogues. Dr. Varela passed away on May 28, 2001.

B. Alan Wallace trained for many years in Buddhist monasteries in India and Switzerland and has taught Buddhist theory and practice in Europe and America since 1976. He has served as interpreter for numerous Tibetan scholars and contemplatives, including His Holiness the Dalai Lama. After graduating summa cum laude from Amherst College, where he studied physics and the philosophy of science, he earned a doctorate in religious studies at Stanford University. He has edited, translated, authored, or contributed to more than thirty books on Tibetan Buddhism, medicine, language, and culture. He has also written about the interface between science and religion. His published works include *Tibetan Buddhism from the Ground Up* (Wisdom Publications, 1993) *Choosing Reality: A Buddhist View of Physics and the Mind* (Snow Lion Publications, 1996), *The Bridge of Quiescence: Experiencing Buddhist Meditation* (Open Court Publishing, 1998), and *The Taboo of Subjectivity: Toward a New Science of Consciousness* (Oxford University Press, 2000). He is also the editor of an anthology of essays entitled *Buddhism and Science: Breaking New Ground,* soon to be published by Columbia University Press.

About the Mind and Life Institute

The Mind and Life dialogues between His Holiness the Dalai Lama and Western scientists were brought to life through a collaboration between R. Adam Engle, a North American lawyer and businessman, and Francisco J. Varela, a Chilean-born neuroscientist living and working in Paris. In 1983 Engle and Varela, who at the time did not know each other, each independently took the initiative to create a series of cross-cultural meetings where His Holiness and scientists from the West would engage in extended discussions over a period of days.

After attending Harvard Law School, Engle's early career included work at an entertainment law firm in Beverly Hills and a year as general counsel for GTE in Teheran. A restless spirit led to his first sabbatical year in Asia, where he discovered a fascination with the Tibetan monasteries he visited in the Himalayas. In 1974 he met Lama Thubten Yeshe, one of the first Tibetan Buddhists to teach in English, and spent four months living at the Kopan Monastery in Kathmandu. When Engle returned to the United States, he settled near Santa Cruz, California, where Lama Yeshe and his disciple Lama Thubten Zopa Rinpoche had a retreat center.

It was through Lama Yeshe that Engle first became aware of the Dalai Lama's long-standing and keen interest in science and His Holiness's desire to both deepen his understanding of Western science and share his understanding of Eastern contemplative science with Western scientists. Engle immediately felt that this was a project he would love to take on.

In the autumn of 1984 Engle, who had been joined on this adventure by a friend, Michael Sautman, met with His Holiness's youngest brother, Tendzin Choegyal (Ngari Rinpoche), in Los Angeles and presented their plan to create a weeklong cross-cultural scientific meeting, provided His Holiness would fully participate in the meeting. Rinpoche graciously offered to take the matter up with His Holiness. Within days, Rinpoche reported that His Holiness would very much like to engage in discussions with scientists, and authorized Engle and Sautman to organize a meeting. This began Tendzin Choegyal's continuing role as a key advisor to what is now the Mind and Life Institute.

Meanwhile, Francisco Varela, also a Buddhist practitioner since 1974, had met His Holiness at an international meeting in 1983 as a speaker at the Alpbach Symposia on Consciousness, where their communication was immediate. His Holiness was clearly happy at the opportunity for discussion with a brain scientist who had some understanding of Tibetan Buddhism, and Varela determined to look for ways to continue this scientific dialogue. In the spring of 1985, a close friend, Joan Halifax, then director at the Ojai Foundation, who had heard about Engle and Sautman's efforts, suggested that perhaps Engle, Sautman, and Varela could pool their complementary skills and work together. The four got together at the Ojai Foundation in October 1985 and agreed to go forward jointly. They decided to focus on the scientific disciplines dealing with mind and life as the most fruitful interface between science and the Buddhist tradition. This became the name of the first meeting and eventually of the Mind and Life Institute.

It took two more years of work among Engle, Sautman, Varela, and the Private Office of His Holiness before the first meeting was held in October 1987 in Dharamsala. During this time, Engle and Varela collaborated closely to find a useful structure for the meeting. Adam took on the job of general coordinator, with primary responsibility for fund-raising, relations with His Holiness and his office, and all other general aspects of the project, while Francisco, acting as scientific coordinator, took on primary responsibility for the scientific content, invitations to scientists, and editing of a volume covering the meeting.

This division of responsibility between general and scientific coordinators worked so well that it has been continued throughout all subsequent meetings. When the Mind and Life Institute was formally organized in 1990, Adam became its chairman and has been the general coordinator of all the Mind and Life meetings; while Francisco was not the scientific coordinator of all of them, until his death in 2001 he remained a guiding force and Engle's closest partner in the Mind and Life Institute and the series of meetings.

A word is in order here concerning the uniqueness of this series of conferences. The bridges that can mutually enrich modern life science and particularly the neurosciences are notoriously difficult to engineer. Francisco had a first taste of this when helping to establish a science program at Naropa Institute (now Naropa University), a liberal-arts institution in Boulder, Colorado, created by Tibetan meditation master Chogyam Trungpa Rinpoche. In 1979 Naropa received a grant from the Sloan Foundation to organize Comparative Approaches to Cognition: Western and Buddhist, probably the very first conference on that topic. Some twenty-five academics from prominent U.S. institutions gathered from various disciplines: mainstream philosophy, cognitive sciences (neurosciences, experimental psychology, linguistics, artificial intelligence), and of course Buddhist studies. The meeting provided a hard lesson to Francisco on the care and finesse that organizing a cross-cultural dialogue requires.

Thus in 1987, profiting from the Naropa experience and wishing to avoid some of the pitfalls encountered in the past, Francisco urged the adoption of several operating principles that have worked extremely well in making the Mind and Life series extraordinarily successful. Perhaps the most important was to decide that scientists would be chosen not solely by their reputations but by their competence in their domain as well as their open-mindedness. Some familiarity with Buddhism is helpful but not essential, so long as a healthy respect for the Eastern contemplative disciplines is present.

Next, the curriculum was adjusted as further conversations with the Dalai Lama clarified how much of the scientific background would need to be presented in order for His Holiness to participate fully in the dialogues. To ensure that the meetings would be fully participatory, they were structured with presentations by Western scientists in the morning session. In this way, His Holiness could be briefed on the basic ground of a field of knowledge. This morning presentation was based upon a broad, mainstream, nonpartisan scientific point of view. The afternoon session was devoted solely to discussion, which naturally flowed from the morning presentation. During this discussion session, the morning presenter could state his or her personal preferences and judgments if they differed from the generally accepted viewpoints.

The issue of Tibetan-English language translation in a scientific meeting posed a significant challenge, as it was impossible to find a Tibetan native fluent in both English and science. This challenge was overcome by choosing two wonderful interpreters, one a Tibetan and one a Westerner with a scientific background, and placing them next to each other during the meeting. This allowed quick, on-the-spot clarification of terms, which is absolutely essential to move beyond the initial misunderstandings between two vastly different traditions. Thupten Jinpa, a Tibetan monk then studying for his *geshe* degree at Ganden Shartse monastery and now the holder of a Ph.D. in philosophy from Cambridge University, and B. Alan Wallace, a former monk in the Tibetan tradition with a degree in physics from Amherst College and a Ph.D. in religious studies from Stanford University, interpreted at Mind and Life I and have continued to interpret in further meetings. During Mind and Life V, while Dr. Wallace was unavailable, the Western interpreter was Dr. José Cabezon.

A final principle that has supported the success of the Mind and Life series has been that the meetings have been entirely private: no press, and no invited guests beyond a very few. This stands in sharp contrast to meetings in the West, where the public image of the Dalai Lama makes a relaxed, spontaneous discussion virtually impossible. The Mind and Life Institute records the meetings on video and audio for archival purposes and transcription, but the meetings have become a protected environment to conduct this exploration.

The first Mind and Life dialogue was held in October 1987 in the Dalai Lama's private quarters in Dharamsala. Varela was the scientific coordinator and moderated the meeting, which introduced various broad themes from cognitive science, including scientific method, neurobiology, cognitive psychology, artificial intelligence, brain development, and evolution. In attendance in addition to Varela were Jeremy Hayward (physics and philosophy of science), Robert Livingston (neuroscience and medicine), Eleanor Rosch (cognitive science), and Newcomb Greenleaf (computer science).

The event was an enormously gratifying success in that both His Holiness and the participants felt that there was a true meeting of minds, with some substantial advances in bridging the gap. Mind and Life I was transcribed, edited, and published as *Gentle Bridges: Conversations with the Dalai Lama on the Sciences of Mind,* edited by J. Hayward and F. J. Varela (Boston: Shambhala, 1992). This book has been translated into French, Spanish, German, Japanese, and Chinese.

Mind and Life II took place in October 1989 in Newport Beach, California, with Robert Livingston as the scientific coordinator, and with the emphasis on neuroscience. Invited were Patricia S. Churchland (philosophy of science), J. Allan Hobson (sleep and dreams), Larry Squire (memory), Antonio Damasio (neuroscience), and Lewis Judd (mental health). It was during this meeting that Engle was awakened by a call at 3 A.M. saying that the Dalai Lama had just been awarded the Nobel prize for peace, and that the Norwegian ambassador would be coming at eight that morning to formally inform him of the award. After receiving the news, the Dalai Lama attended the meeting with the scientists as scheduled, taking time out only to hold a brief press conference about the prize. An account of this meeting is now available as *Consciousness at the Crossroads: Conversations with the Dalai Lama on Brain Science and Buddhism,* edited by Z. Houshmand, R. B. Livingston, and B. A. Wallace (Ithaca, N.Y.: Snow Lion Publications, 1999).

Mind and Life III returned to Dharamsala in 1990. Having organized and attended both Mind and Life I and II, Adam Engle and Tenzin Geyche Tethong, the secretary to the Dalai Lama, agreed that having the meetings in India produced a much better result than holding them in the West. Daniel Goleman (psychology) served as the scientific coordinator for Mind and Life III, which focused on the theme of the relationship between emotions and health. Participants included Daniel Brown (clinical psychology), Jon Kabat-Zinn (behavioral medicine), Clifford Saron (neuroscience), Lee Yearly (philosophy), Sharon Salzberg (Buddhism), and Francisco Varela (immunology and neuroscience). Daniel Goleman edited the volume covering Mind and Life III, entitled *Healing Emotions: Conversations with the Dalai Lama on Mindfulness, Emotions, and Health* (Boston: Shambhala, 1997).

During Mind and Life III a new extension of exploration emerged that was a natural complement to the dialogues but beyond the format of the conferences. Clifford Saron, Richard Davidson, Francisco Varela, Gregory Simpson, and Alan Wallace initiated a research project to investigate the effects of meditation on long-term meditators. The idea was to profit from the goodwill and trust that had been built with the Tibetan community in Dharamsala and the willingness of His Holiness for this kind of research. With seed money from the Hershey Family Foundation, the Mind and Life Institute was formed, which has been chaired by Engle since its inception. The Fetzer Institute funded initial stages of the research project. A progress report was submitted in 1994 to the Fetzer Institute.

The fourth Mind and Life conference, "Sleeping, Dreaming, and Dying," occurred in Dharamsala in October 1992, with Francisco Varela again acting as scientific coordinator. In addition to Francisco and His Holiness, invited participants were Charles Taylor (philosophy), Jerome Engel (neuroscience and medicine), Joan Halifax (anthropology, death and dying), Jayne Gackenbach (psychology of lucid dreaming), and Joyce McDougal (psychoanalysis). The account of this conference is now available as *Sleeping, Dreaming, and Dying: An Exploration of Consciousness with the Dalai Lama,* edited by F. J. Varela (Boston: Wisdom Publications, 1997).

Mind and Life V was held again in Dharamsala in April 1995. The title was "Altruism, Ethics, and Compassion" and the scientific coordinator was Richard Davidson. In addition to Dr. Davidson, participants included Nancy Eisenberg (child development), Robert Frank (altruism in economics), Anne Harrington (history of science), Elliott Sober (philosophy), and Ervin Staub (social psychology and group behavior). The volume covering this meeting is entitled *Visions of Compassion: Western Scientists and Tibetan Buddhists Examine Human Nature,* edited by R. J. Davidson and A. Harrington (New York: Oxford University Press, 2001).

Mind and Life VI opened a new area of exploration beyond the previous focus on life science. That meeting took place in Dharamsala in October 1997 with Arthur Zajonc (physics) as the scientific coordinator. The participants, in addition to Dr. Zajonc and His Holiness, were David Finkelstein (physics), George Greenstein (astronomy), Piet Hut (astrophysics), Tu Weming (philosophy), and Anton Zeilinger (quantum physics). The volume covering this meeting is entitled *The New Physics and Cosmology,* edited by A. Zajonc (New York: Oxford University Press, 2003).

The dialogue on quantum physics was continued with Mind and Life VII, held at Anton Zeilinger's laboratory at the Institut für Experimentalphysic in Innsbruck, Austria, in June 1998. Present were His Holiness, Drs. Zeilinger and Zajonc, and interpreters Drs. Jinpa and Wallace. That meeting was the subject of a cover story in the January 1999 issue of *Geo* magazine of Germany.

The meeting described in this volume, Mind and Life VIII, was held in March 2000 in Dharamsala with Daniel Goleman acting again as scientific coordinator and B. Alan Wallace acting as philosophical coordinator. The title of this meeting was "Destructive Emotions," and the participants were the Venerable Matthieu Ricard (Buddhism), Richard Davidson (neuroscience and psychology), Francisco Varela (neuroscience), Paul Ekman (psychology), Mark Greenberg (psychology), Jeanne Tsai (psychology), the Venerable Somchai Kusalacitto (Buddhism), and Owen Flanagan (philosophy).

Mind and Life IX was held at the University of Wisconsin at Madison in cooperation with the HealthEmotions Research Institute and the Center for Research on Mind-Body Interactions. Participants were His Holiness, Richard Davidson, Antoine Lutz (sitting in for an ill Francisco Varela), Matthieu Ricard, Paul Ekman, and Michael Merzenich (neuroscience). This two-day meeting focused on how to most effectively use the technologies of fMRI and EEG/MEG in research on meditation, perception, emotion, and the relations between human neural plasticity and meditation practices.

Mind and Life X took place in Dharamsala in October 2002. The topic was "The Nature of Matter, The Nature of Life." The scientific coordinator and moderator was Arthur Zajonc, and the participants were His Holiness, Steven Chu (physics), Arthur Zajonc (complexity), Luigi Luisi (cellular biology and chemistry), Ursula Goodenough (evolutionary biology), Eric Lander (genomic research), Michel Bitbol (philosophy), and Matthieu Ricard (Buddhist philosophy).

Mind and Life XI will be the first public meeting of this series. It will be held in Boston on September 13–14, 2003, and will be entitled "Investigating the Mind: Exchanges Between Buddhism and the Biobehavioral Sciences on How the Mind Works." In that meeting twenty-two world-renowned scientists will join His Holiness in a two-day inquiry on how best to institute collaborative research between Buddhism and modern science in the areas of attention and cognitive control, emotion, and mental imagery. For additional information, please see www.investigatingthemind.org.

Beginning in 2000, and as an extension of the research begun in 1990, members of the Mind and Life Institute again began to research meditation in Western brain science laboratories with the full collaboration of meditation adepts. Using fMRI, EEG, and MEG, this research is being carried out at CREA in Paris, the University of Wisconsin in Madison, and Harvard University. Measures of emotional expression and autonomic psychophysiology are being gathered at the University of California at San Francisco and at Berkeley.

Dr. Paul Ekman of the University of California, San Francisco, and a participant in the meeting described in this volume, has developed a research project entitled Cultivating Emotional Balance. This is the first large-scale multiphase Mind and Life research project designed to teach and evaluate the impact of meditation on the emotional lives of beginning meditators. The project has two primary research objectives: design and test a curriculum to teach people to deal with destructive emotional episodes drawing from Buddhist contemplative practices and western psychological research; and evaluate the impact of the curriculum on the emotional lives and interactions of the participants. B. Alan Wallace, another participant in this meeting, has provided advice in the development of the research project and will be the meditation trainer. Ekman recruited Margaret Kemeny to lead the execution of the project, while he continues to provide guidance. The Fetzer Institute has provided initial support for the project, as well as a donation from His Holiness the Dalai Lama.

Mind and Life Institute
2805 Lafayette Drive
Boulder, Colorado 80305
www.mindandlife.org
www.InvestigatingTheMind.org
info@mindandlife.org

Acknowledgments

Over the years, the Mind and Life Institute has been supported by the generosity of many individuals and organizations.

Founders

Without the initial interest and continuous participation and support of our Honorary Chairman, His Holiness the Dalai Lama, the Mind and Life Institute would never have been formed, nor would it continue to flourish. It is truly extraordinary for a world religious leader and statesman to be so open to scientific findings and so willing to devote his time to creating and guiding a meaningful dialogue between science and Buddhism. Over the past fifteen years His Holiness has spent more personal time in Mind and Life dialogues than with any other non-Tibetan group in the world, and for this we are humbled, eternally grateful, and dedicate our work to his vision of seeing the richness of science and Buddhism linked in dialogue and scientific research collaboration, for the benefit of all beings.

Francisco J. Varela was our founding scientist, and we miss him enormously. Both a world-renowned neuroscientist and a very serious practitioner of Buddhism, Francisco actually lived full time at the intersection of cognitive science and Buddhism, and was convinced that a deep and meaningful collaboration between science and Buddhism would be extremely beneficial for both systems, and for humanity itself. The direction he charted for the Mind and Life Institute has been bold and imaginative, while, at the same time, respecting the requirements of scientific rigor and Buddhist sensitivity. Above all, in this high velocity world, he created the time to cultivate the work of the Institute in a careful, logical, and scientifically incremental fashion. We continue on the road he set us upon.

R. Adam Engle is the entrepreneur who, upon hearing that His Holiness was interested in a dialogue between Buddhism and science, seized the opportunity and supplied the persistent effort and ingenuity to put the pieces in place for the work of the Institute to blossom and move forward.

Patrons

Barry and Connie Hershey of the Hershey Family Foundation have been our most loyal and steadfast patrons since 1990. Their generous support has not only guaranteed the continuity of the conferences but breathed life into the Mind and Life Institute itself.

Since 1990, Daniel Goleman has given generously of his time, energy, and spirit. He has prepared this volume and *Healing Emotions* without compensation, as offerings to His Holiness the Dalai Lama and the Mind and Life Institute, who receive all the royalties from their publication.

Over the years, the institute has also received generous financial support from the Fetzer Institute, The Nathan Cummings Foundation, Branco Weiss, Adam Engle, Michael Sautman, Mr. and Mrs. R. Thomas Northcote, Christine Austin, the late Dennis Perlman, Marilyn and the late Don L. Gevirtz, Michele Grennon, Klaus Hebben, Joe and Mary Ellyn Sensenbrenner, Edwin and Adrienne Joseph, Howard Cutler, Bennett and Fredericka Foster Shapiro. On behalf of His Holiness the Dalai Lama, and all the other participants over the years, we humbly thank all of these individuals and organizations. Their generosity has had a profound impact on the lives of many people.

Scientists, Philosophers, and Buddhist Scholar/Practitioners

We would also like to thank a number of people for their assistance in making the work of the institute itself a success. Many of these people have assisted the institute since its inception. First and foremost we thank the scientists, philosophers, and Buddhist scholars who have participated in our past meetings, our current meetings, our research projects, and our advisory boards: the late Francisco Varela, Richard Davidson, Paul Ekman, Anne

Harrington, Arthur Zajonc, Robert Livingston, Pier Luigi Luisi, Newcomb Greenleaf, Jeremy Hayward, Eleanor Rosch, Patricia Churchland, Antonio Damasio, Allan Hobson, Lewis Judd, Larry Squire, Daniel Brown, Daniel Goleman, Jon Kabat-Zinn, Clifford Saron, Lee Yearley, Jerome Engel, Jayne Gackenbach, Joyce McDougall, Charles Taylor, Joan Halifax, Nancy Eisenberg, Robert Frank, Elliott Sober, Ervin Staub, David Finkelstein, George Greenstein, Piet Hut, Tu Weiming, Anton Zeilinger, Owen Flanagan, Mark Greenberg, Matthieu Ricard, Jeanne Tsai, Michael Merzenich, Sharon Salzberg, Steven Chu, Ursula Goodenough, Eric Lander, Michel Bitbol, Jonathan Cohen, John Duncan, David Meyer, Anne Treisman, Ajahn Amaro, Daniel Gilbert, Daniel Kahneman, Georges Dreyfus, Stephen Kosslyn, Marlene Behrmann, Daniel Reisberg, Elaine Scarry, Jerome Kagan, Evan Thompson, Antoine Lutz, Gregory Simpson, Alan Wallace, Margaret Kemeny, Erika Rosenberg, Thupten Jinpa, Ajahn Maha Somchai Kusalacitto, Sogyal Rinpoche, Tsoknyi Rinpoche, Mingyur Rinpoche, and Rabjam Rinpoche.

The Private Office and Tibetan Supporters

We thank and acknowledge Tenzin Geyche Tethong, Tenzin N. Taklha, Ven. Lhakdor, and the other wonderful people of the Private Office of His Holiness. We are grateful to Rinchen Dharlo, Dawa Tsering, and Nawang Rapgyal of the Office of Tibet in New York City, and Lodi Gyari Rinpoche of the International Campaign for Tibet for their help over the years. And special thanks to Tendzin Choegyal, Ngari Rinpoche, who is a board member, a wonderful guide, and true friend.

Other Supporters

Our thanks to Kashmir Cottage, Chonor House, Pema Thang Guesthouse, and Glenmoor Cottage in Dharamsala; Maazda Travel in San Francisco and Middle Path Travel in New Delhi; Elaine Jackson, Zara Houshmand, Richard Gere, John Cleese, Alan Kelly, Peter Jepson, Thupten Chodron, Laurel Chiten, Billie Jo Joy, Nancy Mayer, Patricia Rockwell, George Rosenfeld, Andy Neddermeyer, Kristen Glover, Maclen Marvit, David Marvit, Wendy Miller, Sandra Berman, Will Shattuck, Franz Reichle, Marcel Hoehn, Geshe Sopa and the monks and nuns of Deer Park Buddhist Center, Dwight Kiyono, Eric Janish, Brenden Clarke, Jaclyn Wensink, Josh Dobson, Matt Mc-Neil, Penny and Zorba Paster, Jeffrey Davis, Magnetic Image, Inc., Disappearing, Inc., Sincerely Yours, HealthEmotions Research Institute–University of Wisconsin, Harvard University's Mind/Brain/ Behavior Interfaculty Initiative, Karen Barkow, John Dowling, Catherine Whalen, Sara Roscoe, Jennifer Shephard, Sydney Prince, Metta McGarvey, Ken Kaiser, T&C Film, Shambhala Publications, Wisdom Publications, Oxford University Press, Bantam Books, Snow Lion Publications, Meridian Trust, Geoff Jukes, Gillian Farrer-Halls, Tony Pitts, Edwin Maynard, Daniel Drasin, David Mayer, the Gere Foundation, Jennifer Greenfield, Robyn Brentano, Dinah Barlow, Nick Ribush, and Sarah Forney.

Interpreters

Finally, our very special thanks go to our interpreters over the years: Geshe Thupten Jinpa, who has interpreted for every meeting; B. Alan Wallace, who has been with us for every meeting but one; and José Cabezon, who pitched in for Alan while he was on retreat in 1995. Creating a dialogue and collaboration between Tibetan Buddhists and Western scientists demands excellent translation and interpretation. These friends are quite literally the best in the world.

—R. Adam Engle

To Adam's acknowledgments, I add some of my own. As always, I appreciate the wise advice and loving support of my wife, Tara Bennett-Goleman. I owe special thanks to Zara Houshmand for taking lyrical notes on the meeting and events beyond (some of which have been incorporated into this text), for conducting premeeting and debriefing interviews with participants, and for all her dedicated work in overseeing the production of skillfully edited transcripts. I'm grateful to Alan Wallace for special additional commentary on fine points in the dialogues, and to Thupten Jinpa for consultations on Buddhist texts and on the Dalai Lama's meetings with scientists over the year. Ngari Rinpoche offered invaluable information on the lifelong science interests of his brother, the Dalai Lama. My thanks to Rachel Brod for supplementary research, to Achaan Pasanno, for interviewing Bhikku Kusalacitto in Bangkok, to Arthur Zajonc, Sharon Salzberg, and Joseph Goldstein for answering technical queries on quantum physics and Buddhism respectively, and to Erik Hein Schmidt for consultation on fine points of Buddhism. And especially to Adam Engle for his extraordinary efforts in keeping this train on its track. Without Adam's vision, steady hand, and good energies, this endeavor could never have come this far.

—Daniel Goleman

Index

Page numbers of illustrations appear in italics.